For the traveling runner who may be a businessman, student or vacationer, for every one of the millions of runners and joggers across the country, here is *the* comprehensive guide to places to run in the U.S.A.

One hundred and twenty-five cities and surrounding areas are covered in detail. A descriptive overview for each city presents the factors most affecting local running conditions. Climatological data lists not only weather statistics but altitude and air quality as well. Hotels providing easy access to running courses are recommended, and course descriptions include easy-to-follow directions, distances, terrain, footing, shade, and other information pertinent to each route. Listed also are many available outdoor and indoor tracks, local running clubs, when and where to find local fun-runs and races, and direct contacts—the names, addresses and phone numbers of knowledgeable local runners and running organizations. Travel tips for the runner, a listing of major running stores, and other valuable information make this handy book a must for the adventurous runner.

From the oceanside runs of Hawaii to the evergreen forests of the Northwest, from Pike's Peak to the everglade jungles outside Fort Lauderdale, all the parks, lakes, rivers, mountain trails and in-city routes described in this book are yours for the running!

About the Author

Peter Roth, an officer of the New York Road Runners Club and a director of the New York City Marathon, has written this guidebook from his own recent and extensive travel to each region of the country, and from interviews with hundreds of runner correspondents. He brings to the book his experience of half a lifetime of running and years of contact with many runners through teaching clinics and working within running organizations.

RUNNING USA
The Complete Guide to
Running in 125 American Cities

by Peter Roth

AN AARDVARK BOOK   **NEW YORK**

AN AARDVARK BOOK
PUBLISHED BY BOOKTHRIFT
A SIMON & SCHUSTER DIVISION OF GULF + WESTERN
ONE WEST THIRTY-NINTH STREET
NEW YORK, NEW YORK 10018

Manufactured in the United States of America
Printed and Bound by Interstate Book Manufacturers, Inc.
Production Management by The Book Studio, Inc.

Designed By Donald H. Colflesh
Maps by Visuals Audibles
Photographs: page 39—Dr. Mitch Feingold; page 109—Glenn Angelino;
page 292—Darel Neilson; page 294—Esta Greenfield.
All other text photographs by Peter Roth.
Cover photo of the Brooklyn Bridge by Peter Roth, with thanks to Adidas and Richard Marx.

1   2   3   4   5   6   7   8   9   10

Library of Congress Cataloging in Publication Data

Roth, Peter, 1942-
 Running U.S.A.

 1.   Running—United States—Guide-books.   2.   Jogging—
United States—Guide-books.   3.   United States—
Description and travel—1960-   —Guide-books.
I. Title.
GV1061.2.R67   917.3   79-750
ISBN 0-917384-03-2
ISBN 0-917384-02-4 pbk.

For my mother, Ruth Goldberg,
who has always given me the love
and encouragement to reach out
in the world . . .
and to the memory of my father,
Ben Roth, whose inspiration
I always carry.

Contents

INTRODUCTION

This project began in late February, 1978, when Mike Shimkin, the President of Aardvark Publishing Company, and a longtime runner, called the New York Road Runners Club. Fred Lebow and I were at the office working on club business as usual. He answered the phone, and after a few minutes said, "Peter Roth's the guy you are looking for." I had no idea how it would immediately change my life, and neither did Fred, because I am sure he would not have volunteered my name if he knew he would lose my practically full-time assistance as an officer of the club.

Mike and I met the following day, and he told me of his idea to publish a book on where to run in America. I thought it was a great idea, and began to give him all the advice I could muster. Finally, he said, "Forget the advice, I want you to write it." Not having written anything extensive before, I gambled on my commitment to the subject matter and we shook hands.

Since New York is a large city, and a major crossroads, travelers have frequently heard or read about Central Park and our club, and some call us to provide them with added information about other running areas and courses within the city and the events our club sponsors. Still, there are many occasions when I have met a visiting runner on a training run, kicking himself for not knowing there was a race to enter that morning.

There are many cities in the country with exquisite downtown running courses, and in those very cities there are unknowing runners within a half mile of these courses doing laps around their hotels, or even riding a couple of miles to a "safe" high school track.

A myth exists that hotel personnel and others can point the way to a good course. My experience does not prove this out. Many times when I was told of a nearby course (often just a busy street or a pocket-size park), directions would be vague, and consultations with pedestrians contradictory. Many hotels are located in poor environments for running, locked in by freeways or heavy commercial neighborhoods, or in other areas with adverse conditions. Knowing the right hotel and the best courses can provide the freedom and ease to enjoy and maintain a full running schedule while in a new and unfamiliar place. With this and other valuable information on local running in each city and its surrounding area, I hope this book can be of service not only to traveling runners, but to those interested in the diversity and details of the sport as it exists in the far corners of America.

Covering 125 cities allowed me to reach many climates and terrains that offer fascinating experiences of the breadth of our country. Perhaps *Running U.S.A.* will serve as an inspiration to visit and enjoy many of these different environments. All the in-city routes, all the park, lake, river and mountain trails described in this book are yours for the running. Your interest might be piqued by the unusual desert flora of New Mexico, the dense evergreen parks in the state of Washington, famous Pike's Peak, the popular Phoenix canals, or Honolulu's Mount Tantalus. In Fort Lauderdale, groups go on long runs through an everglade jungle, and in Anchorage, you might feel the exhilaration of a midnight run in broad daylight.

Many people have asked which cities are the best to run in. I do not feel any one city can satisfy everyone. There is so much variety throughout the country that choices can only be personal and subjective. San Diego has beautiful weather, but some people would miss the changing seasons. The Northwest has lush green vegetation and dramatic vistas, but not everyone can appreciate a wet climate. Minnesota has attractive lakes and rivers, but very cold winters. The deep South has beautiful, rolling countryside, but summers can be intolerable. In all of these areas there are people who cherish their own cities and are willing to run through whatever hardships exist in order to enjoy the benefits.

The one thing runners do seem to have in common across the country is the ability to enjoy and appreciate each other's companionship. Among the great experiences you can have while traveling is to meet many of these runners in their hometowns and enjoy the fine hospitality they offer. At the end of my stay in many cities, local runners would part by saying: "Don't forget to tell your readers to call when they get to town, because we sure will be happy to run with them."

The purpose of this book is to provide you with the information to better appreciate and utilize the awaiting opportunities within each city, and to that end I wish you the enrichment and happy miles that our country offers.

PETER ROTH
New York City, 1979

HOW TO USE THIS BOOK

VITAL STATISTICS

The vital statistics for each city are listed first, so that you can make some quick judgments about that city's physical characteristics. I have found many cities to be either larger or smaller than I had originally thought, so I have included population. Unusually high altitude is an important consideration for runners; you may also wish to compare the elevation of different cities.

Average temperature has been listed for January and July, because these months will give you the annual range in temperature. Average precipitation for these two months will give you a clue to yearly patterns, and the number of raindays is a good guide to the amount of raingear you should pack for your trip. In some cases, however, the latter figures may be misleading, as some cities receive largely nocturnal precipitation. The figure for annual average humidity will quickly inform you of the city's arid or moist climate. Air quality has been rated on a scale from excellent to poor.

OVERVIEW

The overview is exactly that, a short description of what each city has to offer runners. It is not intended to be a complete informational or historical rendering, but rather a look at the factors most affecting your run.

HOTELS

Staying at the right hotel is half the battle to enjoying the best workouts on your trip. Many hotels are located in areas in which it is impossible to run safely and effectively, and since advance reservations are imperative in most cities, it is a great help to know which of them are closest to recommended running courses. Read through all the courses for the city to which you are traveling, so that you can choose an appropriate hotel for the type of course you prefer. Not all the hotels I have listed are downtown, so again, study the courses to see which of them appeal to you, and select your hotel accordingly.

Addresses and telephone numbers are not listed as they are easily obtained. Most hotels are associated with large chains, and their central offices will provide you with this information.

RUNNING ROUTES

My main intention has been to describe courses close enough to hotels or hotels close enough to courses to allow for "out-the-door" workouts, as you may not have a car to reach more distant routes. However, some courses which cannot be reached by foot are also described.

Many distances are approximate, and I have identified these with appropriate wording. The purpose of listing mileage is not to give you a distance to judge your speed precisely, but rather to guide you in the general length of a training run.

I usually get confused reading directions, and after a few turns I give them up. To make it easier for you, I have written as concisely as possible. The best way to handle directions is to take a paper and pencil, or write in the margin of the book, and quickly construct your own map from all the lefts and rights. In some instances, overview maps and maps of particular routes have been provided.

In many cases, I have described routes out and back that might be longer than you want to run. I recommend that you run out for half the workout you intend, and then turn back. I have seldom repeated directions back along the same course.

OUTDOOR AND INDOOR TRACKS

Travelers have long resorted to outdoor tracks, particularly at high schools, since they are the most numerous and easiest to find. Many people not willing to venture onto unfamiliar courses will continue to use them, and they will always be valuable for interval workouts. I have listed only tracks that are popular with local runners. Often, they serve as meeting places from which runners head out onto the roads.

School track teams usually prefer not to share their tracks during scheduled workouts, but some six- and eight-lane tracks have room for other runners in the outside lanes. If you feel that your run might coincide with a team workout, or if you have any questions, call ahead to check it out. Many schools have locked their expensive new tracks to prevent excessive wear.

Indoor tracks are seldom available to visitors. Universities normally have strictly enforced regulations, allowing their use only by students and faculty, although you can sometimes be admitted as a guest of someone connected to the university. Most downtown YMCA's have tracks. The majority are small, with 18 to 30 laps per mile, and their policies for accommodating visitors vary greatly. If you are a member of another YMCA, you can always gain entrance, sometimes by payment of a small fee. Some YMCA's limit the number of days you can use their facilities, requiring that you transfer your membership for extended use. Many charge a small fee for non-member guests. Again, this may be limited to a specified number of days. There are some YMCA's that do not allow *any* guests. Call ahead to find out about local requirements.

RUNNING CLUBS AND RACES

Running clubs vary as greatly in style as do the people organizing them. Some are very formal, with their functions well defined, and schedules and times that are strictly adhered to. Others have a more nonchalant attitude and do not put on many ambitious events. If you intend to participate in any races or fun-runs, or attend any other club functions on your trip, I advise that you call or write ahead requesting information about events during your stay. Although a club might hold races on a weekly basis, there may be a time or location change, or even a cancellation. If you write ahead, always enclose a stamped, self-addressed envelope.

TRADITIONAL RACES

The traditional races listed for each city have either been held for several years, or local officials believe they will be held for years in the future. They are not necessarily organized by the local running club, and sometimes they are held in neighboring towns. If you would like to enter these races, the list of contacts will put you in touch with people who know the proper procedures. Also, check with major running magazines that print monthly schedules.

CONTACTS

Contacts are usually people who operate running clubs, or who are longtime local running enthusiasts. They are often runners who have been involved for a long time, and it is reasonable to think that they will be accessible in the future. Many have expressed a willingness to help find other runners with whom visitors can train, and even to provide transportation, on occasion, to get to races.

TRAVEL TIPS

WHAT AND HOW TO PACK

You may discover that you have not packed any raingear when traveling to a surprisingly wet climate, or perhaps not brought your warm-ups to a warm climate where temperatures drop rapidly at night. Knowing what you will find ahead can save you a lot of time and discomfort.

But clothes are not the only preparation you can make. It is not only *what* you pack, but *how* you pack that can make a difference. For example, to be ready for a quick run from an airport, or before you unpack at your hotel, keep your running gear in a separate shoulder bag. A separate bag is also useful for storing your warm-ups for those spur-of-the-moment races or runs you may happen upon. Carrying a supply of plastic bags can also be helpful. Not only will they hold your wet clothes, they are great for ice packs, using your hotel's ice supply.

Be sure to pack an extra pair of shoes for extremely wet or hot climates. If you are uncertain about the temperature, bring many layers of light clothing to bulk up; a cap and gloves are a good precaution. I always throw in a pair of Orlon tights for extra warmth without having to overload my suitcase. One of those aluminum blankets that are handed out at the end of marathons is always a good item to keep in your running bag for those days when you have had a hard run, and the air begins to chill.

Your running club or race T-shirts are great for meeting other runners (or even friends and relatives of runners). Do not forget about light-colored clothes and reflector tape for night runs. I also recommend packing some Vaseline to guard against chafing, and to protect you from extreme cold. Chapstick and suntan lotion can also save you from discomfort.

After my first trip, when I was loaded down with too much running gear, I learned to pack some soap for washing clothes in the hotel sink. That meant I could bring less gear, and after a long run, I noticed that my already drenched clothes dried a lot faster after a quick washing.

AIRPORT RUNS

With long stopovers and flight delays, many runners slip on their flats and shorts and head out for a run until flight time. Few airports have showers, but all have storage lockers or baggage check-ins, and decent restrooms. Most runners can get by temporarily with a quick rinse at the sink after a hard run.

Airport routes have quite similar characteristics. Terrain is flat, at least near the facility, so it is difficult to lose sight of the airport tower. An access road will lead to an exit where service roads often circle around part of the airport's perimeter. Farmland or commercial property usually surrounds the area, as it is too noisy for residential development. Be sure not to wander too far away; one wrong turn can mean one missed flight.

UPON ARRIVAL

When traveling from the airport to the hotel, I always try to ask questions. "See many runners around town? Do they run near the hotel at which I will be staying? Are there any good parks or lakes nearby? Do cars give runners a tough time?" Sometimes a taxi driver will take a quick detour to show me a nearby park, and I always use the trip to take bearings on north/south and to get a view of the terrain. By the time I reach my hotel, I am always psyched up and excited about the city.

At the hotel desk, I have more questions. "Have you seen any runners? Where do they run? Have they mentioned any of their experiences?" By the time you read this, hotels will have had many more runners pass through, and will have more answers.

Quite a few hotels already realize the interest in running among their customers and are providing new services for them, such as "jogging maps" for local routes, or providing transportation to and from local parks for workouts.

A map of the city can be your best friend when local streets are very complicated. The newsstand in your hotel will usually have one, otherwise try a nearby gas station or a car rental office at the airport.

THE LOCAL SCENE

If you are interested in joining up with local runners, or participating in a local race or fun-run, the people listed in the book will be glad to help you. There might even be a club meeting that evening. If the city is not listed in this book, you can call a number of different organizations, including the YMCA, a sporting goods store, a university athletic department, the city parks and recreation department, or the daily newspaper sports department.

Planning your individual run will depend on a number of different factors. Some cities are unsafe for night runs. Traffic, unlit courses, or crime areas may limit your run to daylight hours. The cleaner air and lesser traffic of early morning make it a preferable part of the day. Also, there are fewer pedestrians and almost no bicycles to compete with for narrow sidewalk space. Very early in the morning, you can beat almost all the traffic, and dictate your own courses over empty city streets. In New York, many runners can be seen traveling up and down Fifth Avenue at 5:00 and 6:00 A.M.

Group runs are common in the early morning, and it is easier to find companionship at that time. In some hot climates, groups start out as early as 4:00 A.M. Downtown YMCA's often have early-bird groups that welcome visitors. Even if you are not a member, you can meet them on the street to join their workout.

Most cities require some traversing along busy streets to reach parks, lakes or rivers. Of course, rush hours are the worst time to compete with traffic. If you do not like waking up very early, you can have a relatively safe run after the evening rush hour. Lunchtime runs have many avid participants in large cities. Even on hot days, this is the only time some people can work out. YMCA's are again the best place to find group runs during the week, and some running stores can also be good meeting and starting points. Running alone on city streets is great for sightseeing, but a pack of runners draws you into the pace, and pedestrians and cars will be more cautious.

Getting to distant running courses from your hotel can be a problem. If the course begins and ends at a YMCA or another place with a pay phone, you might want to take a taxi there, knowing you can call for one to take you back. Public transportation is not always the best bet; you may not be comfortable riding in a bus or subway wearing minimal running clothes, and when you are through, it might be chilly waiting around at the station in your wet clothes. Sometimes you can predetermine your finishing time and location, and call for a taxi to meet you just as you complete your workout.

If you are interested in entering a local race, call or write for an entry blank before your trip. Many big races close months ahead of time. You can usually post-enter small races, but it is wise to call ahead to check about schedule or location changes.

A FEW WORDS OF WARNING

Women should consider running alone only during daylight hours and along well-trafficked routes. If you are not familiar with the territory, do not consider it safe. It only takes one secluded spot for a mugger or rapist to be lurking. Suburban, residential neighborhoods are usually the safest areas, since there is so much visibility from homes, and not many dangerous types loiter about.

Men seem to be more immune to attack, although now that running gear is becoming so expensive (*e.g.*, shoes, warm-ups, and stopwatches) there may be an increase in muggings. I enjoy night runs through hilly sections of Harlem, in New York. This is not a neighborhood I would ever walk through at night, but during runs, the only incidents that occur are groups on street corners shouting "Rent-a-car, superstar!" or "Marathon!"

It may be that so-called "redneck" neighborhoods are the most dangerous. The people who live there are much more sensitive to strangers crossing their "turf," and react with occasional violence. On rural roads, runners are frequent targets for beer cans or tobacco juice, and in a few isolated cases have even been shot at or killed.

A lesser evil, a curious or pesty dog can change a beautiful course into a frightening experience. Usually, if enough runners use a course, sufficient pressure can be exerted to have a dog penned. For this reason, it is best to seek out well-used routes. Of course, friendly dogs can also be a problem, and people strolling with an unleashed canine along running paths do not realize the number of runners that have been tripped and injured by dogs underfoot.

ALTITUDE, CLIMATE AND POLLUTION

Do not bother worrying about high altitude. It will have an affect on your running until your body adjusts to it, and thats that. Expect to run more slowly at first, and after you have acclimated, you will still be a bit slower than at sea level. Take it extremely easy at very high altitudes, shortening your runs considerably. High altitude goes hand in hand with low humidity. This is a concern that you *can* do something about. If you notice that your mouth and throat become parched during a long run, the best solution is to chew gum to keep saliva present. If your mouth should become extremely dry, hop into a steamed-up room after your run, and inhale plenty of moist air.

The greatest threat in a dry climate is dehydration. Sweat evaporates so fast that your body seems not to perspire at all. Without realizing it, you can lose pounds of fluid, and before you know it body temperature can be up to a dangerous level. Make sure you have checked out the water supply along the route before you begin, or provide for your own supply. An effective and comfortable water belt for runners has recently been patented.

Air pollution can be another problem. Of the many pollutants in the atmosphere, photochemical oxidants are considered the most harmful to runners. These are produced by chemical reactions between hydrocarbons (*i.e.*, gasoline vapors) and nitrogen oxides (which are formed from the nitrogen and oxygen in the air when anything is burned). Sunlight is the major cause of these chemical reactions, and the resultant photochemical oxidant is commonly known as ozone. Once the chemical reactions in the atmosphere take place, mostly over areas of heavy automobile use, ozone then drifts into outlying areas. Since sunlight is required to produce ozone, it does not usually drift into these unsuspecting suburban and rural communities until nightfall, so you may want to keep this in mind when scheduling your runs in some suburban areas.

NEW SPACES

Cities all across America are building new parks and installing bike paths and "jogging trails." Very often these are along riverbanks where industrial areas previously sealed off a river to public use. Now that industry is moving away from downtown areas, the cities are reclaiming their right to these lands.

Parks in many cities have been usurped by golf courses which try to keep runners off. A few running clubs have successfully tested the legality of being kept off recreational land they maintain through taxes. Golf course perimeters normally measure close to 2½ miles, and runners are seldom bothered along the outside edges.

A last resort, and a popular one in some cities, can be found on cemetery roads. Physically, a cemetery can be an ideal location—quiet roads, no dogs, and real solitude. Psychologically, it might not be an "up" experience.

Jerry Barkann collects bridges. When he visits a new city, he looks for bridges to run. This can mean the excitement of the Golden Gate in San Francisco or the George Washington Bridge in New York with their towering structures and magnificent views, or the satisfaction of a long run over the eleven bridges on the Charles River in Boston. Not all bridges in big cities are crossable, but those that are can provide a chance to see the city from a different vantage point. In many flat cities, they can be the only chance for some hill work.

Each city warrants a different type of preparedness. Whether you consider climate, terrain, footing, running at night, traffic or high crime areas, it is best to know the situations that lie ahead on your trip. You will find much of this information for the 125 cities listed in this book.

RUNNING U.S.A.

Birmingham

Population: 290,000	Humidity: 72%
Elevation: 382–608 ft.	Av. Temperature: (Jan.) 44°F.; (July) 80°F.
Air Quality: Fair to poor	Inches of Rainfall: (Jan.) 4.84; (July) 5.22 Raindays: 117

OVERVIEW

Birmingham has a clean environment, and the dynamic, undulating landscape will entice many visiting runners. Mountains cross through the city east to west, creating lush green valleys for flat, shaded runs.

Red Mountain borders the south edge of downtown, and an interesting, winding route can be found nestled along its near side. On the other side of the mountain, a popular route runs along Shades Creek Parkway and Lake Shore Drive, and this is where you will find many local runners.

The downtown area has no unobstructed runs, and if you must stay in a hotel there, a nearby high school provides a mediocre track. The airport is only about 4 miles northeast of town, and 1 mile beyond is another popular running site, East Lake Park.

Some of the better hotels are located away from downtown, and close to good running. There are not a lot of races here, but you will find plenty of friendly runners.

HOTELS

Sheraton Mountain Brook Inn, Best Western Kahler Plaza, Passport Inn, Hyatt House

LAKE SHORE DRIVE

A couple of miles south of Red Mountain, this straight, scenic route runs along both sides of Shades Creek, and past the Samford University Campus. The Sheraton Mountain Brook, on Route 280, is perhaps the best hotel from which to enjoy running in Birmingham. The hotel is very convenient to this course. Run south on 280 for ½ mile to Shades Creek Parkway. Turn right onto the Parkway, which after ¾ of a mile becomes Lake Shore Drive. At that point there is also a gas station for the only water stop on the course. Shades Creek Parkway has many beautiful, old mansions. Continue on Lake Shore Drive for 2½ miles along a wooded section of young trees. At the end, the road curves south into South Lake Shore Drive, which parallels the route back until it curves north, back into Lake Shore Drive. The South Drive is a two-lane, seldom used road with a new, soft and smooth blacktop surface.

HIGHLAND AVENUE

This course is convenient to the Kahler Plaza, just south of the downtown area. Run south from the hotel, slightly uphill toward Red Mountain for about ⅓ mile to a left turn on Highland Avenue. Follow the avenue for about 3 miles as it winds through a residential neighborhood. Terrain along the road is generally flat. At the far end, you will reach Boswell Golf Course, where you can run 2½ to 3 miles around its grass perimeter. The Golf Course is on very hilly terrain. Follow the same route back to the hotel.

EAST LAKE PARK   Take Route 11 northeast to East Lake Park. There are no hotels nearby. A 1-mile gravel and paved path skirts around East Lake. Terrain is flat and shaded, and water fountains are available. You will find many other runners here.

OUTDOOR TRACKS   Downtown, Phillips High School, only a few blocks from the Civic Center and the Hyatt House, has a hard-surfaced, 5-laps-per-mile track. It also has a playing field for softer footing.

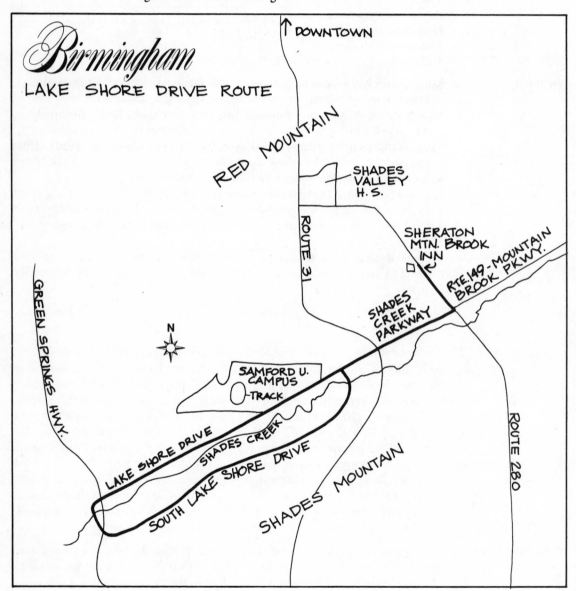

The University of Alabama in Birmingham has a ¼-mile, all-weather track. Passport Inn is located near the track.

Samford College, along Lake Shore Drive, has a ¼-mile cinder track.

INDOOR TRACKS   The Downtown YMCA has a 13-laps-per-mile banked track; the Shades Valley YMCA has a 20-laps-per-mile track; and the Jewish Community Center has a 22-laps-per-mile track.

CLUBS AND RACES   The Birmingham Track Club puts on a number of races during the year (listed under Contacts, below).

TRADITIONAL RACES   Birmingham Marathon: February
Vestavia Dogwood Run, 6 miles: April
Talladega 5-Mile: Early May
Zayre to Zayre Run, 7.5 miles: August
Homewood Labor Day Run, 10 kilometers
Montclair 10-Kilometer Run: October
Vulcan Run, 10 kilometers and 2 miles: November

CONTACTS   John Spink, Birmingham Track Club, 1741 Marryvale Road, Birmingham, AL 35243. (205) 822-6598.
Versal Spalding, Spalding Running South, 3105 Cahaba Road, Birmingham, AL 35223. (205) 879-2148.
Downtown YMCA, 526 20th Street North, Birmingham, AL 35203. (205) 324-4563.
Shades Valley YMCA, (205) 871-7373.
Jewish Community Center, (205) 879-0411.

HUNTSVILLE

Population: 135,000	Humidity: 72%
Elevation: 610–636 ft.	Av. Temperature: (Jan.) 40.2°F.; (July) 79°F.
Air Quality: Fair	Inches of Rainfall: (Jan.) 5.13; (July) 4.88 Raindays: 121

OVERVIEW

Located geographically at the top of the state, Huntsville has been building a reputation as the top running city in Alabama. The Huntsville Track Club is known across the country for its informative newsletter and the superb quality of its running events. Sophisticated handling of its Rocket City Marathon has drawn the New York City Marathon to study its structure and methods in order to improve its own race. Harold Tinsley, a 2:33 master marathoner, has been the prime force behind the club's success.

Downtown Huntsville contains many old, restored homes and buildings, and its quiet, tree-lined streets can provide safe and scenic runs. The city has spread out, taking much of the bussle away from downtown thoroughfares. Four miles east of town, 2,140-acre Monte Sano State Park sits on top of 1,800-foot Monte Sano Mountain. Many local runners come here for their quality workouts.

Just south of downtown, a new cross-country course has been built at the Old Huntsville Airport, and to the west, a popular route circles around the University of Alabama at the Huntsville Campus.

HOTELS

Sheraton Motor Inn, Carriage Inn Motor Hotel, Ramada Inn

MONTE SANO PARK

A popular route, and part of the marathon course, begins at the Monte Sano School, on Monte Sano Boulevard. You must drive to this course, and you can reach it from downtown via Highway 431 east to a left turn on Monte Sano Boulevard. The course is basically a two-lane road traveling through the park and residential areas. Most of it is tree-lined, and many little hills provide a constant variety of pace, none of which can be considered very steep.

Head south from the school for ¼ of a mile to a left on Panorama Drive, which loops around the top of the mountain. The first mile comes at the point where the road makes a sharp right. At 1.7 miles the road crosses Monte Sano Boulevard on the far side of the loop. Continue on the drive until you can make a left onto the Boulevard at 2.35 miles. Head north on Monte Sano Boulevard, and just after the 3-mile point (from the start), turn right on Nolen Avenue and enter the park. The 4-mile point is at the entrance to the camping area. At 4½ miles, you will pass the park overlook and then the road makes a sharp left, and you exit the park onto Bankhead Parkway. Now it is an easy downhill along the contour of the mountain to a left on Fearn Street. Take Fearn up a steep grade back to Monte Sano Boulevard, and return to the starting point for a run just short of 8 miles. Water fountains and rest rooms can be found at the Park Office, soon after the 4-mile mark.

OLD HUNTSVILLE AIRPORT
Located about 2 miles south of downtown along busy Memorial Highway, the airport contains a new, mostly grassy and flat, cross-country course. The Ramada Inn, on Memorial Highway, is only a ½ mile north of the airport, via an access road.

The course begins at the south end of the north/south runway. Do not worry about airplanes, as they no longer use the facility. Three-foot-tall cement markers have been placed every ¼ mile for direction and mileage. About 20 percent of the course goes through nearby woods, where you will find one small hill. No water fountains or rest rooms have been installed as yet.

UNIVERSITY OF ALABAMA CAMPUS
About 2½ miles west of downtown, the university campus is circled by the South Loop Road and the North Loop Road. Together they comprise a 2½-mile loop around the entire campus. The four-lane road is flat, and no cars park along it; however, traffic can sometimes be a problem before and after evening classes.

Grass areas beside the road offer softer footing on occasion, and sidewalks are sometimes available. Water fountains and rest rooms can be found at Spragins Hall on the northeast side of the course.

The Sheraton Inn is located just across University Drive from the course, and the Carriage Inn is about a mile east on University Drive.

CLUBS, FUN-RUNS AND RACES
The Huntsville Track Club produces a great many excellent events throughout the year, including an all-comers program in the summer. Fun-runs are held every Saturday at 9:00 A.M. at the Old Huntsville Airport.

TRADITIONAL RACES
Winter Winds, 4 and 2 miles: Mid-February
UAH Spring Races, 6 and 2 miles: March
Rocket Run, 10 and 3 miles: May
A & M Road Race, 10 kilometers: June
American Cancer Society, 15 kilometers: Late July
Monte Sano Road Races, 6 and 3 miles: September
Rocket City 20-kilometer: November
Joe Steele Rocket City Marathon: December

CONTACT
Harold Tinsley, Huntsville Track Club, 8811 Edgehill Drive, Huntsville, AL 35802. (205) 881-9077.

MOBILE

Population: 195,000	Humidity: High — 76.5%
Elevation: 8 – 300 ft.	Av. Temperature: (Jan.) 51°F.; (July) 82°F.
Air Quality: Fair	Inches of Rainfall: (Jan.) 5; (July) 8.9 Raindays: 123

OVERVIEW

If you can handle the humidity, Mobile is a beautiful city to run in. Canapes of oak trees cover downtown streets, where runners busily churn their way back and forth, especially along popular Government Street. Terrain varies between flat downtown courses and the hilly western suburbs.

Fortunately, an area containing downtown hotels, the Municipal Auditorium and the YMCA marks the beginning of the Government Street course. A greater variety of distances have been measured from the Murphy High School track, just west of town, and close to the Government Street course.

The hills west of town contain pretty residential communities, with winding, tree-lined streets. Two college campuses here offer grassy, cross-country courses.

During warm months, afternoon showers are frequent between 2:00 and 4:00 P.M., due to the city's close proximity to the Gulf of Mexico.

Clubs are just beginning here, and races are not frequent, but many runners have created groups for informal workouts.

Two notable hazards here are fire ants and local drivers. The ants have a sting that some people are allergic to. Their mounds are very large, but tall grass can hide them. A number of local drivers enjoy littering the roads, and they sometimes use runners as targets.

HOTELS

Holiday Inn — I-10, Sheraton Inn, Malaga Inn

GOVERNMENT STREET

This most popular course begins in front of the YMCA, and heads west for exactly 2.5 miles to the Old Cannon Monument at Houston Street. The flat course is well shaded by oaks, and running is limited to the sidewalks, which have occasional uneven footing. Many intersections must be crossed. Water can be obtained at frequent gas stations.

Runners often detour to the south of Government Street, between Ann Street and Broad Street, to run through the Beautiful Oakleigh Garden District.

ROUTES FROM MURPHY HIGH SCHOOL

Located ½ mile northwest of the Old Cannon Monument, many different distances can be run from the Murphy High School track by heading north on Carlen to Dauphin Street, and turning east toward downtown. As you run east on Dauphin through the Dauphin Way District, you will reach different streets heading south to Government Street. By taking these different streets, progressively further from the high school, your loops will be progressively longer distances. If you turn south on Ann Street and head back to the high school on Government Street, your run will measure 3¼ miles. If you do the same on Broad Street, instead of Ann Street, you will go 4½ miles. Likewise, if you run south on South Washington Avenue you will go 5 miles; on South Conception, the loop will measure 6 miles; and at Water Street, your run will total 6½ miles.

Turning down South Washington Avenue will take you past the Public Library; and turning down South Conception will take you through the architecturally historic Bienville Square.

To reach the high school from the Old Cannon Monument, head west as Government Street turns into Old Government Street, and then make a right onto Carlen Street.

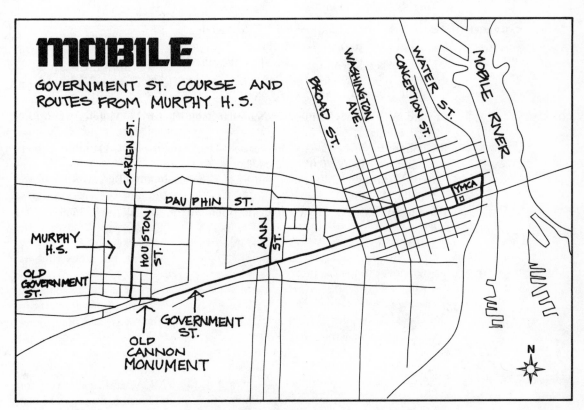

MUNICIPAL PARK

You will find many runners in this hilly, scenic park, 8 miles west of downtown. The site contains many paths, footbridges, lakes, and fences to climb over. The perimeter measures 2¼ miles, and can be run on grass alongside the road. The park is well shaded, and water fountains and rest rooms can be found near the pavilions.

If you follow the road through the park on the south side and continue southwest, you will reach the University of South Alabama at about 2 miles. Many runners use the hilly terrain on the campus for unmeasured cross-country workouts.

Following the road through the north side of the park, and continuing west, you will be on a 3-mile route to the Fairgrounds. This road has flat terrain, and a grass median borders the road on both sides.

SPRING HILL
COLLEGE

This campus, in the western suburbs, offers beautiful hilly and grassy cross-country running through a shaded, oak-tree environment. Park at the shopping center next to the campus.

OUTDOOR TRACKS

The Chandler YMCA, 10 miles west of town, has a ¼-mile asphalt track. A 400-meter Chevron track is available at the University of South Alabama.

INDOOR TRACKS

The Downtown YMCA has an air-conditioned, banked, 34-laps-per-mile track.

CLUBS, GROUP RUNS
AND RACES

The Mobile Track and Field Federation schedules races during the year. The Murphy Fun Runners meet most afternoons at the Murphy High School track. On weekends, they meet at 5:30 P.M. during summer, and 3:30 or 4:30 P.M. during the colder months.

TRADITIONAL RACES

Azalea Trail Run, 10 kilometers: Late March
Memorial Day 10- and 5-Mile Run
National Jogging Day Run, 4 and 2 miles: Early October
Turkey Trot, 3.3 miles: Mid-November
Tee-Shirt Race, 5 miles: Early December

CONTACTS

Richard W. Overbey, American National Bank, Box 1628, Mobile, AL 36629. (205) 433-0511.
Richmond P. Brown, City Recreation Department, 2900 Dauphin Street, Mobile, AL 36606. (205) 438-7472.
Charlie Matlock, Mobile Track and Field Federation, 4654 Bit and Spur Road, Mobile, AL 36608.
Downtown YMCA, 61 South Conception Street, Mobile, AL 36602. (205) 432-3621.

ANCHORAGE

Population: 202,101	Humidity: 71%
Elevation: 114 ft.	Av. Temperature: (Jan.) 11.8°F.; (July) 57.9°F.
Air Quality: Good	Inches of Rainfall: (Jan.) .84; (July) 2.07 Raindays: 113

OVERVIEW

Running has been a popular sport in Anchorage for many years, and contrary to what one might expect, climate does not seem to present any major problems. Many local runners are able to put in high mileage all year long. Winter temperatures rarely go below zero, so normal winter running gear will be suitable here. In addition, snowshoe running and cross-country skiing are real naturals as an adjunct to a running program in this climate, and equipment is easily obtainable.

Short winter days create the greatest problem for a runner's schedule. Routes are not well lit at night, so it is best to plan a workout between 10 A.M. and 3 P.M. During summer, daylight hours can include a midnight run.

Anchorage runners have great spirit and sense of community within the sport, and you will find a strong exhuberance and camaraderie at their events.

HOTELS

Holiday Inn, Sheffield House, Westward Hilton, Travelodge

CHESTER CREEK BIKE TRAIL

This unobstructed bike trail can be reached from downtown hotels by running south on C or E streets for about ¾ of a mile. If you head west on the trail, toward the mountains, you can run 4 miles. Heading east, you can run 1½ miles to the end of Westchester Lagoon. The course is flat and wooded. Keep in mind that the more isolated parts of the trail can be dangerous—some muggings have occurred in these areas. In winter, footing is often difficult.

THE PARK STRIP

Located only a few blocks from downtown, this popular mile-long strip is bordered by Cordova and N streets on the east and west respectively, and 9th and 10th avenues north and south. A full circuit is about 2.5 miles. Street crossings intersect the flat course, but with little interference from traffic. Rest rooms are available, and there are water fountains open in summer. At the west end, you can experience nice views of Mt. McKinley and the Alaskan Mountain Range.

STUCKAGAIN HEIGHTS ROAD

Drive south on C Street or Gambell to Tudor Road. Turn left (east) and drive to Stuckagain Heights Road, .6 miles beyond the stoplight at Boniface Road. This dirt road is hard to find, so keep your eye out for Kingston Drive, identified by about twenty mailboxes on a stand, located across the street from the Stuckagain course. The long, uphill route runs 5 miles to the top. At the 2.5-mile mark, you will cross Tank Trail Road, the only intersecting road on the course.

The road travels to a classy restaurant and a few homes near the top, so there is not much traffic to worry about. Spectacular views can be seen from the top of the course.

You may encounter a moose or bear occasionally, but it is usually no problem. If you are worried about it, just sing or yodel along the way, just as you would on any mountain trail if you do not want to surprise anything.

CLUBS, FUN-RUNS AND RACES

The Pulsator Running Club holds a full schedule of running events throughout the year (see Contacts). Fun-Runs take place every Saturday at 9:00 A.M. at Stuckagain Heights Road. The racing calendar is heaviest during the summer months and lighter in the winter.

INDOOR TRACKS

There are no indoor tracks, but some of the local schools have gyms or hallways that are open for evening running.

TRADITIONAL RACES

Glacier Marathon: Mid-May
Women's 10-Kilometer: Early June
Mayor's Midnight Sun Marathon: Mid-June
Seward's Mountain Marathon Race: Fourth of July
Resurrection Pas Trail Marathon: Early August

CONTACTS

John and Marcie Trent, Pulsators Running Club, 1700 Tudor Road, Anchorage, AK 99507. (907) 279-2975.

Roy Reisinger, 1046 West 20th, Anchorage, AK 99503. (907) 277-1065, or 279-6602 (work).

Terry Martin, 3960 Reka Drive, B-6, Anchorage, AK 99504.

The Athlete's Foot, 900 West Northern Lights Boulevard, Anchorage, AK 99503. (907) 274-4633.

Anchorage Parks and Recreation Department, (907) 264-4366.

FAIRBANKS

Population: 27,116	Humidity: 63.5%
Elevation: 436 ft.	Av. Temperature: (Jan.) −11.9°F.; (July) 60.7°F.
Air Quality: Poor	Inches of Rainfall: (Jan.) .6; (July) 1.9 Raindays: 102

OVERVIEW

Located much further north in Alaska than Anchorage, Fairbanks has colder winters, but receives less snow. Winter running is limited to plowed roads or shoveled sidewalks. A second drawback to winter running here is a condition known as "ice fog." Its major pollutant is carbon monoxide, and during the coldest months ice fog pervades the atmosphere to the great detriment of runners. Needless to say, most local runners resort to cross-country skiing beyond the city area during this time.

For most of the year, running centers around the University of Alaska, where there are marked and measured cross-country trails of varying distances between 2 and 12 miles. The University is located about 4½ miles west of downtown, and can be reached partway via bike path. An elaborate system of bike paths course through the city, providing many interesting routes. The outskirts of town have a lot of dirt roads and hills.

The Equinox Marathon, in September, has been held since 1963, and it offers one of the toughest courses in the country, with winning times just under three hours.

HOTEL

Chena View Hotel

ROUTE TO THE UNIVERSITY

Chena View Hotel is located along the Chena River, on First Avenue. From the hotel, head west on First Avenue, beside the river on a bike path. After about 1¼ miles, turn south on Peger Road and follow it to the Airport Road Access Street, where you will turn west to University Avenue, again continuing west to the Ice Arena at the university. Other than the bike path on First Avenue, you will be running on fairly unobstructed sidewalks. Terrain is generally flat.

UNIVERSITY RUNNING AND CROSS-COUNTRY SKIING TRAILS

From the University Ice Arena, distances have been measured for 2, 4, 6, 9 and 12 miles through the woods to the north and west of campus. All the trails are marked and easy to follow over the rolling hills. Residential roads surround the area, making it hard to become stranded.

FARMERS LOOP ROAD

From downtown, you can run an interesting 13½-mile loop by following the route to the university, and then heading north on Farmers Loop Road, running on its bike path for 8 miles. Upon nearing downtown, head south on Old Steese

Highway for ½ mile to the Chena River, and follow the river west for another ½ mile back to the start.

INDOOR TRACKS
There are no indoor tracks in Fairbanks, but if it is necessary for you to resort to the indoors, some runners use Patty Gym at the university. Gym facilities are open to the public for a small fee.

CLUBS AND RACES
Running Club North holds a large number of races during the warmer months.

TRADITIONAL RACES
Equinox Marathon: Late September

CONTACTS
Dr. John Gilmore, Mark Woldseth or Bill Smith, Athletic Department, University of Alaska, Fairbanks, AK 99701. (907) 479-7205.

Judge Bill Taylor, Running Club North, Room 434, 604 Barnette, Fairbanks, AK 99701. (907) 452-1556 (work).

PHOENIX & SCOTTSDALE

Population: Phoenix—700,000 Scottsdale—82,000	Humidity: 40%
Elevation: 1,200 ft.	Av. Temperature: (Jan.) 51°F.; (July) 91°F.
Air Quality: Poor	Inches of Rainfall: (Jan.) .1; (July) 1.3 Raindays: 35

OVERVIEW

The variety of running conditions and courses in American cities is broadened even further by the unique characteristics of Phoenix. Hot, dry air and a desert environment create distinct problems for visiting runners. Activity flourishes mainly during morning hours, often earlier than most other runners are used to. A weekly Saturday morning group begins their long run at 4:30 A.M. during the hottest months. Other months, they may meet as late as 5:30 A.M. Early runs eliminate the need for shade trees, which do not exist anyway. Sometimes a big rock can provide a cool respite. Rain seldom falls outside of July and August.

Locating a running course can be as simple as finding your nearest neighborhood canal, and running along the side on dirt paths. These canals, which meander in odd directions throughout the city, were built by the Salt River Project, an irrigation project started under Teddy Roosevelt, with hydroelectricity added later. Terrain on the canals is level, except for occasional sudden dips, and the running surface is smooth. Very few roads cross the canals to interfere with your pace.

Streets are laid out in a grid pattern, with major roads every mile. Mountains surround the city, and its suburbs provide good hill work in some of the outlying parks. Both Phoenix and Scottsdale are major resort towns, only about 10 miles apart from downtown to downtown. The two cities share the same canals, and even the same running organizations. Races are quite numerous most of the year, to make up for their absence during the hot summer.

Most visitors stay in resort hotels away from the downtown area of Phoenix, which does have its own excellent hotels. Downtown running is limited to fairly busy streets, and small Encanto Park.

HOTELS

Phoenix: Adams Hotel, Del Webb's Townehouse, Hyatt Regency, Arizona Biltmore
Scottsdale: Radisson Resort Hotel, Holiday Inn, Scottsdale Hilton, Safari Hotel

ENCANTO PARK

This course begins at the YMCA, only a few blocks from the downtown hotels. Run north on 2nd Avenue for two blocks, and turn west on Roosevelt for one block. Then turn north on 3rd Avenue for 1½ miles to a west turn onto Encanto Boulevard for four blocks to the beginning of the park. Continue west, running through the parking lot, past the band shell and under about 100 yards of shade trees to 15th Avenue. Turn north on 15th and follow the pathway for ¾ of a mile into the park, always holding a northerly direction as other paths veer off to the side. A small clubhouse along the way has water. Two hundred yards later, you will reach the northern edge of the park. Head east along the perimeter of the golf course, on the grass inside the fence, for about ¾ of a mile until you have to turn south, staying in the golf course for 1 mile back to Encanto Boulevard. A small fence must be jumped to get back on the road. Return back to the YMCA along the same roads on which you reached the park. The total distance for this course is 5 miles.

The course to and from the park has the luxury of a bike path for part of the way on 3rd Avenue. It is recommended that you never run this route in the dark, but it is safe during the day.

ARIZONA CANAL
This is perhaps the most popular running course (or courses) in both Phoenix and Scottsdale. Plural, because many different segments of the canal are used over a 23.67-mile distance between Thunderbird Road to the west, and Pima Road along the eastern border of Scottsdale. For a long run, you can try the entire length. Many interim distances have been measured. East from Thunderbird Road to Central Avenue is 8.62 miles. Central Avenue to 24th Street mesaures 3.95 miles, and 24th Street to Scottsdale Road is 7.18 miles. Scottsdale Road to Pima Road is 3.92 miles. Each year, the canal is dredged, and the bottom sand is graded over the running paths on each side of the water-way.

The Arizona Biltmore, one of the most luxurious resorts in the country, is located along the canal close to 24th Street. The hotels listed in Scottsdale are within a short distance of the canal, near Camelback and Scottsdale roads.

There are few amenities along the canal, except for other friendly runners, and the soft footing. Water fountains, rest rooms and shade are nonexistent.

SQUAW PEAK PARK
About 7 miles north of downtown Phoenix, this park is situated in the small Phoenix Mountain Range, within the city. Although you can have great views of the city skyline from the top of Squaw Peak, the trail to the summit can be very dangerous for runners inexperienced with shale footing. The loose rock makes it very easy to turn an ankle. The main trail begins at the parking lot and climbs via a switchback route, for 1¼ miles on a 1,500-foot rise. Water is located at the base of the mountain. A number of shale rock horse trails wind around the mountain range, and you can cover about 6 miles without repeating yourself. These trails are fairly flat.

SOUTH MOUNTAIN PARK
This large 15,357-acre park is located about 7 miles south of downtown Phoenix. For a rolling 11-mile run from the entrance, head southwest on the road to San Juan Point and back. A challenging hill course will take you up the road to the top of South Mountain. This 8½- to 9-mile course rises 1,500 to 2,000 feet.

PAPAGO PARK
Just south of Scottsdale, this small, hilly park has many smooth, worn trails. None are measured. Water and rest rooms can be found at the zoo.

CLUBS, FUN-RUNS AND RACES
The Arizona Road Racers is the major running organization in the area. They hold one to two races every weekend during the cooler months. An informal group of its members meets every Saturday at 4:30 A.M. in summer, and 5:30

A.M. other months, at 4250 Union Hills, about 20 miles north of Phoenix. A car rides along with them to hand out water on their long runs.

The Arizona Marathon Society puts on a couple of races during the year, plus they hold a Run for Fun every Sunday.

OUTDOOR TRACKS   Phoenix College, ¼ mile north of Encanto Park, on 15th Avenue, has a ¼-mile dirt track. Many runners include this for extra mileage on their runs around the park. The YMCA has an 18-laps-per-mile track. Arizona State University has a ¼-mile, all-weather track, and three junior colleges have outdoor tracks.

TRADITIONAL RACES   Biltmore 10-Kilometer: Early February
YMCA/Police Academy Half-Marathon: March
S.P.A.E.C. Half-Marathon: Early April
Mormon Lake Half-Marathon: Mid-August
Jerome Hill Climb, 5 miles: Labor Day
South Mountain 11-Mile Run: End of September
Marston South Mountain Hill Climb, 9 miles: October
North Bank 10-Kilometer: Early November
Fiesta Bowl Marathon: Early December

CONTACTS   Charlie Rice, Arizona Road Racers, 10055 East Cactus Road, Scottsdale, AZ 85260. (602) 948-6294.
Mitch Tillotson, Arizona Road Runners, (602) 993-8183.
Dr. Art Mollen, Arizona Marathon Society, 6825 North 18th Place, Phoenix, AZ 85016.
Phoenix YMCA, 350 North First Avenue, Phoenix, AZ 85003. (602) 253-6181.

TUCSON

Population: 310,000	Humidity: 39%
Elevation: 2,400 ft.	Av. Temperature: (Jan.) 51°F.; (July) 86°F.
Air Quality: Fair	Inches of Rainfall: (Jan.) .8; (July) 2.4 Raindays: 50

OVERVIEW

Tucson will please the adventuresome spirit of your running heart. You can enjoy running through colorful desert terrain with its inherently beautiful, natural environment; the giant saguaro cactus or a vast array of desert creatures can be readily experienced. Or try the surrounding hills, offering challenging workouts along dramatic canyon routes.

Many local runners say this is the best running environment you can find. When there is much rainfall, it usually occurs at night, and the terrain will be dry for a morning run. Summer heat presents a problem only during the middle of the day. The desert climate provides cool night temperatures, and mornings are very comfortable.

This spread-out city has very few available courses for centralized running; the popular in-town running routes can be found 5 or 6 miles from the center of the city, and are listed below. If you must stay close to the center, a dry riverbed runs through the downtown area, but would be the last choice, other than streets, for a decent workout.

Beware of the dry climate, and remember to drink plenty of fluids during your run.

HOTELS

Doubletree Inn, Best Western Aztec Inn, Rancho de Rio Motel

RANDOLPH PARK

Located close to 6 miles east of downtown, this is the most convenient, popular place to run in Tucson. Doubletree Inn sits right across the street from the park on Alvernon. Aztec Inn, also on Alvernon, is within ½ mile of the park. The city is laid out in square-mile blocks, and the park lies within one of these blocks, bounded by Alvernon on the east, Broadway on the north, Country Club on the west, and 22nd Street along the south. A 4-mile loop can be run around the perimeter of the park. Terrain is flat, and footing is divided between grass and pavement. Almost no shade can be found along the route. Water and rest rooms can be found on the inside of the park.

A grouping of three baseball fields within the park provides an oval loop of ½ mile. This is very popular among shorter distance runners. Nearby water fountains and grass footing make this loop desirable. The golf course is fenced off to keep runners out.

SABINO CANYON

This exciting, challenging course can be found 12 to 13 miles northeast of town. Take Tanque Verde Road to Sabino Canyon Road, and continue north to the Visitors' Center. You can park your car at the Visitors' Center parking lot, as the road within the Canyon has now been completely closed to cars. Rancho de Rio Motel is not far from the canyon.

This very hilly course follows Sabino Creek through Sabino Canyon, crisscrossing over the creek many times. You will travel over ten bridges on this 7½-mile, out-and-back, paved route. Rolling hills constitute the initial 1.2 miles to the first bridge. Then it is mostly up, climbing several hundred feet to the turnaround. The road doubles back on itself, so it is easy to follow.

Rest rooms can be found along the entire course, but water is available only the first third of the way; *do not* drink water from the creek. Beware, at times the creek can run dangerously high, washing over some of the bridges. People have been swept into the water and drowned.

An alternate route can be run from the canyon road. If you turn right at .6 miles onto Bear Canyon Road, you will be on a 4- to 4½-mile out-and-back course. This is not quite as hilly as the Sabino Canyon Road.

No shade trees are available in the area, although in Sabino Canyon the canyon walls will often block out the sun.

OLD SPANISH TRAIL

If you head east on Broadway, you will hit Sarnoff Road at about 8 or 9 miles and .2 miles later, you will be at the Old Spanish Trail. This old road provides some interesting and hilly desert running for as much as 17 miles one way, arriving at Colossal Cave, a tourist attraction.

SAGUARO NATIONAL MONUMENT ROAD

The entrance to Saguaro National Park can be found 6.4 miles along the Old Spanish Trail. You can drive to the monument and leave your car in the parking lot. The road loops around this cactus-filled park for 8.3 miles. Interesting wildlife can be found along the hilly terrain. Coral snakes and Mojave rattlesnakes are common here, but the broad road gives you plenty of room to run wide of any danger. Do not worry about the poisonous Gila monsters, as they would have to gnaw away at your leg for a while to do any damage. After a heavy rain, tarantulas abound along the road. Contrary to their bad reputation, they are harmless.

Water and rest rooms can be found at the entrance to the park. Mileage markers do not exist, but the 4.1-mile mark is at the pull-off parking lot at the top of the first big hill; and the 6.3-mile mark is at a picnic area which has rest-room facilities.

PIMA COLLEGE CROSS-COUNTRY COURSE AND OUTDOOR TRACK

Four or 5 miles west of town, the Pima College all-weather track remains lit at night during the summer for the public to take advantage of the cool night air. Next to the track is the start of an interesting desert cross-country course. There are many alternative routes, from 2 to 6 miles in length. They are all difficult to follow, so it is best to find a local runner to guide you through. The footing is mostly on dirt and over rocks.

CLUBS, FUN-RUNS AND RACES

The Southern Arizona Road Runners Club holds fun-runs every Sunday morning at Sabino Canyon. They also hold races on a weekly schedule.

TRADITIONAL RACES

Tucson Sun Run, 15 kilometers: March
Cottonwood Lane, 10 kilometers: Late April

Saguaro National Monument Loop Run, 8.3 miles: Labor Day
Turkey Trot, 4 miles: Weekend before Thanksgiving
Sabino Canyon Cross-Country Race, 20 kilometers: Late November or early December

CONTACT Chuck Kerr, Southern Arizona Road Runners Club, 8230 East Broadway, Suite W2, Tucson, AZ 85710. (602) 886-9552, 296-4830.

Little Rock

Population: (met.) 207,000	Humidity: 70%
Elevation: 291 ft.	Av. Temperature: (Jan.) 39.5°F.; (July) 81.4°F.
Air Quality: Fair	Inches of Rainfall: (Jan.) 4.2; (July) 3.4 Raindays: 102

OVERVIEW

Situated in the geographical center of the state, Little Rock is located alongside the Arkansas River across the bank from North Little Rock, a separate and important city in Arkansas. The two cities together comprise the Little Rock metropolitan area.

Good running courses can be found in both cities, although the best areas are not reachable by foot from any of the hotels. Terrain varies greatly, from very hilly areas to flat riverside runs. Burns Park has been well prepared for visiting runners with colored markers placed to guide the unfamiliar. Humidity is noticeably high throughout the year.

HOTELS

Sheraton Motor Inn (Little Rock), Holiday Inn (North Little Rock)

BURNS PARK

About 1½ miles south along busy I-40 from the Holiday Inn, Burns Park must be reached by car. Many runners in the city prefer to train here. Cross over the bridge to the south side of the freeway near the golf course and the Arkansas River. Follow park signs to the Archery Range. At the range, you'll find three different sets of colored markers at the first intersection; follow the arrow of the color you select, and continue to follow the arrows of the same color at all other intersections. This will provide a 4-mile course over hilly terrain with some cross-country paths. There are three different courses, each designated by a different color.

Water fountains and rest rooms are available. The park is not considered a good place to run at night.

MACARTHUR PARK

Downtown Little Rock provides this attractive park for convenient workouts. The Sheraton is only about one block away. A flat, 1½-mile perimeter road circles around the park and the Arkansas Art Center within the park. However, the surrounding area is not considered safe, nor is nighttime running in the park.

ARKANSAS RIVER ROUTE

Starting about 4 miles from downtown, the river run passes through a scenic area at the river's edge. A road or bike path will take you along a 4-mile stretch from the Arkansas River Dam to the "old clubhouse." This flat, shady course normally has light traffic. At the Arkansas River Dam, the course begins just off Resamen Park Road. Parking is available at either end of the course.

OUTDOOR TRACKS	A good all-weather track is located downtown at Scott Field on the grounds of Forrest Heights Junior High School on University Avenue, ½ mile south of Cantrell Avenue, a main artery. In North Little Rock, the Old Main High School track is ¼ mile north of the Holiday Inn.
INDOOR TRACK	The downtown YMCA at 6th and Broadway has an indoor, banked oval track of 16 laps to the mile.
CLUBS	Two running clubs are active in the Little Rock area: the Little Rock Road Runners Club holds weekly fun-runs and monthly races; the Little Rock Hash House Harriers also hold weekly fun-runs and sponsor several 25-kilometer races during the year.
FUN-RUNS	LRRRC fun-runs are held every Saturday morning and are organized through the Finish Line Sports store (address given below). The Hash House Harriers meet at 4:00 P.M. every Sunday during most of the year, and at 7:00 P.M. on Mondays during the summer. The locations of all fun-runs vary, and the appropriate sponsors should be contacted for details.
TRADITIONAL RACES	Arkansas 5-Kilometer Championships: April Fourth of July 4-Mile Run Arkansas 20-Kilometer Championships: November Roadhog Road Race, 6 miles: December
CONTACTS	Lloyd Walker, Little Rock Road Runners Club, 28 Pleasant Cove, Little Rock, AR 72211. (501) 225-9018. Gary Smith, Finish Line Sports, 5623 Kavanaugh, Little Rock, AR 72207. Rick Pruett, Little Rock Hash House Harriers, 1034 Grayland, Jacksonville, AR 72076. (501) 982-7301.

LAKE TAHOE

Population: Not available	Humidity: Not available
Elevation: 6,230 ft.	Av. Temperature: (Jan.) 27°F.; (July) 61°F.
Air Quality: Good	Inches of Rainfall: (Jan.) 6.13; (July) .26 Raindays: Not available

OVERVIEW

Bordered along magnificent Lake Tahoe, this high altitude city contains excellent running facilities, and has been used as an Olympic training site. It lies on a flat plain, surrounded by craggy peaks of the Sierra Mountain Range. Downtown running provides none of the hill work that can be found in the ski areas close to town. Also, many mountain roads and trails provide an infinite choice of routes.

Early September brings the first snowfalls, and local runners turn into avid skiers as well. No races or fun-runs are held during ski season, but training continues throughout the year, even with annual heavy snowfall. Roads are well plowed, and temperatures seldom remain below freezing during the day, which quickly melts the snow and keeps the roads from freezing. Runners claim to have excellent footing all winter long.

The major focus in town is the newly resurfaced 400-meter Tartan track at the Intermediate School. A number of world-class athletes come here for summer training to take advantage of the altitude and the great track. They also can support themselves with convenient part-time work in the gaming casinos.

HOTELS

This is a resort town loaded with variably priced hotels. The track is centrally located, as are most hotels.

ROUTE FROM INTERMEDIATE SCHOOL TRACK

From the track, head out Al Tahoe Boulevard, along its wide dirt shoulder, to a right turn onto Johnson Road. Follow this dirt road for 1 mile until you can turn right across a meadow, following a creek back to the track. The course is flat, well shaded, and marked for directions. This 3-mile loop can hook onto another 2-mile loop for a figure-eight, 5-mile run. The 2-mile loop is marked for direction as well. Both loops come back to the track, where water and rest rooms are available.

ROUTE FROM HIGH SCHOOL TRACK

Heading west from the high school, follow the horse trail to a fork, stay to your right and you will be heading out to Fallen Leaf Lake, which you will reach after 3 miles. The half-paved, half-dirt road around the lake measures 7 miles. The entire route is flat, and pine trees provide substantial shade.

OUTDOOR TRACKS

The 400-meter track at the Intermediate School can be used at all hours. Runners even train here at night, although the track is not lit. The high school has a ¼-mile dirt track.

CLUBS, FUN-RUNS
AND RACES

The South Tahoe Track Club holds events at the Intermediate School Track during summer months. Fun-runs are every Saturday at 10:00 A.M., and track meets are held every Thursday at 5:30 P.M.

TRADITIONAL RACES

Tahoe 72-Mile Relay (seven-person teams): June
Incline Marathon: Late June
Ponderosa Ridge Run: Mid-July
Tahoe 72-Mile Run: Late September

CONTACTS

Austin Angell, South Tahoe Track Club, Box 1521, South Lake Tahoe, CA 95705. (916) 541-5224; (916) 544-7337 (where he is Chef de Cuisine at the Christiania Inn).
Lake Tahoe Track Club, Box 5983, Incline Village, NV 89450.

LOS ANGELES

Population: (met.) 9,200,000	Humidity: 61%
Elevation: 0– 5,074 ft.	Av. Temperature: (Jan.) 55°F.; (July) 73°F.
Air Quality: Poor	Inches of Rainfall: (Jan.) 3; (July) .05 or less Raindays: 35

OVERVIEW

This densely populated city consists of many small towns and areas that, to an outsider, are hardly distinguishable from each other. Running was not considered in the design of the city, and few good courses are convenient to any hotels. It is almost impossible to get around town without a car, as mass transit and taxis are scarce. In a city of this great size, only a handful of decent and popular courses are available, and a car is necessary to get to most of them.

If you are staying in downtown Los Angeles, there are no convenient runs through parks or other scenic environments. The only solution is the unobstructed area around the Convention Center.

Griffith and Elysian parks, located on the northeastern side of the city, provide some excellent hill training as well as some scenic views of the Los Angeles skyline. Many runners come to Griffith Park to avoid some of the heavy smog found closer to downtown.

Smog is the worst enemy in this city, and many days of high pollution can interfere with a good training schedule. But runners tend to challenge the elements, be they natural or man-made, and Los Angeles is no exception. Marty Cooksey, one of the top women distance runners in the world, is somewhat stoic about the problem. "I liken days when I can't get enough oxygen to the positive effects of altitude training." There are some days when smog is just too heavy, and a "Stage 3 Alert" is enforced. During this time, driving is restricted, and it is recommended to stay indoors.

The most popular running course in town is the grass median on San Vicente Boulevard. Somehow, I had pictured this as a busy commercial avenue where runners brave choking auto fumes and dangerous intersections. My mind is now at rest, as I found an attractive, residential avenue winding peacefully down to the ocean in Santa Monica. The oceanfront in Los Angeles, although busy, provides many miles of long, flat sidewalks and bike paths.

San Fernando Valley, lying north of Los Angeles, is home to more than another million metropolitan residents. Its flat terrain provides few running facilities for this large population to enjoy. Woodley Park and the Balboa Sports Center, at the Sepulveda Flood Control Basin and Dam, attract many runners to the flat, open miles along golf courses, ball fields and agricultural projects.

HOTELS	Downtown hotels are all within an easy to moderate run of the Convention Center.
	Holiday Inn—Convention Center, Holiday Inn—Santa Monica, Holiday Inn—Brentwood, Bel Air Sands—Brentwood
CONVENTION CENTER	It is less than ½ mile from your downtown hotel to the Convention Center. Holiday Inn is located right across the street. From the other hotels, run to Figueroa Street, and then go south to 11th Street, which borders the Convention Center on the north. Figueroa continues along the eastern edge, Pico on the south, and Sentous on the west. One loop on the sidewalk along these streets measures about 1 mile. This flat run has almost no shade. Water is available at the Convention Center, when it is open.
ELYSIAN PARK	About 3 miles north of downtown, this park can be reached on foot along city streets by heading north on Hill Street, over the Hollywood Freeway, and continuing north another ⅓ of a mile before turning west onto College Street. After another ⅓ mile, go north on Chavez Ravine Place, followed by a quick left onto Stadium Way for the last mile to the park.

There are no set courses in Elysian Park, and the roads are so winding and contorted that a map is not even helpful. If you drive here, park at the Police Academy on Academy Road. You might find some other runners at the Academy, or obtain more detailed advice on how to follow the myriad curving and hilly roads. If you give yourself enough running time to allow for becoming lost, about 5 or 10 minutes, you will probably have no trouble returning to your car.

I ran this course with Marty Cooksey, who seemed to know her way around. If we were ever lost, she kept the secret very well. She told me that this was the area where the hillside strangler was active, and she would enjoy the opportunity for the strangler to try and catch her. I questioned what would happen if the strangler were a world-class runner. She replied, "There would be a new world's record." Seeing her handle these hills, I believed her.

It is best to run here early or late, as there is little shade and little water, except at the Academy, picnic areas and park buildings. There are some dirt trails, although most running is on the road. Great vistas can be experienced of the city below, and the San Gabriel Mountains to the north and east.

GRIFFITH PARK	Located about 5½ miles north of downtown, Griffith Park has a vast number of roads and trails, and a variety of running surfaces and terrain. On over 4,000 acres, the park contains 53 miles of trails that zigzag in a disorderly manner. The 15 miles of paved roads seem easier to follow, and you will find many runners using the grass and dirt paths along them. Water can be found at picnic areas along the roads.

A good hill run can be had up to the Observatory. Approaching the park on the Golden State Freeway, exit at Los Feliz Boulevard and follow signs to the Observatory. Leave your car at Los Feliz, and begin your run into the park. Using the grass median or sidewalk, follow the road past the Greek Theater and some picnic areas. At about halfway there will be rest rooms to your left. When you reach the fork, take the road to the right, going through the tunnel and up to the top of the mountain. The course measures 1.9 miles, one way. Shade is plentiful, and the view from the top is spectacular.

A pleasant, flat run can be found along the eastern side of the park. At Los

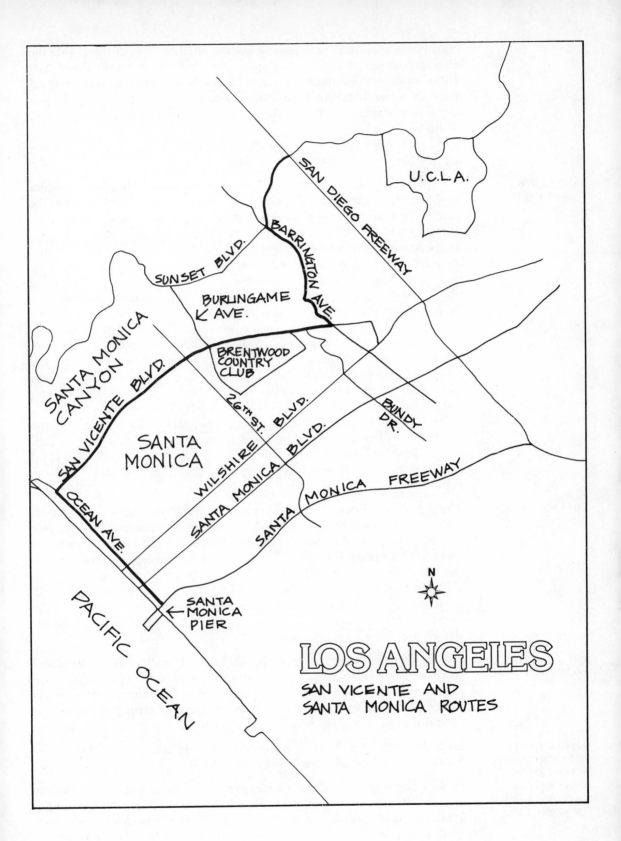

U.C.L.A.

SAN DIEGO FREEWAY

SUNSET BLVD.

BARRINGTON AVE.

BURLINGAME AVE.

SANTA MONICA CANYON

BRENTWOOD COUNTRY CLUB

SAN VICENTE BLVD.

26TH ST.

WILSHIRE BLVD.

SANTA MONICA BLVD.

BUNDY DR.

SANTA MONICA

SANTA MONICA FREEWAY

OCEAN AVE.

N

SANTA MONICA PIER

PACIFIC OCEAN

LOS ANGELES

SAN VICENTE AND
SANTA MONICA ROUTES

Feliz, follow signs to the zoo, and park at the Shetland Pony Stables. Take the sidewalk into the park, staying to your right where there is some shade. You will be on Crystal Springs Drive. At 1.1 miles there are rest rooms, and at 1.3 miles are water fountains. From here, continue on a dirt path along the golf course for a shady 1.2 miles to the zoo parking lot, to complete the 2.5-mile course, one way.

In Los Angeles, and even in Griffith Park, it is best to run early in the morning to avoid the worst hours of air pollution.

SAN VICENTE
BOULEVARD

This popular, attractive course runs through Brentwood and Santa Monica west, slightly downhill, to the ocean. From the usual start at 26th Street to the water is 2½ miles. The Boulevard east of 26th Street becomes somewhat commercial. From 26th Street east to Bundy Drive is exactly 1 mile. The grass median along the Boulevard is intersected by cross streets, which create the only obstacles. Surprisingly, some early morning runners have seen coyotes along the course. Apparently they come south out of the hills. Short, overhanging trees shade the path at regular intervals. Occasional gas stations, and a Baskin-Robbins provide water.

When you reach the ocean, cross the road to run along the grass and sidewalk on the palisades overlooking the beach. If you head south along Ocean Avenue, you will reach the Santa Monica Pier after 1½ miles. The run along the palisades is lined with palm trees, and easy footing and the lack of dogs and bikes make this run truly enjoyable. Later in the day, this area becomes congested with people relaxing in the shade. A Holiday Inn is located at the pier.

On the eastern end of the San Vicente course, another Holiday Inn and the Bel Air Sands Motel, both on Sunset Boulevard at the San Diego Freeway, are within easy reach—about a 1½-mile run from San Vicente Boulevard. Head west on Sunset to a left turn onto Barrington Avenue, which will take you to the Boulevard.

LOS ANGELES
AIRPORT

The airport borders along the ocean, providing moderate accessibility to beach runs. If you have a long layover, then head out the airport exit and run south for 1 mile on Sepulveda Boulevard to Imperial Highway and turn west for another 2.3 miles to the beach. A paved bike path runs along the beach for many miles in each direction.

If you run north on Sepulveda, staying left onto Lincoln Boulevard, you will reach Gonzaga Avenue after about 2 miles. Turn north for almost ½ mile to the Loyola University Campus. The grounds have many grassy areas for pleasurable cross-country running.

SEPULVEDA DAM
RECREATION AREA

Located along the southern edge of the San Fernando Valley, this enclosed area provides many miles of flat, easy, unobstructed paved and dirt pathways. Many runners meet at the parking lot between the Balboa Golf Course and the Sports Center. Routes vary considerably as there are many different golf courses and cornfields to skirt around, as well as grassy ball fields in the western section.

CALIFORNIA STATE
UNIVERSITY, LONG
BEACH CAMPUS

Located south of Los Angeles, many runners come here to enjoy the campus cross-country course on the rolling hills and fields.

UNIVERSITY OF
CALIFORNIA, LOS
ANGELES CAMPUS

In West Los Angeles, UCLA provides excellent facilities that visiting runners can use. The campus contains 413 acres of hilly, grassy terrain with a perimeter 2-mile loop on cinder, dirt and grass trails. At the Sunset Boulevard-Westwood

Leal-Ann Reinhart, along Ocean Avenue in Santa Monica

entrance on Circle Drive, you will see a sign posted with course descriptions. Many parts of the campus have excellent shade, and water fountains and rest rooms are located throughout the area. On Sunset Boulevard, along part of the perimeter course, you can run up a hill measuring 508 yards. This has been named "Veterans Hill."

At Drake Stadium, there is a grass field with a 1,000-meter perimeter. Plans are to eventually put down a Tartan surface on this loop to lessen the heavy use of the track. Parking around UCLA can be a problem.

OUTDOOR TRACKS

At Drake Stadium on the UCLA Campus, a ¼-mile Tartan track is available at all hours except during team practice. Santa Monica College, at 17th Street and Pico Boulevard, has a dirt ¼-mile track. From October to April, it is open and lit on weekday nights from 5:15 to 7:30 P.M. The Santa Monica Track Club works out here. Pierce College, in San Fernando Valley, has a ¼-mile dirt track. Many high schools in the area have good, available tracks.

INDOOR TRACKS

Few indoor tracks exist in this mild, mostly dry climate. A number of YMCA's do have small tracks.

CLUBS AND RACES

A few very serious clubs are active in this city. The San Fernando Valley Track Club has a world-class women's team, as well as top men athletes, and trains under the guidance of the famous Laslo Tibori.

The Santa Monica Track Club has top runners and coaches. Membership is quite costly.

The Seniors Track Club is more interested in the average runner and publishes a newsletter; they are also beginning to put on some races.

"In the Long Run" is a group set up as a clearinghouse of information for runners. Many clinics are held, and some fun-runs. The organizer of the group is sport sociologist, Dr. Jonathan Brower.

The Southern Pacific Association AAU publishes an annual schedule of races.

TRADITIONAL RACES

Brentwood 10-Kilometer: Memorial Day
Palos Verdes Marathon: June
Marina Venice Race, 10 kilometers: July
Santa Monica Marathon: Last Sunday in August
Perrier 10-Kilometer: September
Culver City Marathon: First Saturday in December

CONTACTS

Southern Pacific Association AAU, 10917 Riverside Drive, North Hollywood, CA 91603. (213) 877-0256.
John Rupp, Seniors Track Club, Box 2161 TA, Los Angeles, CA 90051.
Ed Stotsenberg, Santa Monica Track Club, 9418 Wilshire Boulevard, Beverly Hills, CA 90212. (213) 274-8288.
In the Long Run, Box 67824, Los Angeles, CA 90067. (213) 553-3899.
UCLA Track Office, (213) 825-1822.

Oakland

Population: 331,000	Humidity: 71%
Elevation: 0 – 1,754 ft.	Av. Temperature: (Jan.) 49°F.; (July) 63°F.
Air Quality: Fair to poor	Inches of Rainfall: (Jan.) 4.2; (July) .01 Raindays: 63

OVERVIEW

Oakland residents say that if you haven't lived there, you wouldn't know what a great city it is. Most visitors only look at the city across the bay from San Francisco; large hotels do not even exist in downtown Oakland. But this quiet town has some amenities that runners can appreciate. For example, Lake Merritt, a saltwater lake, is tucked within the downtown area, and its perimeter provides a very scenic route. The Oakland hills, shooting up over 1,700 feet, create challenging workouts through rustic redwood forests.

The Bay Area Rapid Transit System connects Oakland with San Francisco and Berkeley to provide easy access to the running opportunities in those cities.

HOTELS

Hotel Leamington, Best Western Boatel Motor Lodge, Best Western Thunderbird Lodge

LAKE MERRITT

This attractive downtown lake is bordered by office buildings on the north and east sides, while residential communities border the south and west. The old Leamington Hotel, with fair accommodations, is the only convenient hotel, located about ¼ of a mile directly north of the lake.

The lake circumference measures 3.2 miles on a flat and mostly paved path. Grass is often available alongside. A few boathouses have water and rest rooms, and you will find occasional, but little shade.

EMBARCADERO

A popular place for visitors to stay is Jack London Square, along the bay. The Boatel and Thunderbird lodges are located here. As the neighborhoods around the square are not very pretty or interesting, and there are no scenic running courses along the bay, most runners head out on the Embarcadero, an industrial road along the estuary, a channel between San Francisco Bay and San Leandro Bay. Because the road parallels the freeway, it carries little traffic. A flat shoulder provides adequate footing for a run. You can run 5 or 6 miles one way in a southerly direction.

JOAQUIN MILLER PARK AND REDWOOD PARK

These two contiguous parks offer ideal running conditions. Located 4 or 5 miles north, in the Oakland hills, they can be reached by taking MacArthur Boulevard Freeway northeast to Fruitvale Avenue. Go two blocks up Fruitvale and turn left onto Lincoln. This becomes Joaquin Miller Road, which will take you to the park.

If you think you might enjoy running on solid dirt trails over hilly terrain through beautiful redwood forests, then you might consider this area. On days when the air pollution is unhealthy, the forest air remains clean, and is normally cool.

Check at the ranger station for maps of the trails, and once you pick your route, there will be markers along the trails to guide you. Water fountains and rest rooms can be found periodically en route. During heavy rains, footing becomes very difficult, and many runners change over to the Skyline Boulevard route.

SKYLINE BOULEVARD

Skyline Boulevard runs between Joaquin Miller Park and Redwood Park. Many runners begin this course at the Joaquin Miller Park parking lot. Head left on the undulating, shady road, and after 3 miles you will arrive at Skyline Gate parking area, where you can obtain water. Continuing north, at 5 miles you will come to a firehouse where water is again available. Here you will be at the junction of Snake Road and Colton. You can continue north for another 10 or 15 miles, or you can turn back.

OUTDOOR TRACKS

Numerous colleges, in and around the city, have good all-weather tracks. Laney College is in the downtown area. Merritt College is in the hills, and the College of Alameda is 10 minutes south of town through the tube under the estuary.

INDOOR TRACKS

The Oakland YMCA has a gym where you can run 20 laps per mile. The Y is only three blocks from Lake Merritt.

Lake Merritt, Oakland

CLUBS

A number of clubs are active in Oakland. Between the East Bay Road Runners Club and the Lake Merritt Joggers and Striders, you can find many running events to choose from.

TRADITIONAL RACES

Woodminster Cross-Country Run, 9¼ miles: Early June
Lafayette Rim Run, 5 miles: Late August

Oakland Brass Pole Run, 10 kilometers: Late September
Marine Air Reserve Run, 6 and 3 miles: Late September
Berkeley Moraga Run, 13 miles: Mid-October

CONTACTS

Gail Wetzork, East Bay Road Runners Club, 1940 Webster Street, Oakland, CA 94612. (415) 522-3724.

John Notch, Lake Merritt Joggers and Striders, 230 Marlow Drive, Oakland, CA 94605. (415) 562-2210.

Oakland YMCA, 2101 Telegraph Avenue, Oakland CA 94612. (415) 451-5711.

Oakland Parks and Recreation Department, Burton Webber, Public Relations, (415) 273-3091.

Laney College, Special Services Department, (415) 834-5740.

PALM SPRINGS

Population: 30,000	Humidity: 45%
Elevation: 420 ft.	Av. Temperature: (Jan.) 54°F.; (July) 91°F.
Air Quality: Fair to poor	Inches of Rainfall: (Jan.) 1.1; (July) .24 Raindays: 16

OVERVIEW

Running through a desert can be a challenging experience. If that's what you want to do, then Palm Springs is perhaps the safest and most stylish place to do it. The city lies very flat at the base of Mount San Jacinto, and the mountain casts its shadow over the town in the late afternoon, creating more time for late-day runs out of the sun.

Warm weather (or hot) prevails year 'round, with temperatures in the summer becoming unbearable for all but early morning workouts. Later in the day, the sun heats up the road so much it can practically burn your shoes off. And a further warning: because the air is dry, the normal high temperatures seem cooler, yet your body can dehydrate very quickly here without exhibiting a lot of perspiration.

There are no large parks to run in, so most mileage is gained along the local roads which are basically laid out in a square-grid pattern. Golf courses can be attempted, although some will not allow runners.

Being a resort town, hotels are plentiful. The preferred location for runners is the southern part of town where there are more golf courses with available water, more opportunities for grass running, and less wind to fight.

HOTELS

Canyon Hotel, Vagabond Hotel, Royal Inn, Riviera Hotel

SOUTHERN ROUTE

The Vagabond and Royal Inn sit close to each other along with about six other motels. The same route can be run from all of them. Head south for about 1⅓ miles on Palm Canyon, turning east onto Murray Canyon for 1 mile. Then go north on Toledo for 1 mile; then west on LaVerne for 4/5 of a mile. You will then be back on Palm Canyon, where you head north to your hotel for the last ⅓ mile. The total distance is about 4½ miles.

The Canyon Hotel and the few motels around it lie more to the south, but one can follow the same route starting from a different part of the course. Start east on Murray Canyon, then north on Toledo, west on LaVerne, and south on Palm Canyon for about a 4-mile loop.

NORTHERN ROUTE

From the Riviera and the few motels around it, you can follow another easy grid course for 5 miles. Go south on Indian for 1½ miles, turning east on

Tahquitz-McCallum for 1 mile. Then turn north on Sunrise for 1½ miles until you go west on Vista Chino for the last mile.

AERIAL TRAMWAY ROAD

The Tramway Road leads off from Palm Canyon, a major thoroughfare through town. The Riviera Hotel is about 1 mile south of the road, and just one block east of Palm Canyon.

Climbing over 1,800 feet over 4 miles, the Tramway Road presents a real challenge. The entire road is paved, and no shade is available until the last mile, where you will find a creek bed and several trees. There is no water along the route. At the top of the road, you will reach the base station for the tramway and can obtain water, and perhaps a lift down if you are not into downhill running.

FUN-RUNS

There are fun-runs every Sunday morning at Palm Springs High School at 8:00 A.M., and in Palm Desert at the College of the Desert at 9:00 A.M.

CLUBS AND RACES

It will only be a matter of time until the local runners organize a club. A few 10-kilometer runs are scheduled nearby at Banning, Indio and Blythe, California.

TRADITIONAL RACE

Big Macathon, 10 miles, Palm Desert: Saturday before Christmas

CONTACTS

Jack T. Warren, 1653 San Lucas Road, Palm Springs, CA 92262. (714) 327-6809.

J. Clayton Taylor, 250 Debby Drive, Palm Springs, CA 92262. (714) 327-9180.

SACRAMENTO

Population: 260,700	Humidity: 66%
Elevation: 17 ft.	Av. Temperature: (Jan.) 45°F.; (July) 73°F.
Air Quality: Fair to poor	Inches of Rainfall: (Jan.) 1.9; (July) .1 Raindays: 57

OVERVIEW

Very few cities can boast of good street running in their downtown areas. The local runners in Sacramento actually recommend it. The city is known for its shade trees, and small parks along the way can provide water and rest rooms. With these positive aspects, add to it the driver awareness that busy street running will create, and the situation starts to approach sanity.

Although Sacramento lies slightly northeast of San Francisco, its valley climate is characterized by hot summers, and the typical Northern California moist, mild winters.

HOTELS

Red Lion Inn, Mansion Inn, Best Western Ponderosa, Vagabond, Motel 6

DOWNTOWN RUNS

Most runners favor running along J and H streets. The terrain is flat, the scenery interesting, and the people are friendly. The Mansion Inn, Best Western, Vagabond, and Motel 6 are good downtown hotels.

AMERICAN RIVER BIKE TRAIL

This winding, scenic, wooded bike trail travels along a river where tranquility was interrupted in 1848 when gold was discovered. Now it's runners' gold as this 13-mile-long trail accommodates a large population utilizing the paved and dirt footing. There are mileage markers every mile and water fountains every 5 miles. You can reach the bike trail 2 miles north of downtown in Discovery Park, at the confluence of the Sacramento and American rivers. The Red Lion Inn is about ½ mile south of the trail.

WILLIAM LAND PARK

A flat, 4-mile loop around this park provides excellent grass footing under heavy shade. The route follows the perimeter, although many cutoffs and variations are possible. The park contains a golf course, gardens and a zoo, as well as plenty of water fountains. Hotels are *not* close to this facility, 2½ miles south of town.

TRACKS

The Sacramento Central YMCA has an outdoor dirt running track, 14 laps per mile, and an indoor gymnasium where you can run the perimeter of 20 laps per mile.

CLUBS

The Buffalo Chips Running Club organizes most of the races in the area; see address and phone number below.

FUN-RUNS

The Rancho Cordova Park District, 10 miles east of downtown, puts on weekly fun-runs every Saturday morning. McIntoshes Sports Cottage puts on monthly fun-runs, 10 miles northeast of downtown, also on Saturday mornings.

TRADITIONAL RACES

Sacramento Marathon: October
Pepsi 20-Mile Run: November

CONTACTS

John McIntosh, Buffalo Chips Running Club, McIntosh's Sports Cottage, 4120 El Camino Avenue, Sacramento, CA 95821. (916) 488-7182.

Sally Edwards, Fleet Feet, 2408 J Street, Sacramento, CA 95814. (916) 442-3338.

Rick Baugher, Central YMCA, 2021 West Street, Sacramento, CA 95818. (916) 452-5451.

SAN DIEGO

Population: (met.) 1,520,000	Humidity: 64%
Elevation: 0–823 ft.	Av. Temperature: (Jan.) 55°F.; (July) 69°F.
Air Quality: Poor	Inches of Rainfall: (Jan.) 1.7; (July) trace Raindays: 42

OVERVIEW

A city with ideal running conditions year 'round is indeed difficult to find. Of course, "ideal" is very subjective, and there are many runners who love harsh winters or hot, wet, humid climates. However, most runners would agree that San Diego is an ideal city for running. During most of the year, temperatures are moderate, with few super-hot days.

Numerous courses can be found throughout the city, and wherever you stay you will be very close to an excellent route. The airport is only 2 miles from downtown, and you will find great running practically outside the door of the plane.

Although you can run along the ocean, about 5½ miles from downtown, San Diego Bay, at the city's edge, is a beautiful harbor with parks and islands awaiting your pleasure. Another popular waterfront run is along Mission Bay and Mission Bay Park, just to the north of town.

If waterside running is not your thing, there is yet the pride of San Diego, Balboa Park. This is a beautiful park situated at the northeast corner of the downtown area. It contains the famous San Diego Zoo, the Natural History Museum, two art galleries, the Museum of Man, the Hall of Champions, and numerous recreational facilities.

HOTELS

Any hotel along the bays or the ocean. At Balboa Park, the Holiday Inn—Harbor View, and the Balboa Park Travelodge.

BALBOA PARK

There are no easy routes to be followed in this park, with all the measured courses involving figure eights and other maneuvers. Most of the running is done on the west side of the freeway, which runs through a valley in the park. This area provides good workouts on Powder Hill, and two other hills known as The Snake, and Switchback. Flat areas can be found along 6th Avenue on the western edge and along El Prado over the bridge to the big water fountain. Drinking fountains are mostly found along 6th Avenue. Shade is plentiful.

Groups of runners meet frequently in front of the Municipal Gym at Pan American Plaza; 11:30 A.M. to noon is a favorite time.

MISSION BAY PARK

Mission Bay is an inland recreational waterway about 4 miles north of downtown. Although a large segment of the park is still undeveloped, there are trails and roads that can be utilized for short to long runs. A popular starting point is at the information booth on the eastern side of the bay at the foot of Clairemont Drive. From here, it is a 5-mile loop if you run north to the De Anza Parking Lot and then south onto the Fiesta Island Bridge, returning from there to the information booth. This run is through the developed section of the park, allowing you to choose between grass and concrete footing. You can see many sailboats and water-skiers in the bay alongside the route. There is no shade in the entire Mission Bay area and the terrain is all flat.

If you run over the bridge onto Fiesta Island, the road looping around the island will add 4 miles to your run. You can park near this island to isolate the loop. Being undeveloped, the island offers no amenities, just wild grass and sand, with a paved road to run on.

For a more varied experience of the bay area, you can follow an 8-mile loop using a causeway to circle around much of the bay. Heading south from the information booth on East Mission Bay Drive, and staying right at 1½ miles onto Sea World Drive, follow the drive to a right onto Perez Cove Way going north over the Ingraham Street Causeway. Take your first right at the end of the bridge onto Crown Point Drive, and then after a mile go left onto Morell Street for nearly ⅓ mile before a right turn onto Grand Avenue. Following this road, you will end up back on East Mission Bay Drive, arriving at the information booth. Be sure to have plenty of water during the first 2 miles, as there will be no fountains after that.

OCEAN ROUTE

On the western side of Mission Bay is the oceanfront, a populated area with a concrete walkway alongside the beach. Good beach running can be enjoyed at low tide. The distance between Crystal Pier in the north, and the jetty at the south end is 2.5 miles.

SAN DIEGO BAY

If you stay along San Diego Bay, there are some areas that offer beautiful waterside runs. The downtown area fronts on the east side of the bay and the harbor is clean with much to see. A Holiday Inn sits across the street from the *Star of India* windjammer at the Embarcadero. Try a run through the Embarcadero in the early morning when the fishermen are preparing their nets. Heading west along the bay toward the airport is a stretch that will soon be developed into an attractive park similar to the one you will reach a little further west past the airport.

When you reach the airport on your right, you will also see a road to your left going out onto Harbor Island. The island is 1½ miles long, and contains some excellent hotels. Along the bay side of the island, for its full length, is a beautiful park providing a choice of grass or pavement running. Rest rooms and water fountains are frequent.

Back out on the road, west along the bay, is a newly developed park. Here you can have a choice of three running surfaces: a smooth dirt path at the water's edge, a paved path, or an even grass surface. As with all parks along the water in San Diego, there are plenty of rest rooms and water fountains.

After the park, you will be passing Naval Training Centers until you reach Scott Street. Make a left here, and then after ¼ mile make another left onto Shelter Island. Again, you will find yourself on another beautiful island with excellent hotels and an attractive waterside park extending for just over a mile.

Wherever you stay along the bay, all these areas are available for an exciting run. From the downtown harbor to the end of Shelter Island is a distance of 6 miles, one way.

CUYAMACA RANCHO STATE PARK

As you travel inland from San Diego, the altitude and the temperature climb together. There is challenging hill work not far from town. If you are willing to travel 45 to 50 miles east, you will find many miles of trails at Cuyamaca. Pick

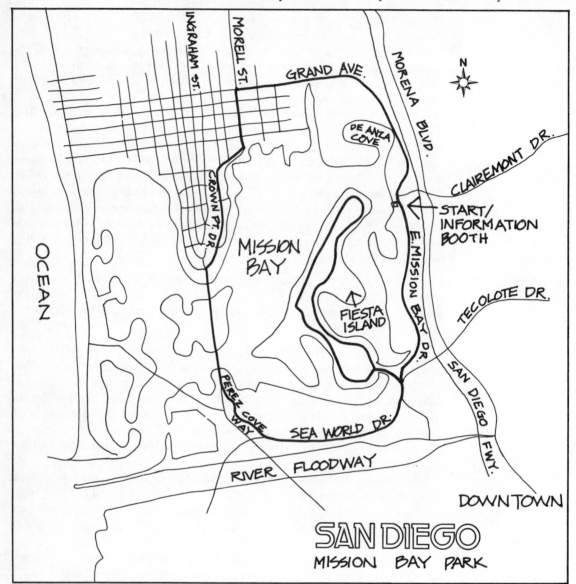

up a state park map at the entrance to Green Valley Falls Campground, or Paso Picacho Campground, and choose a trail. The "Harvey Moore Loop" in the East Mesa area is recommended for seeing a lot of wildlife.

LA JOLLA SHORES

This beach, about 6 miles north of Mission Bay, is considered the best in the area for good, flat runs, regardless of the tide. The 1-mile-long route is very popular.

Balboa Stadium, downtown near Balboa Park, has a ¼-mile rubberized asphalt track that is sometimes available. Call the San Diego Recreation Department to find out when. Point Loma College, about 7 miles from downtown near the entrance to the harbor, has a ¼-mile dirt track. Southwestern College, in Chula Vista, south of town, has a ¼-mile rubberized asphalt track.

San Diego State College has installed a new ¼-mile Tartan track, but is restricting its use. Until it is more available, runners are using a ½-mile loop around the lower grass field. The college can be reached 10 miles east of I—5, on I—8. Grossmont College, 16 miles east of town, has a ¼-mile Tartan track.

The San Diego Track Club averages about three races every two weeks.

The Mission Bay Marathon Clinic meets every Sunday at 8:30 A.M. at the

Harbor Island, San Diego

Mission Bay Information Center. After a warm-up, groups run from 3 to 15 miles or more.

The San Diego Recreation Department sponsors an exercise and fun-run class every Monday, Wednesday and Friday at 5:30 P.M. in Balboa Park. The class is led by Donna Gookin.

Bob Day, at Phidippides Running Store, holds a clinic every Tuesday at 6:30 P.M.; a run is included.

TRADITIONAL RACES

Mission Bay Marathon: Second Saturday in January
Balboa Park 8-Mile: Late August
Aztec "Invitational" Cross-Country, 6 and 4 miles: Third Saturday in October
Mission Bay 25-Kilometer: Three weeks before Marathon

CONTACTS

Dave Baxter, San Diego Track Club, 1940½ Thomas Avenue, San Diego, CA 92109. (714) 483-0909.

Ozzie Gontang, Mission Bay Marathon Clinic, 2903 29th Street, San Diego, CA 92104. (714) 281-7447.

Bill Stock, San Diego Track Club, 7160 Baldrich Street, San Diego, CA 92041. (714) 465-7099.

Bob Day, Phidippides Running Store, 3740 Sports Arena Boulevard, San Diego, CA 92110. (714) 222-7161.

San Diego Recreation Department Information, (714) 236-5740.

San Francisco

Population: (met.) 4,500,000	Humidity: 70%
Elevation: 0–934 ft.	Av. Temperature: (Jan.) 50°F.; (July) 59°F.
Air Quality: Fair	Inches of Rainfall: (Jan.) 4.4; (July) .05 or less Raindays: 67

OVERVIEW

The Golden Gate City rests on a hilly peninsula between the Pacific Ocean and San Francisco Bay. Exhilarating vistas can be experienced on runs along the bay and across the Golden Gate Bridge. As city hills are very steep, and present all the inherent problems of city street running as well, most runners prefer routes along the bay, and in Golden Gate Park, a very large and beautiful area jutting in from the ocean towards downtown. I always thought this park was connected to the bridge, but it is actually over 2½ miles to the south.

The downtown area is not practical for accommodations unless you stay along the bay at Fisherman's Wharf or the Embarcadero. Hotels at Union Square or in Chinatown offer only city street running unless you stay at the Hyatt on Union Square, which offers a shuttle service for runners to Marina Green on the bay.

Excellent running courses can be found in all directions as you head away from the city. Lakes, bays, mountains and the ocean all provide runners with diverse and exciting experiences. The popularity of the sport here is so great that practically every area has developed its own club. Of course, the major organization has long been the Dolphin South End Runners Club, founded by the famous Walt Stack. Walt's inspiration of long, slow, steady mileage, and participation in running events, at any level, has guided the growth of running in much of the country. At every race, when he hands out the awards, he tells the winners that "If it weren't for us slobs, you would have no one to beat."

The weather in San Francisco can be cloudy and cool much of the year. However, it is possible to hit hot weather in the spring, summer, and especially in the early fall. Mark Twain is quoted as saying: "Coldest winter I ever spent was a summer in San Francisco."

HOTELS

Holiday Inn–Fisherman's Wharf, Sheraton at Fisherman's Wharf, Ramada Inn, Travelodge at the Wharf, Hyatt Regency, Holiday Inn–Embarcadero, Hyatt on Union Square

GOLDEN GATE PARK

Golden Gate Park has some magnificent runs passing sumptuous gardens and many small lakes. This is one of the most beautiful parks in America. Many local runners prefer to live close by to take full advantage of its great running environment. Unfortunately, no major hotels exist near the park, which is about 3½ miles southwest of downtown.

It's length is slightly over 3 miles, plus the "panhandle," a thin strip extending east for another ¾ of a mile. Except for the panhandle, the width is about ½ mile, forming a rectangle with the narrow side abutting the ocean.

Recommended courses are very complicated and require familiarity with landmarks. The best bet is to park at the popular starting points, the Polo Field or Stowe Lake, and join up with local runners or head through the park on your own. The main roads are fairly direct and easy to follow. The North and South Drives can be run in a loop, and many roads and paths connect the two drives along the way. Nine lakes dot the park, and the larger ones are encircled with roadways. You'll find grassy areas alongside many roads for safer footing, and sidewalks can help avoid traffic on park roads, which are closed to cars only on Sundays. Shade, water fountains and rest rooms are abundant. The terrain is mostly flat, with a gradual drop-off to the west.

A book about trail runs and path mileage in the park will soon be published. The author is Tom Benjamin.

THE EMBARCADERO

This section is located along the bay just north of the Bay Bridge (which leads to Oakland and Berkeley). You can choose a run northwest to Golden Gate Bridge, or a run south along China Basin. Both runs are along the water.

If you run toward Golden Gate Bridge, head east from your hotel to the Embarcadero, the roadway that runs along the piers. Turn left, and follow the sidewalk for 2 miles to Fisherman's Wharf. It is a flat run with no shade and no water. Most of the piers are fronted by buildings, so there are few views offered along this area. The course becomes more interesting from Fisherman's Wharf to the bridge.

The run along China Basin offers the same scenery as the Embarcadero. Follow the road along the piers for about 2½ miles. These are industrial areas and traffic can be a nuisance during working hours.

FISHERMAN'S WHARF

Proceeding west along the bay from Fisherman's Wharf, stay on Jefferson Street, and after about ½ mile you will be at Van Ness Avenue with Fort Mason directly in front. Run through the fort, which is on a small hill, for the only change in elevation on the entire route, and pick up Marina Boulevard on the other side. In a few hundred yards, you will reach Marina Green, one of the most popular running areas in town.

MARINA GREEN AND GOLDEN GATE PROMENADE

The Green, a large lawn, is about ½ mile long with a yacht basin alongside. Many people do laps around the Green. A series of exercise stations begins here and extends west toward the bridge. No shade is available anywhere along the bay, except at Fort Mason. No water fountains or rest rooms are available either.

Run past the Green, staying on Marina Boulevard for another ½ mile to a right turn into the parking lot at St. Francis Yacht Club. At the water's edge, turn left toward the bridge again. From here it is 1.85 miles along the Golden Gate Promenade to Fort Point, an old Civil War fort that sits under the Golden Gate Bridge. The footing along the promenade alternates between pavement and dirt and sand. Total mileage from Fisherman's Wharf to the bridge and back is about 9 miles.

Views along the run are spectacular—sailboats in the bay, Alcatraz Island,

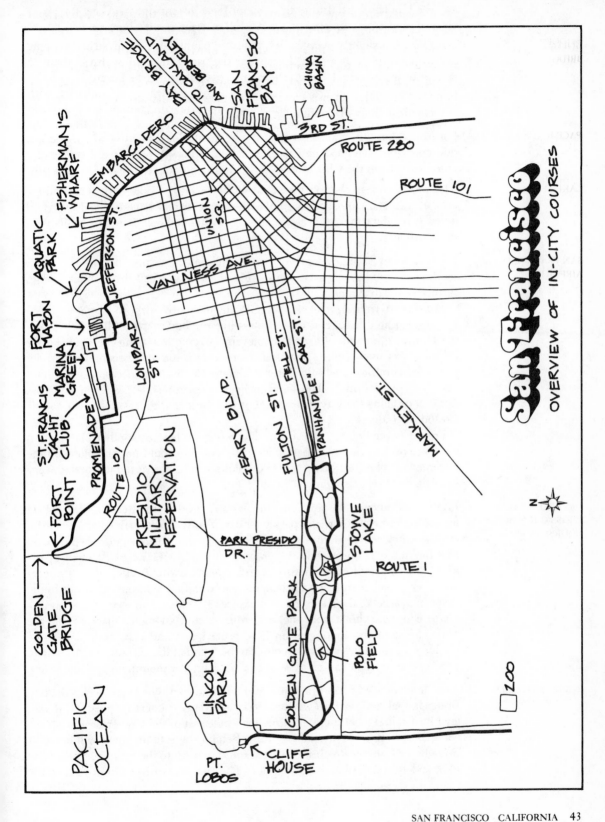

San Francisco

OVERVIEW OF IN-CITY COURSES

PACIFIC OCEAN

GOLDEN GATE BRIDGE

FORT POINT

ST. FRANCIS YACHT CLUB

MARINA GREEN

FORT MASON

AQUATIC PARK

FISHERMAN'S WHARF

EMBARCADERO

BAY BRIDGE

TO OAKLAND AND BERKELEY

SAN FRANCISCO BAY

CHINA BASIN

3RD ST.

ROUTE 280

ROUTE 101

UNION SQ.

JEFFERSON ST.

VAN NESS AVE.

PROMENADE

LOMBARD ST.

ROUTE 101

PRESIDIO MILITARY RESERVATION

GEARY BLVD.

FULTON ST.

FELL ST.

OAK ST.

"PANHANDLE"

MARKET ST.

PARK PRESIDIO DR.

STOWE LAKE

ROUTE 1

GOLDEN GATE PARK

POLO FIELD

LINCOLN PARK

PT. LOBOS

CLIFF HOUSE

N

100

and the Golden Gate Bridge are some of the constant sights. Along the promenade, waves crash up against the seawall offering a refreshing spray.

GOLDEN GATE BRIDGE

A run across the Golden Gate Bridge is a must for visiting runners. You can reach the bridge on foot by running from Fort Point, up the hill to the toll plaza. If you are driving, you can park your car at the vista points at either end of the bridge. The bridge span is close to 1.67 miles, and the distance between vista points is just short of 2 miles.

PACIFIC OCEAN

For ocean running, you can park at the beach at Golden Gate Park, and at low tide you will have good hard-packed sand footing. A measured distance of 3 miles starts from the Cliff House on the north and goes to the zoo at the south.

LAKE MERCED

This pretty run, in the southwest corner of the city, follows a path around the lake. If you start and end at the boathouse, you will have covered exactly 5 miles. It is a flat run with occasional shade. Water and rest rooms are available at the boathouse.

SAN FRANCISCO AIRPORT

Located about 12 miles south of San Francisco, the airport has an easy route south along the bay, or a fabulous place to run if you can drive about 8 miles further south to Belmont.

From the terminal, it is ¾ of a mile out to South Airport Boulevard. The Hilton is located here, and many hotels line the boulevard to the south. From the Hilton, run south along the boulevard, staying left along the bayfront for 2½ miles to Coyote Point. Just after the hotel area the road becomes very quiet and free of traffic. The only drawback along this route is occasional pollution due to airplane fumes. The bayfront is very picturesque, and you will pass duckblinds along the way. Coyote Point was the site of the last settlement of the Costonoan Indians.

From Coyote Point, you can travel on along the bay for another 2½ miles on the levee over a wide macadam pathway. Women should not run alone on the lower levee. The road down to Coyote Point can be run at night. By day, very little shade covers the route.

CRYSTAL SPRINGS CROSS-COUNTRY COURSE IN BELMONT

From San Francisco Airport, take the freeway south to the Belmont Exit. Head for the highest elevation, and park your car. You will have arrived at a beautiful cross-country course along Crystal Spring Lake that has been designed by runners for runners. Located on the grounds of the San Francisco Water Department, the course offers a mixture of trails, paths, switchbacks and hills to provide every level of runner a challenging and fulfilling workout. Laid out in the shape of a large Y, the basic course measures 3½ miles. Some cutoffs are available to eliminate the steeper inclines. Mileage and kilometer markers line the route. Most of the footing is on hard-packed dirt and clay under moderate shade. Two fountains and rest rooms can be found at the entrance to the course. During the run you can enjoy views of the bay, the mountains and the lake.

BERKELEY FIRE TRAIL

Traveling outside of San Francisco, you will find some good runs across the Bay Bridge in Oakland (*see Oakland*) and Berkeley. Many runners frequent the Berkeley Fire Trail. To get there, drive about 1 mile east of the University of California at Berkeley, to Memorial Stadium. Behind the stadium, you will come to Strawberry Canyon Road. Follow that for ½ mile up to the Strawberry Canyon Park and Recreation Area parking lot. The run starts here, uphill next to the swimming pool and alongside a fence for ¼ mile, to a small dirt parking lot on the right. About 50 feet ahead is a dirt road with a chain across it and a sign saying "Fire Trail."

The road is easy to follow as it winds around for 1½ miles until it reaches the far end of the park. Turn left here up a steep hill for about 200 yards to the Upper Fire Trail. This road will take you another 3 miles until it ends at the Space Sciences Laboratory. Along the entire course you will experience an overall rise in elevation of about 1,000 feet.

Great vistas can be seen of San Francisco, the bay, and the bridges. Since the area is heavily wooded, the Fire Trail functions as an access route to fight potential forest fires. During the week, a shuttle bus can take you back to campus from the Space Sciences Laboratory if you do not appreciate downhill running.

CLUBS, FUN-RUNS AND RACES

San Francisco, the Bay Area, the Peninsula, and Marin County are loaded with vital, active running clubs. The Dolphin South End Running Club, known as the DSE, has a large participatory following. Members score points with their training mileage and the mileage run in races to become eligible for a trophy at the end of the year. The club has a monthly newsletter and holds weekly races.

The West Valley Track Club has developed a great reputation for national and world-class competition. Their women's marathon team has always won high honors in international events. The club is also famous for its publication, the *Nor-Cal Running Review*, an excellent running magazine published six times a year. These activities overshadow other aspects of the club, such as the frequent local races they hold.

Walt Stack on the Golden Gate Promenade, San Francisco

The Camino West Runners Club is another large organization that puts on many races throughout the year.

The Tamalpa Runners holds fun-runs on a magnificent course, 20 minutes north of San Francisco in Marin County. On Saturdays at 9:00 A.M., runners meet at Mountain Home Inn Restaurant on Panoramic Highway. The run goes around and over Mount Tamalpais, a beautiful redwood forest area. Afterward, the group breakfasts in the Mill Valley vicinity.

Forty-five minutes south of San Francisco in Los Altos Hills, the guiding light of fun-runs, *Runner's World* magazine, holds weekly fun-runs on Sundays at 9:30 A.M., starting at the Foothill College lower parking lot.

The Embarcadero YMCA has many groups heading out during the day on runs north and south along the bay. They hold an official fun-run every Friday afternoon at 12:15 P.M.

TRADITIONAL RACES
West Valley Marathon: February
Bay to Breakers, 7.6 miles: Late April, early May
Dipsea, 6.7 miles: Summer
Golden Gate Charity Run, 10 kilometers: August
Times 9, 9.9 kilometers: Labor Day
Double Dipsea, 13.4 miles: Early September
Bridge to Bridge, 10 kilometers: October
Excelsior West End, 10 kilometers: November
Livermore Marathon: December
Christmas Relays, 50 miles: December

CONTACTS
Walt Stack, 321 Collingwood Street, San Francisco, CA 94114.
Jack Leydig, *Nor-Cal Running Review*, Box 1551, San Mateo, CA 94401. (415) 341-3119.
Pete Michon, Camino West R.C., 174 Crestview Drive, San Carlos, CA 94070.
Bob Anderson, Rich Benyo, *Runner's World* magazine, 1400 Stierlin, Mountain View, CA 94043. (415) 965-8777.
Don Capron, Tamalpa Runners, 4808 Fulton Street, San Francisco, CA 94121. (415) 668-3875.
Ed Ducazau, Embarcadero YMCA, 166 Embarcadero, San Francisco, CA 94105. (415) 392-2191.

SAN JOSE

Population: 570,000	Humidity: 58%
Elevation: 100 ft.	Av. Temperature: (Jan.) 49.2°F.; (July) 68.2°F.
Air Quality: Poor	Inches of Rainfall: (Jan.) 2.7; (July) trace Raindays: 80

OVERVIEW

Located 50 miles south of San Francisco in the Santa Clara Valley, San Jose participates in the intense running atmosphere of the Bay Area. The Santa Cruz Mountains rise up along the western edge of the city, providing some beautiful scenic runs above the flat valley. Terrific climate is the keynote here. Santa Clara Valley maintains warm, comfortable temperatures year 'round, while mountains separate the city from moist ocean air. Your carbohydrate and mineral needs can easily be met by making use of the abundant supply of fruits and vegetables grown in this agriculturally rich environment.

Downtown, runs basically include tolerable city streets, often with bike lanes, and many small parks where you can run around ball fields. High schools have good tracks. For the best courses and good accommodations, many runners prefer to stay in the foothills west of town. Here you will find less traffic, more shade, and a more challenging terrain. The hillside environment is truly magnificent, and the area is convenient to downtown.

HOTELS

La Hacienda Inn Motor Hotel, Los Gatos Lodge

VILLA MONTALVO ARBORETUM

Beginning at La Hacienda Inn on Highway 9, proceed west, staying to the left in the bike lane and continuing past the traffic lights to a gate on the left. This is the entrance to the Aboretum, a scenic retreat for artists, nestled in the foothills. You will see beautiful gardens, a bubbling creek, plenty of shade with tall trees, birds and deer. You will *not* see any dogs.

Follow the main road until it crests at the main building, and then head downhill, past the stop sign and back out onto Highway 9 and return to the Inn. The run measures 5 miles. Gates to the Arboretum close at 5:00 P.M.

VASONA PARK

Head east on Highway 9 toward Los Gatos. Turn left at the first set of traffic lights onto Winchester Boulevard, and then right at the next traffic light onto Blossom Hill Road. Continue down the hill, staying left, and turn left into Vasona Park after you pass the creek. From here, you can follow paths around a small, pretty lake or run on one of the grass fields surrounding the park. Return along the same route. This course measures 4.5 miles out and back from La Hacienda Inn. Early morning runs are best to avoid traffic on this route.

OCEAN RUNS

Northern California always has beautiful routes along the ocean. A 30-minute drive south on Highway 17 will take you to Santa Cruz beaches.

OUTDOOR TRACKS	Many high school and college tracks are available. Two popular tracks in the foothills can be found at West Valley College and Los Gatos High School.
CLUBS, FUN-RUNS AND RACES	The West Valley Joggers and Striders have a run every Saturday morning at West Valley College at 8:00 A.M. at the track. Running events are normally printed in the *San Jose Mercury-News* Sports Section on Saturday morning. The famous *Runner's World* fun-runs are held every Sunday at 9:30 A.M. at Foothill College in Los Altos Hills, north of San Jose.
TRADITIONAL RACES	Paul Masson Marathon: January *San Jose News* Race, 6 miles: March Dammit Run, 5.593 miles: August
CONTACTS	Ken Napier, West Valley Joggers and Striders, 1612 Bearden Drive, Los Gatos, CA 95030. (408) 379-1420. Valley Athletic Sporting Goods, 1424 Saratoga Sunnyvale Road, San Jose, CA 95128. (408) 446-2727.

BOULDER

Population: 78,600	Humidity: Not available
Elevation: 5,354 ft.	Av. Temperature: (Jan.) 33°F.; (July) 74°F.
Air Quality: Fair to poor	Inches of Rainfall: (Jan.) .8; (July) 1.7 Raindays: 56

OVERVIEW

Boulder is a special town. Sitting right at the base of the Flatiron Range of the Rockies, the high altitude and dry mountain air create an ideal atmosphere for serious distance training. Many of the nation's elite runners either live here or travel here to utilize Boulder's gifted environment.

Some of the local runners include Frank Shorter, Rick Rojas, Ted Casteneda, John Gregorio and Guy Arbogast. In 1977, after Lasse Viren ran the New York City Marathon, he went to check out Boulder to see what he was missing.

The city itself is flat, with hills rising up from the southwest to the Flatirons, Flagstaff Mountain and the Table Mesa area. Hotels are located along the eastern perimeter of town, a distance of about 2 to 3 miles to the foothills.

HOTELS

Holiday Inn, Broker Inn, Best Western Golden Bluff, Hilton Harvest House

CHAUTAUQUA PARK ONTO MESA TRAIL

Chautauqua Park lies at the base of the Flatirons in the southwest corner of town. It can be reached from the above hotels, located near 28th Street and Arapahoe Avenue, by running west on Arapahoe to 6th Street, and turning left to the park at Baseline Road. For a more scenic route, you can follow the river just south of Arapahoe along a trail which can take you to 6th Street.

The Mesa Trail begins at the rear of the big green theater building in the park. A very scenic, hilly run, the trail heads south for about 10 miles with many offshoots. It has a rocky footing that often gets washed out. The Parks and Recreation Department works at grooming the trail with logs and rocks. They don't want to make it too smooth in order for it to remain a challenge to hikers. The Mesa Trail and the offshoot trails are all marked for direction and are color-coded for degree of difficulty for hikers. Easy, Green trails are considered difficult enough for running.

It's uphill for the first 2½ to 3 miles along the trail. After that, it varies between flat and up. At about 3 miles from Chautauqua Park, you can return along Bear Creek by turning left onto the service road. It is a small, loose gravel road that follows the creek back to town. A bike trail skirts the southern edge of town and you can head back along it to the eastern hotel area.

Although there are no shade trees on the Mesa Trail, a sharp rise borders the west side, giving the sun an early setting.

DAKOTA RIDGE

For terrific vistas of Boulder and its surroundings, many runners head uphill to the west of town. If you run north on 4th Street along the edge of town, you will see a left going uphill, which is Mapleton. Take this to a small park which is the trailhead to Dakota Ridge. From here it is a 2-mile run uphill to the vista point. Runners say that on a clear day you can see as far as Kansas.

OUTDOOR TRACK
With a large number of elite runners in town, a complete training regimen necessitates an outdoor track for those important interval workouts. A new ¼-mile polyurethane track has been built by the University of Colorado at 30th Street and Colorado Avenue. The public is welcome to use it.

INDOOR TRACK
Balch Fieldhouse is located west of the football stadium and is attached to it near the intersections of Colorado and Folsom. The Fieldhouse contains a ⅛-mile Tartan track. Balch is open to anyone when classes are not in session. Dinnertime or weekends are the best bet to get in a workout.

FUN-RUNS
Fun-runs are held monthly on the second and fourth Saturdays at the South Boulder Recreation Center at 9:00 A.M. The third Saturday of each month is reserved for women only.

CLUBS AND RACES
The Colorado Track Club holds races once a month during the cold season and twice a month in warmer weather.

TRADITIONAL RACES
Flatiron Sun Run, 5 miles: Late June
Run for the Roses, 10 kilometers (men); 5 kilometers (women): Late August

CONTACTS
Frank Shorter Sports, 1129 Pearl Street, Boulder, CO 80302. (303) 449-2130.
Rich Castro, 2330 Kalmia, Boulder, CO 80302. (303) 449-6650 (office).

Colorado Springs

Population: 200,000	Humidity: 49%
Elevation: 6,145 ft.	Av. Temperature (Jan.) 29°F.; (July) 65°F.
Air Quality: Fair	Inches of Rainfall: (Jan.) .3; (July) 3.1 Raindays: 87

OVERVIEW

This city provides some of the most scenic runs in the country. From here you can also run the toughest hill climb, the famous course of the Pikes Peak Marathon. Nestled at the foothills of the Rockies, Colorado Springs is a haven for altitude training and many top runners come here to utilize its vertical offerings. Jay Longacre, the adventure-runner who conquered the Himalayas, lives and trains here.

Located 65 miles south of Denver, Colorado Springs is also the home of the U.S. Air Force Academy. The Academy's grounds provide some beautiful runs. Another interesting and scenic locale is the Garden of the Gods which contains large, unusual rock formations, including the famous Balanced Rock.

Some precautions are necessary for running here. When heading up into mountain trails, it is best to run with a companion. Footing can be treacherous, and you do not want to be stranded with an injury. If you plan to stop your run at a higher altitude than when you started, bring some extra clothes, as temperatures drop considerably as you ascend. Do the same if you are driving to a higher altitude for a run. In summer, an afternoon thunderstorm can deliver very cold rain and chilly breezes.

HOTELS

Antlers Plaza Hotel, Four Seasons Motor Inn, Sheraton Motor Inn (near the Air Force Academy)

MONUMENT VALLEY PARK

This park provides an easy run, convenient to the Antlers Plaza Hotel and the Pikes Peak YMCA/USO. From both starts, the run measures 5 miles. Starting at the Antlers Plaza, head downhill on Pikes Peak Avenue to a right turn on Sierra Madre Street. Enter the park and follow the path under the Bijou Street overpass, along the railroad, and continue on the path north to the end of the park. Doubleblack to the start.

From the Y/USO, run west across Acacia Park, continuing west on Platte Street, across Cascade Street, and still west on Boulder Crescent to the park. Turn right on the gravel path, following it to the end of the park. Return along the same route.

The routes are flat and scenic. Monument Valley Park is a long, narrow strip along both sides of a creek. Many runners use this course by day, and it can also be run at night. However, keep in mind that water and rest rooms are not available; and trees in this part of the country do not provide adequate shade.

ROUTE FROM FOUR SEASONS MOTOR INN	An easy, flat run on seldom used roads is available from this inn. If you go left on the winding dirt road from the back door of the inn, and continue to where Las Vegas meets the Hancock Expressway, and return, the distance measures 2.8 miles. If you continue on Las Vegas to the traffic light at Nevada, and then return, the distance is 5.2 miles. There are no intersections to cross. The course can be run at night; water and rest rooms are not available.
AIR FORCE ACADEMY GROUNDS	From the Sheraton Motor Inn, head left on Academy Boulevard and enter the Academy on Southgate Boulevard. A run of different distances can be had, the further into the grounds you go; exact distances have been measured out and back to the inn. Terrain is rolling and becomes steeper as the foothills rise up within the grounds. The altitude is over 7,000 feet. Water and rest rooms can be found in different buildings.
	If you continue on Southgate Boulevard, turning back at Stadium Boulevard, your run will be 4 miles. If you turn right when you reach Stadium Boulevard and continue to Academy Drive, then turning back, you will go 7 miles. Turning back at the Parade Loop will make it 9 miles, and to Northgate Boulevard will make it 10 miles (all on Stadium Boulevard).
	If you turn left on Northgate Boulevard, which becomes Academy Drive, and loop around the Cadet area on the running path along the left side of the road, you will end up back at Stadium Boulevard, and after returning to the inn, you will have done 17 miles.
GARDEN OF THE GODS	The course here, beginning at the parking lot, is shaped like a figure eight with a small tail. Take a left onto Gateway Road, and then your first right, following that road up and around the Hidden Inn parking lot, past the Hidden Inn and across the intersection below the inn which will put you on Ridge Road. Proceed on Ridge Road, up the hill past the Visitors' Center, taking the first right, and then the first paved left, and you will find yourself above the inn. Continue on this road, passing the Balanced Rock, to the El Paso Street intersection. Follow the same route back for a 10-mile run.
	This very unusual, scenic park provides good, tough hills on blacktop footing. You must be cautious of slow-moving traffic. Many other runners use this course. Water and rest rooms are located at rest areas.
PIKES PEAK	This course begins at the Cog Railway and Incline Railway parking lot, about 6 miles west of town. Run up Ruxton Street past the power plant onto the dirt road up to the chlorine treatment plant, which is at the start of the Barr Trail. Head up the Barr Trail.
	The distance to the top of the Incline Railway, round trip from the parking lot, is 6 miles. To Barr Camp, it is 15 miles. To the A frame at the timberline, 21 miles, and to the summit, 27 miles. The total rise in elevation is about 7,300 feet.
RAMPART RANGE ROAD	Another exciting, scenic hill climb begins at the Garden of the Gods into this range of small, very old mountains. An old dirt jeep road heads up into the range between Pikes Peak and the Air Force Academy. When snow is on the ground, the sun hits the road early in the morning and melts it quickly. There are beautiful vistas overlooking Colorado Springs and the Eastern Plains. The road climbs gradually and relentlessly from 6,300 feet to 9,300 feet in 12 miles. The top of Black Canyon is 2 miles from the start. When you can look out onto a concrete excavation, it will be 5 miles, and the first scenic overlook is 11 miles.

INDOOR TRACKS	The new fitness center at the Pikes Peak YMCA/USO has an excellent 22-laps-per-mile banked track.
CLUBS	The Pikes Peak Road Runners Club holds different running events throughout the year.
TRADITIONAL RACES	Garden of the Gods, 10 miles: Mid-June Pikes Peak Marathon, 28.4 miles: Mid-August
CONTACTS	R. Carl McDaniel, Pikes Peak Road Runners Club, 3360 Red Onion Circle, Colorado Springs, CO 80918. (303) 598-4006. Pikes Peak YMCA/USO, 207 North Nevada, Colorado Springs, CO 80903. (303) 471-9790.

DENVER

Population: (met.) 1,310,000	Humidity: 45%
Elevation: 5,130 – 5,470 ft.	Av. Temperature: (Jan.) 29°F.; (July) 73°F.
Air Quality: Poor	Inches of Rainfall: (Jan.) .6; (July) 1.8 Raindays: 87

OVERVIEW

Denver is a beautiful city, lying just east of the white-capped Rockies. Long vistas reveal Pikes Peak to the south, jutting up above its surrounding sea of mountains. North, your eye can travel to the foothills overlooking the city of Boulder. A large, flat plateau spreads through the eastern part of town and continues as far east as the horizon.

Like Boston, Denver has few square miles, with many little towns tucked in around it to comprise the metropolitan area. A great number of parks dot the cityscape, all capable of providing some sort of workout. A few are, of course, more popular than others. Washington Park, close to downtown, receives the most attention.

Few cities have as many outstanding courses to choose from, as well as weather conditions void of any great extremes. Winter is seldom too cold and snow accumulation is moderately low. Pollution is perhaps the greatest nuisance, and the high altitude will be apparent to most visitors.

The South Platte River runs north to south through Denver, and has been the site of a major park development program. Known as the Greenway, it will eventually total 40 to 50 miles of uninterrupted running. The finished section through downtown has already been used for a number of marathons.

Another long waterway through Denver is the Highline Canal, which runs for over 30 miles through the east and southeast sections of town. Its soft footing and long distances between cross streets provide a comfortable route for visiting interesting parts of the city.

A large number of clubs carry on the running programs in town, each with its own unique contribution. There are plenty of races over easy terrain, as well as some grueling hill climbs. Nearby Colorado Springs and Boulder contribute additional events within easy reach.

HOTELS

Downtown hotels are all about 1 mile or so east of the Greenway.
Aurora: Holiday Inn – East, Dunes Motor Hotel

WASHINGTON PARK

Two miles southeast of downtown, this park is the site of thirty to forty races per year. A shaded, mostly flat road loops around the park for 2.2 miles. When traffic is allowed on the road, a grass and clay trail just beyond the road provides a 2.5-mile loop. Markers for all mileages and kilometers have been placed along the road. Five rest rooms can be found in the park, two of which are always open, and water fountains are numerous.

PLATTE RIVER GREENWAY

As of the end of 1978, 13 miles of the Greenway have been completed. It begins at 40th Avenue North, at the Coliseum, and runs south. An additional 10 miles will be added in 1979, to extend the park down to Chatfield Dam. The Greenway's width varies between 20 and 60 feet along the river, and in the downtown area, runs through a warehouse section and railroad yard. A paved bike path travels the length of the park, crossing the river occasionally on a wood-planked bridge. Although city terrain is basically flat beside the river, the path climbs up and down the riverbank to make your run more interesting. Water fountains are located every 1 to 1½ miles, and rest rooms will eventually be installed. Some areas of the course have shade from older trees, in other areas it will take some time for new trees to fill out.

The Greenway can be reached from downtown by running northeast on 15th Street, or east along Colfax.

HIGHLINE CANAL

This clay and gravel trail runs flat along the 10- to 20-foot-wide canal. Shade trees cover most of the route that travels through horse country and residential communities. You can run at ½- to 1¼-mile intervals before having to deal with intersections. Water and rest rooms can be found at nearby gas stations.

The canal trail runs northeast from Waterton, and passes through the town of Aurora, about 8 miles east of downtown. The Holiday Inn and Dunes Motor Hotel lie close to the course, along Colfax Avenue near the Veterans' Hospital. The distance between Waterton and County Line Road measures 15.8 miles. From South Havana Street to Colfax Avenue is 12.4 miles.

CHEESMAN PARK

At East 8th Avenue and Franklin Street, and only about 1½ miles southeast of downtown, this park sits on a hill looking out on the capitol dome and across to a magnificent view of the Rockies. Mostly flat, a dirt trail circles its perimeter for just under a mile. Denver's Botanic Gardens lie adjacent to the park for an interesting side trip.

CITY PARK

Between 17th and 26th avenues, York Street, and Colorado Boulevard, this largest park in the city has many paved pathways for circuitous routes. A golf course and lake can be found here. However, many runners avoid this park because it is in a troublesome part of town.

SLOAN'S LAKE PARK

About 4 miles northwest of town, a 2.75-mile paved trail loops around the lake. There are some small hills over both shaded and open sections. Great views of the mountains can be had from this course. Water fountains and rest rooms can be found in the summer at the boathouse on the north side, and the restaurant on the south side.

OUTDOOR TRACKS

There are many tracks around town, but most of them are not open to the public.

INDOOR TRACKS

The Downtown YMCA has a 24-laps-per-mile, banked track. About fifteen health clubs in town have excellent indoor tracks, but you can only use them as the guest of a member.

CLUBS, FUN-RUNS AND RACES

The Rocky Mountain Road Runners Club is the principal running organization in Denver. They hold about twenty-four races each year. One race each month is a handicap event, and a popular tune-up series precedes the Boston Marathon.

The Colorado Masters Running Association puts on a race each month, usually between 5 and 15 kilometers.

The Denver Track Club sponsors short runs and track events in town, and a few long runs out of town.

The Colorado Track Club, in Boulder, puts on races there, and publishes the *Rocky Mountain Running News*.

The Timber Ridge Runners, up in the mountains, puts on about twenty races per year. Half of them are fun-runs and the other half are tough hill climbs.

The Colorado Columbines is a women's running club that has weekday group runs, and fun-runs twice a month. They also put on a number of clinics.

The Downtown YMCA puts on a number of popular races each year.

TRADITIONAL RACES

Mile-High Marathon: May
Firecracker 4.4-Mile: Fourth of July
Mt. Evans Hill Climb (over 14,000 ft.), 15 miles: July
Watermelon Race, 5 miles: July
Vailfest 10-Kilometer and 5-Kilometer: September
Denver Marathon: October
Turkey Trot, 4 miles: Thanksgiving Day
Sunset Mountain Hill Climb, 5 miles: New York's Eve

CONTACTS

Bill Michaels, Rocky Mountain RRC, 1035 Corona Street, Apt. 6, Denver, CO 80218. (303) 831-1687.

Nancy Hamaker, Colorado Masters Running Association, 1525 South Lansing Street, Aurora, CO 80012. (303) 750-9043.

Steve Kaeuper, Denver Track Club, 2263 Krameria, Denver, CO 80207. (303) 388-8180.

Rick Rojas, Colorado Track Club, 1410 19th Street, Apt. 8, Boulder, CO 80302.

Garry Phippen, Timber Ridge Runners, Box 1262, Evergreen, CO 80439. (303) 674-7161.

Phil Guries, Downtown YMCA, 25 East 16th Street, Denver, CO 80202. (303) 861-8300.

HARTFORD

Population: 138,300	Humidity: 70%
Elevation: 10–290 ft.	Av. Temperature (Jan.) 25°F.; (July) 73°F.
Air Quality: Fair to poor	Inches of Rainfall: (Jan.) 3.3; (July) 3.4 Raindays: 125

OVERVIEW
: Located in the center of Connecticut, Hartford, the state capital, has undergone major redevelopment to make the downtown area a clean, modern business center. Running here focuses on Bushnell Park, a small, centrally convenient haven for daily workouts. For a more challenging course, many runners head out to the West Hartford Reservoir, a 20-minute drive from downtown.

HOTELS
: Hartford Hilton, Governor's Motor House

BUSHNELL PARK
: Although Bushnell Park's perimeter is only .7 miles, local runners make the most of it by running over as many square feet of the park as possible. There is plenty of grass to wander over as well as paved roads and walkways. Shade covers about fifty percent of the terrain and the small hills will present little challenge. Water and rest rooms can be found across the street at the YMCA. The Hilton borders the park. Automobiles are prohibited.

WEST HARTFORD RESERVOIR
: The West Hartford Reservoir is an ideal place to put in quality mileage. Located only 15 to 20 minutes from downtown via Farmington Avenue, this hilly, shady area contains about 30 miles of roads and trails, all closed to automobile traffic. Water is available, and in winter the roads are plowed.

FUN-RUNS
: The Hartford YMCA sponsors fun-runs on the first and third Sundays of each month at the West Hartford Reservoir.

TRADITIONAL RACES
: Capital City Mini-Marathon, 10 kilometers: April
Manchester 5-Mile Run: Thanksgiving Day

CONTACT
: David G. Arnold, Hartford YMCA, 160 Jewell Street, Hartford, CT 06103. (203) 522-4183.

NEW HAVEN

Population: 125,000	Humidity: 70%
Elevation: 15 – 150 ft.	Av. Temperature: (Jan.) 29°F.; (July) 72°F.
Air Quality: Poor	Inches of Rainfall: (Jan.) 3.2; (July) 3.1 Raindays: 131

OVERVIEW

New Haven, famous for the home of Yale University, has a cultured, cosmopolitan population in a New England setting. The traditional Green, a grassy common located in the center of town, draws many runners to its convenient, flat and safe course. A few other parks close to town provide more challenging terrain.

Parts of the city contain old and dying industrial areas with typical urban problems. Running is not considered safe in the city at night. Streets take unpredictable twists and turns, names change abruptly, and directions can be confusing. Do not assume that cars here will stop for you. The city is notorious for motorists squeezing through changing lights.

HOTELS

Sheraton Park-Plaza Hotel, Holiday Inn – Yale University

THE GREEN

The Sheraton is located adjacent to the Green. One full lap of this well-tended historical site measures roughly ½ mile. Water can be found at the southeast corner. The Yale Campus sits close to the Green, and you might enjoy some pleasant runs through its rustic and colorful environment.

EDGEWOOD PARK

From the Sheraton, head to the Green, and as you reach it, turn left on Chapel Street and run for about 1 mile to Boulevard. Sections through Chapel Street are run-down, but the street is safe as it is a major artery. Cross Boulevard and enter the park. Follow the interior road, out and back, for a 2-mile distance. Side paths and other roads are available, and if lost, you can key to a large, 25-foot-high, concrete sundial that is impossible to miss. Water is available next to the sundial. This park has pleasantly rolling terrain under excellent shade.

EAST ROCK PARK

This time, turn right on Chapel, cross Church Street, and at the next street, Orange, turn left. Follow Orange Street for about 1½ miles to East Rock Park. Here you will find two areas that runners utilize. A 2- to 3-mile loop can be run around the ball fields and along a small river. Most runners prefer to work their way up the 350-foot East Rock. This course measures about 4 miles if you start from where Orange Street reaches the park, and then turn left to run around to the far side of the rock before reaching a complicated set of roads. Local runners feel the directions from here are too complicated to explain, and suggest heading up the hill in the company of other runners. This park is definitely not recommended for after-dark running.

SLEEPING GIANT STATE PARK

About 8 miles north of town, this park provides some of the best running in the area. You will need a map to get there, as directions are impossible. One loop of the park is 8.3 miles, including a very tough hill as well as some less challenging terrain. The Sleeping Giant Pacers call this territory home.

INDOOR TRACKS

Coxe Cage at Yale University, next to the Yale Bowl, is open in the afternoons for runners who carefully follow track etiquette. You must call ahead for permission to use this 220-yard facility.

The Central Branch YMCA has a 21-laps-per-mile track. Groups of runners from this Y head out to nearby parks at different hours during the week. The Y is located only about ⅛ of a mile from the New Haven Green, along Chapel Street.

OUTDOOR TRACKS

The Yale track, across the street from Lampham Fieldhouse, measures ¼ mile on cinders. The track is open to visitors anytime, although it is not lit at night.

CLUBS, FUN-RUNS AND RACES

The New Haven Runners Club sponsors clinics and fun-runs in Edgewood Park on the weekends. The Sleeping Giant Pacers meet at 9:00 A.M. every Sunday for a run around the "Giant."

TRADITIONAL RACES

Milford 3-Mile Run: June
Fair Haven 4½-Mile Race: Late June
Cheshire 6.5-Mile Run: June or July
New Haven Labor Day 20-Kilometer Run
Guilford 10.2-Mile Run: Mid-September

CONTACTS

Bill Fasula, President, Sleeping Giant Pacers, 84 Burke Street, Hamden, CT 06514. (203) 776-5124.
Al Furbush, Sleeping Giant Pacers, 111 Standish Avenue, North, Haven, CT 06473. (203) 239-2133.
Steve Mick, 1632 Chapel Street, New Haven, CT 06511. (203) 789-8489.
Bob Hensley, Phidippides, Milford, CT 06460. (203) 874-8091.
Central Branch YMCA, 52 Howe Street, New Haven, CT 06511. (203) 865-3161.
Coxe Cage, Yale University, (203) 436-4751.

New London

Population: 27,700	Humidity: 70%
Elevation: 40 ft.	Av. Temperature: (Jan.) 29°F.; (July) 71°F.
Air Quality: Fair to poor	Inches of Rainfall: (Jan.) 3.7; (July) 3.3 Raindays: 127

OVERVIEW

New London has always been famous as a seagoing town with an excellent deepwater port. Only longtime runners know that its real claim to fame is its contribution of many world-class runners. Obviously, the running must be good in this town to produce such runners as two-time Olympic marathoner John Kelley, Boston Marathon winner Amby Burfoot, New York City Marathon winner Norm Higgins, 20-mile world-record holder Fred Norris, and 1,500- and 3,000-meter American record holder Jan Merrill.

The Connecticut College campus and surrounding area provide the best local running, and the nearby seashore also has some excellent courses.

HOTEL

Holiday Inn, Route 95

CONNECTICUT COLLEGE CAMPUS

The campus is located 1 mile east of the Holiday Inn. The road that circles through the campus is 1.1 miles long, but the campus' extensive grassy lawns make it possible to loop around and zigzag your way through many miles of running, almost entirely on grass alone. Even better than the campus running is the trail that courses along three of its sides.

CONNECTICUT COLLEGE ENVIRONS

To the west lies the justly famous Arboretum, a gorgeous 250-acre natural area with many miles of trails winding around the centrally situated pond. The shortest loop around the pond is about ½ mile, and the longest, which includes some rocky cliff running, is about 1½ miles.

Just to the north of the campus and the Arboretum are the Thames Science Center trails. The longest of these stretches about 2 miles before it connects with William Street, which leads back to the Center.

Across Route 32, on the east side of the campus, are several miles of trails that make up part of the Coast Guard Academy's cross-country course. The most spectacular of these crosses a damp salt marsh to Mamacoke Island, which is the best place to spy on the atomic submarines across the way at the Groton Naval Base. The trail follows the island's perimeter for a 1-mile loop. The interior portion of the island is high, flat and rocky. A perfect perch for sunbathing and picnicking after the run.

THAMES RIVER AND LONG ISLAND SOUND

You will reach these bodies of water 4 miles south of the Holiday Inn. They offer many miles of unobstructed running. Three contiguous pieces of property in Waterford (the Eugene O'Neill Theatre, Waterford Town Beach and Harkness Memorial Park) make for good seaside running with alternate grass, sand and asphalt footing.

RACES   Local races are held mostly in the summer and early fall.

TRADITIONAL RACES   Groton Recreation Department, 5 miles: Mid-June
                        Norwich Rose Arts, 10.6 miles: Late June
                        Ocean Beach — John Kelley, 11.6 miles: First Saturday in August

CONTACT   Amby Burfoot, *Runner's World* East Coast Office, 416 Williams Street, New London, CT 06320. (203) 447-2157.

wilmington

Population: 66,200	Humidity: 71%
Elevation: 0–135 ft.	Av. Temperature: (Jan.) 32°F.; (July) 76°F.
Air Quality: Fair to poor	Inches of Rainfall: (Jan.) 3.2; (July) 4.3 Raindays: 122

OVERVIEW

A modest metropolis in a modest-size state, Wilmington's running gets right to the point with convenient and popular downtown routes. Everything seems to be located close together to make life easy for the traveling runner. A good hotel, the YMCA and a running store all sit at the start of the downtown runs. It is only ½ mile to the Brandywine River where the runner has a choice of two directions, both taking advantage of the scenic environment.

HOTEL

Hotel DuPont

ROUTE TO ROCKFORD PARK

Go out the hotel entrance on Delaware Avenue and head northwest, continue past the Central YMCA at two blocks and Marathon Athletic Shoes at three blocks, to Adams Street after another 200 yards. Turn right, and it is straight downhill to Park Drive along Brandywine Park and the river. Go left on Park Drive (not into the park) until it ends, a distance of about 1 mile. Take a right on Lovering Avenue, and then 30 yards later, another right onto Kentmere Parkway and continue to Rockford Park, which you will reach at 2 miles. The park has a beautiful, shaded 1½-mile loop with a slight grade up and a slight grade down. A water fountain can be found at the tower. Follow the same route back to the hotel for a 5½-mile course.

BRANDYWINE PARK RUN

Follow the same route as above to the bottom of Adams Street and Park Drive. Instead of turning left, cross over the Drive and enter Brandywine Park, then go left on the small path for ½ mile to an interesting swinging bridge. Cross the bridge over the river and follow the path to the right past the zoo to the Market Street Bridge. Cross the bridge and turn right on Park Drive for the ½ mile back to Adams Street. This 2.1-mile loop along the Brandywine River is marked by arrows. The total run from the hotel and back is 3.1 miles.

For both courses from downtown, beware of rush-hour traffic for the first ½ mile on city streets.

INDOOR TRACKS

The Central YMCA has an indoor, banked, 22-laps-per-mile track.

CLUBS AND FUN-RUNS

The Delaware Sports Club and the YMCA Runners Club put on running events during the year. Marathon Athletic Shoes sponsors fun-runs each week at Rockford Park. From April to October it's on Thursday evenings at 6:00 P.M., with distances from ¼ to 4 miles.

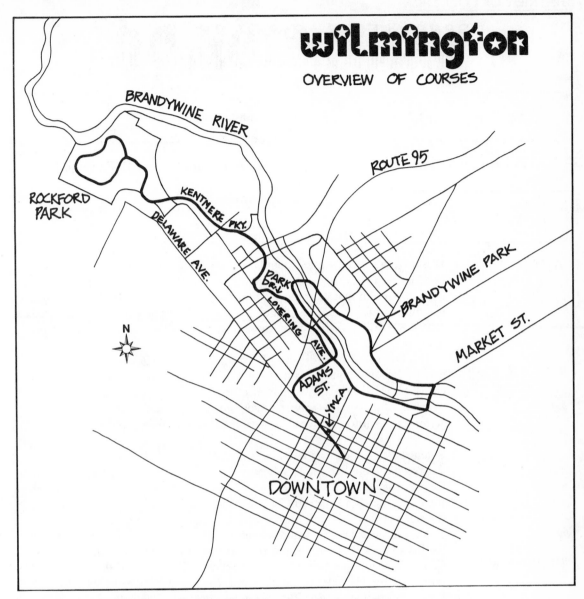

wilmington

OVERVIEW OF COURSES

BRANDYWINE RIVER

ROUTE 95

ROCKFORD PARK

KENTMERE PKY.

DELAWARE AVE.

PARK DR.

LOVERING AVE.

BRANDYWINE PARK

MARKET ST.

ADAMS ST.

YMCA

N

DOWNTOWN

TRADITIONAL RACES	Caesar Rodney Half-Marathon: Early April Run for Cancer, 10 kilometers: End of April Newark Turkey Trot, 10 kilometers: Thanksgiving Day
CONTACTS	Wayne S. Kursh, Marathon Athletic Shoes, 623 Delaware Avenue, Wilmington, DE 19801. (302) 654-2354. Central YMCA, 11th and Washington Streets, Wilmington, DE 19801. (302) 571-6900.

WASHINGTON, D.C.

Population: (met.) 3,200,000	Humidity: 68%
Elevation: 1–410 ft.	Av. Temperature: (Jan.) 37°F.; (July) 78°F.
Air Quality: Fair to poor	Inches of Rainfall: (Jan.) 2.9; (July) 4.1 Raindays: 120

OVERVIEW

Washington's sophisticated population has enthusiastically adopted the sport, flooding major courses with energetic runners. A city where individual visibility is important, many people prefer to run at lunchtime when they can discover old and new acquaintances plugging away at their miles. Fortunately, the best routes are easily reached from downtown, providing convenient and efficient workouts.

The Potomac River, dividing Washington from neighboring Virginia, flows past Georgetown, the Kennedy Center and the Lincoln Memorial at the western end of the Mall. Many government offices and monuments surround the Mall, which is a flat, open, grassy area, good for easy workouts. If runners head west across the Mall to the river, they have a choice of four excellent courses.

Two small parks, at the river, sit on either side of the Tidal Basin. East Potomac Park, to the southeast, and West Potomac Park, to the northwest, have flat, scenic loops. If runners head north along the river, past the Kennedy Center, they will pick up the start of the Rock Creek Park Bike Path, which soon after heads away from the river in a northeast direction for many miles through the city and into Maryland.

A very unusual course begins along the Potomac River in Georgetown, where the Rock Creek Bike Path begins to head away from the river. This is the C & O Canal Towpath on a strip of land between the Potomac and the canal, heading northwest for 185 miles to Cumberland, Maryland. Originally used for pulling barges through the canal, it is now an unobstructed, flat running path.

The beauty of running in this city lies in the close proximity of all these courses to one another, and the large number of runners taking advantage of every course.

HOTELS

Watergate Hotel, L'Enfant Plaza Hotel, Shoreham Americana Hotel, Sheraton Park Hotel

THE MALL

Close to 2 miles long, the Mall is a long, open park, stretching between the Capitol Building on the east end, to the Lincoln Memorial next to the Potomac River at the west end. The Washington Monument is located between the two. Many runners loop around the Mall on grass or wide sidewalks. There are few intersecting streets.

WEST POTOMAC PARK Just below the Lincoln Memorial and adjacent to the Mall, this park is a peninsula between the Potomac and the Tidal Basin. A paved walkway loops around flat terrain for a 2-mile course. Shade is sparse.

EAST POTOMAC PARK Crossing a bridge from West Potomac Park, or 15th Street, will put you on the island containing East Potomac Park. This park has a concrete walkway along its perimeter beside the Potomac River and Washington Channel. The park is also known as Hains Point.

Cool breezes from the river will refresh you on this 4-mile loop. Vistas across the water on all sides take in well-known landmarks. Some runners enjoy peaceful workouts here at night. L'Enfant Plaza Hotel is located across the Channel from the park.

ROCK CREEK PARK Heading north from the Lincoln Memorial, along the river, will put you on the Rock Creek Park Bike Path, just below Kennedy Center. For a while, this is a narrow strip beside the river until it passes the Watergate Hotel, as it turns inland where Rock Creek flows into the Potomac. The park then winds its way northward broadening into a thickly wooded area on both sides of the creek. The bike path runs alongside park roads which are often heavily traveled by automobiles.

You can enter the park at many points along the route. A few miles north, the Shoreham Americana and Sheraton Park hotels are located only a block or two uphill from the park.

Just north of this area, Rock Creek flows through the National Zoo, offering an opportunity to visit with some distant cousins. Continuing north, the park becomes even broader as it reaches up into the corner of the city, and then thins down a bit as it enters Maryland. The bike trail ends a couple of hundred yards north of Pierce Mill, which is slightly north of the zoo. Beyond that, your choice is the road, or bridle paths which are not very simple to follow. A dirt path next to the road is helpful a good part of the way. Some fine hills can be found at the zoo, and the terrain remains as challenging as you continue toward the Maryland border. It is about 9 miles to the far end of Washington, and the park continues in Maryland for at least another 10 miles. Water fountains and rest rooms are infrequently available.

C & O CANAL TOWPATH Your ultra-marathon fantasies can come true on this almost endless dirt path beside the C & O Canal. Beginning in Georgetown, the narrow strip of land that runs 185 miles west to Cumberland, Maryland, has been designated a national park. Terrain is flat, and there are no cars to deal with the entire route. Mileages have been painted on small posts, and the only things missing are water fountains and rest rooms.

TWO BRIDGES LOOP An interesting diversion from the more traditional routes can be run by heading over the Memorial Bridge at Lincoln Memorial, and running south along the river bike path on the Virginia side down to the 14th Street Bridge, and across to East Potomac Park and back up along the river through West Potomac Park.

All the parks and routes close to the Potomac have periodic water fountains and rest rooms. Shade is not an abundant commodity, though.

PRESIDENT'S TRAIL From Memorial Bridge, a pleasant bike trail runs south down to Mount Vernon, through Virginia. Once over the bridge, take the bike trail along the river and follow it south, sweeping past the National Airport and through Alexandria.

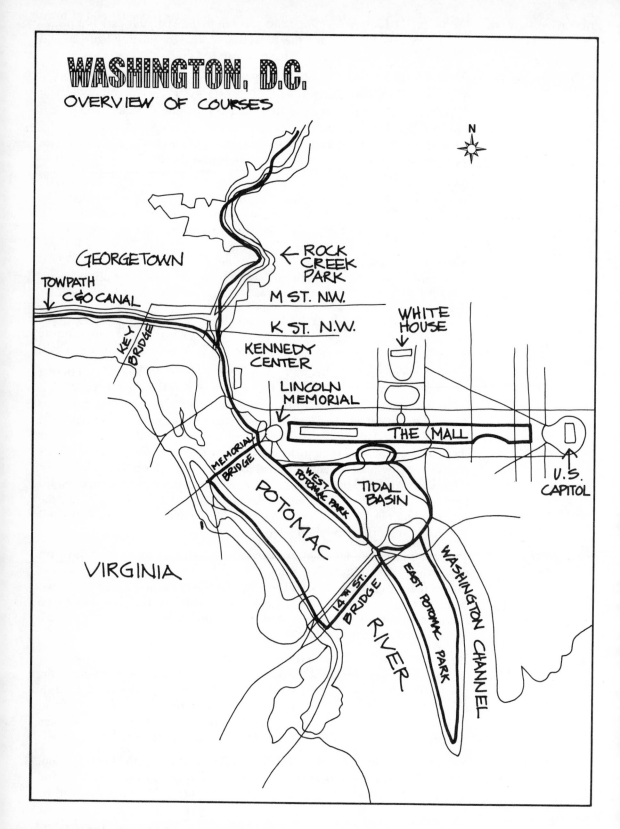

WASHINGTON, D.C.

OVERVIEW OF COURSES

N

GEORGETOWN

TOWPATH
C&O CANAL

← ROCK
CREEK
PARK

M ST. N.W.

K ST. N.W.

KENNEDY
CENTER

WHITE
HOUSE

KEY
BRIDGE

LINCOLN
MEMORIAL

THE MALL

MEMORIAL
BRIDGE

POTOMAC

WEST
POTOMAC PARK

TIDAL
BASIN

U.S.
CAPITOL

VIRGINIA

14TH ST.
BRIDGE

EAST
POTOMAC
PARK

WASHINGTON CHANNEL

RIVER

Here you will have to follow signs through local streets to the far end of town where the bike path picks up along the highway. The run is about 14 miles round trip.

NATIONAL
ARBORETUM

About 3 miles northeast of downtown Washington via Maryland Avenue, this beautifully maintained park provides about 6 miles of roads over rolling terrain. Traffic is light, and you can enjoy the magnificent gardens and unusual trees and shrubs.

OUTDOOR TRACKS

Georgetown University has a new, 400-meter, Chem-Turf, granular surface track. It is located at Kehoe Field, on campus.

INDOOR TRACKS

Georgetown University also has a new 200-meter, Chem-Turf, smooth surface indoor track. A policy has not yet been established as to its availability. The new National Capital YMCA has an 18-laps-per-mile, banked track.

CLUBS, FUN-RUNS
AND RACES

The D.C. Road Runners Club is a sophisticated organization with clinics, newsletters and weekly running events. Their Snowball Series in the winter consists of seven races to prepare for the Washington's Birthday Marathon. Race-walkers also participate in club events. Individuals do not compete for the club, but do run in club races.

The Potomac Valley Seniors put on a number of running events during the year, and the D.C. Harriers are equally active. A number of local clubs compete in races here, as well as on a national level. The Washington Runners Club, D.C. Striders and Washington RunHers all have excellent teams.

Fun-runs are held at Greenbelt Lake Park, off Crescent Road, at 9:00 A.M. every second and fourth Saturday.

TRADITIONAL RACES

Washington's Birthday Marathon: Washington's Birthday
Bethesda Chase, 10 kilometers: March
Perrier Cherry Blossom, 10 miles: First Sunday in April
Marine Corps Marathon: Early November
Alexandria Turkey Trot, 5 miles: Thanksgiving Day

CONTACTS

David Gottlieb, D.C. Road Runners Club, 3115 Whispering Pines, Silver Spring, MD 20906. (301) 460-8858.
Don Perkins, Potomac Valley Seniors, (202) 931-8656.
David Theall, D.C. Harriers, 6443 Old Chesterbrook Road, McLean, VA 22101. (703) 356-7837.
Georgetown University Track Office, (202) 625-4293.
National Capital YMCA, 1711 Rhode Island Avenue, Washington, DC 20036. (202) 862-9622.

Fort Lauderdale

Population: 185,000	Humidity 74%
Elevation: 10 ft.	Av. Temperature: (Jan.) 67°F.; (July) 82°F.
Air Quality: Fair	Inches of Rainfall: (Jan.) 2; (July) 6 Raindays: 123

OVERVIEW

This bustling running community, on the southeast shoreline of Florida, has developed a very complete running program. Races, group runs and social activity centered on running form a major part of the area lifestyle. Holiday Park, the popular gathering place for runners, is centrally located, and a run starting from there will provide you with company much of the day or evening.

Just south of Ft. Lauderdale, at Port Everglades, a large, mostly undisturbed tropical jungle is often visited by adventuresome runners from the north. Many Saturday mornings a group heads through this exciting environment for their long run.

Most of the parks in the area are well maintained, and although some charge twenty-five or fifty cents to use, the clean rest rooms and free showers are well worth the cost.

HOTELS

Holiday Park is bordered by U.S. 1, Sunrise Boulevard, 14th Avenue and 6th Street. Many hotels can be found within an easy run from the park. Birch State Park lies along North Ocean Boulevard, where many good motels can also be found.

HOLIDAY PARK

Most runners meet near the gym and tennis center at the park. Free showers are available in the gym. An exercise course has been developed in the park over a 1.26-mile loop, and the perimeter of the park has a grass pathway measuring 1.67 miles. No shade exists, but there is plenty of water.

BIRCH STATE PARK

Birch State Park, along the ocean, contains a 2-mile loop on the main road, or on a sand and pine-needle path alongside the road. Excellent foliage throughout the park will protect you from the sun. Rest rooms are located at the north and south ends. No fountains are available. An entrance fee of twenty-five cents is required to use the park. A tunnel goes under Route A1A to the beach for a swim after your run. Showers are available at the beach.

T.Y. PARK

This is a very pretty 200-acre park with a small man-made lake in the center. It is located south of Ft. Lauderdale, in Hollywood, about ¼ mile west of I-95 along Sheridan Street. A perimeter bike path measures 2 miles. About ⅓ of the path lies in shade. There are plenty of rest rooms and water fountains, and there are free showers. A fifty cents per person and fifty cents per car entrance fee are charged.

JUNGLE RUN

This run usually starts at Holiday Park, about 5 miles from Port Everglades. The Port is bordered by the ocean, the 17th Street Causeway, Route 1, and the Dainia Cutoff Canal. It is best to enter the jungle from Route 1 at the 17th Street Causeway and head to the southeast corner, making your own course.

The terrain requires a *fartlek* type of running in that frequent stops or changes of pace are necessary. Numerous mud puddles, fallen trees and fences are interspersed throughout the Port. Many unforeseen circumstances can occur, including occasional encounters with alligators, or flooded-out footbridges. The short runner is at an advantage when running with a taller partner who can knock down the spiderwebs in the dense pine-tree forest section. At certain times of the year, bananas and coconuts can be obtained through the tree farm section.

It is most enjoyable to approach the run with other runners so the unusual sights can be shared. However, it can also be enjoyable to run alone, in that this is one of the few uninhabited areas in a fast-growing urban region.

CLUBS AND RACES

The Ft. Lauderdale Road Runners Club holds a race every weekend, usually on Sundays at 9:00 A.M. Distances and location vary, with a short and long distance at each event. Long group runs usually start at 7:00 A.M. on Saturday mornings, at Holiday Park.

TRADITIONAL RACES

Heart Run, 7.6 miles: Early April
Meet of Miles, 1 mile: Late May
Fourth of July 15-Kilometer
Mid-Summer Classic, 6 miles: Early August
Holiday Classic, 6 miles: Late December

CONTACTS

Andy Riska, Running Sports, 1326 S.E. 17th Street Causeway, Ft. Lauderdale, FL 33316. (305) 763-5555.
Lynn Tunks, Athletic Attic, 826 North Federal Highway, Ft. Lauderdale, FL 33304. (305) 761-1131.
Pete Jeff, Ft. Lauderdale Sports Editor for the *Miami Herald*, One Herald Plaza, Miami, FL 33101. (305) 462-1550.

GAINESVILLE

Population: 80,000	Humidity: 73%
Elevation: 185 ft.	Av. Temperature: (Jan.) 57°F.; (July) 81°F.
Air Quality: Fair	Inches of Rainfall: (Jan.) 3; (July) 8 Raindays: 91

OVERVIEW

Gainesville was long considered a quiet college town until such famous runners as Frank Shorter, Marty Liquori, Barry Brown and Jeff Galloway began competing for the Florida Track Club. Since then, and after these runners left the team, the town has blossomed into a true mecca for running. As in other meccas, such as Eugene, Boston and Honolulu, runners abound in every direction.

The most popular route is a 2-mile course on the University of Florida Campus. As many as a thousand people use this course each day. Most other routes take in city streets and country roads with loops of varying distances both north and south of University Avenue, a major thoroughfare through town. The University and a Holiday Inn are both located along the Avenue. Bike paths can be found along many city streets.

For a change of scenery and terrain, some people work out on the dirt trails at Devil's Millhopper State Park, northwest of town. Marty Liquori prefers to train here. The park contains a large sinkhole, where a portion of land has caved in to form a 100-yard-deep, ¼-mile-wide bowl.

HOTEL

Holiday Inn — University Avenue

UNIVERSITY CAMPUS COURSE

The track on the university campus is located 1 mile west of the Holiday Inn, along University Avenue. From the track, a 2-mile dirt and wood-chip trail leads out at a gradual downhill and travels through some woods before returning uphill to the track. Mileage is posted every ½ mile. Water fountains and rest rooms can be found at the track. There are also locker and shower facilities open to the public.

"TOBACCO ROAD"

This 12-mile rectangular loop begins by heading west for 2 miles along University Avenue from Holiday Inn. Other starting points are the university track, 1 mile west of Holiday Inn, and the Athletic Attic Running Store, 2 miles west of Holiday Inn. At Athletic Attic, the route heads south for 4 miles on 34th Street to "Tobacco Road," a dirt road that earned the nickname from its rundown condition. "Tobacco Road" goes east for 2 miles to Southwest 13th Street (or Route 441), at the Brown Derby Restaurant. From the restaurant, complete the loop by running north for 4 miles back to University Avenue.

Shorter versions of the course can be made by heading east from 34th Street on closer cross streets. Archer Road is only 2 miles south of University Avenue, and Willston Road is 3½ miles south.

The course utilizes a number of bike paths on generally flat and open terrain, except for "Tobacco Road," which has rolling hills under good shade. Water and rest rooms can be found at occasional gas stations.

NORTHERN LOOP

A similar 10-mile course can be run to the north of University Avenue, although it is not preferred by local runners because it has no dirt roads. From Holiday Inn, head north to Northwest 13th Street for 3 miles to 39th Avenue. Turn west for 2 miles to 34th Street, and then south for 3 miles to University Avenue, heading east on University for the last 2 miles back to the start.

The route is flat and mostly along bike paths. Shorter versions of 5, 6 and 9 miles respectively can be had by turning west at 8th Avenue (½ mile north), 16th Avenue (1 mile north), and 23rd Boulevard (1½ miles north, running diagonally north to 34th Street). The 16th Avenue cross street has some good hills.

DEVIL'S MILLHOPPER STATE PARK

From the corner of 39th Avenue and 34th Street, 5 miles away from Holiday Inn, on the northern loop, you can continue on to the park by staying west for another mile on 39th Avenue, and then turning north for 1 mile on Millhopper Road. This is a heavily wooded area with a lot of underbrush crisscrossed with numerous motorcycle trails. Running surface is mainly loose dirt on fairly flat terrain except for the big sinkhole. There are no defined courses, and it is possible to become lost for short intervals. The park measures about 1 square mile. Rest rooms can be found at the Nature Center.

OUTDOOR TRACKS

A ¼-mile Chevron track is located at the University of Florida, on University Avenue. It is not lit at night. 1 mile south, at P.K. Yonge High School, you will find a ¼-mile grass track.

CLUBS AND RACES

The Florida Track Club is the major running organization in Gainesville. Races are held about once a month, usually on a Saturday morning. During the summer, there are occasional All-Comers Meets on Thursday nights. The Master Gators Track Club is a competitive wing of the Florida Track Club; and the Athletic Attic Track Club, an elite competitive club, has a number of world-class runners.

TRADITIONAL RACES

Sun Run, 10 miles: Mid-February
Florida Relays Marathon: First weekend in March
Floriday Relays: Last weekend in March
Micanopy Half-Marathon: Mid-October
Florida AAU Cross-Country Championships, 10 kilometers: December

CONTACTS

Lenny Rhine, Florida Track Club, Box 12463, Gainesville, FL 32604. (904) 373-0292.
Roy Benson or John Creer, University of Florida Track Office, Box 14485, Gainesville, FL 32601. (904) 392-0673.
Athletic Attic, 2300 S.W. 34th Street, Gainesville, FL 32605. (904) 377-5289.

Jacksonville

Population: 590,000	Humidity: 75%
Elevation: 25 ft.	Av. Temperature: (Jan.) 55°F.; (July) 81°F.
Air Quality: Fair to poor	Inches of Rainfall: (Jan.) 2.8; (July) 7.4 Raindays: 116

OVERVIEW

Named after Andrew Jackson, this city has long been a busy port on the St. Johns River. Located about 13 miles from the ocean in northeastern Florida, the downtown area lies along an S curve of the river. There are no large parks here, and no pathways for any length beside the riverbank. Downtown courses start in small Friendship Park and head north and south on tree-lined streets. Like most of Florida, the terrain is flat, and bridges are used for hill workouts.

Many visitors to Jacksonville stay at the ocean, and routes here are very simple. At low tide, the beach provides miles of hard-packed sand; high tide pushes runners up onto First Avenue where mileage is limited to a 2½-mile stretch.

In addition to these popular courses, street running in-town generally is good. Some runners enjoy a run from downtown to the beach, and nearby colleges offer grassy or wooded cross-country courses.

The Jacksonville Track Club is very active with training and fun-runs, but limits its number of races, for the most part, to big annual events with large fields.

HOTELS

Downtown: Hilton Hotel, Travelodge Motel
Jacksonville Beach: All motels are convenient to the beach.

ROUTES FROM
FRIENDSHIP PARK

The above hotels are located next to Friendship Park, at the river. By going directly south from the park along San Marco Boulevard, you can run until San Marco becomes Hendricks Avenue. At the south end of the San Jose Shopping Center, you will have run 1½ miles. When Hendricks and San Jose split, the distance is 2¼ miles, and when they meet up again, it is 4 miles. Lakewood Shopping Center is at 5 miles, and Beauclerc Road is at 9 miles.

This route travels along a wide road with extra parking lanes, which runners frequently use, and sidewalks if you prefer being closer to the trees and on a flatter surface.

For a run through one of Jacksonville's oldest and best-preserved neighborhoods, run northwest from the park, over the Acosta Bridge, turning west along Riverside Avenue. The YMCA Health and Fitness Center is 1 mile out, and Memorial Park is 2 miles. King Street is 3 miles, and Boone Park is 4.1 miles. The only real hazard on this route is the uneven sidewalk, where large tree roots have pushed up the flagstone. Water stops are available about every mile along both of these routes.

For those who desire a hill workout, two bridges, the Acosta and Main Street bridges, flank Friendship Park. One loop over the two bridges measures 1.8 miles. There is no problem with traffic here. A water fountain is located in the park.

JACKSONVILLE
BEACH

Many visitors naturally prefer to stay at the beach. Most sun worshippers and runners are concentrated between Atlantic Boulevard on the north, and Beach Boulevard to the south, a stretch of exactly 2.5 miles. If you run north of Atlantic to the south end of Hanna Park, you will have covered another 2.5 miles. South from Beach Boulevard to the Ponte Vedra/St. John's County Line Iron Fence is another 2.5 miles. The total distance along the three consecutive areas measures 7.5 miles. At high tide, only the 2.5 miles between Atlantic and Beach is navigable on the road closest to the beach, First Avenue.

Water spiggots are available behind the Atlantic and Beach Boulevard Life Guard Stations, with rest rooms at about the center of the boardwalk, and portable toilets at the pier.

A run between the beach and downtown easily follows Atlantic Boulevard for the entire 16 miles, crossing the Main Street Bridge, next to Friendship Park, in downtown.

During summer, due to the high heat and humidity, beach runs make the most sense, because you can always jump into the ocean when symptoms of hyperthermia begin.

CROSS-COUNTRY
COURSES

Three local colleges provide good cross-country running. Jacksonville University, 5 miles northeast from downtown on University Boulevard North, next to the St. Johns River in Arlington, has hills and woods. The University of North Florida, 13 miles east along Beach Boulevard, has narrow trails through dense woods surrounding the campus. This is real wilderness, and you can become seriously lost without a local guide. Florida Junior College's South Campus, 1 mile north of the University of North Florida on Beach Boulevard, has flat, grassy, measured courses of 2 and 2½ miles. These are marked, and located between the woods and the campus.

OUTDOOR TRACKS

Typical to much of Florida, tracks are very poor. Jacksonville University has a ¼-mile asphalt track.

CLUBS, FUN-RUNS
AND RACES

The Jacksonville Track Club is the major organization for running in Northeast Florida. Their regularly scheduled program consists of a monthly meeting, a monthly fun-run, and a weekly training run.

Meetings are held on the second Tuesday of each month at 7:30 P.M. at the Downtown YMCA. Fun-runs are held on the second Saturday at Florida Junior College's South Campus at the rear parking lot. A 4-mile cross-country race is included. The events begin at 9:00 A.M. during summer months, and 10:00 A.M. in winter.

Each Saturday at 8:30 A.M., except Fun-Run Saturdays, a training run starts and ends at Friendship Park.

Small groups within the JTC and other local organizations are initiating more "minor" races and fun-runs. The club's newsletter lists all of these events.

TRADITIONAL RACES

Winter Beach Race, 10 miles: Early February

Jacksonville River Run, 15 kilometers: Early April
Beaches Run, 5 miles: Late August

CONTACTS   Jacksonville Track Club, Box 515, Jacksonville, FL 32201.
Jay Birmingham, Phidippides Running Center, 775 University Boulevard North, Jacksonville, FL 32211. (904) 743-6063.

Population: (met.) 2,420,000	Humidity: 74%
Elevation: 0–30 ft.	Av. Temperature: (Jan.) 67°F.; (July) 82°F.
Air Quality: Fair	Inches of Rainfall: (Jan.) 2.2; (July) 6.9 Raindays: 129

OVERVIEW

The City of Miami's downtown area lies along Biscayne Bay. Easy access to the Venetian Causeway gives runners a pleasant route over to Miami Beach, where running is confined to the many golf courses. Coral Gables and South Miami, both close to downtown Miami, have popular courses and considerable running activity. The Miami Runners Club is located in South Miami.

Miami has a lot of automobile traffic, and these hot cars on hot roads can leave you very cold. Fortunately, there are some roads which are not heavily used, such as the Venetian Causeway, which charges a toll (vehicles only). Also, the many golf courses allow runners to use their perimeters.

Due to year 'round warm weather and the lack of convenient large parks with abundant water fountains, many local runners favor short loops where they can return to a water supply, often to a cooler in their cars. Humidity is usually 20 percent higher in the mornings, when the air is about 10 degrees cooler, so there is a trade-off of humidity for coolness during morning runs.

HOTELS

Omni International Hotel, DuPont Plaza Hotel, Howard Johnson's – Midtown, Holiday Inn – Downtown Coral Gables, Coconut Grove Hotel

VENETIAN CAUSEWAY

This convenient downtown run begins along Biscayne Boulevard, the avenue closest to the bay. Bay Front Park lies across the boulevard along the water's edge for a distance of about ½ mile. You can head north along the boulevard, or through the park, which is sometimes populated by bothersome loiterers. At the end of the park, stay on Biscayne Boulevard, going north for about 3/5 of a mile to the Venetian Causeway at N.E. 15th Street. The Omni International is at the causeway entrance. Turn right and you will be heading over the bay. Due to the toll and a two-lane road, many motorists avoid this causeway, making it safe for runners. It's flat with occasional islands, offering detours onto residential streets. The distance across to Miami Beach is 2½ miles. Shade can sometimes be found on the islands; there is no water on the causeway.

Once you reach the other side, you can continue on Dade Boulevard for ½ mile to Bay Shore Golf Course on your left for some grass running.

CORAL GABLES

Located closer to Miami International Airport than Miami itself, Coral Gables has a convenient run through downtown and out to a nearby golf course. If you

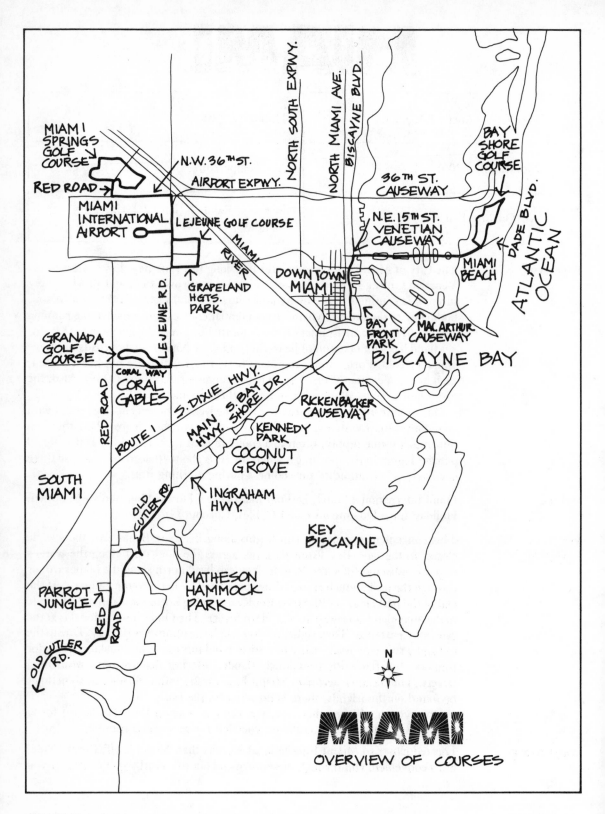

MIAMI

OVERVIEW OF COURSES

start at the Holiday Inn on LeJeune Avenue, head south for about ⅓ mile to a right on Coral Way. Continue on Coral for about ¼ mile to the Granada Golf Course where you can run the 2.3-mile perimeter. The beaten-down track at the edge of the course has very good footing. Follow the same route back to the hotel.

MATHESON HAMMOCK PARK AND OLD CUTLER ROAD

Miami is a flat city, and the only small hills in town are found in South Miami along Old Cutler Road near Matheson Hammock Park. The Miami Runners hold many fun-runs and races beginning at the park, and many runners travel here for their workouts. The park contains rest rooms and showers, along with plenty of shade and a concession stand for after-the-run relaxation. Normally, runners only start and finish here, with most mileage gained along Old Cutler Road. There are many trees along this route, providing excellent protection against the hot Florida sun.

From the entrance to the park, you can run either north or south along Old Cutler Road. The road to the north goes 2 miles to the traffic circle, and the road south continues for 10 miles. Going south, you will run into Red Road after about a mile, but keep heading south and the road will become Old Cutler again. A bike path exists along both the north and south routes.

Many runners who use the Old Cutler Road course begin their run from Parrot Jungle on Red Road. This is only about ⅓ mile north of the intersection with Old Cutler Road.

KENNEDY PARK COCONUT GROVE

The Coconut Grove Hotel is just up Bay Shore Drive from the Kennedy Park Vitacourse. This small bayfront park attracts many joggers over its grassy lawns and exercise route.

Venetian Causeway, Miami

MIAMI
INTERNATIONAL
AIRPORT

Just south of the airport entrance, and across LeJeune Road, you can run on LeJeune Golf Course and through Grapeland Heights Park. If you head north on LeJeune for ¾ of a mile to N.W. 36th Street, turning left and following 36th for 1½ miles to a right turn on Red Road, you will arrive at Miami Springs Golf Course.

CLUBS AND
FUN-RUNS

The Miami Runners Club has been growing very rapidly. Although running has been booming, many clubs cannot keep up with the growth unless many selfless runners are willing to put a lot of their time into the hard work that is needed. Hans and Laurie Huseby have been making that effort in Miami. The club puts on fun-runs every Sunday morning starting at Matheson Hammock Park.

TRADITIONAL RACES

Orange Bowl Marathon: January
Podiathon 20-Kilometer: Early May
Jordan Marsh 10-Kilometer: Early September
Key Biscayne 10-Kilometer: Early October
Race of the Americas, 7.6 miles: Late November

CONTACT

Hans Huseby, Miami Runners Club, Foot Works, 5724 Sunset Drive, South Miami, FL 33143. (305) 667-9322.

ORLANDO

Population: (met.) 500,000	Humidity: 74.5%
Elevation: 127 ft.	Av. Temperature: (Jan.) 60.8°F.; (July) 82.3°F.
Air Quality: Fair	Inches of Rainfall: (Jan.) 2.28; (July) 8.29 Raindays: 116

OVERVIEW

If you look at a map of Orlando, you might expect to find many lakeside courses. This busy tourist city has dozens of lakes amidst its beautiful residential communities. However, most of the lakes are bordered by private land, forcing runners to use surrounding residential streets which do not usually circumvent the lakes, requiring complicated routes through these neighborhoods.

Lake Eola, downtown, is enveloped by Eola Park to become the one lake where a waterside loop is possible. Although small, it is the only unobstructed course available, and thus a popular running site.

Just west of town, Disney World has recently become enlightened about running. For years, they considered runners a nuisance, but now they are promoting some recently designated jogging trails. Surrounding hotels can usually provide guests with easy routes on flat country roads through orange grove territory.

HOTELS

Best Western Kahler Plaza Inn, Howard Johnson's Executive Center, Hyatt House
Disney World—Contemporary Resort Hotel, Polynesian Village Resort Hotel, Lake Buena Vista Townhouse Hotel

LAKE EOLA

Kahler Plaza is located right at the lake. Howard Johnson's is only about 1 mile away if you run east on Colonial Drive for ½ mile and then south on Broadway to the lake. A paved sidewalk runs around the lake through Eola Park. You can also run part of the way on grass. This flat, .6-mile course has plenty of shade and one water fountain and rest room. The Central YMCA has daily groups that run to and around the lake.

WINTER PARK

This is one of the most beautiful residential areas in Orlando, and many local runners do their workouts on its quiet streets. Jon Hughes, from the Track Shack, took me on an interesting run here, but I would be unable to show anyone the course we took. Stop by the store (address listed below, under Contacts), and Jon or the other runners there will be happy to give you directions. There are some excellent hotels in Winter Park, and you might enjoy the ambience of the neighborhood.

DISNEY WORLD

From each of the hotels listed for Disney World, a separate jogging course has been laid out through the facilities. All three courses have mostly paved surfaces over a distance of not quite 2 miles. They are easy to follow and are well marked, both for direction and mileage. Some intersections must be crossed, except on the well-shaded Lake Buena Vista course, which outlines a golf course. Water fountains and rest rooms are adequately placed over the flat terrain.

HYATT HOUSE

This hotel, near Disney World, is surrounded by many acres of woods. Hyatt House has taken a strong interest in running, and even sponsors an annual 10-kilometer race around the hotel grounds.

OUTDOOR TRACKS

The Central YMCA has a 1/5-mile asphalt track. A track at Seminole Junior College is also available. Many high schools have excellent tracks, as this is a strong track-oriented city.

CLUBS, FUN-RUNS AND RACES

The Orlando Runners Club holds frequent races during the year. Many other groups, including the Track Shack, also put on numerous running events. The Winter Park YMCA holds fun-runs on Saturdays at 8:00 A.M.

TRADITIONAL RACES

Citrus Open Cross-Country Run, 8 miles: Late February
Windermere 10-Kilometer Run: Late April
Winter Park 10-Kilometer Run: June
Lady Track Shack 5-Kilometer Run: Mid-September
Hyatt 10-Kilometer Run: Late November
Tangerine Bowl Mini-Marathon, 13.1 and 2 miles: Mid-December

CONTACTS

Bill or Sally Childers, Orlando Road Runners Club, (305) 647-0523.
Don Wilson, Orlando Recreation Department, 649 West Livingston Street, Orlando, FL 32801. (305) 849-2288.
Tracy Dent or Jon Hughes, Track Shack, 1313 North Mills Avenue, Orlando, FL 32803. (305) 898-1313.
Central YMCA, 433 North Mills Avenue, Orlando, FL 32803. (305) 896-6901.
Winter Park YMCA, Bobby Dale, 1201 North Lakemont, Winter Park, FL 32792. (305) 644-1509.
Disney World Jogging Information, (305) 824-4781.

st. petersburg

Population: (met.) 649,000	Humidity: Not available
Elevation: 0–50 ft.	Av. Temperature: (Jan.) 65°F.; (July) 85°F.
Air Quality: Fair	Inches of Rainfall: (Jan.) 2.6; (July) 9.1 Raindays: 103

OVERVIEW

St. Petersburg sits on the southern tip of a large peninsula on the west coast of Florida across the bay from Tampa. The St. Pete Beach draws the most runners because of the refreshing dips you can take during a run. Numerous scantily clad, languid bodies along the course cannot be overlooked as another factor for its popularity. Negative aspects must be mentioned as a balance. These include stray frisbees and keeping your eye on a setting sun for a dangerously prolonged time. In summer, beware of late afternoon lightning storms.

HOTELS

All beach hotels are fine for beach running; Hilton–Downtown

ST. PETERSBURG BEACH

With flat, hard-packed sand, especially at low tide, this is an excellent 7-mile back-and-forth run. The distance from Sharkworld Aquatarium at the north end to Passa-A-Grille Channel and Pier at the south end measures 3½ miles. Shade is unheard of on the Suncoast and water must be sought out at establishments off the beach.

TAMPA BAY ROUTE

From the Hilton, a beautiful run exists to the north along Tampa Bay. For 2 miles out, you can run on sidewalk or grass passing interesting sights such as the Yacht Club and the Municipal Pier. Again, there is no shade. Return on the same route along the bay.

CLUBS

The Suncoast Runners is an active club headed by Dr. Tom White. They received some national attention when they boycotted a major Florida race because of an unduly high entry fee.

FUN-RUNS AND RACES

Fun-runs are held every Saturday at the Azalea Middle School at 7:30 A.M. The Suncoast Runners have an active schedule of races, including the Sundown Beach Races, held from June to August every other Friday; distances vary.

TRADITIONAL RACES

Bay-to-Bay Race, 7.5 miles: Memorial Day
Mini-Marathon, 13.1 miles: Early February

CONTACTS

Dr. Tom White, Suncoast Runners Club, 1250 Jungle Avenue North, St. Petersburg, FL 33710.
Greg Holzwart, 5914 43rd Avenue North, St. Petersburg, FL 33709. (813) 546-8682.
Athletic Attic, Tyrone Square #760, 6901 22nd Avenue, St. Petersburg, FL 33710. (813) 344-1542.

TAMPA

Population: (met.) 541,000	Humidity: 74.5%
Elevation: 15 ft.	Av. Temperature: (Jan.) 60°F.; (July) 82.3°F.
Air Quality: Fair to poor	Inches of Rainfall: (Jan.) 2.3; (July) 8.4 Raindays: 108

OVERVIEW

Located midway along the Gulf Coast of Florida, this flat, open city boasts many outstanding runners. Track and field also reigns in Tampa and there are world-class athletes training here. Shot-putter Doug Price operates two of the running stores along with runner Pete Foret.

Tampa Bay snuggles right up to downtown, and waterside running from here is convenient and pleasurable. Few cities in America get hotter in the summer, and the lack of good shade warrants pre-dawn or dusk runs.

HOTELS

Holiday Inn—Central, Riverside Hilton Inn, Sheraton—Tampa, Tampa Airport Resort Golf and Racquet Club, Host International, Bay Harbor Inn, Causeway Inn Beach Resort

BAY SHORE BOULEVARD

This downtown course can be run from the Holiday Inn, Hilton or Sheraton. Go to South Ashley Avenue (at the Hilton door) and then south to a right turn on Brorein, following it over the canal bridge. Take your first left, go two blocks, and then turn right onto Bay Shore Boulevard.

Bay Shore Boulevard runs for about 7 miles along beautiful Hillsboro Bay on one side, with luxurious residential homes on the other. The Gasparilla Road Race utilizes this course. Much of the route can be run on grass, and occasionally you can find an apartment house that has an outdoor water faucet.

DAVIS ISLAND

Near the start of the Bay Shore course, along the Boulevard, you will see a bridge going over to Davis Island. If you take this bridge, you will be on a man-made island of beautiful homes with a roadway covering 5 miles. A gem of a run.

COURTNEY CAMPBELL CAUSEWAY

Beaches line most of this causeway between Tampa and Clearwater, offering excellent running along the water. A dirt road borders the beach for 3 miles to the causeway bridge. The Bay Harbor Inn and the Causeway Inn both sit on the Tampa side of this route, and two rest-room areas can be found along the way.

LIFE CLINIC AT BRANDON

Dr. George Greenwell owns the Life Clinic which is located in Brandon, about 20 miles west of Tampa. The clinic has an international reputation for its research into running. Many miles along dirt country roads and through phosphate pits can begin from here, and when you are through, you can shower at the clinic. Take Highway 60 to Beverly Road, and the clinic will be on your right.

AIRPORT RUNS   Close to the airport there are many flat, straight country roads to wander over. The Host International and the Tampa Airport Resort are fine accommodations from which to start your runs.

CLUBS   The Tampa Bay Track Club carries a full schedule of races and clinics throughout the year.

TRADITIONAL RACES   Gasparilla Classic, 15 kilometers: Early February
Tampa Bay Classic, 10 miles: Late October

CONTACTS   Tampa Bay Track Club, 344 Westshore Mall, Tampa, FL 33609. (813) 876-9347.
Starting Block, Brandon Mall, Brandon, Florida 33511. (813) 681-3505.

West Palm Beach

Population: West Palm Beach—62,000 Palm Beach—8,600	Humidity: 74%
Elevation: 0–18 ft.	Av. Temperature: (Jan.) 61°F.; (July) 82°F.
Air Quality: Fair	Inches of Rainfall: (Jan.) 2.5; (July) 6 Raindays: 131

OVERVIEW

Situated along the east coast of southern Florida, this city's focus on recreational activities has naturally led to a strong interest in running. Although it appears there would be many beach runs and numerous scenic routes, most runners tend to congregate at the popular "Bridges" course, utilizing the bike paths along both sides of Lake Worth and two bridges that cross it.

West Palm Beach, the populated business area, sits across the inland waterway from less populated Palm Beach. The "Bridges" course includes both cities. This area's proximity to many other nearby resorts creates an active environment.

HOTELS

Holiday Inn–Downtown (West Palm Beach), Travelodge (West Palm Beach), Heart of Palm Beach Motor Hotel

"BRIDGES" RUN

This route forms a loop by using the North Bridge and the South Bridge over Lake Worth, the inland waterway. A bike trail exists along either side of the waterway. From the two West Palm hotels, head north on the bike trail along Flagler Drive to the North Bridge. Go over the bridge and turn south onto the bike trail along the waterway down to the South Bridge, going over South Bridge and back across to West Palm Beach and the Flagler Drive bike trail, heading north back to the hotels. The total distance is 2¾ miles.

From the Heart of Palm Motor Hotel, head west to the bike trail along the waterway, and then follow the same route as above, looping over the two bridges, and then back to the motel. This distance is 3 miles.

The YMCA, located near the bike trail in West Palm Beach, is used by many runners as the starting point for the course. It is also a good stop-off for water and rest rooms. This route can be used safely day or night.

BIKE TRAIL NORTH

This excellent route involves a trip across the North Bridge and north on the bike trail in Palm Beach. From the YMCA starting point, the course is 9 miles to the end of the island and back. To the Sailfish Club and back it is 7 miles. Water is available at the far end of the Sailfish Club.

JOHN PRINCE PARK

Just south of West Palm Beach in Lake Worth, you will find this scenic park with fine cross-country running over grassy lawns. A course has been measured along a bike trail that stretches along a pretty lake. Although the trail is 5 miles long, the measured and marked area extends for only 2½ miles. The park has partial shade and adequate water and rest room facilities.

CLUBS, FUN-RUNS AND RACES
The Palm Beach Runners Association is an active, growing club with a full schedule of races. Many different groups in nearby communities hold frequent fun-runs, and the PBRA can give you the details (see address below).

TRADITIONAL RACES
Anniversary Run, 15 kilometers: Early February
Shamrock Run, 10 miles: Sunday closest to St. Patrick's Day
Easter Classic, 6 miles: Easter Sunday
Law Day Run: Early May
Turkey Trot, 10 kilometers: Sunday after Thanksgiving

CONTACTS
Palm Beach Runners Association, P.O. Box 8205, West Palm Beach, FL 33407. Justus W. Reid, 250 Royal Palm Way, Palm Beach, FL 33480. (305) 659-4800.

ATLANTA

Population: (met.) 1,760,000	Humidity: 71%
Elevation: 738 – 1,086 ft.	Av. Temperature: (Jan.) 45°F.; (July) 80°F.
Air Quality: Fair to poor	Inches of Rainfall: (Jan.) 4.3; (July) 4.9 Raindays: 115

OVERVIEW

Atlanta would seem to have it all, and for local runners who use their own neighborhoods, it does offer an excellent training environment. There are rolling hills, cool winters, but admittedly, hot summers. The major problem to out-of-town runners is a lack of downtown courses.

Some of the most beautiful hotels in America are located in the heart of downtown. The Hyatt Regency here launched that chain's luxurious line, and the new Peachtree Center is a magnificent landmark for Western International. From these and other exceptional downtown hotels, you must run nearly 2 miles on city streets to reach a small but satisfactory city park.

Running organizations in Atlanta are exceptional, with the Atlanta Track Club a leading, superactive force in the country. The Atlanta Running Center, headed by Jeff Galloway, who also heads up the Phidippides chain, is an innovative organization working on clinics and scientific experiments to understand and improve our lot.

HOTEL

Colony Square Hotel

PIEDMONT PARK

The only running accessible to downtown hotels can be found at Piedmont Park. A small lake in the park has a perimeter pathway with a number of exercise stations. One loop around the lake and the adjacent ball field will total 1 mile. A golf course in the park can only be used on Mondays, when it is closed to golfers. The terrain is mostly flat under good shade, and water and rest rooms are available.

The Colony Square Hotel, an excellent accommodation, sits only a few hundred yards from the park entrance on 14th Street. From the other downtown hotels, about 2 miles away, head east a couple of blocks to Piedmont Avenue, and turn north for a direct route to the park. The sidewalk is wide with few intersections over small rolling hills. Near the park, the neighborhood becomes residential. If you stay on Piedmont Avenue, past the park, you will reach Ansley Mall after another ½ mile. The Atlanta Running Center is located here at the Phidippides running store, and Wednesday night clinics are held here throughout the year.

GEORGIA TECH
UNIVERSITY CAMPUS

This downtown campus can provide some grassy areas to wander around during a workout. It is in closer proximity to the downtown area than Piedmont

Park, and for a short run might be just the place to head to. Go north on Spring Street from the hotel area to a left on Linden. Total distance to the campus is ¾ of a mile.

EMORY UNIVERSITY CAMPUS

The Emory Campus, about 5 miles northeast of downtown, contains a 2-mile cross-country course beginning at the President's Estate driveway on Clifton Road. The path over the campus and through Druid Hills is easy to follow.

The ¼-mile cinder track on campus receives a lot of use from local runners. Nighttime is popular, with lights from the nearby tennis courts illuminating the track.

STONE MOUNTAIN COURSES

Sixteen miles east of U.S. 78, this tourist attraction has two excellent routes for hilly, shady runs. You can either start from the train station parking lot or go through the East Gate on the walkway to the mountain. The least hilly of the two routes is the 5-mile loop around the mountain. For the hillier 8-mile loop, stay on the road that circles around the lake. Due to the many tourists, it is best to run here in the early morning or late in the day.

KENNESAW MOUNTAIN TRAILS

A challenging wilderness area can be found 20 miles northwest of town on U.S. 41. Kennesaw Mountain offers 19 miles of trails. The terrain is extremely hilly. Routes are not marked for distance, although you might meet some runners who are familiar with the trails.

CLUBS AND RACES

The Atlanta Track Club is the major running organization in town. They also sponsor competitive men's and women's teams for international events. Their annual schedule includes two to three races each month, usually held in diverse

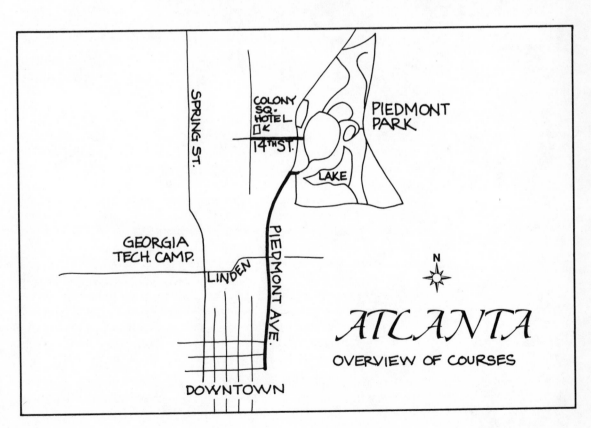

locations around Atlanta; a different race director handles each race. During the summer, an all-comers track meet is held weekly on Wednesday nights.

The Atlanta Running Center is a non-profit organization created to promote running for fitness. Among its activities is a weekly Wednesday night clinic held at the Phidippides running store.

TRADITIONAL RACES   The Atlanta Marathon: Late January
Peachtree Road Race, 10 kilometers: Fourth of July

CONTACTS   Atlanta Track Club, P.O. Box 11556, Atlanta, GA 30355.
Atlanta Running Center, Phidippides, Ansley Mall, 1544 Piedmont Road, N.E., Atlanta, GA 30324. (404) 875-4268.

SAVANNAH

Population: 110,000	Humidity: 73%
Elevation: 42 ft.	Av. Temperature: (Jan.) 50°F.; (July) 81°F.
Air Quality: Fair	Inches of Rainfall: (Jan.) 2.9; (July) 7.9 Raindays: 112

OVERVIEW

This beautiful port city is located on the Savannah River, close to the ocean. Many small squares and tree-lined streets attract local runners as well as tourists, and its grid pattern makes for easy street running through historic neighborhoods. Some hotels provide easy access to the Talmadge Memorial Bridge, which will take you over its span, on the only hill in the city, to the South Carolina side of the river.

Many members of the Savannah Striders put in their daily mileage out at Lake Mayer, about 7½ miles south of downtown. Year 'round humidity appears to be the biggest obstacle to running here, and long, hot summers compound the discomfort.

HOTELS

Holiday Inn–Downtown, Howard Johnson's–Downtown, Ramada Inn, Quality Inn–Heart of Savannah, Desoto Hilton, John Wesley Hotel, Days Inn Motel, Downtowner Motel

TALMADGE MEMORIAL BRIDGE

Holiday Inn, Howard Johnson's and Ramada Inn all sit at the foot of this bridge. It is an old structure with a narrow sidewalk that can be a little dangerous when big trucks sweep by. Local runners use this route for their hill workouts. A great scenic view of Savannah can be seen from the span. At 3 miles, you will be on the bridge over the Buford County line in South Carolina.

DOWNTOWN AND RIVERFRONT RUNS

This city can really be appreciated by running through its historic district, which is sandwiched in by East Broad Street, West Broad Street and the river. The distance along the river measures close to ¾ of a mile. A bike path has been built about 30 feet from the water's edge through the cobblestoned wharf area. The Quality Inn and John Wesley Hotel are located close to the river.

Loops can be run by using the Broad streets at either end of the district, the river bike path, and the wide transverse streets that cross east/west, south of the river. If you cross at Oglethorpe Avenue, where the Downtowner is located, the loop measures 3 miles, and if you cross at Liberty Street, where the Hilton is located, the loop measures 4½ miles.

FORSYTH PARK

This park is located within the historic district, a couple miles south of the river. A sidewalk perimeter measures just over 1 mile. Water fountains and rest rooms are available. Local runners suggest you do not use this park at night.

DAFFIN PARK	Daffin Park can be reached a few miles southeast of downtown along Victory Drive. There are many open fields here to run around, and water and rest rooms are available. Unfortunately, dogs have been a big problem in this park, and so the majority of runners avoid coming here.
LAKE MAYER	This most popular course can be reached from downtown by driving south on Abercorn to a left turn (east) onto Victory Drive. Turn right (south) onto Waters Avenue, and continue to a left (east) on Montgomery Cross Road to the lake. Days Inn is about a 2¼-mile run from the lake. Head east down Mall Boulevard for ½ mile to Waters Avenue. Follow Waters south for ¼ mile and then turn west onto Montgomery Cross Road for 1½ miles to the lake.
	The lake is bounded by a 1½-mile asphalt track. Little shade can protect you from the sun, but there are water fountains, rest rooms, and free showers. Mileage markers are placed at the first quarter mile, and then each half-mile. For a longer loop, the perimeter of the recreational area around the lake measures 3½ miles.
OUTDOOR TRACKS	The Savannah YMCA has a ⅛-mile jogging track.
CLUBS, FUN-RUNS AND RACES	The Savannah Striders hold fun-runs frequently on Saturday mornings at Lake Mayer. In hot weather they are at 8:00 A.M., and during cool months, at 10:00 A.M. Races are held monthly.
TRADITIONAL RACES	St. Patrick's Day 5,000-Meter Torchlight Run, 4 and 2 miles: May Wilmington Island Run, 10 and 5 miles: Early December
CONTACTS	Bob Phillips, 9219 Melody Drive, Savannah, GA 31406. (912) 354-1302, 234-6616 (work). Cedric Stratton, 506 East 57th Street, Savannah, GA 31405. Gary Siebert, (912) 897-4490. Savannah YMCA, 6400 Habersham Street, Savannah, GA 31405. (912) 354-6223. Larry Graves, Savannah Striders, (912) 354-9957, 233-9257 (work). Savannah Striders Track Club, Stan Friedman, P.O. Box 9846, Savannah, GA 31402.

HONOLULU

Population: 375,000	Humidity: 67%
Elevation: 7 ft.	Av. Temperature: (Jan.) 72.3°F.; (July) 80.1°F.
Air Quality: Good	Inches of Rainfall: (Jan.) 4.4; (July) .6 Raindays: 102

OVERVIEW

Honolulu claims to be the running capital of the world, and they have plenty of evidence to support their claim. Most astonishingly, they turn out over 2,000 runners every Sunday morning for the Marathon Clinic in Kapiolani Park. And that's at 7:30 A.M.! Not only is running big in size, but a great deal of organization lies behind it. The Mid-Pacific Road Runners Club and the Honolulu Marathon Association take full responsibility to provide the best running environment possible. Honolulu's Department of Parks and Recreation has published a brochure entitled "Jogging," which maps out over twenty recommended routes. Also, the first of its kind, a runner's guidebook was published in 1977, with details of routes for the island of Oahu.

As active as the city is with runners, it also has many other outdoor enthusiasts, resulting in busy streets and paths. Picnickers infest the parks, and autos create danger on park roads and other popular routes. To ensure safety, pedestrians, including runners, are subject to a fifteen-dollar fine for running a red light.

The most frequented course in parks along the beach can be reached in minutes from Waikiki hotels. Every aspect of these courses has been scrutinized and analyzed by local aficionados, and you certainly will not find yourself running alone on any of these designated routes.

The weather in Honolulu has few deterrent qualities. It is almost always warm and sunny. Although there are few very hot days, coming here from a cold climate will necessitate some adjustment. Early morning and night runs are perhaps the most sensible. The hilly Tantalus run, north of town, has frequent cloud cover to provide respite from the heat and sun.

HOTELS

A great variety of hotels can be found in the Waikiki area—about 2½ miles from the business district.

KAPIOLANI PARK

Kalakaua Avenue is the key to running from the Waikiki hotels to the popular running courses north, east or west. On the eastern edge of Waikiki Beach lies Kapiolani Park. Head down Kalakaua Avenue east to Monsarrat Avenue. Here you can start a loop around the park. It is .4 mile across the park to Paki Avenue, then a right turn and .6 mile along Paki to Kalakaua, and another right along the ocean back to the start to complete 1.8 miles. This triangular course remains flat over the paved roadway or dirt path and shade is moderate. Water fountains and rest rooms are frequent.

DIAMOND HEAD

A run around Diamond Head Crater is a favorite among local runners. This scenic course begins at the same place as the Kapiolani Park loop, heading out Monsarrat. Continue on Monsarrat past the park until it joins Diamond Head Road, keeping right around the crater on Diamond Head Road, until it takes you back to Kalakaua Avenue at Kapiolani Park, and along that to the starting point. Total distance is 4.6 miles. The route is often run in the reverse direction as well.

A tiny, triangular-shaped park at the far end of the course contains a water fountain, and the course measurement includes a detour around the fountain. Parts of this course are flat, and some moderate hills are located along the ocean side of the crater. Footing is sidewalk and road under occasional shade. Water fountains are also located along the ocean side and inland side of the crater, one on each side. During the Marathon Clinic, residents supply water on their front lawns.

Kahala Beach is located just beyond the Diamond Head course. From the Kahala Hilton, Diamond Head Road can be reached by running west along Kahala Avenue 1.6 miles. It meets the course at the small park with the water fountain.

ALA WAI CANAL

This is an easy, convenient loop, located just north of the Waikiki Beach area. Heading north from the beach, just about any street between Kapiolani Park and the canal inlet will take you to the sidewalk along the canal. Follow the sidewalk along the near side of the canal, crossing it at McCully Street. Take McCully a few hundred yards to a right turn on Kapiolani Boulevard. Stay on the boulevard for .6 mile to Date Street. Turn right and continue straight on Date for .8 mile, passing the Ala Wai Golf Course. At the far side of the course, go right on Kapahulu Avenue for .4 mile to the Waikiki Library, where you will make another right onto Ala Wai Boulevard and continue on the sidewalk to where you started.

It is not as complicated as it might sound. The loop has five sides over flat terrain, and shade is practically nil. Water is available about midway along the canal, and on the ball field just after the canal bridge. You will also find a rest room at the ball field. Uneven grass and dirt paths are available along Date Street. The canal loop measures 3.4 miles.

ALA MOANA PARK

Across the street from the giant Ala Moana Shopping Center, west of Waikiki, you can run an easy loop around the park. One loop around the perimeter measures 2 miles. Magic Island extends into the ocean from the park, and one loop around the island will give you another mile. From here, a great view can be had of the Waikiki skyline and Diamond Head.

The park has plenty of water fountains, rest rooms and showers. Occasionally you can run on grass or dirt instead of sidewalk. Masses of people use this park, especially on weekends.

MOUNT TANTALUS

This is a challenging and very scenic run. A great experience for any runner visiting Honolulu. Part of the run travels through a tropical rain forest where misty vistas produce exquisite rainbows. Views of the city are spectacular with the entire spread of Honolulu Harbor and Waikiki below you.

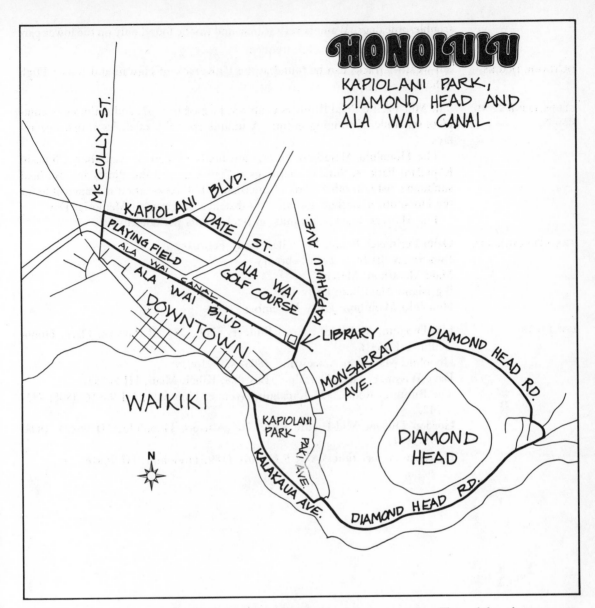

HONOLULU

KAPIOLANI PARK,
DIAMOND HEAD AND
ALA WAI CANAL

Run out Kalakaua Avenue toward the mountains. Turn right when you can run no more. Go one block to Punahou Street and turn left. Run on Punahou until you reach Wilder Avenue. Turn left on Wilder and run to Makiki Heights Drive. The Tantalus course begins here.

Run up Makiki Heights Drive for 1.3 miles to Tantalus Drive. Turn right and continue on Tantalus to the top of the mountain. The route starts out with a gradual incline and continually gets steeper. At the top, continue around on Round Top Drive for a more gradual descent to the starting point. The route over Tantalus is 10.1 miles, and it is about 2 miles from Waikiki to the starting point.

Danger persists the entire way up the mountain and down. The road is narrow, and cars whip around the curves. Near the top, beware—there are some troublesome dogs. Water is very scarce, and can be found only on the lower part of Round Top Drive.

OUTDOOR TRACKS

All-weather tracks can be found at the University of Hawaii and Kaiser High School.

CLUBS, CLINICS AND RACES

The Mid-Pacific Road Runners Club was formed in 1962, and maintains a complete schedule of running events. A unique specialty of theirs is distance relays.

The Honolulu Marathon Association holds its famous Marathon Clinic in Kapiolani Park on Sunday mornings at 7:30 A.M., and the clinics are also held simultaneously on other parts of the island. The Association is responsible for the Honolulu Marathon and an ultra-distance program on Memorial Day.

The Masters Track Club puts on track events periodically.

TRADITIONAL RACES

Oahu Perimeter Relay, 133 miles: Early February
Run-Swim Biathlon: Late February
Maui Marathon: March
Big Island Marathon: Early July
Honolulu Marathon: Early December

CONTACTS

Lou DiSanto, Mid-Pacific Road Runners Club, 3832-B Pukalani Place, Honolulu, HI 96816.
Honolulu Marathon Association, (808) 839-2160.
Dave Wissmar, Maui Marathon, Box 888, Kihei, Maui, HI 96753.
The Running Room, 821 Kapahulu Avenue, Honolulu, HI 96816. (808) 737-2422.
Gordon Dugan, Mid-Pacific RRC, 704 Ainapo, Honolulu, HI 96825. (808) 395-5474.
Hawaiian Association AAU, P.O. Box 7189, Honolulu, HI 96816.

BOISE

Population: 110,00	Humidity: 57%
Elevation: 2,739 ft.	Av. Temperature: (Jan.) 29°F.; (July) 75°F.
Air Quality: Good	Inches of Rainfall: (Jan.) 1.5; (July) .2 Raindays: 91

OVERVIEW

Below the Sawtooth Mountains, in the southern part of Idaho, many river valleys have created a belt of busy towns across the state. Boise is located to the west, along the Boise River. Boise, its name derived from the French *"les bois,"* the woods, has abundant trees available for your shaded runs.

The city has climate and terrain to satisfy most every runner. A high and dry atmosphere provides comfortable running all year. Summers get hot, but cool morning air can be very refreshing. In winter, snowfall never reaches obstructive accumulations.

Terrain varies from a flat riverbed area to foothills rising quickly to the northeast. Within several miles they can take you over 1,000 feet above the valley floor.

Boise lifestyle is slow to pick up new trends, and running here has been an undeveloped sport until just recently. Drivers have yet to appreciate runners along the road, and occasional harassment prevails. Staying on the footpaths along the river is the easiest and most convenient running, although the foothills offer challenge and some solitude.

HOTELS

All downtown hotels are located within ½ mile of the Boise River, including the Boisean Motel, Boulevard Motel, Ramada Inn and International Dunes Motel.

BOISE RIVER GREENBELT

Construction of a bike/footpath began in 1978, and when completed will provide 50 miles of beautiful, unobstructed running next to the Boise River. As of publication of this book, 4½ miles have been developed through the downtown area. The pathway travels along both sides of the river and passes through two municipal parks. Trees have been undisturbed during this construction, and provide wonderful shade. Plenty of water fountains and rest rooms are available.

Courses have not been marked along the path, and a variety of routes, utilizing the bridges that cross the river every ¾ to 1 mile, can be run—just create your own loops around both sides of the river.

FOOTHILLS

Within ½ mile northeast of town, the foothills are available for very challenging hill workouts. Many routes are possible over the residential streets, varying in degree of difficulty. The downtown YMCA is measuring fifty-two different routes, and will provide maps with directions. Some of these are now ready.

A popular 5.8-mile route begins at the YMCA on State and 10th streets, and heads north five blocks on 10th to Thatcher Street. Turn right and run two blocks over to 8th Street. From here you head north again for eight blocks along shaded 8th Street, to a right turn on Brumback Street, which quickly turns into Boise Hills Drive. The road then heads uphill into Boise Heights.

After a few hundred yards, turn right, continuing uphill on Crestline Drive. As the uphill ends, in a little over a mile, take a right onto a dirt road and follow it for about 1/3 mile to some motorcycle trails on your left, and then follow the trails for close to a mile before reaching Mile High Road. Turn left onto this dirt road and follow it back into 8th Street, and onto the route back to the YMCA.

CLUBS, FUN-RUNS AND RACES

Quite a number of different clubs and organizations are involved with running in Boise. The YMCA and the West Side Optimist Club both put on frequent running events. The Optimist Club holds fun-runs every third Sunday at 11:00 A.M. during the cooler months, and 7:00 P.M. when it is hot. They hold races every fourth Sunday at 9:00 A.M.

A new club, the Treasure Valley Road Runners, has been formed to bring together these diverse groups to create a cohesive running environment.

TRADITIONAL RACES

Table Rock Road Run, 9 miles: End of June
Dam-Statesman Fun-Run, 6.4 and 2.4 miles: Late September
Les Bois Marathon: Early November

CONTACTS

Basil Dahlstrom, Sport Life, 451 Main Street, Boise, ID 83702. (208) 343-0371.
Bill Crookham, Treasure Valley Road Runners, Box 520, Caldwell, ID 83605. (208) 459-7451 (work).
Boise YMCA, 1050 State Street, Boise, ID 83702. (208) 344-5501.

CHICAGO

Population: (met.) 7,650,000	Humidity: 66%
Elevation: 579 – 673 ft.	Av. Temperature: (Jan.) 27°F.; (July) 75°F.
Air Quality: Poor	Inches of Rainfall: (Jan.) 1.9; (July) 4.1 Raindays: 120

OVERVIEW

This hearty city has numerous possibilities for interesting runs. Foremost, of course, is the lakefront, with terrific vistas of the Chicago skyline. On days when the water is pounding up on the shore with a biting spray to cool your run, you can experience a thrilling sense of slipping between the power of nature from the lake, and the contrasting strength of mankind in the cityscape. Certainly a run not to miss in Chicago. Different parks and beaches along the lake provide an everchanging environment over 14 measured miles.

Problems occur on cold days when the wind blows down from the northeast. If you head downwind for the first part of your run, when you eventually turn back into the wind you can experience up to a 30 degree drop in the wind/chill factor. At the latter stages of a workout, your body is often too tired to generate enough heat to overcome this.

Away from the lake, many parks are frequented by runners living nearby. There are active neighborhood running clubs that utilize their parks for races and fun-runs. No one major running club dominates Chicago running, but the small clubs are now developing a cohesiveness that will improve the quality of running events in the city.

Many visitors stay in hotels near O'Hare Airport. At first, it appears to be a difficult area to run in, with many highways and commercial streets wherever you look. Miraculously, if you run only about ½ mile east, the Des Plaines Forest Preserve provides miles of wooded terrain.

HOTELS

Many hotels are located along the lakefront. The most convenient are along Lakeshore Drive. These include: Holiday Inn – Lakeshore, Howard Johnson's, Playboy Towers, and the Ambassador East. Quite a number are located just a few blocks in from the lake. Hotels along South Michigan Avenue also sit at the lakefront, across from Grant Park.

LAKEFRONT

The lakefront course can be reached from downtown hotels by heading east to Lakeshore Drive. To cross the drive north of Navy Pier, use the underpasses at North Avenue, Oak Street, or Chicago Avenue, or cross at the light at Erie Street. These crossings are about ⅓ mile apart. You will find a cement pathway next to the water's edge. The course is not closely marked, and every couple of miles you will see a mileage marker.

The 1½-mile stretch between the Navy Pier at the south end, north to the southern tip of Lincoln Park, is known as the Gold Coast. Lincoln Park extends north of the Gold Coast for 5 miles. Here the path sits a little further back from the water's edge, creating a chance to run on grass or dirt instead of concrete. Occasional shade and water fountains can be found in the park, but no rest rooms.

A very scenic run heads south from Navy Pier for a distance of 7½ miles to Jackson Park, measured along the water. Crossing over the Chicago River, you will be in Grant Park. It contains a stand of 2,000 American elm trees, one of the last remaining stands of elms in the world. This beautiful, formal park also contains Buckingham Fountain, the largest fountain in the world. On a warm day, with a good northeasterly wind, its spray will be very refreshing. To the left is Monroe Street Harbor where the water is often dotted with small sailboats. Continuing south, you will reach Planetarium Drive, leading onto a peninsula where you can detour out and back for an additional measured mile. Close to the peninsula is the Field Museum and Shedd Aquarium. The entire lakefront can be run at night under good lighting. If you are on the peninsula at night in April, when the smelt are running, you will find many fishermen along the way bringing them in with nets.

Continuing south, you can run into Burnham Park, which extends 5 miles south. This quiet and peaceful park is considered a haven by many local runners. At the bottom of the park, you will reach Promontory Point at 55th Street. Here you can either head back north or cross under the drive into Jackson Park.

JACKSON PARK

The University of Chicago Track Club uses the park's 2.2-mile loop for its winter races. The distance is measured on the paved path around the perimeter. The fact that winter races are held here does not mean the pathway gets cleared of snow. Chicago runners are very tough.

MIDWAY TO WASHINGTON PARK

A pleasant run can be had from Jackson Park heading west along the Midway. This is a wide, grassy boulevard that was formerly a World's Fair grounds, measuring exactly 1 mile to Washington Park. The park has been the site of a number of national AAU cross-country races. These are run in the southern half of the park, twisting complicatedly around a central lagoon. A perimeter pathway around the entire park would be about 2½ to 3 miles. All the parks in Chicago are flat, and most have adequate shade. Water fountains and rest rooms are almost always available.

MARQUETTE PARK

Home of the Marquette Park Track Club, and located about 4 miles west of Washington Park, this facility contains a 3-mile and a 2-mile loop. You can run on grass alongside the asphalt path. Although the paths lie flat, some interior toboggan hills provide the only hill workout available in all of Chicago.

DES PLAINES FOREST PRESERVE

Located about ½ mile east of O'Hare area hotels, this heavily wooded preserve has an excellent dirt trail about 5½ miles long. The Des Plaines River runs the length of the preserve, and the dirt bridle path can be found along its east bank. Depending on which hotel you begin from, you will probably enter the park at the northern half to third section. The course runs north to Oakton Street, and south to Belmont Avenue. There are few water fountains here.

NORTH BRANCH AND SKOKIE DIVISION FOREST PRESERVES

Home of the Windy City Striders, this area, located about 5 miles east of the Des Plaines Forest Preserve, can be reached from the airport by following Kennedy Expressway southeast to Nagel Avenue, turning north on Nagel for ¾ of a

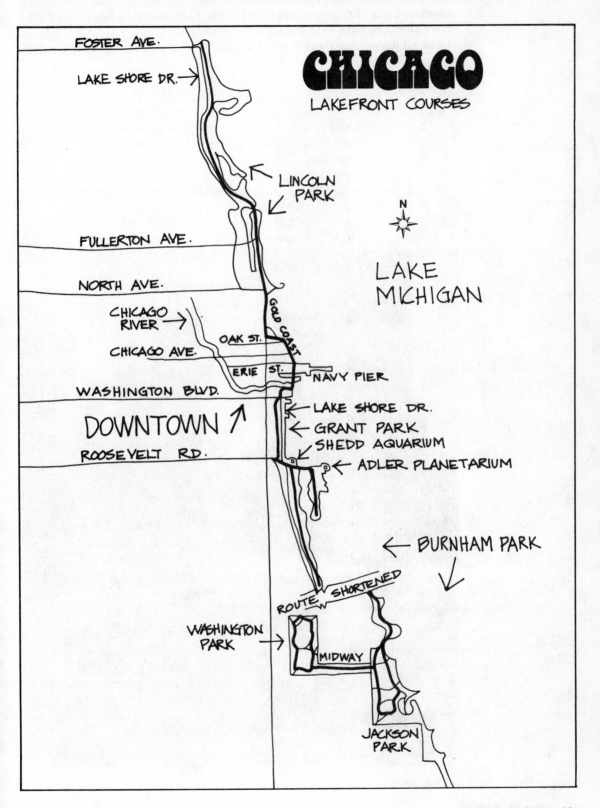

CHICAGO
LAKEFRONT COURSES

FOSTER AVE.

LAKE SHORE DR.

LINCOLN PARK

FULLERTON AVE.

NORTH AVE.

N

LAKE MICHIGAN

CHICAGO RIVER

CHICAGO AVE.

GOLD COAST

OAK ST.

ERIE ST.

NAVY PIER

WASHINGTON BLVD.

DOWNTOWN

LAKE SHORE DR.

GRANT PARK

SHEDD AQUARIUM

ROOSEVELT RD.

ADLER PLANETARIUM

BURNHAM PARK

ROUTE SHORTENED

WASHINGTON PARK

MIDWAY

JACKSON PARK

mile until it dead-ends. Turn right for 50 yards to the Caldwell Woods Park entrance. From downtown, follow Kennedy Expressway to Bryn Mawr Avenue, then turn right onto Nagel to the dead end.

The Chicago River flows through this preserve area, and a 7-mile bike path

Lakefront, Chicago

runs alongside it. You can run on dirt alongside the paved path. Water fountains are available.

The Leaning Tower YMCA, just east of the preserve, has morning and noon groups that utilize this course.

RIIS PARK

The Riis Park Striders lay claim to this turf. Located about 7 miles west of downtown, and 6 miles southeast of O'Hare Airport, it can be reached from the airport by following Kennedy Expressway to Austin Avenue, and then south for 3½ miles to Fullerton Avenue. Turn right for two blocks to the park. From downtown, go north to Fullerton and then west to the park.

Here you will find a 1-mile loop around the perimeter of this attractive park. There are some small hills and plenty of grass to run on. Water fountains and rest rooms are available, and there is a fieldhouse with free lockers and showers. The park is lit at night, and in winter the course is well plowed.

OUTDOOR TRACKS

Lakeshore Park is located in downtown Chicago at Lakeshore Drive and Chicago Avenue. This small recreational facility, about one square block in size, has a ¼-mile cinder track around its perimeter. It is narrow, and the turns are sharp. Adjacent to the park is a small building with a gym, lockers, and showers that are available to the public at certain hours. The park is right across the drive from the lakefront, providing a choice between track and lakeshore running. Lakeshore Park is headquarters for the Azteca Running Club.

Marquette Park has a 1/6-mile cinder track, and 400-meter cinder tracks can be found at Jackson Park and Riis Park.

Stagg Field, at the University of Chicago, and across the street from Washington Park, has an excellent ¼-mile all-weather track. The University of Chicago Track Club, under the directorship of the famed Ted Haydon, works out here. Many world records have been held by members of the team. Visiting runners may use the track at different times.

INDOOR TRACKS

The Lawson YMCA on Chicago Avenue has a 30-laps-per-mile track.

CLUBS, FUN-RUNS AND RACES

The Riis Park Striders hold races every Sunday morning at 10:00 A.M. at the park. The Windy City Striders hold races mostly on Saturday mornings at Caldwell Woods Park. In winter, some of their races are held on Sunday mornings. The University of Chicago Track Club holds their winter races in Jackson Park on Sundays at 11:00 A.M. In spring, they have races on the track at 4:30 P.M. on Sundays; and in summer, races are held on the track at 5:00 P.M. on Thursdays.

The Midwest Masters hold races monthly at different locations around the region. The Athlete's Foot Running Club meets at Belmont Avenue and the lake at 7:00 P.M. Wednesdays and 10:00 A.M. Sundays for training runs. The Marquette Park Track Club meets weekdays at 5:30 P.M. for training runs. The Run Chicago Clinic meets the first Sunday of every month at the Chicago Academy of Sciences. After a discussion, there are group runs. In Western Springs, at Bemis Woods, fun-runs are held on Saturdays at 8:00 A.M.

The *Chicago Tribune* publishes a section called "Venture" each Wednesday, and all weekly running events are listed here in the "Go Guide." If you miss the Wednesday issue, you can call the Venture office.

TRADITIONAL RACES

Chicago Lakefront, 10 miles: May
Chicago Distance Classic, 20 kilometers: Sunday of July Fourth Weekend
Mayor Daley Marathon: Late September (subject to change)

Mike Martorano, Riis Park Striders, 3428 West Parker, Chicago, IL 60647. (312) 227-5961.

Milan Mitrovic, Windy City Striders, 5459 North Lamon, Chicago, IL 60630. (312) 545-4674.

Ted Haydon, University of Chicago Track Club, 5640 South University, Chicago, IL 60637.

Wendell Miller, Midwest Masters, 180 North LaSalle, Chicago, IL 60601.

Jack Bolton, Marquette Park Track Club, (312) 425-1491.

Chicago Academy of Sciences, 2001 North Clark Street, Chicago, IL 60614.

Jesse Garcia, Azteca Running Club, (312) 973-1279.

Athlete's Foot Running Club, 2828 North Clark Street, Chicago, IL 60657.

Chicago Tribune "Venture" Section, (312) 222-4543.

Lawson YMCA, 30 West Chicago Avenue, Chicago, IL 60610. (312) 944-6211.

Leaning Tower YMCA, 6300 Touhy, Niles, IL 60648. (312) 647-8222.

PEORIA

Population: 125,300	Humidity: 72%
Elevation: 488 ft.	Av. Temperature: (Jan.) 24°F.; (July) 75°F.
Air Quality: Fair	Inches of Rainfall: (Jan.) 1.8; (July) 3.1 Raindays: 109

OVERVIEW

Located in northcentral Illinois, Peoria sits in a rich agricultural area alongside the Illinois River. No large parks exist in or around the city that are available for runners. It's mostly city street running with some small parks to break up the monotony. The riverbank has no pathways or trails. Downtown running is popular over the hilly streets near the Peoria YMCA. A park and cemetery can be reached from the Y.

HOTELS

Continental Regency, Downtown Motel, Ramada Inn

YMCA TO GLEN OAK PARK

The YMCA acts as headquarters for downtown running. Many runners head out from here throughout the day, especially in the early morning and at noon. All routes start at the corner of Fayette and Glendale. The three hotels mentioned are within a few blocks of the Y. Push off on Fayette from the YMCA building to Monroe Street. Turn left and follow the flat terrain through a safe, low-income neighborhood until you make another left onto Abington. You will soon make a right past Perry into Glen Oak Park. It is 1.6 miles to the park entrance. Keep to your right on a shaded road that travels over a number of hills. Turn left at the tennis court stop sign and head straight to the intersection of McClure and Prospect. Turn left here onto Prospect (2½-mile mark) and start back to the Y, making a half-right onto Glen Oak Street, following over its mild hills until you make a left at the 4-mile mark onto Knoxville. Then take a left onto Fayette to the Y.

If you wish to do extra mileage, you can make loops of the park by taking your first left after the tennis court stop sign. Each loop is a mile. Water fountains are available in the park.

YMCA TO SPRINGDALE CEMETERY

Springdale Cemetery sits adjacent to Glen Oak Park. There is no direct connection between the two. To get there, follow the same route from the Y, and just short of the park entrance, go right on Perry. The cemetery will be on your right. It is extremely hilly with very winding roads. There are no directions or courses laid out, and it is easy to become lost. The cemetery does a lot of business that way. Although there is shade, no water fountains are available. You can take Perry directly back to the Y.

OUTDOOR TRACK

Meinen Track, a ¼-mile rubberized track, is very popular among local runners,

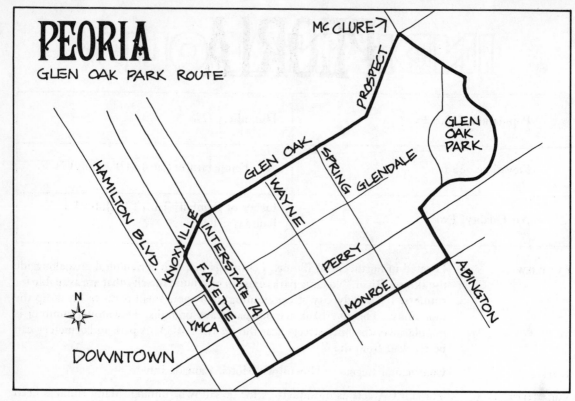

and many events are held here. The track is not always open, so at times runners have to climb over the fence. You can get to it by driving out I-74 to the University Exit North, about 6 or 7 miles from downtown.

INDOOR TRACKS

The YMCA does not have a track, but the gym floor gets a lot of use in the winter. It is 18 laps per mile.

CLUBS, FUN-RUNS AND RACES

The Illinois Valley Striders is a very active organization. Fun-runs are held every Sunday morning at 9:00 A.M. at Meinen Track. During spring, summer and fall, there are two races each month. In the winter, only one each month.

TRADITIONAL RACES

Steamboat Classic, 15 kilometers and 4 miles: June
Turkey Trot, 4 miles: November

CONTACTS

Steve Shostrom, Illinois Valley Striders, 3018 North Bigelow, Peoria, IL 61604. (309) 671-7077, 688-7758.
Dan Osterman, Peoria YMCA, 714 Hamilton Boulevard, Peoria, IL 61603. (309) 671-2722.

INDIANAPOLIS

Population: 750,000	Humidity: 73%
Elevation: 664 – 845 ft.	Av. Temperature: (Jan.) 28°F.; (July) 75°F.
Air Quality: Fair	Inches of Rainfall: (Jan.) 2.9; (July) 3.7 Raindays: 121

OVERVIEW

Situated close to the geographical center of Indiana, Indianapolis provides local runners with easy access to the excellent running opportunities throughout the state. Bloomington to the south, and Indiana Dunes to the north, have widespread reputations for their outstandingly beautiful and interesting parks. Although Indianapolis has few races, nearby towns can easily fill up a race calendar.

The downtown area has a couple of small parks convenient to hotels, which will provide a sufficient workout. A great attraction among local runners is the Water Company Canal, which extends 18 miles north to Broad Ripple Park. Only certain sections are open for running, as some parts are fenced off by private landowners. It is best to begin a run 3 miles north of downtown, at Riverside Park.

Fort Benjamin Harrison, about 15 minutes northeast of town, has free access to its hilly golf course and wooded trails, while northwest of town is the popular Eagle Creek Park. The suburban areas are not well plowed during winter snows.

HOTELS

Indianapolis Hilton, Holiday Inn – Downtown, Howard Johnson's – Downtown

UNIVERSITY PARK

A couple of blocks north of the Hilton, and several blocks north of Monument Circle in the heart of downtown, University Park and the adjacent World War Memorial Plaza provide a 1-mile loop of flat grass and sidewalk running. The area is well shaded, and only a small number of intersections need to be crossed. Plenty of water fountains are available, but no rest rooms. This course is lit and safe for night running.

MILITARY PARK

Only three blocks north of the Holiday Inn and Howard Johnson's, this small park has a perimeter slightly short of 1 mile. Terrain is flat, and footing is all grass. Water fountains and rest rooms are available. Night running is not recommended here.

RIVERSIDE PARK

You can reach this park by heading a few miles north on Meridian Street, then turning west on 30th Street for about ½ mile. Many runners use the 930 acres of flat, shady terrain. A perimeter road, measuring about 2½ miles, is mostly free of traffic, and in the center of the park you can find a 1-mile cross-country course. The loop begins at the baseball diamond next to the Army Reserve Building. Follow the trees marked with orange dots.

WATER COMPANY
CANAL ROAD

Many runners begin this course at Riverside Park. An old dirt and gravel one-lane road runs along the edge of the canal. It is a very scenic environment with enough shade trees overhead to protect you from a light rain. Going north, you will pass the Museum of Art on the opposite bank, and then for a little while you will be sandwiched in between the canal and the White River. At 3 miles, Butler University will be on your right. The Butler Baseball Diamond is a popular starting point for the canal run. Seven more miles will take you to Broad Ripple Park, at the end of the road. No water fountains are available along the canal.

EAGLE CREEK PARK

About 10 miles northwest of town, Eagle Creek Park has many dirt trails meandering over its 3,000-acre site. Terrain is hilly in some sections. Many small ponds and a large reservoir add to its natural beauty.

FORT BENJAMIN
HARRISON

About 10 miles northeast of town, Fort grounds are available and well used. Many runners enjoy the hilly roads and golf course. A large section of the fort site is undeveloped and heavily wooded, and excellent trails can be found here. If you park at the golf course, you will be north of the congested areas.

For a 3-mile course, head east on Shafter road for about ½ mile and turn north (left) on Lee Road, following it to 63rd Street. Turn left on 63rd, and run along the edge of the golf course until you reach Shafter Road, where you will make a left back to the start.

OUTDOOR TRACKS

Butler University has a ¼-mile cinder track that can be used most of the time. Usually you have to jump the fence to get in, but no one will bother you.

INDOOR TRACKS

At Butler University, the gymnasium has a concrete-floor balcony track, not banked, with 6 laps per mile. Visiting runners are not kept off the track, but use of the showers and lockers is questionable.

The Jordan Branch YMCA has a new, banked track of 24 laps per mile.

CLUBS AND
FUN-RUNS

The Indianapolis Jogging Club and the Hoosier Track Club co-sponsor a weekly fun-run on Saturdays at 9:30 A.M. at Park Tudor, north of the Fieldhouse at Butler University. Fun-runs are also held on Sundays at Fort Benjamin Harrison at the Golf Lodge at 10:30 A.M.

The Hoosier Road Runners Club, also known as the Indiana Striders, holds races periodically throughout the year.

TRADITIONAL RACES

Indianapolis "500" Mini-Marathon, 13.1 miles: Friday of Memorial Day Weekend

CONTACTS

Rich Radez, Indianapolis Jogging Club, 3410 Sherburne Lane, Indianapolis, IN 46222. (317) 635- 4551.

Chuck Koeppen, Hoosier RRC, 1815 East 116 Street, Indianapolis, IN 46032. (317) 844-1823.

Don Poland, Hoosier Track Club, 4923 North Kendwood, Indianapolis, IN 46206. (317) 251-0249.

The Runner's Forum, 852 North U.S. 31, Greenwood IN 46142. (317) 882-1800.

Jordan YMCA, (317) 253-3206.

DES MOINES

Population: (met.) 323,000	Humidity: 72%
Elevation: 800 ft.	Av. Temperature: (Jan.) 21°F.; (July) 76°F.
Air Quality: Fair	Inches of Rainfall: (Jan.) 1.1; (July) 3.3 Raindays: 105

OVERVIEW

This quiet city also provides a quiet place to run—the most popular route is in a cemetery! Although there are other attractive runs, the city is mostly flat and the cemetery provides the best hill training around. In winter, its roads are always well plowed.

The Des Moines River runs through the downtown area. Very little industry surrounds it, and the town and river are clean and attractive. There are not many large hotels in Des Moines. The main confluence of them is just to the north of the downtown area and adjacent to the Veterans Auditorium where many conventions are held. Routes along the river are convenient from these hotels. Slightly south of downtown, Water Works Park provides many miles of runs through its peaceful, wooded environment.

The home of the Drake Relays and Drake Marathon, running is popular here, although it is informal and many loosely organized groups put on races throughout the year.

HOTELS

Holiday Inn – South, Holiday Inn – Downtown, Ramada Inn, Howard Johnson's, Midtown Motor Inn

DES MOINES RIVER ROUTE

The Holiday Inn – Downtown, Howard Johnson's, Ramada and Midtown are all situated very close to the river. If you run over to the Veterans Auditorium and behind it, you will be on a road alongside the river. For a 6-mile run on pavement, you can head north, or for a potentially longer run, partly on grass, you can run south.

Going north, you will reach University Bridge after ⅓ of a mile. You can also reach the bridge by running directly north from your hotel up 6th Avenue to University Avenue, and turning right. Cross the bridge and continue straight on University Avenue to Lutheran Hospital at Pennsylvania Avenue. To this point it is about ¾ of a mile. Turn left and continue on Pennsylvania for about 1¼ miles, until you see a small parking lot on your left with a little building containing rest rooms; there is also a water fountain here. At the far side of the lot is the start of a cement running path that meanders through a park alongside the river. This path is marked every quarter mile for 1 mile, and the plans are to extend the path to 10 miles. Follow the same route back to your hotel.

Going south from the auditorium, hug the river on the grass or pavement. At about 1 mile you will reach the Oaks Minor League Ball Park. Here, the Raccoon River flows to your right and you can run up on the grass levee for a couple of miles to Water Works Park.

WATER WORKS PARK

This large, flat site contains 14 miles of gravel and dirt roads, plus bridle paths and small levees to run on. There are no prescribed courses and it is possible to lose your way. However, other runners will be glad to show you the routes, and you can use the river and outer boundaries as guides. A central picnic area contains rest rooms and a water pump.

This is a very pretty park, with lush vegetation and plenty of small animals scurrying around the many walnut trees amidst the interesting landscape.

Holiday Inn – South is perhaps the most convenient hotel for running in Des Moines. It is located on Fleur Drive, directly across from the Water Works.

GLENDALE CEMETERY

If you are not overly sensitive about graveside running, Glendale Cemetery can give you an excellent workout. It is located about 3½ miles northwest of downtown. The majority of the area is very hilly, although the northern portion is flat. The roads are highly crested and their winding, intersecting pattern can give you the choice of numerous routes. If you stay to your right near the perimeter, you can run a loop of about 2½ miles. Parts of the cemetery have good shade. Water faucets used for sprinkling are numerous, and there is one rest room available.

WAVELAND GOLF COURSE

The golf course is located on the other side of University Avenue, opposite Glendale Cemetery. As the name implies, the land is very wavy, and excellent and challenging cross-country running can be had over the hilly links. A paved road used by golf carts is also available. There is ample shade throughout the course. Runners can use the facility during off-season, or during in-season at off-hours when golfers are not present.

OUTDOOR TRACKS

The Drake University ¼-mile track is normally open to visitors. All of the high schools have quality tracks, which are also available.

INDOOR TRACKS

The Des Moines YMCA, located at the river and Grand Avenue, has a beautiful, new 19-laps-per-mile track.

FUN-RUNS

The YMCA has an active group that runs from the Y periodically during each weekday. A small group meets at Glendale Cemetery at 9:00 A.M. on Saturdays and Sundays throughout the year.

CLUBS AND RACES

No large, cohesive clubs exist in Des Moines. The two major organizations that sanction races in the area are the Iowa AAU and the Iowa U.S. Track and Field Federation. Any individual or small group can go to them and request sponsoring a race. Both organizations publish an annual schedule.

Saturday races are frequently held in Water Works Park—in the fall at 10:00 A.M., and in the summer at 6:00 P.M.

TRADITIONAL RACES

Washington's Day Run, 10 miles: Mid-February
Drake Relays Marathon: Late April
Covered Bridge Marathon, Winterset: Early October
Turkey Trot, 5 miles: Thanksgiving Day

CONTACTS

Iowa USTFF, 615 Securities Building, Des Moines, IA 50309. (515) 288-9741.
Ken Kopecky, 1641 68th Street, Des Moines, IA 50310. (515) 279-6348.

Des Moines YMCA, 101 Locust Street, Des Moines, IA 50309. (515) 288-0131.
Stan Smith, 2428 Grand, Apt. 218, Des Moines, IA 50312.
Iowa AAU, 810 8th Avenue, N.W., Independence, IA 50644.

Water Works Park, Des Moines

WICHITA

Population: 270,000	Humidity: 62%
Elevation: 1,285 ft.	Av. Temperature: (Jan.) 31°F.; (July) 81°F.
Air Quality: Fair to poor	Inches of Rainfall: (Jan.) 0.8; (July) 4.3 Raindays: 82

OVERVIEW

The largest city in the state, Wichita is located in the southcentral section, along the Arkansas River (pronounced like Kansas). Its terrain lies perfectly flat, while the river curves its way past the downtown area. A bike path along the river makes this an easy city for a visiting runner. It is a quiet city for running activity, as many local runners use their residential streets for training, and the local club is somewhat low-key.

The crazy winds of Kansas do not seem to have much of a reputation in the downtown area.

HOTELS

Broadview Hotel, Holiday Inn – Plaza, Ramada Inn – Central

ARKANSAS RIVER BIKE PATH

To reach the bike path, cross over the river from the Broadview Hotel, on the Douglas Avenue Bridge. Holiday Inn is a couple of blocks west of the river, just north of Douglas Avenue. Ramada Inn is about five blocks west of the river, close to the Kellogg Bridge.

The path runs along the east bank of the river to the south. You can follow it into Watson Park and around the lake until the path ends and you must doubleback. The distance one way from the Douglas Avenue Bridge is about 4¼ miles. Shade is scattered, as are the water fountains and rest rooms along the way. Night running is possible with light from automobile traffic.

MULTI-PARK LOOP

If you continue north on the bike path for another ½ mile, you will reach Seneca Bridge. Cross the river into Sim Park. This is the point where the Little Arkansas River flows into the Arkansas River. Both rivers curve into the area, forming a bowl lined with city parks. You can run east or west here, staying in the parks along the river. North Riverside Park sits on the far bank of the smaller river on the right, and, after running through South Riverside Park, can be reached by a small bridge over the river. Following the perimeter of that park, you can get back across the river a little further north along the Eleventh Street Bridge. Eleventh Street, after a few residential blocks, connects with Sim Park.

The parks are very grassy and open with an opportunity to wander around, running for time. If you stay on the perimeter loop, the distance is considered to be about 6 miles.

CLUBS AND RACES

The Wichita Running Club schedules a race every month. They also have group workouts which welcome visiting runners.

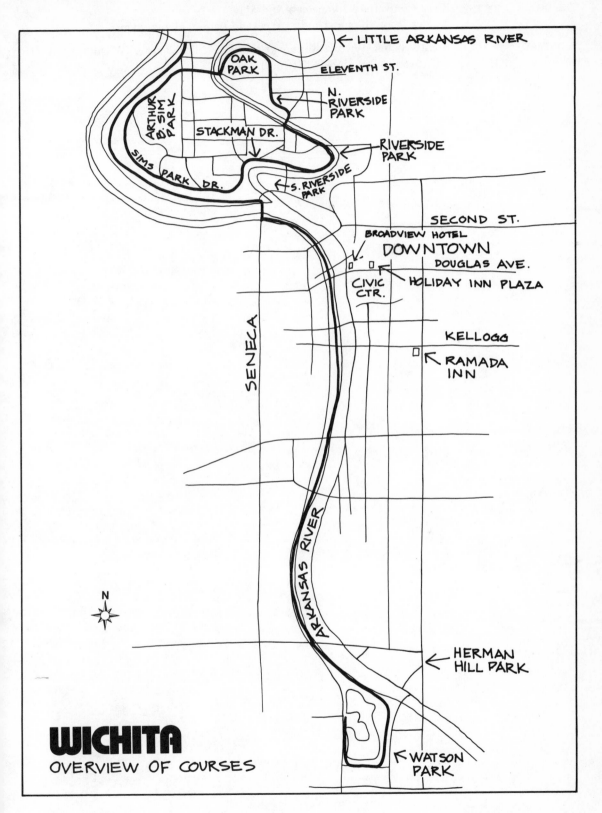

WICHITA
OVERVIEW OF COURSES

TRADITIONAL RACES River Festival, 10 kilometers: Mid-May
Turkey Trot, 10 and 2 miles: Weekend before Thanksgiving

CONTACT Brent Wooten, Wichita Running Club, 3054 South Custer, Wichita, KS 67217.
(316) 942-4560, 268-4480 (work).

Lexington

Population: 193,000	Humidity: 72%
Elevation: 990 ft.	Av. Temperature: (Jan.) 33°F.; (July) 76°F.
Air Quality: Fair	Inches of Rainfall: (Jan.) 3.9; (July) 4.6 Raindays: 128

OVERVIEW

This is horse farm country. Miles of running alongside bluegrass pastures and plank fences over rolling hills give local runners an idyllic environment for their daily workouts. Although you would have to stay several miles outside of town to be near these routes, you would be happy to have the opportunity to experience them. Remember that these places smell as "farmy" as they look.

The University of Kentucky is located in Lexington, bringing in a young and active running population. The U. of K. track has become a popular meeting place, both for track and road running.

HOTELS

Hilton Inn, Holiday Inn, Hyatt Regency

COLDSTREAM FARM COURSE

This quiet, scenic route lies within 1 mile of the Hilton and Holiday Inn. Run from the hotels toward downtown on the Newton Pike to the Carnahan House and head up the long driveway. Behind the house, jump over a stone wall and head right on the roadway. It's 4½ miles one way to Spindletop Farm. The hilly road offers no shade, and you'll find no water.

UNIVERSITY OF KENTUCKY TRACK AND ROADS

The Hyatt Regency appears to be the closest hotel, only 2 miles northwest of the track. The ¼-mile rubberized asphalt track sits adjacent to about a ½-mile perimeter of playing fields for some short, unobstructed runs. It's easy to find groups of runners heading out from here for longer runs on the nearby residential streets.

FUN-RUNS

The Todds Road Stumblers meet, naturally, at Todds Road in Clark County, about 8 miles from downtown, every Saturday morning starting at 7:00 A.M. The runs are usually for 6, 9 or 15 miles, with routes marked at ½-mile intervals. Call Jim Bell to arrange for a ride.

All year, Saturday fun-runs are held at the University Track at 4:00 P.M. All Comers Track is Wednesday nights at 6:00 P.M. throughout the summer.

TRADITIONAL RACES

Downtown 10-Kilometer: July 4th
One-Hour National Track Championship: June

CONTACTS

Jerry Stone, Route 3, Georgetown, KY 40324. (606) 232-6582 (days).
Jim Bell, Farmington Road, Lexington, KY 40502. (606) 278-1596 (nights).

LOUISVILLE

Population: (met.) 870,000	Humidity: 68.5%
Elevation: 382−761 ft.	Av. Temperature: (Jan.) 35°F.; (July) 78°F.
Air Quality: Fair	Inches of Rainfall: (Jan.) 3.5; (July) 3.8 Raindays: 122

OVERVIEW

Louisville, situated along the Ohio River, has beautiful parks and scenic river runs to provide a diversity of courses. It is a quiet town where many runners work out in their own communities. The large number of parks spread out through the suburbs has eliminated a desire for runners to utilize downtown courses. Thus, you might readily find yourself alone on a peaceful run along the river's edge. The Indiana side of the river is easily reachable and offers vistas of the Louisville skyline.

The excitement of the Kentucky Derby is not lost among runners, as the biggest footrace of the year takes place during Derby festivities on the preceding weekend.

HOTELS

Downtown: Galt House, Stouffer's Louisville Inn, Holiday Inn−Midtown, Howard Johnson's−Downtown, Rodeway Inn, Louisville Travelodge
Along the River: Holiday Inn−Rivermont, Best Western America's Host
Fairgrounds: Executive Inn, Executive West

RIVER ROAD

From downtown, head to the river and turn right (east), running under the elevated I-64 and I-71. The first mile, along River Road, goes through a commercial area which is not heavily traveled outside of rush hours. After that, the road opens up and some small grassy parks line the road. At 2 miles you will come to a golf course that has a grassy path around its perimeter. At 2½ miles, Zorn Avenue breaks off to the right, offering a nice long straightaway, out and back. After Zorn Avenue, there are numerous playing fields along River Road. Beyond the fields, the road becomes very rural, and can be followed for 10 miles from downtown.

CLARK MEMORIAL BRIDGE

Second Street, downtown, will carry you onto the Clark Memorial Bridge. One mile across to Indiana, and the scenery is very different. There is no city here. Once off the bridge, turn right and run to the river. Riverside Drive follows the river east and west of the bridge for a mile on either side. On the west side, after a mile, you can run up on the floodwall and enjoy its grassy footing for another mile or two west.

SENECA AND CHEROKEE PARKS

These two adjoining parks offer a variety of footing and terrain. They can be found a few miles east of downtown. Seneca Park is the most popular meeting place for runners in Louisville. A wide open area with grassy playing fields and tennis courts, many runners warm up doing laps over a 2-mile loop. A common starting point is at the tennis courts. From here you can run out to Cherokee Park for more serious mileage. Cherokee Park has winding roads over semihilly terrain where you can run a 7-mile loop plus some interesting side roads. However, take warning: the routes can be confusing and you might become lost.

Automobiles travel through the park, so it is possible to ask directions of motorists from time to time. Shade is more predominant in Cherokee Park, and rest rooms are available there.

IROQUOIS PARK

Several miles south of town, Iroquois Park is large and beautiful, yet many runners avoid it due to the busy roads and occasional harassment. At quiet times, the park has an excellent and challenging route. A 3.2-mile road loops around the outer sections over moderate hills. An inner road goes 1½ miles uphill to a flat 1-mile loop at the top. The park is woody and very shady. Water fountains and rest rooms are easy to come by.

You can run out from the park on Southern Parkway along a grassy strip for about 3 miles. A slight grade downhill will lead you out.

KENTUCKY FAIR AND EXPOSITION CENTER

The Fairgrounds are located only ½ mile from the airport. Signs will direct you on your run from the airport. Executive Inn and Executive West sit right at the entrance to the Fairgrounds. Huge parking lots are surrounded by grass to create a flat, 2-mile loop. Forget about shade.

INDOOR TRACKS

The Downtown Center YMCA has a new 22-laps-per-mile track.

CLUBS, FUN-RUNS AND RACES

The Metropolitan Parks and Recreation Board, through its Operation Gap, has an extensive road running program. The Cherokee Road Runners is a fairly new club and schedules a couple of races every month. The Mason-Dixon Athletic Club sponsors the Mason-Dixon Games each February, and occasional road races. They also support a competitive team.

TRADITIONAL RACES

Kentucky Derby Mini-Marathon, 13.1 miles: Monday before Kentucky Derby
Joe Binks Memorial Cross-Country Run, 10 kilometers: Early September

CONTACTS

Ken Combs, Metropolitan Parks and Recreation Board, Box 1334, Louisville, KY 40213. (502) 459-0440.
Frank Starks, Cherokee Road Runners, 1414 La Fontenay Court, Louisville, KY 40223. (502) 245-2796.
Charlie Zipprich, Mason-Dixon Athletic Club, 9616 Elm Lake Drive, Louisville, KY 40291. (502) 239-1402.
Downtown Center YMCA, 555 South Second Street, Louisville, KY 40202. (502) 587-6700.

NEW ORLEANS

Population: 1,125,000	Humidity: 76%
Elevation: 5 – 25 ft.	Av. Temperature: (Jan.) 55°F.; (July) 82°F.
Air Quality: Fair	Inches of Rainfall: (Jan.) 4.5; (July) 6.7 Raindays: 114

OVERVIEW

New Orleans is a city of many attractions. The French Quarter, its cosmopolitan atmosphere and true southern tradition flavor the city's environment. Running here has its distinct characteristics as well. The city is bordered on the south by a curve of the Mississippi River, creating the "Crescent City" nickname, and along the north by Lake Pontchartrain. Waterside running has much popularity here, as well as utilization of the large, beautiful city parks. You can choose among runs along a famous river levee, a sailboat-dotted lake, or a trip through stands of majestic oaks with spanish moss dripping over the path.

A thrill-seeking run from downtown would be to follow the grassy St. Charles Avenue "neutral ground" out to Audubon Park, jumping from track to track to avoid the frequent trolley cars. This happens to be a popular route.

The constant among all the different courses in New Orleans is the pervasive flatness of the terrain. Running up the bank of the river levee or the rise on a bridge span offers the only possible vertical ascents. It is not a place to train for the Pikes Peak Marathon. In the summer, heat is another constant, necessitating early morning runs.

The New Orleans Track Club has charted all its popular courses, and can provide maps for many distances with variations on each course.

HOTELS

The French Quarter and nearby hotels are not very convenient, but you may not want to miss staying there; Fountain Bay Club Hotel (near City Park)

ST. CHARLES AVENUE
NEUTRAL GROUND

St. Charles Avenue heads west through the city until it makes contact with the river on the far western side, after about 4½ miles. It passes Audubon Park after about 3½ miles. At the river, Carrollton Avenue goes northeast for 3½ miles, directly to City Park. These two avenues combine to create an 8-mile course, one way, to the park. Grass footing will carry you the whole way, except when you run on pavement at intersections. The Charles Street trolley uses the same grass median strip known as the "neutral ground." Many runners head down the middle of the tracks, and when a trolley comes, they jump over to the other tracks. Of course, sometimes a trolley is coming the other way, and then it gets tricky. The drivers know to look out, but sometimes a runner can slip or trip at the wrong time. To make matters worse, cars cross at the intersections. Good shade trees line the course along the avenues.

NEW ORLEANS

CITY PARK

LAKE PONTCHARTRAIN

SEABROOK BRIDGE

BREAKWATER

WEST END

LAKE AVE.

ROBERT E. LEE BLVD.

17ᵀᴴ ST. CANAL

PONTCHARTRAIN BLVD.

WEST END BLVD.

CANAL BLVD.

ORLEANS AVE.

MARCONI DR.

WISNER BLVD.

GERNON BROWN GYM

MARIBEAU AVE.

HARRISON AVE.

CITY PARK

CITY PARK AVE.

ESPLANADE AVE.

ORLEANS AVE.

CARROLLTON AVE.

TULANE AVE.

CANAL ST.

N

DOWNTOWN

AUDUBON PARK   The park is situated between St. Charles Avenue and the Mississippi River. Magazine Street runs through the park, parallel to St. Charles Avenue. All measured routes follow loops on the park drive between St. Charles Avenue and Magazine Street. A basic 2-mile loop goes once around, and along Magazine Street, heads in on the path past the rest rooms. Sections of the route lie in heavy shade, and you can head out on the open grass for softer footing or run along the bridle path under the trees.

Tulane University and Loyola University are located across St. Charles Avenue, attracting many students onto this course.

CITY PARK   This giant park is designed along the lines of Central Park in New York, and Golden Gate Park. At the north end of the park is Lake Pontchartrain. Marconi

Drive on the west, and Wisner Boulevard on the east, border the length of the park. A favorite meeting place for local runners is at Gernon Brown Gymnasium on the corner of Marconi Drive and Harrison Avenue.

The Fountain Bay Club Hotel, located at the corner of Carrollton and Tulane avenues, is only about 1¼ miles south of City Park, along Carrollton.

You can run a measured distance of just about any length from a start at the Gernon Brown Gym. Most routes utilize the park's perimeter, or parts thereof, and different distances along the lakefront. One lap around the perimeter of the park is just short of 8 miles. Beginning at the gym, one mile north will get you to Lee Boulevard. From here, courses generally turn west for another mile to West End Boulevard. Then it is a right turn (north) and you can either go straight to the lake, or for an interesting diversion, turn west onto Lake Avenue and run out onto the breakwater out in the lake. You will end up coming back to West End Boulevard after 2 miles, out and back. Then heading north, you will reach the lakefront. Running east along the lakefront, it is 5 miles, one way, to Seabrook Bridge.

For a simple 10-mile run, head north from the gym and over to West End Boulevard and up to the lake. Follow the lakeshore east, passing Wisner Boulevard, and go over the Bayou St. John Bridge. As you come off the bridge, turn left and circle under the bridge, heading south along the bayou. When you reach Lee Boulevard turn right, back to Wisner, and go south around the perimeter of the park back to the gym. To make it a 12-mile run, do the 2 miles onto the breakwater.

In the park, you can run on the road or the adjacent grass. Water fountains are abundant, and shade is fair. Along the lakefront, sidewalks or grass are available on top of the levee. Shade is sparse, but there is plenty of water.

It is possible to run to City Park from downtown, but traffic can be very difficult. From the northeast back end of the French Quarter, the park is only 2 miles away along Esplanade Avenue. Buses leave the downtown area frequently for the lakefront at West End Park.

MISSISSIPPI RIVER LEVEE

The river, along the downtown area, offers no running possibilities due to heavy commercial activity. The best starting point, along the east New Orleans bank, is at Audubon Park. From here the levee provides a flat, scenic run on a crushed-shell roadway. Other than that there are no other amenities—no water, rest rooms, shade or mileage markers can be found. At about 4 miles, heading west, you will pass the Causeway road, and at 14 miles you will come to Williams Boulevard in Kenner.

Along the west bank, in Jefferson Parish, you can begin a run at City Hall opposite Jackson Avenue on the east bank. Heading west, you will reach 10 miles at the point when the river turns southwest after its northerly direction. A slight detour will have to be made just after the first mile, in order to cross the bridge over the Harvey Canal.

SUPERDOME

Downtown, across the street from the Hyatt Regency, the Superdome offers a possibility of unobstructed running. The large concrete promenades surrounding it are often empty. Although the distance has not been measured, one lap around is about ¾ of a mile. There is no shade; water and rest rooms can be found at the Hyatt.

CLUBS, FUN-RUNS AND RACES

The New Orleans Track Club provides a full schedule of running activities throughout the year. Clinics and fun-runs are held every Saturday morning at

St. Charles Avenue "Neutral Ground," New Orleans

10:00 A.M. at the St. Charles entrance to Audubon Park. Also, on Saturday mornings at 8:00 A.M., runners meet at the Gernon Brown Gym for a long run. Races are held about twice a month.

TRADITIONAL RACES   Jackson Day Race, 5½ miles: Early January
Mardi Gras Marathon: Early February
Turkey Day Race, 5 miles: Thanksgiving Day

CONTACT   New Orleans Track Club, Box 30491, New Orleans, LA 70190. (504) 522-6682.

SHREVEPORT

Population: 185,000	Humidity: 71%
Elevation: 254 ft.	Av. Temperature: (Jan.) 47.2; (July) 83.2
Air Quality: Fair	Inches of Rainfall: (Jan.) 4.04; (July) 2.89 Raindays: 97

OVERVIEW

Shreveport lies in the northwest corner of Louisiana, close to Texas. The city first became a viable location when Captain Shreve barged into the jammed-up Red River, to cut a channel through 165 miles of wooden debris. Now the city has become a viable running town after a park and bike trail have been built next to the Red River. This is basically a one-course city, where local runners also run in their own neighborhoods. A high school track, just a few miles south of town, receives some attention as well.

Climate here is not as steamy as in the Gulf cities, but summer heat must be highly respected. The Shreveport Track Club meets for group training runs twice a week, and also puts on small, frequent races.

HOTELS

Chateau Motor Hotel, Captain Shreve Hotel

FANT PARKWAY TRAIL

The above hotels are located very close to the Red River, and the Fant Parkway Trail, which runs between the river and Fant Parkway for 4 miles to the south. The course is bordered by the Texas Street Bridge at the northern end, and the Shreveport-Barksdale Bridge on the south end. Mileage markers can be found every ½ mile.

The trail runs through a pretty park with many shade trees, and offers a nice view across the river. A few small hills provide some interest. Although parkway lighting makes the trail navigable at night, it runs close to a tough neighborhood, so be cautious. No water fountains are available.

OUTDOOR TRACKS

Three miles south of downtown, via Line Avenue, a ¼-mile cinder track is available at Byrd High School, at the intersection of Line and Kings Highway.

INDOOR TRACKS

The YMCA, four blocks west of the Fant Parkway Trail, has a banked, wooden, 20-laps-per-mile track.

CLUBS, FUN-RUNS AND RACES

The Shreveport Track Club meets on Wednesday evenings at 7:30 P.M. during the summer, and at 6:00 P.M. during winter months at the south end of the Fant Parkway Trail for group runs. They also meet on Saturdays at 7:00 A.M. during the summer, and 8:00 A.M. other seasons for group runs or races. Locations for these vary.

TRADITIONAL RACES

YMCA St. Patrick's Day Run, 8 and 4 miles: Nearest Saturday to St. Patrick's Day

YMCA Fall Run, 25 and 10 kilometers: Mid-December
Shreveport Track Club Holiday in Dixie Run, 10 and 5 miles: Late April

CONTACTS

Ronny Davis, Shreveport Track Club, 437 Elmwood, Shreveport, LA 71104. (318) 861-6134.
Richard Rogers, Central YMCA, 400 McNeil, Shreveport, LA. (318) 221-5151.

PORTLAND

Population: 56,000	Humidity: 74%
Elevation: 0 – 187 ft.	Av. Temperature: (Jan.) 21°F.; (July) 70°F.
Air Quality: Good	Inches of Rainfall: (Jan.) 3.6; (July) 2.3 Raindays: 125

OVERVIEW

On the Maine coast, Portland has water surrounding it on three sides, with residential communities across the water to the north and west. This is where you will find the major running routes. Along the western Back Bay, a grassy strip runs north next to Baxter Boulevard, providing excellent views of downtown Portland. Local runners claim this to be one of the most beautiful running courses in the Northeast. Several miles northwest of town, an isosceles triangle describes a 5,000-meter course that becomes more popular in the winter when Baxter Boulevard freezes over. This course is also very convenient to some outlying motels.

During the summer, coastal breezes keep the city relatively insect-free, but further inland, running can be uncomfortable amidst black clouds of bugs over the grassier areas.

Tradition is an important quality to Mainites, and is reflected in the five annual running events held each year. Not one is less than ten years old, and there have been no new upstarts, as yet, to upset the calendar.

HOTELS

Holiday Inn – Downtown, Portlander In-Town, Holiday Inn – West, Howard Johnson's

BAXTER BOULEVARD

Less than ½ mile from downtown, the Boulevard can be reached by running downhill on High Street and turning west on Forest Avenue. You will come to the Boulevard on your right, identified by a sign. A band of grass about 15 yards wide, to the side of the road, was privately donated to the city. The course is actually along a section of Route 1. Trees, about 40 to 50 yards apart, line the road. This flat, 2.2-mile route, one way, has a worn dirt path that most runners use. If you drive to the course, you can leave your car in Payson Park, about ⅛ mile west of the Boulevard, and a little bit north of the southern end.

There is no formal starting place for the course, most runners just pick it up in their neighborhoods. The northern end is at Tukey's Bridge, where Route 1 meets Route 295.

RIVERSIDE LOOP

From Holiday Inn, and Howard Johnson's, head west on Riverside Street along its wide shoulder for about 1¾ miles. After crossing Route 302, you will be heading west on Riverside Industrial Parkway. This is the first leg of the

5,000-meter course. Riverside Municipal Golf Course will be on your left. The road goes under the Maine Turnpike and then up a steep hill for about 100 yards. At the top of the hill, turn right and stay on that road for about 1¼ miles. This second leg of the course is lit and good for night running. When you reach Route 302, turn right for about ¼ mile back to where the course started at the Parkway. There is not a lot of shade along this course, and no water or rest rooms, but traffic will not be a problem and most of the course is fairly flat.

MACKWORTH ISLAND
A couple of miles north of town, along Route 1, the Downeast Court Club charges a small daily fee for use of its sauna, whirlpool, etc. From the club, a scenic 5½-mile run is available. This course goes up Route 1 for 2 miles to the Mackworth Island Bridge. On the island, there is a really pretty loop for 1½ miles on a dirt road. The course is basically flat, but traffic can sometimes be a nuisance on Route 1.

OUTDOOR TRACKS
A ¼-mile, all-weather track is available at Portland Stadium, behind the Portland Exposition Building on Park Avenue.

CLUBS AND RACES
The Maine Masters Track Club holds five annual races. The Central Maine Striders are not very active in the city, and hold races in other parts of Maine.

TRADITIONAL RACES
Roland Dyer Memorial 10-Kilometer and 5-Kilometer: Third Saturday in March
Father's Day 4-Mile Race: Mid-June
Portland Midi-Marathon, 13.1 miles: First Sunday in October
Falmouth, Maine, 5.8-Mile Race: First Sunday in November
Cape Elizabeth Turkey Trot, 5.8 miles: Sunday before Thanksgiving

CONTACTS
Vern Putney, Portland Press Herald, 390 Congress Street, Portland, ME 04102.
Rick Krause, Central Maine Striders, 1 Summer Street, Pittsfield, ME 04967.
Ken Flanders, 62 Providence Avenue, South Portland, ME 04106. (207) 799-6681.
Downeast Court Club, 170 Route 1, Falmouth, ME 04105. (207) 781-4281.

BALTIMORE

Population: (met.) 1,870,000	Humidity: 69%
Elevation: 0–489 ft.	Av. Temperature: (Jan.) 37°F.; (July) 79°F.
Air Quality: Fair to poor	Inches of Rainfall: (Jan.) 2.9; (July) 4.1 Raindays: 122

OVERVIEW

Downtown Baltimore can appear very ominous to runners looking for carefree workouts on unobstructed routes. Fortunately, local runners are just discovering a brick walkway that follows the harbor into downtown from historical Fort McHenry. The 10-kilometer route to the fort and back creates a viable convenience from downtown hotels.

This is a busy running town, with many interesting parks found in outlying communities. Some can be reached on foot from nearby motels. Hills characterize the suburban terrain, with roads and paths winding through rustic woods and around small lakes and reservoirs. The popular courses have been well measured, and are frequently used by the active Baltimore Road Runners Club. The city's proximity to Washington, D.C., provides an even greater accessibility to weekend races.

HOTELS

Baltimore Hilton, Lord Baltimore, Holiday Inn–Downtown, Holiday Inn–Loch Raven Boulevard, Holiday Inn–Cromwell Bridge Road, Hunt Valley Inn

DOWNTOWN TO FORT MCHENRY

From the downtown hotels, head east to St. Paul Street and turn south (right). St. Paul runs into Light Street. This is the Inner Harbor where you can stay off the street and run along a broad brick path next to the harbor. Follow Light Street into Key Highway, and stay on Key along the harbor until you reach Lawrence Street. Turn right on Lawrence for a few hundred yards until you make a left on Fort Avenue. This middle part of the route is both an industrial and residential area. When you reach Latrobe Park, make a right turn to circle around it, and then continue on Fort Avenue to Fort McHenry. If you make one loop through Fort McHenry and return along the same course (without circling the park) to the end of the Inner Harbor, you will have run 10 kilometers.

A complete loop in Fort McHenry measures exactly 1 mile. Here the course runs along a seawall, with magnificent views of the harbor and bridge. The Fort is open from 9:00 to 5:00, seven days a week. Flat terrain and little shade characterize the course. Public toilets can be found at the Inner Harbor and in the Fort.

DRUID HILL PARK

One of the more interesting parks in the city, Druid Park can be reached from downtown via a busy shortcut, or a longer, pleasant run on a seldom used road. Either way, the first mile begins at the Baltimore Civic Center on Hopkins Place. Go north 1 mile on Park Avenue to Biddle Street. If you continue north on Mount Royal, you will reach Druid Lake, in the park, just short of the second mile. To take the longer route, make a right on Biddle, and a quick left on Maryland Avenue. On the other side of the expressway, go left on Falls Road. Follow Falls along the river, and past a few factories. After the flashing yellow light at Mount Vernon Mills, about 2½ miles out, make three consecutive right turns, and cross over the expressway again before entering the park.

If you turn left once inside the park, you will soon reach Druid Lake. A flat, 1½-mile loop can be run on the road circling the lake. For a hilly, 5-mile loop of the park, turn right at the swimming pool, and follow the mostly traffic-free perimeter road through intermittent shade. Water and rest rooms can be found at the entrace to the zoo in the western section.

LOCH RAVEN
RESERVOIR

You will find runners on this busy route day and night. Located about 12 miles north of downtown, this hilly, out-and-back course runs along Loch Raven Road between Sander's Ice Cream Store at Cromwell Bridge Road in the south, and Peerce's Restaurant at Dulaney Valley Road in the north. The distance is 4½ miles, one way. Wooded landscape frames views of the adjacent, scenic Loch Raven Reservoir.

Automobiles are kept off the course on Sundays from 10:00 A.M. to 4:00 P.M. A dirt parking lot just off Cromwell Bridge Road is the only place to legally park your car. Mileage markers along the route measure a section of the Maryland Marathon, these are orange numerals in small white squares.

Two Holiday Inns are located near the course. If you drive from downtown, take Calvert Street north to 33rd Street. Go east to Hillen, then north to Perrin Parkway and left onto Satyr Hill Road, which will take you to Cromwell Bridge Road. Turn right to Sander's Ice Cream Store.

LAKE MONTEBELLO
PARK

This major training/racing area in the city can be reached on a fairly direct 4½-mile stretch from downtown. Head east from downtown hotels to Calvert Street. Run or drive 3 miles north to 33rd Street. Turn right for 1½ miles, passing Baltimore Memorial Stadium, to the park.

An inner loop of 1.35 miles borders the lake on an almost traffic-free, hard-surfaced road over flat terrain. There is no shade close to the lake. An outer loop utilizes the 2.9-mile perimeter of the park on a mixture of sidewalk, road, grass and dirt, over rolling terrain. Runners work out here both day and night. Water fountains and rest rooms can be found north of the lake, close to Harford Road.

HERRING RUN PARK

Located across Harford Road from Lake Montebello, this park boasts a beautiful cross-country loop on a wood-chip path through woods and fields over hilly terrain. One loop measures 2 miles.

PATAPSCO STATE
PARK

This beautiful run along the Patapsco River is located 9 miles southwest of downtown. Take I-95 south to Rolling Road. Go west to Gun Road, and south to the park. The run begins at the parking lot. Head east to the bridge, cross the river and run west along the river on the abandoned, paved road until it ends. Repeat the course back to the start for a total mileage of 5½ miles. This flat, wooded terrain is very scenic alongside the river gorge. A water fountain is located near the park office, and toilets can be found in the woods.

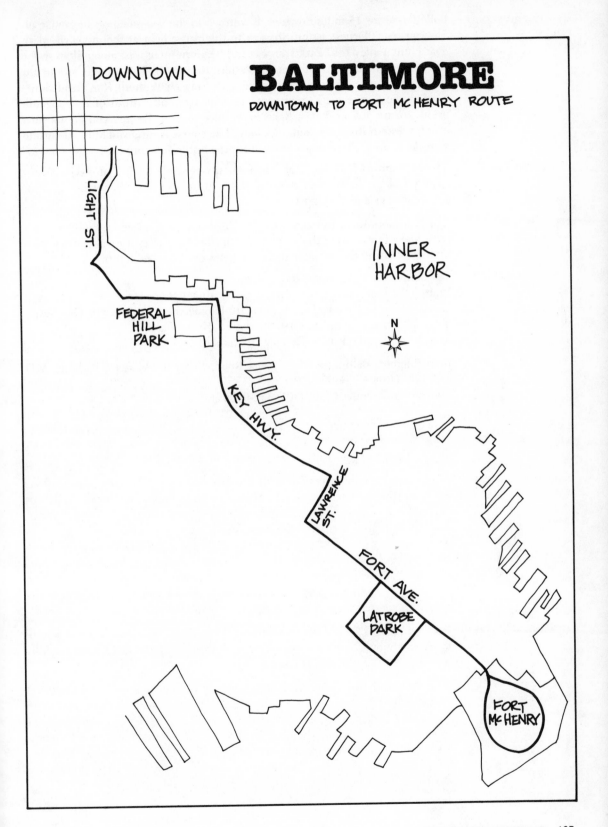

WESTERN RUN ROAD COURSE	Follow I-83 for 15 miles north of downtown to the beginning of the course on Shawan road. Drive east on Shawan to the traffic light at the industrial park near Hunt Valley Inn. Park your car and begin running west along Shawan for about ⅔ of a mile to a right turn on Western Run Road. The complete route is 6 miles, one way, and every mile is marked. Stay on Western Run Road until, nearing the 6-mile mark, you come to a bridge, and instead of crossing the bridge, turn right on Belfast Road to the final marker. Be sure you do not turn off on Western Road at about 2½ miles. The course is rural and hilly, alongside a creek. A great place to get away from the hubbub of city life.
INDOOR TRACKS	The Downtown Racquet Club has a 23-laps-per-mile track. Catonsville Community College, in the west suburbs, has a 10-laps-per-mile track which is available mornings and evenings.
CLUBS, FUN-RUNS AND RACES	The Baltimore Road Runners Club is a very active organization, holding many races and clinics during the year. You can run in a race every week, usually on Sunday. During the summer there are races on Tuesday nights.
TRADITIONAL RACES	Lady Equitable, 10 kilometers: March Jones Falls Express, 4 miles: First Sunday after Labor Day Constellation to Fort McHenry Race, 10 kilometers: September or October Satyr Hill Race, 12 miles: First Sunday in November Maryland Marathon: First Sunday in October
CONTACTS	John Roemer, Baltimore RRC, Evna Road, Route 1, Box 246, Parkton, MD 21120. (301) 472-4197. Downtown Racquet Club, (301) 332-0906.

BOSTON

Population: (met.) 3,850,000	Humidity: 67%
Elevation: 0 – 330 ft.	Av. Temperature: (Jan.) 29°F.; (July) 72°F.
Air Quality: Fair to poor	Inches of Rainfall: (Jan.) 3.7; (July) 2.7 Raindays: 127

OVERVIEW

The oldest and most famous race in America is, of course, the Boston Marathon. Beginning in the suburb of Hopkinton, it travels west for the 26 miles, 385 yards to the Prudential Building in the center of downtown.

This Patriot's Day race is only the highlight of running here each year, as Boston is truly a mecca for the sport. Many reservoirs, rivers and bays have created unlimited possibilities for exciting runs, and the largest student population of any American city streams over these routes.

The Metropolitan area of Boston consists of many small towns surrounding the city on three sides, with the Inner Harbor to the east. Downtown running focuses along the Charles River, separating Boston from Cambridge, where a total loop of 16.78 miles can be run beside the riverbank. Close to downtown hotels, the route is not only very convenient, but it also provides outstanding vistas of the city and the river with sailboats and sculls plying their way back and forth between the many bridges. These eleven bridges allow for different length runs by crossing over and heading back at many places along the way.

West of downtown, in Brookline, runners congregate at Bill Rodgers Running Center on Chestnut Hill Avenue. From here they have a choice of crossing the street to Chestnut Hill Reservoir, or to try the famous Heartbreak Hill, nearby on Commonwealth Avenue. A very popular course is the Fresh Pond Reservoir, northwest of Cambridge. Many people meet at the parking lot and socialize as runners pass through on each lap around the paved 2¼-mile loop.

A continuous run from the Boston Common at the center of downtown to the west takes in many Boston attractions. Commonwealth Avenue, the Back Bay Fens, the Riverway, Jamaica Way, Jamaica Pond and Arnold Arboretum together create a chain of parks and paths to provide a long morning or afternoon of leisurely, scenic running. The Arboretum's traffic-free roads wind through interesting landscape for peaceful, carefree workouts. Many local runners consider this their favorite course.

Because of Boston's long history as a running mecca, its social environment has developed to satisfy an active population. Every evening at the Eliot Lounge, on Commonwealth Avenue, you can share in tales of the great Boston races, or a discussion of those to come. With so many Boston runners among the world's greatest (*i.e.*, Bill Rodgers, Randy Thomas, Alberto Salazar, Bobby

Hodge and Mike Roche), the city buzzes with debate about present and future prospects.

HOTELS

All downtown hotels are within easy reach of good courses.
Cambridge: Hyatt Regency

CHARLES RIVER

The river can be reached by running north a short distance from any downtown Boston hotel. You may have to run along some sidewalks next to Storrow Drive before you can cross over to the Charles River embankment. Here you can run a popular 3.79-mile loop utilizing the Charles River Dam to the east, and the Harvard Bridge to the west. An even shorter loop of 2.82 miles uses the Longfellow Bridge to the east, instead of the dam.

Longer loops can be run by crossing at any of the eight more bridges to the west. Massachusetts Institute of Technology occupies much of the northern bank across from downtown, and the Hyatt Regency Hotel lies slightly west of the Harvard Bridge, at M.I.T. This hotel provides jogging maps to its customers.

The only danger to be aware of on these river routes is that on occasion, runners have been mugged along the riverbanks. During snowy winter days, 2½ miles are plowed along the Boston side of the river.

BOSTON COMMON AND PUBLIC GARDENS

In downtown Boston, the Common is a small park contiguous to the Public Gardens. For a short workout, the wide walk around both parks measures about 1½ miles. The north side of the course has a slight grade, and the entire loop lies under abundant shade. Water fountains and rest rooms are available.

COMMONWEALTH AVENUE ESPLANADE

Beginning at the Public Gardens and heading west, this grassy mall runs down the center of Commonwealth Avenue for slightly over 1 mile. The flat course has a paved walkway, and many trees line the mall. One negative aspect is the frequent crossroads.

BACK BAY FENS

At Charlesgate, near the end of the Commonwealth Avenue Esplanade, take the bridge left over the railroad tracks, and run down into the Fens. This is a marshy area surrounding the Muddy River. You can run south on walkways through here for about 1 mile to Riverway, which heads south for close to another mile to Jamaica Way. Both areas are flat and have adequate shade.

JAMAICA POND

Along Jamaica Way, this pond has a 1.4-mile loop on a paved, flat pathway. There is plenty of shade, and you can find a water fountain and rest rooms at the entrance to the pond on Jamaica Way. If you drive, park on local streets adjacent to the pond.

ARNOLD ARBORETUM

About ½ mile south of Jamaica Pond is the entrance to the Arboretum. This beautiful nature park has winding roadways with some rolling hills and one fairly nice incline of about ⅓ mile, near the center of the park. It is called Bussey Hill.

Cars are prohibited in the Arboretum, and parking near the entrance can sometimes be a problem. There are many water fountains, and some portable toilets are located close to the park entrance. Shade is ample. This is a great place to get away from the crowds.

FRESH POND RESERVOIR

The Reservoir can be reached from Harvard Square by heading out Brattle Street and taking a right onto Fresh Pond Parkway. A paved walkway circles around the Reservoir next to a chain-link fence. A distance of 2¼ miles can be

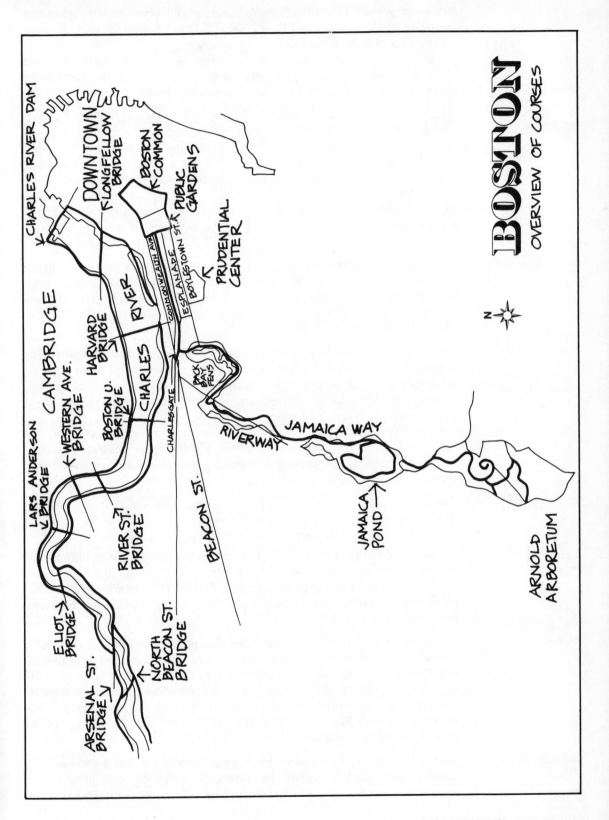

run if you pass directly through the parking lots. Between the parking lots and the water is a small park, and if you take the detour around the park, you can add another ¼ mile to the loop.

Mileage markers are painted on the path every ⅛ mile. The course is flat, and shade is sporadic. You can find a water fountain in the parking lot, but there are no rest rooms. Plows keep the course runable all winter.

CHESTNUT HILL
RESERVOIR

This reservoir lies across Chestnut Hill Avenue from the Bill Rodgers Running Center in Brookline. Go 200 yards west on Beacon Street to the reservoir gate. The city wants to keep runners away from the water's edge, so they have been building a running trail along the outside of the fence below the dike. The water level is above street level and you cannot see the reservoir unless you climb up on the dike. Unfortunately, the fence restricts this. Until a satisfactory trail is installed, many runners climb the 5-foot wrought-iron fence and run on a 2-mile dirt path next to the water. Little shade exists, and there are no water fountains or rest rooms.

HEARTBREAK HILL

This famous obstacle near the end of the Boston Marathon course is actually four medium-size hills that follow each other in Newton, on Commonwealth Avenue. They cover about 3 miles overall. If you head up Chestnut Hill from the Bill Rodgers Running Center and turn left onto Commonwealth Avenue, you will meet them very quickly.

PLEASURE BAY

In South Boston, this is a beautiful loop around a small bay on a peninsula jutting out into Boston Harbor. The 2.2-mile course travels along a paved walkway through parks and across a narrow causeway which encloses the bay. The busy life in the harbor creates some interesting distractions. Winter winds can be cold and fierce along here.

If you run west from the bay on the L Street Beach, or alongside it, you will reach the L Street Bathhouse after .7 miles. The bathhouse has lockers, steam-baths and showers, and parking is available. It is closed on Sundays during winter.

FRANKLIN PARK

About 3½ miles southwest of Boston, this large park was formerly used for many running events. Now the park is considered too dangerous to recommend. At a recent race, some runners were stopped and beaten.

MIDDLESEX FELLS
RESERVATION

About 7 miles north of Boston, Route 93 passes through this large, hilly nature preserve. The facility is so large that it reaches into several different towns. Bridle paths travel all through the area, and it is easy to become lost. Remember which town you park your car in, and when you are lost, you can ask directions back to that town.

SPOT POND

Within the Middlesex Fells Reservation, this pond is surrounded by a hilly 5-mile loop. Much of it is on roads, and the wide shoulder offers some protection from traffic. The course will give you a good workout, and many top runners, including Bill Rodgers, frequently train here. Shade covers the route at intervals; water can only be found at commercial establishments. Once you can see the pond from Route 93, exit at Roosevelt Circle, and you will be able to park at a number of different places.

OUTDOOR TRACKS

Boston College, on Commonwealth Avenue in Newton, has a 480-yard all-weather track which is available to visitors. At night, it is only lit when the adjacent ball fields are in use. Tracks at other universities are restricted.

The Metropolitan YMCA, on Huntington Avenue in Boston, has a 12-laps-per-mile, banked track. The Cambridge Family Y has a banked 33⅓ track, and a lot of runners also use the 20-laps-per-mile gym floor. The roof has a 22-laps-per-mile track. Indoor tracks at Tufts University, M.I.T., and Boston College all have restrictions, but occasionally unaffiliated runners find their way on.

The North Medford Track Club is perhaps the most active club in the region. They hold weekly fun-runs at Fresh Pond Reservoir on Saturdays at 10:00 A.M. These are 2½- and 5-mile runs. They meet at the low-end parking lot where pipes are stored. During the summer they have runs on Tuesday evenings as well, and races are held every Sunday through the winter. These are at many different locations within a 40-mile radius of Boston.

The Boston Athletic Association has been responsible for the Boston Marathon since it began in 1897. Now the club works with the Prudential Insurance Company to put on the race.

The Cambridge Sports Union holds a series of eleven Thursday races during the summer at 6:30 P.M. at Fresh Pond Reservoir. Distances are 2½ and 5 miles. They also put on a variety of other running events during the year.

The Greater Boston Track Club, under the coaching of Bill Squires, has one of the best competitive teams in the world. Bill Rodgers and Randy Thomas are their two most famous members. The club is also well known for directing the Labatts Freedom Trail Run. Membership is open to all runners. Track workouts are held on Tuesday nights at Boston College.

The Wingaersheek Runners are located in Rockport, Massachusetts, on the shore of Cape Ann. They invite visiting runners to join their Saturday practice runs along the ocean, through "posh oceanside neighborhoods, along a road with a beach on one side and a pond and marshes on the other, along a winding

Charles River Embankment, Boston

road past coves, and a surf-crashing shore looking over a twin lighthouse island." The club puts on about six races a year.

TRADITIONAL RACES

Lowell V.F.W. Qualifier Marathon: March
Cambridge Greek Church 15-Kilometer: Mid-March
Brighton Knights 15-Kilometer: Late March
Boston Marathon: Third Monday in April
Marsh Post 12-Mile Handicap: Late April
Haverhill 10-Mile: July
Chelmsford Elks 7-Mile: August
Falmouth Road Race, 7.1 miles: Mid-August
Labatt's Freedom Trail Road Race, 8 miles: Late September
Foxboro Marathon: November
Falmouth Otis A.F.B. Marathon: December

CONTACTS

Fred Brown, North Medford Track Club, 157 Walsh Street, Medford, MA 02155. (617) 391-1899.

John Cedarholm, Boston Athletic Association, 180 Beacon Street, Boston, MA 02155. (617) 536-4768.

Will Cloney, Director, Boston Marathon, Box 223, Boston, MA 02199.

Mark Yesley, Cambridge Sports Union, 1 Chatham Road, Newtonville, MA 02160. (617) 527-5735.

Dave Ellis, Cambridge Sports Union, Box 1163, Brandeis University, Waltham, MA 02154.

Don Spittle, Wingaersheek Runners Club, 203 South Street, Rockport, MA 01966. (617) 546-7592.

Larry Newman, Greater Boston Track Club, 47 South Central Street, Bradford, MA 02830. (617) 372-2948.

Eliot Lounge, 370 Commonwealth Avenue (at the corner of Massachusetts Avenue), Boston, MA 02115. (617) 262-8823.

Robert S. Campbell, New England AAU, 39 Linnet Street, West Roxbury, MA 02132. (617) 742-2248.

Metropolitan YMCA, 316 Huntington Avenue, Boston, MA 02115. (617) 536-7800.

Cambridge Family Y, 820 Massachusetts Avenue, Cambridge, MA 02139. (617) 876-3860.

Springfield

Population: 160,000	Humidity: 71%
Elevation: 75 – 200 ft.	Av. Temperature: (Jan.) 27°F.; (July) 73°F.
Air Quality: Fair	Inches of Rainfall: (Jan.) 2.9; (July) 3.6 Raindays: 123

OVERVIEW

This southcentral Massachusetts city, in character with the rest of the state, has become a hotbed of running activity. Springfield lies along the Connecticut River, creating the core of a large metropolitan industrial region, including Chicopee and Holyoke.

Springfield College, a school devoted to physical education, contributes an unusually high population of running enthusiasts. This enthusiasm has spread throughout the region as the number of quality races offered here is as high as some of the largest cities in the country.

There are no accommodations adjacent to any unobstructed courses, and most of the suggested routes involve some mileage on city streets.

HOTELS

Holiday Inn, Marriott Hotel, Springfield YMCA

VAN HORN PARK

The YMCA is a popular starting point in the downtown area for runs to this park. Holiday Inn is across the street from the Y, and the Marriott is within ½ mile south of the Y. The route from the Y to Van Horn Park measures about 1½ miles along mostly residential streets. Start west on Chestnut Street for ¼ mile to Carew Street. Turn north and head uphill for most of the ⁴/₅ mile to Armory Street. Turn left (west) for the last ¼ mile to the park.

Follow the road in the park, staying left at the fork. When you reach Cunningham Street, you can either head east along Armory Street to complete a 1½-mile loop of the park, or follow Cunningham west and then south to Springfield Street to get back to the Y. When Springfield reaches Chestnut, turn east and take Chestnut for about 1 mile back to the Y. The complete distance from the Y to the park, once around the park, taking the Cunningham to Springfield route back to the Y, measures 5 miles.

If you take a full loop around the park to where you entered, and then follow the same route on your return, you will have covered 4½ miles. Of course, you can add additional loops in the park. The park road is covered by adequate shade; the terrain offering a few small hills. Water and rest rooms can be found at the ball fields. The course is considered difficult to run at night, and traffic can occasionally present a problem.

FOREST PARK

Forest Park is located about 2 miles south of downtown, in South Springfield.

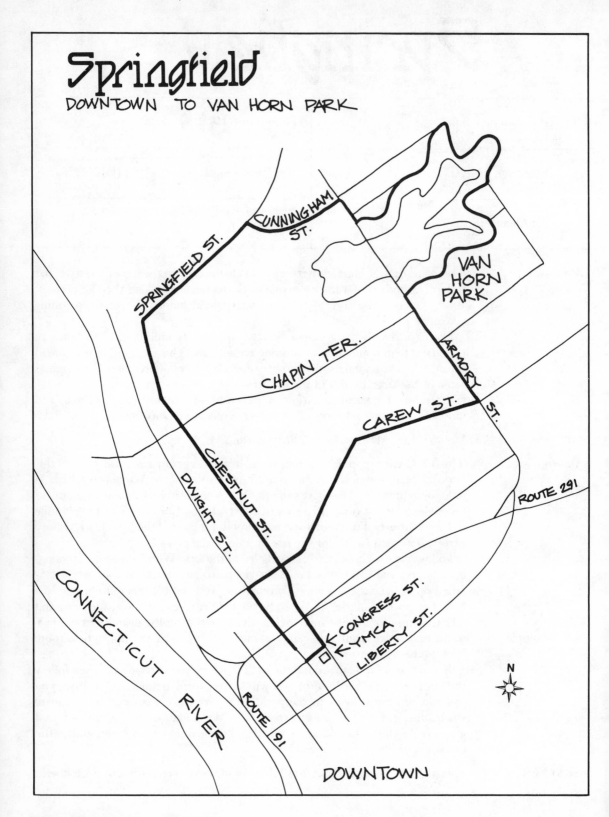

Springfield
DOWNTOWN TO VAN HORN PARK

VAN HORN PARK

CUNNINGHAM ST.

SPRINGFIELD ST.

CHAPIN TER.

ARMORY ST.

CAREW ST.

CHESTNUT ST.

DWIGHT ST.

ROUTE 291

CONNECTICUT RIVER

ROUTE 91

CONGRESS ST.
YMCA
LIBERTY ST.

N

DOWNTOWN

The route from the Civic Center to the park can be easily followed. Take Main Street about 2 miles south to Fort Pleasant Avenue, then turn right up the hill for ½ mile to a left turn on Sumner Avenue. It is then a flat ½ mile to Forest Park.

You have a choice of many roads and trails in this 800-acre park. The most popular route is a 1-mile loop around the ball fields and rose gardens. The perimeter road of the park will give you a run of about 7 miles. All courses in the park contain excellent shade, over mostly flat terrain. Water can be found within the central areas.

SPRINGFIELD COLLEGE CROSS-COUNTRY COURSE
Located near the downtown area, the cross-country course travels around the campus, past Duggan Junior High School and through the neighboring campgrounds. A difficult course to follow, it is best to meet runners at the college track, which is the starting point, and let them show you around. At 4:00 P.M. on Thursdays, the college team invites the public to join its workouts.

OUTDOOR TRACKS
Springfield College has a ¼-mile all-weather track. The YMCA has a $\frac{1}{10}$-mile, good-quality macadam track.

INDOOR TRACKS
The YMCA has a 20-laps-per-mile cork indoor track.

CLUBS AND RACES
The Springfield Harriers is the only official club in town, but they are not a major force, as practically every organization in town is involved in running. Many different groups hold races during the year.

TRADITIONAL RACES
Holyoke St. Patrick's Road Race, 8.3 miles: March
WAQY 5-Mile Race: End of April
YMCA Anniversary Run, 5 miles: Early May
Heart Fund Race, 5 miles: Mid-May
Springdale Mall Memorial Day, 6.5 and 3.2 miles
Holyoke Marathon: Early June
Fourth of July, 6 miles
Downtown Pancake Run, 5 miles: Early October
Columbus Day Road Race, 10 kilometers
Springfield College Mike Swirsky Memorial Run, 5.3 miles: Late October
Galaska Road Race, 10 kilometers: Early November

CONTACTS
Springfield YMCA, 275 Chestnut Street, Springfield, MA 01104. (413) 739-6951.
Dr. Jack Mahurin, Springfield College, 263 Alden Street, Springfield, MA 01109. (413) 787-2066.
Walter Childs, AAU, (413) 566-3145.

DETROIT

Population: (met.) 4,400,000	Humidity: 71%
Elevation: 573 – 672 ft.	Av. Temperature: (Jan.) 26°F.; (July) 73°F.
Air Quality: Poor	Inches of Rainfall: (Jan.) 1.9; (July) 3 Raindays: 132

OVERVIEW

There is no city in America where adversity has been a deterrent to running. Somehow local runners persist in overcoming both natural and man-made obstacles. Detroit has two particular enemies. As the automobile capital, its lobby is sufficiently strong to maintain full-time use of the roads on Belle Isle, the most popular running area in Detroit. The city is located between Lake Erie and Lake St. Clair on the Detroit River across from Windsor, Canada. Belle Isle sits in the middle of the river, only a couple of miles from downtown. A very common activity here is to go for a drive on Belle Isle, creating a constant traffic nuisance.

The second nemesis of runners is the high crime rate. Residents must resort to their automobiles to avoid crime-ridden public transportation. Running courses are confined to safe neighborhoods. Many parks are unsafe, as well as downtown routes to some of the safer areas. If your plans are such that you can stay out of the downtown area, many people prefer accommodations in nearby Dearborn, about 12 miles to the west.

Some of the residential neighborhoods are very hilly and conducive to good workouts. The social nature of local runners allows for many group workouts. Courses are hard to follow, and it is recommended to meet up with these groups if you are going to run in their areas.

HOTELS

Downtown: Hotel Ponchartrain, Radisson-Cadillac Hotel
Dearborn: Holiday Inn, Dearborn Inn, Hyatt Regency, Fairlane Gold Key Inn, Dearborn Travelodge

BELLE ISLE

This popular course can be easily reached by car from the city freeways. Two miles east of downtown, take the Belle Isle Bridge from East Jefferson Avenue. Parking is never a problem. A flat, wooded island, it contains a perimeter road measuring 5.5 miles. By taking the bridge across to East Jefferson and back, the loop is extended to 7 miles, and you get a little hill work on the ramps of the bridge.

Early morning runs are recommended, as traffic becomes very heavy during the day. Night runs are risky. Running to the island from downtown is also considered risky. Head in a clockwise direction because autos travel counterclockwise. A nice cooling breeze comes off the river, and there is plenty of shade. Seven or eight water fountains line the course, and rest rooms can be found at the parking lots and the casino. Unfortunately, views from the island are not very exciting, as industrial areas line both sides of the river.

PALMER PARK

Not really a park, this area is a residential neighborhood 6 miles north of downtown, containing a golf course on the west side of Woodward Avenue, between McNichols and Seven-Mile roads. Woodward Avenue is one of the main arteries through the city. A sidewalk skirts the golf course for a 2.9-mile loop alongside a fence. Terrain is flat and well shaded. No water fountains or rest rooms are available. The course is safe for women running alone, but perhaps not at night. Motels are not located near here.

CRANBROOK COLLEGE

Sixteen miles north of town, in the community of rich Bloomfield Hills, the college campus provides miles of wooded, hilly terrain. Runners often meet at the parking lot of the Church of the Latter Day Saints on Woodward Avenue, north of Big Beaver Road. The roads around the campus are equally hilly, and fairly void of traffic. The quiet neighborhood offers scenic views alongside its well-appointed homes. Directions are impossible for routes both on and off campus, as roads and trails are poorly marked. Mike Cunney, who has run here many times, still prefers to run with people who are more familiar with the courses. Very few water fountains can be found here.

LEVAGOOD PARK

One mile north from Dearborn motels on Telegraph Road, and three blocks west on Wilson Avenue, you will arrive at small, flat Levagood Park. A blacktop track measuring .6 mile circles the park around its ball fields. The course is shaded and there is a water fountain.

HENRY FORD COMMUNITY COLLEGE

Near the Fairlane Shopping Center in Dearborn, there is a hilly, wooded area adjacent to the college track. Dirt trails have excellent footing, but again, they are hard to follow, and it is best to run with knowledgeable people. You will often find other runners at the track, where there is a water fountain and rest rooms. This area is considered very safe.

OUTDOOR TRACKS

The Henry Ford Community College, in Dearborn, has a ¼-mile cinder track around the soccer field behind the tennis courts.

INDOOR TRACKS

The Downtown YMCA has a 24-laps-per-mile, banked track.

CLUBS, GROUP RUNS AND RACES

The Motor City Striders are the major club in Detroit. They hold frequent races, mostly on Belle Isle at 10:00 A.M., Sundays.

The Belle Isle Striders meet at the Casino on Belle Isle at 7:00 A.M. every Saturday, Sunday and public holiday throughout the year. In winter, they meet at 7:30 A.M. After the run, in warm weather, they often go for a swim in the Detroit River at the Bathhouse. Later they gather for breakfast at the Big Boy Restaurant on East Jefferson, at the foot of the Belle Isle Bridge.

During the summer, track meets are held on Wednesday evenings at McComb Junior College, about 12 miles east of town.

Running events are listed in the Sports Section of the *Detroit News* every Thursday.

Joe Arendt, a doctor who runs with a group of cardiac patients, has expanded his group to include other runners. They meet every Sunday at 8:00 A.M. for runs through and around Cranbrook College. You will find them gathering at the Church parking lot. Afterwards they meet for breakfast at the Maple House, in the shopping center at the junction of Maple Road and Coolidge Highway.

TRADITIONAL RACES

Ernest Smith 5-Mile Run: Early March
Pontiac Wide Track Festival, 11 miles: June
International Freedom Festival, 10 miles: Early July
Burgquist and Brennan Memorial, 5.4 miles: Early September
Chauncey Longwhite Memorial, 10 miles: Early October
Motor City Marathon: Late October

CONTACTS

Edward Kozloff, Motor City Striders, 10144 Lincoln, Huntington Woods, MI 48070. (313) 544-9099.
Ken Isherwood, Downtown YMCA, 2020 Witherell Street, Detroit, MI 48226. (313) 962-6126.

ℜalamazoo

Population: 80,000	Humidity: 72%
Elevation: 775 ft.	Av. Temperature: (Jan.) 25°F.; (July) 73°F.
Air Quality: Fair	Inches of Rainfall: (Jan.) 2.0; (July) 3.5 Raindays: 133

OVERVIEW

In the southwest section of Michigan, Kalamazoo's industrial and university activity create a busy atmosphere. Many runners can be seen on city streets. Not in parks, because none are conveniently located. The most frequented course is only ½ mile from the center of town along two quiet residential streets.

The convenient Western Michigan University cross-country course provides some challenging hills over open and grassy terrain. Local runners prefer not to get too busy putting on big or frequent running events, since many good races can be found in nearby cities. Camaraderie is high here, and visiting runners can easily find company for a workout.

HOTELS

Holiday Inn—West, Kalamazoo Hilton

OAKLAND DRIVE, WINCHELL AVENUE COURSE

These two streets, at right angles to each other, provide the most convenient, year 'round running in town. They can be reached easily from the Hilton, located in the heart of downtown. Head west on Michigan Avenue for five long blocks to Oakland Drive. Turn left (south) and run down Oakland to Winchell (2½ miles from the hotel). Make a right (west again), and follow Winchell for 1.3 miles until it dead-ends.

The five blocks on Michigan have wide sidewalks, and on Oakland it is best to stay on the sidewalks. There are a number of intersections, but they do not seem to slow many runners down. Along Winchell, you can safely run in the street. There are some gradual hills en route, and Oakland will provide you with good shade. Water and rest rooms are not easy to come by.

KLEINSTUCK FOREST PRESERVE

Follow the same route out along Michigan and Oakland, but about ¼ mile short of Winchell, turn left on Maple. One-fourth of a mile down Maple will bring you to the YMCA. Directly behind the Y is the forest preserve. A dirt path can be followed through the woods for a loop just 60 yards short of ¾ of a mile. Obtain water and rest room facilities at the Y.

WESTERN MICHIGAN CROSS-COUNTRY COURSE

To reach the course from downtown, run down West Michigan past Oakland and across the university campus. When you reach the Campus Theater, turn right down Howard for ½ mile. When the road turns right onto Kendall, cross the road and run up the grassy hill and through the fence. You will see a dirt path in front of you. Take it in either direction for a $1\frac{7}{10}$-mile loop of the outer part of the course. The inner course is complicated to follow and you will need another runner to show you the way.

HOLIDAY INN – WEST COURSE	Located only 2 miles from downtown, a pleasant run through farm country can be had from this hotel. Head west on Stadium Drive for 1.6 miles to the little town of Oshtemo. Turn north (right) at the traffic light onto 9th Avenue and run along its gravel shoulder to KL Avenue. Turn west (left) on KL and again, staying on the shoulder, follow this shady, hilly road to 4th Avenue. At this point you will be 2½ miles from the start. From here you can doubleback, or head south on 4th to Stadium Drive (which also might be called West Michigan) and turn east back to the hotel. Fourth Avenue also has some tough hills. Out in farm country, watch out for non-vicious dogs. An asphalt bike path makes running safer between Oshtemo and the Holiday Inn. Water and rest rooms will be a problem on this course.
OUTDOOR TRACKS	Two outdoor tracks are located across the street from each other. From West Michigan and Oakland Drive, head up Stadium Drive, and you will quickly be between the ¼-mile all-weather track at Western Michigan University and Angell Field at Kalamazoo College, which contains a ¼-mile cinder track.
INDOOR TRACKS	The YMCA on Maple Street has a banked indoor track measuring about 20 to 22 laps per mile.
CLUBS AND RACES	The Kalamazoo Track Club holds low-key races in the spring and summer on alternate Thursday evenings. In the fall, they hold cross-country races every other Saturday.
TRADITIONAL RACES	Two-Runner 10-Mile Relay: Late August 25-Kilometer Race: October
CONTACTS	Terry Doxey, President, Kalamazoo Track Club, (616) 385-2949. Tom Coyne, 1584 Spruce Drive, Kalamazoo, MI 49008. (616) 383-1752, 349-9307.

LANSING

Population: 130,000	Humidity: 73.5%
Elevation: 863 ft.	Av. Temperature: (Jan.) 22.6°F.; (July) 70.9°F.
Air Quality: Fair	Inches of Rainfall: (Jan.) 1.91; (July) 2.82 Raindays: 139

OVERVIEW

Located in the central part of the state, Lansing, Michigan's state capital, has a small downtown area surrounded by both heavy industry and rural farmland. The Grand and Red Cedar rivers flow through town, and parks along the rivers provide scenic runs. Just north of downtown, many runners begin at Lansing Community College for a 3-mile loop beside the Grand River, but closer to the capital, only a one-block-square park is available.

A couple of miles south of town, Potter Park has 80 acres to run through, but perhaps the most popular route is found 4½ miles southeast, near Michigan State University. Here there are 4- and 5-mile, easy-to-follow courses along rural roads. The university campus itself is huge (5,100 acres), and runners are constantly churning out miles over its many roads.

Every Saturday at 10:00 A.M. sharp, the starting gun goes off for the weekly road race. Most runs are small, and there is plenty of competition.

The city is building running trails in several different parks. Three golf courses, Sycamore, Groesbeck and Red Cedar, allow runners to make use of their facilities.

HOTELS

Capital Park Motel, Hospitality Inn, Red Roof Inn

RIVERFRONT PARK

Downtown, the Capital Park Motel is across the street from a small park with a perimeter of 2½ laps per mile. It is also in close proximity to the capitol building and the YMCA.

To reach Riverfront Park from downtown, run north on Grand for about ⅔ of a mile to Lansing Community College. Take a right across the river on the Old Railroad Bridge. Then head south (right) along the river on a new dirt trail which circles around the City Market and then back north, again along the river to the far end of Burchard Park. From the park, doubleback to the Old Railroad Bridge, and across to the starting point. The total distance from and back to the college is close to 3 miles. Water fountains and rest rooms are being installed, and the course is lit at night and considered marginally safe.

SOUTHEAST ROUTE

This course can be reached via the Jolly Road Exit on I-496, about 4½ miles southeast of town. The Hospitality and Red Roof inns are located here on Dunckel Road. From these inns, head east for a short distance to Collins Road and turn north (left). Stay on Collins for 1 mile to a right on Forrest Road. This road travels alongside a golf course for 1 mile to College Road, where you turn right and continue on College for 1 mile, until you come to a road going right under the power lines. If you take this road, it will bring you back to Collins and the inns for a 4-mile run.

If you continue straight on College for another ½ mile, you will reach Jolly Road. Jolly has more traffic than the other roads, but a right here will take you back to Collins Road after 1 mile, and another right on Collins will take you back to Dunckel after ½ mile.

The course passes many well-kept farms and livestock, and much of the land is owned by Michigan State University. The roads are blacktop with good shoulders. Water can be found at the MSU farms. There is no night lighting, but that does not seem to deter many of the runners who use this course.

MICHIGAN STATE
UNIVERSITY CAMPUS

The campus is located in East Lansing and can be reached on a 2½-mile route from the Dunckel Road Inns. Follow the same course as above, and continue along Forrest Road to a left on Harrison Road, which will take you to the campus.

The Red Cedar River flows through campus, and many people enjoy runs along both sides of it. You will see runners using every path and roadway throughout this fairly level facility.

POTTER PARK

This park is a little more than 2 miles from downtown. To get there, go east on Michigan Avenue for 1 mile, and then south on Pennsylvania Avenue to the park entrance. Follow the roadway in the park for about a 1-mile loop. The course heads downhill to the Red Cedar River, along the river, and then back uphill (gradual) and around to the entrance. The park is lit at night and considered safe. Water fountains and rest rooms are available.

OUTDOOR TRACKS

Michigan State University has a ¼-mile rubberized asphalt track.

INDOOR TRACKS

The YMCA has a 22-laps-per-mile track. Dennison Field House at Michigan State has a 220-yard track which is not open to outsiders, although many use it anyway.

CLUBS AND RACES

The Mid-Michigan Track Club holds weekly races at various locales every Saturday morning at 10:00. During warm months, races are also held Tuesdays at 6:00 P.M.

TRADITIONAL RACES

Fourth of July 10-Kilometer
State Journal 10-Kilometer (Women): Early October
East Lansing 10-Kilometer: November

CONTACTS

Raymond D. Warner, Mid-Michigan Track Club, 4922 Tenny Street, Lansing, MI 48910. (517) 372-9400 (work).
Gordon Schafer, Mid-Michigan Track Club, 4378 West Holt Road, Holt, MI 48842.
Lansing Parks and Recreation Department, (517) 487-1270.
Lansing YMCA, 301 West Lenawee Street, Lansing, MI 48914. (517) 489-6501.

Minneapolis

Population: 360,000	Humidity: 69.5%
Elevation: 687 – 1,060 ft.	Av. Temperature: (Jan.) 13°F.; (July) 72°F.
Air Quality: Fair	Inches of Rainfall: (Jan.) .7; (July) 3.2 Raindays: 113

OVERVIEW

Up in the North Country, Minneapolis has a fresh, vigorous atmosphere that draws many runners onto its roads and paths. This modern, cultural city is surrounded by beautiful rolling countryside and scenic waterside runs. Twenty-two lakes can be found in the city, many of which are frequented by the hearty running population. Streams and rivers also abound, and the Mississippi flows through town with high bluffs on either side offering exciting vistas from its famous course, the River Road.

A chain of lakes, beginning with Lake of the Isles at the southwest corner of downtown, have the most popular appeal, as their peaceful loops can take you through attractive residential communities. Connecting these lakes to the Mississippi River, Minnehaha Creek runs east through a narrow, rustic park, past Minnehaha Falls, which Longfellow characterized as the "laughing water."

Winters are cold and difficult, yet local runners seem to thrive on the adversity of it. Many world-class athletes live and train in this environment, including Garry Bjorklund, Mike Slack, Steve Hoag, Ron Daws and Alex Ratelle. If this is the result, there must be something many of us do not know about winter running.

HOTELS

Holiday Inn – Downtown, The Radisson, The Leamington

LORING PARK

Loring Park is located in the southwest corner of the downtown area. It can be reached by running south on any of the downtown avenues to Grant Street. Turn right here and it's only a short run to the park. If you run the perimeter, it's a fraction short of 1 mile. Flat and mostly grassy, there is occasional shade. A large noontime running population utilizes this course.

There is poor lighting for night runs, although with fairly even footing, the course is possible. In winter, the park is used extensively for cross-country skiing and there are many hard-packed trails that are excellent to run on.

In the middle of the park you will find a wooden bridge crossing a small pond. There is a water fountain here, and you might take a look at the many thousands of goldfish colonizing the pond. A building in the park contains rest rooms and a water fountain, but it is not often open.

The Holiday Inn – Downtown, one of that chain's more luxurious hotels, is only two blocks east of Loring Park. The Convention Center is four blocks east, and The Radisson, located within the famous skyway system, a complex of buildings and blocks connected by enclosed walkways, is ¾ of a mile from the park.

ROUTE TO LAKE OF THE ISLES

After passing through Loring Park, there are two different routes to reach Lake of the Isles, the first of three closely connected lakes. For the shortest route, 1¼ miles, follow Lyndale Avenue south, then turn right onto West Franklin Avenue, proceeding the final ¾ of a mile to the lake.

The longer route is to head west on Kenwood Parkway past the Tyrone Guthrie Theater. Stay on Kenwood over its hilly course to Kenwood Park and through to the lake. This route is close to 1¾ miles.

LAKE OF THE ISLES

This lake has a curving shoreline and you never are far from the opposite shore. There is a nice scale and intimacy about it. Measuring 2.8 miles along a flat, paved pathway, the course has moderate shade and occasional grassy areas to provide soft footing. No water fountains are available.

LAKE CALHOUN

There are only about 300 yards between the southeast corner of Lake of the Isles and the northeast corner of Lake Calhoun. This is a larger, rounder lake with a flat circumferential path of 3.2 miles. Plenty of shade exists, and the northeast corner has a water fountain and rest rooms.

LAKE HARRIET

Going south from Lake Calhoun for ⅓ mile along William Berry Parkway, you'll reach Lake Harriet. This body of water is similar to Lake Calhoun, but is only 3 miles in circumference. At the northwest corner of Lake Harriet is a water fountain and rest rooms.

A loop around the three lakes measures about 10 miles. This is an area frequented by many romantic couples and the sights can be very distracting. It is reported that Ron Daws had a sudden romance with a tree while noticing some of the local activity.

MINNEHAHA PARKWAY

The course continues beyond Lake Harriet and heads east toward Lake Nokomis and the Mississippi River. It follows the Minnehaha Creek through a wooded park belt next to the Minnehaha Parkway. The run is about 4 miles to Lake Nokomis along slightly rolling hills.

LAKE NOKOMIS

There is an exercise course at Lake Nokomis Park, plus water fountains and rest rooms. A 2.8-mile pathway runs around the lake.

MINNEHAHA PARKWAY CONTINUED TO MINNEHAHA FALLS

You do not need to run around the lake to continue east along Minnehaha Creek. After another 2 miles you'll reach Minnehaha Falls. This is where Longfellow lived and was inspired to do his writing. If you stay to the left for another ¼ mile you'll be on the bluff directly over the Mississippi River.

RIVER ROAD LOOPS

Along both sides of the Mississippi River is the popular River Road. The length of this course varies as different bridges can be used to make up different loops. The northern limit is Washington Bridge at the University of Minnesota. The southern limit is Ford Bridge at Minnehaha Park. The loop utilizing these two bridges is 11 miles. From Washington Bridge, a loop south to Franklin Bridge is a fraction short of 3 miles, and again from Washington Bridge a loop south to Lake Bridge is 6.2 miles. These loops are on the bluff above the river and they are basically flat with decent shade. The river roads are not near any major

Lake of the Isles, Minneapolis

hotels. Runners staying in downtown hotels can possibly run the 3½ miles along busy streets to the course by heading south to Franklin Avenue and then east to the river.

19-MILE LOOP   Utilizing all of the courses previously mentioned, a good 19-mile run can be created. You can head south from downtown through Loring Park, passing the three close lakes, then head east along Minnehaha Creek and northwest on the River Road, finally turning west on Franklin and back to downtown.

WIRTH PARK   Wirth Park is located just 2½ miles west of downtown. Take Route 12 to Wirth Parkway north. A number of cross-country trails begin at or near the parking lot. On the west side of the lot, the trails are dirt and wood chip, and on the east side they are paved with asphalt. There are no marked courses or distances and it is easy to feel lost. There are few runners here to show the way, though the park is not so large that you'll be lost for very long. The hills in this park are short and steep and drinking water is not available. The Mud Ball Race is held here every April, and if the terrain isn't wet enough, it's given some help by the race directors. Steve Hoag has said that if a runner finishes the race with both of his shoes still on his feet, he hasn't run his hardest.

MORE HILLS   Many runners do their hill training near the University of Minnesota, utilizing the pathways up from the river flats to the bluff. Garry Bjorklund does a lot of his hill work in Columbia Park in northern Minneapolis and also at Nine-Mile Creek in Bloomington, south of the city.

OUTDOOR TRACKS   Northrop College has a ¼-mile track located ¼ mile west of Loring Park. The

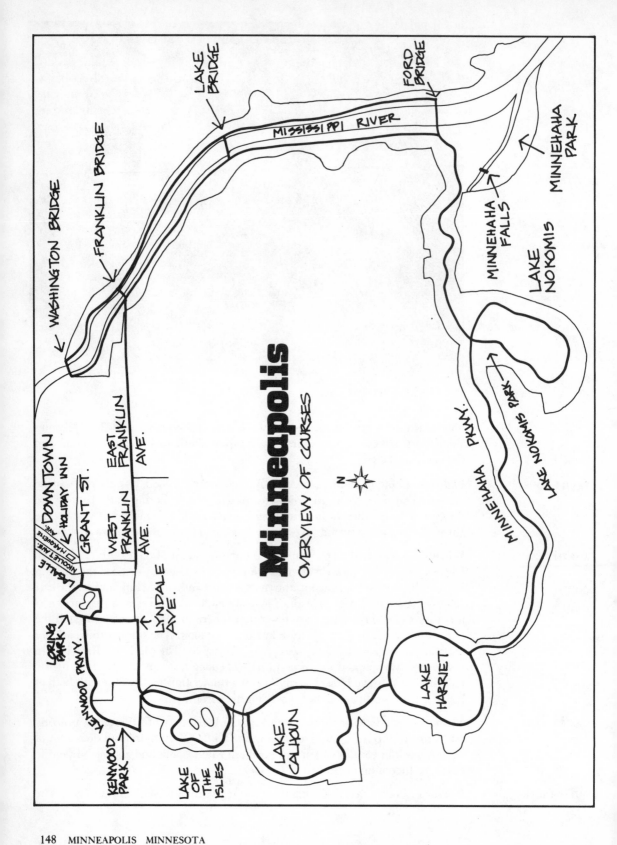

Minneapolis
OVERVIEW OF COURSES

LAKE BRIDGE

FORD BRIDGE

MISSISSIPPI RIVER

FRANKLIN BRIDGE

WASHINGTON BRIDGE

MINNEHAHA PARK

MINNEHAHA FALLS

LAKE NOKOMIS

MINNEHAHA PARK

DOWNTOWN

HOLIDAY INN

GRANT ST.

EAST FRANKLIN AVE.

WEST FRANKLIN AVE.

LASALLE

NICOLLET AVE.

MARQUETTE AVE.

LYNDALE AVE.

LORING PARK

KENWOOD PKWY.

KENWOOD PARK

LAKE OF THE ISLES

LAKE CALHOUN

LAKE HARRIET

MINNEHAHA PKWY.

LAKE NOKOMIS PARK

N

most popular outdoor track is Bierman Track at the University of Minnesota. This is on S.E. 15th Avenue between S.E. 5th and 6th streets.

INDOOR TRACKS

For a city with cold, snowy winters, there are not many indoor facilities available to visiting runners. The Downtown YMCA at 30 South 9th Street has a good 19-lap-per-mile track. Washington Bridge at the University of Minnesota has an enclosed walkway over the bridge. This accommodates students during the day, but at other times there is room to run the quarter-mile distance.

AIRPORT

The airport is located at the juncture of the Mississippi and Minnesota rivers. Across the service road to the airport is Fort Snelling State Park. You can find some trails running through it or you can run north to the Mississippi and along the river up to Minnehaha Park about 3 miles away.

HOTELS ALONG I-494

L'Hotel Sofitel, Radisson – South, Howard Johnson's

I-494

Along I-494 about 7 miles due west of the airport in Bloomington are a few hotels used for conventions which are particularly close to Hyland Lake Park Reserve. From these hotels run west to E. Bush Lake Road, then south ⅓ mile to the park. You will find excellent cross-country courses here with variable terrain. Mike Slack considers this one of the best and most challenging cross-country areas in America. You can also choose to stay west along E. Bush Road for about 1½ miles until you come to Bush Lake with about a 3-mile circumferential road.

CLUBS

The major running club in Minneapolis is the Minnesota Distance Running Association. It has an active schedule of races and clinics throughout the year. The good running stores in town can supply information about weekly events.

There is a very active women's running club in Minneapolis called the Northern Lights Track Club. They hold many fun-runs and races, mainly for women and occasionally for men. They also have an excellent monthly newsletter.

TRADITIONAL RACES

Mud Ball Run, 4.5 miles: First weekend after the Boston Marathon
Pea Soup Days, 10 kilometers: Late June
Hopkins Raspberry Festival, 5 miles: Late July
City of Lakes Marathon: October

CONTACTS

Jim Ferstle, Editor, *Minnesota Distance Runner*, 1480 Carroll, St. Paul, MN 55104. (612) 644-6697.
Jan Arenz, Northern Lights Track Club, 4094 Flowerfield Road, St. Paul, MN 55112. (612) 786-1197.
Garry Bjorklund or Mike Slack, Bjorklund Sports, 831 Marquette, Minneapolis, MN 55402. (612) 333-4832.
Steve Hoag, *Running World*, 3511 West 70th Street, Edina, MN. (612) 925-1411.
Downtown YMCA, 30 South 9th Street, Minneapolis, MN 55402. (612) 332-2431.

ST. PAUL

Population: 280,000	Humidity: 69%
Elevation: 687 – 1,060 ft.	Av. Temperature: (Jan.) 15°F.; (July) 74°F.
Air Quality: Fair	Inches of Rainfall: (Jan.) .7; (July) 3.2 Raindays: 113

OVERVIEW

St. Paul, the capital of Minnesota, adjoins Minneapolis to create a giant metropolitan area. The proximity of the cities is such that the identity of each becomes lost within certain activities. Many people live in St. Paul and work in Minneapolis as well as the other way around. The organization of running has not developed along city lines, and clubs draw membership equally from both cities. The one factor that remains true to its own city is the geographical location of the running courses.

Downtown St. Paul sits close to the Mississippi River. In contrast to Minneapolis, the roads along the river are more commercial, and although adequate for running, do not offer the natural beauty that the Minneapolis River Run provides. St. Paul has a number of good runs leading out from downtown along grassy malled, residential boulevards. Not only are these courses enjoyable on their own, but they will lead you to some beautiful city parks and lakes.

HOTELS

Holiday Inn, Best Western Capp Towers, Howard Johnson's – I-94 at White Bear, Radisson Hotel

SUMMIT AVENUE

This scenic avenue runs from downtown directly west to the Mississippi, hitting it along the popular Minneapolis River Run, part of which passes through St. Paul. You can reach Summit Avenue from Holiday Inn by heading south on Marion Street to St. Paul School, staying left to Ireland Boulevard, and going right to Summit-Irvine Avenue up the hill to Summit Avenue, continuing west. It is about 1 mile from Holiday Inn to Summit Avenue.

Summit Avenue is a long, flat, straight road on a plateau with beautiful mansions alongside. A grassy mall provides excellent soft footing under luxuriantly shady trees. After about 3½ miles on the plateau, you will reach a downhill to the river, meeting it about ½ mile south of Lake Bridge. See Minneapolis for a description of the River Run.

HARRIET ISLAND PARK

From Capp Towers or the Radisson, run west a few blocks to Wabasha and turn south, going over the bridge to the island. It is a fairly steep grade downhill going out, and you will have to come back the same way. Once on the island, the course is flat and shaded. The island is not very large, perhaps 1½ miles round trip.

SHEPARD ROAD RIVER RUN

This route is not highly recommended because it takes you along a commercial road with considerable auto and truck traffic during the day. The road becomes less commercial the further you run from downtown. Shepard Road heads west along the river from the downtown area close to the Radisson Hotel. Mike Slack, a world-class runner, used this route frequently when he worked in downtown St. Paul. It is convenient, and basically unobstructed. Mileage is not limited, as the road continues into Minneapolis.

COMO PARK

Como Park can be reached by a run of about 2 miles from downtown at the State Capitol, heading north on Rice Street for a few blocks to Como Avenue and then following a straight route out Como, northwest to the park. A sidewalk will carry you over flat, shady terrain. Traffic can be a problem on this route.

When you reach the park, you can follow a bike path around Lake Como for 2 miles. A couple of steep hills can be avoided by taking the roadway in those areas. Como Park has 448 acres to wander over, with many paths and trails. A golf course can provide good grass mileage without any hassle from the golfers.

PHELAN PARK

Phelan Park provides a running environment similar to Como Park. Situated about 3½ miles northeast of town, the newly enlarged golf course, and Lake Phelan, with a 3.1-mile perimeter, are considered good training facilities.

Phelan Park can be reached from Howard Johnson's by running south on White Bear Avenue, and then west for a hilly mile to Johnson Parkway at Indian Mounds Park. The parkway provides soft footing over its grassy mall for the 2¼ miles north to Phelan Park.

Some small lakes north of the park can be easily reached by footpaths and can be run for additional miles. Keller Lake, within ½ mile, is heavily frequented by park runners. Another popular route is to head west from the golf course, along Wheelock Parkway, for 4½ miles to Lake Como. This road also contains a grassy mall for comfortable running between the parks.

INDOOR TRACKS

There are no indoor tracks in St. Paul, although the downtown YMCA has a 20-laps-per-mile gym floor that receives a lot of use in adverse weather. Many runners leave in groups from the Y for daily workouts. Summit Avenue and Harriet Island are their two most popular routes.

CONTACTS

St. Paul YMCA, 475 Cedar Street, St. Paul, MN 55101. (612) 222-0771.
Steve Hoag, *Running World*, 1656 Grand Avenue, St. Paul, MN 55105. (612) 690-5488.

HATTIESBURG

Population: 38,000	Humidity: Not available
Elevation: 145 ft.	Av. Temperature: (Jan.) 50°F.; (July) 81°F.
Air Quality: Fair	Inches of Rainfall: (Jan.) 4.7; (July) 5.8 Raindays: 78

OVERVIEW

Like many small cities in the country, especially those with large universities, Hattiesburg has developed an active running population. Again, like other university towns, the popular running courses have been measured and marked near to the campus. Hattiesburg, lying in the southern sector of the state, is also part of the Longleaf Pine Belt, and involved in the production of lumber.

HOTELS

Southernaire Hotel, Holiday Inn—North

UNIVERSITY ROUTE

Running centers around the University of Southern Mississippi, located about 2½ miles west of downtown. The Southernaire is the closest hotel to the university, about ½ mile south. The Holiday Inn is located 2 miles to the north of campus.

Start at the University parking lot adjacent to Green Coliseum. This is convenient and centrally located. Proceed out 4th Street west, and remain on 4th for the entire route out and back. This 20-kilometer AAU-certified course is marked every mile. This hilly terrain rolls through countryside containing a smattering of houses and stands of longleaf pines. Be prepared for a few dogs between the 2- and 3-mile marks. Water and rest rooms are hard to come by along the course.

CLUBS AND RACES

The Hattiesburg Track Club holds races twice a month. The time and the day of the week vary.

TRADITIONAL RACES

Magnolia Classic 10-Kilometer Run: April
Golden Eagle 20-Kilometer Run: November

CONTACT

John L. Pendergrass, Hattiesburg Track Club, Box 1230, Hattiesburg, MS 39401. (601) 584-6211.

JACKSON

Population: 170,000	Humidity: 71%
Elevation: 295 ft.	Av. Temperature: (Jan.) 47°F.; (July) 82°F.
Air Quality: Fair to poor	Inches of Rainfall: (Jan.) 4.5; (July) 4.3 Raindays: 108

OVERVIEW

Jackson, the state capital and largest city of Mississippi, is located along the Pearl River in the southwest section of the state. It is a hilly city with plenty of foliage. The Old South retains its character here and a popular downtown run tours through a beautiful and old area of town. Most of the marked courses are found outside of town, either to the north or the south.

Running is still in its early stages here, and local runners are excited about visitors coming through and enjoying their courses and their hospitality. If you drive out to some of the prescribed courses on the outskirts of town, you might want to check out the course with your car and deposit containers of water along the way.

HOTELS

Jackson Hilton Inn, Holiday Inn—Southwest, Jacksonian Master Hosts Inn

DOWNTOWN ROUTE

The downtown area does not have any specific courses. No large parks or river runs are available. The Downtown YMCA serves as runners' headquarters, and groups head out into a hilly residential area for their daily mileage. Beautiful trees line the streets to protect runners from the sun, but there are too few street lights to guide runners at night.

The Jackson Hilton is the most convenient hotel to this area. From the hotel, run a few blocks north and turn east onto Fortification for about 1 mile. Cross over the interstate and you will be at the YMCA.

NATCHEZ TRACE PARKWAY SOUTH

South Jackson, where the new Metrocenter is located, has become an active and vital part of town. A beautiful and popular course begins not far from here. The Natchez Trace Parkway South has been part of the long history of Jackson, and is maintained by the U.S. Park Service. Very few automobiles use the road, creating a haven for runners. The asphalt road or grassy shoulder can provide a run of 50 miles. The first 8'miles are marked on the road surface. Terrain is flat under moderate shade; no water is available.

Accommodations close to this route can be found at the Holiday Inn—Southwest. Take I-20 3 or 4 miles west to the Natchez Trace Parkway exit, and head south for ¾ of a mile to the course parking lot.

RIVERSIDE PARK

This small park can be found several miles north at the Lakeland exit of I-55. The circumference measures 1¼ miles. Shade is sparse, although the many water fountains can help you on a hot day. The hilly-terrained route has no mileage markers. Many runners extend their workouts along Lakeland Drive East for as far as 10 miles out. Heavy traffic can be a problem except during early morning or weekends.

PEARL RIVER RUN

Only a local runner can guide you to and along this route. It is a beautiful, scenic run under excellent shade. No water exists for the 5- to 10-mile distance. Snakes present the greatest hazard to unsuspecting runners. It could even be more of a hazard if you run the course in a terrified state.

HIGHLAND VILLAGE ROUTE

Located several miles north of town at the Northside exit of I-55, a 10,000-meter marked course begins at the Highland Village Shopping Center. The local Phidippides Running Store has created this hilly, residential route out and back, marking it with arrows. The Jacksonian Inn is only about ½ mile from the shopping center.

VICKSBURG CIVIL WAR PARK

Local runners highly recommend this historic park for a quality hill workout. It is located 50 minutes west of Jackson along I-20.

TRACKS

A new $^4/_5$-mile outdoor asphalt track has been built by the Downtown YMCA. If you prefer to run indoors, they also have a 15-laps-per-mile indoor track.

FUN-RUNS

The Phidippides Running Center, at Highland Village Shopping Center, conducts fun-runs on a frequent but unscheduled basis.

CLUBS AND RACES

The Mississippi Track Club holds races mainly during the cooler months. The club's quarterly newsletter provides a schedule of the many races available in the area.

TRADITIONAL RACES

Mississippi Marathon: Early December

CONTACTS

Dr. Walter Howell, Mississippi Track Club, P.O. Box 4006, Clinton, MS 39058.
Phidippides Running Center, Highland Village Shopping Center, Jackson, MS 39211. (601) 981-3583.
Downtown YMCA, 800 East River Place, Jackson, MS 39205. (601) 948-3090.

KANSAS CITY

Population: (met.) 1,235,000	Humidity: 64%
Elevation: 741 ft.	Av. Temperature: (Jan.) 30°F.; (July) 81°F.
Air Quality: Fair	Inches of Rainfall: (Jan.) 1.3.; (July) 3.8 Raindays: 98

OVERVIEW

Situated on a large hill above the Missouri River, the downtown area of Kansas City is strictly commercial. I researched this city during a physical education convention when many runners were staying in downtown hotels and heading out during breaks to get in their workouts. Many came back with somber stories about endless city streets and too many dead ends. Those who headed downhill to the north quickly arrived at the Missouri and found no routes along the river's edge. The luckier ones headed downhill to the south where they eventually came to Liberty Memorial Park.

Actually, there are two Kansas Cities. The major metropolitan area is in Missouri, where life follows an urban style. The other Kansas City is in Kansas, just across the river to the west, and pursues a comfortable existence as a moderate-sized western town. The two together constitute Greater Kansas City along with their sprawling suburbs.

Although there are some small and popular parks downtown, much running activity takes place in the western suburbs where many people train on their local neighborhood roads. Shawnee Mission Park, west of town, is a popular site used for many races. Quite a number of large running clubs in town provide local runners with an abundance of events, and the clubs work well together to produce a full annual schedule.

HOTELS

Holiday Inn – City Center, Phillips House, Radisson Muehlebach Hotel, Intercontinental Hotel, Alameda Plaza Hotel, Raphael Hotel, Crown Center Hotel

LIBERTY MEMORIAL PARK

A straight shot south on Main Street for 1.1 miles, Liberty Memorial Park can comfortably be reached from the downtown hotels, notably the Holiday Inn, Intercontinental, Radisson, and Phillips House. Head a few short blocks west from the hotels to Main Street and then it's a right turn and downhill most of the way. You will pass Union Train Station on your right just before reaching Pershing Street. Then continue on Main Street uphill for .6 mile to Memorial Drive, a right turn into the park.

Three loops can be run in the park. The first one on your right lies perfectly flat, over grass with good shade trees, and the other two are slightly hilly with little shade. Three loops together can be run in a figure-eight fashion, with each loop being about the same distance for a three loop total of 1½ miles. No water fountains or rest rooms exist in the park.

Crown Center Hotel, a luxury Western International Hotel, sits on the corner of Main Street and Pershing Street at the southeast corner of Liberty Memorial Park. It operates a health club for its guests. This is probably the most convenient hotel in Kansas City for runners, although it is quite expensive.

PENN VALLEY PARK

Liberty Memorial Park is actually a part of Penn Valley Park, covering a large area to the west. You can extend your run in this direction and follow its low-lying pathways for its ½-mile length. The park can be entered at its northern end by heading west on Pershing and then turning south onto Pennway.

LOOSE PARK

At this small, attractive park, about 3½ miles from downtown, you will find the greatest number of runners. The entrance at Wornall and 51st Street can be reached by following Broadway south from downtown. The Alameda Plaza and the Raphael Hotels, directly across the street from each other, are at Wornall and Ward Parkway, only ½ mile north of the park.

A 1-mile paved pathway loops around the mostly grassy, undulating park, with mileage markers every ¼ mile. At the start of the course you will find a water fountain and rest rooms. During the winter the path is well plowed. A large number of races are held here, but the pathway is very narrow, limiting the number of participants.

SWOPE PARK

Swope Park, one of the largest city parks in America, is located about 7 miles southeast of downtown. Although the park contains an excellent cross-country course near the zoo and Starlight Theater, many runners feel the park is too dangerous for a workout. Five years ago, a race had to be stopped due to harassment. If that turns you on, then you will be glad to know that it's a 2-mile undulating route following the tree line.

SHAWNEE MISSION PARK

Excellent road and grassy cross-country courses are available at Shawnee Mission Park at 79th Street and Bonner Road, 35 minutes by car from downtown. The perimeter of the park will give you a 5.2-mile route, for perhaps the hilliest workout in the park. The loop around the lake is 4.5 miles, and if you follow the inner roadway, the distance is 1.7 miles. Near the main entrance is a 2-mile cross-country course.

INDOOR TRACKS

The Downtown YMCA has an indoor track, 26 laps per mile.

CLUBS AND RACES

The Mid-America Masters Track and Field Association maintains a year 'round schedule of road racing and track and field. Their publication *Master-Pieces* comes out seven times a year. The members enjoy social get-togethers the second Friday evening after work each month.

The Missouri Valley AAU organizes many races through its LDR Chairman, Carl Owczarzak. These are often held at Shawnee Mission Park or at the Shawnee Mission West High School track.

The Kansas City, Kansas Track Club is a new organization founded by Rich Ayers in order to provide more local races and clinics.

The Kansas City, Missouri Parks and Recreation Department has been holding races and fun-runs.

TRADITIONAL RACES

Hospital Hill Run Quarter and Half-Marathon: Early June
Run for Your Life, 10 Kilometers: Early May

CONTACTS

Russ Niemi, MAMT and FA, 8229 Eby, Overland Park, KS 66204. (913) 967-6242.

Carl Owczarzak, 6823 West 77th Terrace, Overland Park, KS 66204. (913) 341-6864.

Rich Ayers, 2413 North 57th Terrace, Kansas City, KS 66104. (913) 287-2667.

Bill Taft, Kansas City Parks and Recreation Department, 5606 East 63rd Trafficway, Kansas City, MO 64130. (816) 523-3401.

Brad Flick, Downtown YMCA, 404 E. 10th Street, Kansas City, MO 64106. (816) 842-8920.

Loose Park, Kansas City

ST. LOUIS

Population: (met.) 2,250,000	Humidity: 67%
Elevation: 385 – 614 ft.	Av. Temperature: (Jan.) 33°F.; (July) 81°F.
Air Quality: Fair to poor	Inches of Rainfall: (Jan.) 1.9; (July) 3.7 Raindays: 106

OVERVIEW

The Missouri River empties into the Mississippi just north of this major cosmopolitan city. Eye-catching Gateway Arch reaches up from a park at the bank of the Mississippi as the river flows south past the downtown area. This very small park provides the only opportunity to run close to either river. A 5,000-meter course has been measured through downtown streets and under the Arch for an urban, trafficked route. The local YMCA sends groups of runners out on this course in the early hours before autos obstruct the roads.

Road running goes back to 1904 in St. Louis, when the city's first marathon was held during their internationally famous World's Fair. The 1,400-acre site of this exposition has now become Forest Park, a popular haven for the city's runners. Located only 4 miles west of downtown, its adjacent hotels provide visitors with convenient accommodations close to excellent running.

The St. Louis Track Club has long been an ambitious organization, and offers local runners a very busy year 'round schedule. Sometimes there are as many as two races per weekend, or even two on one day.

HOTELS

Rodeway Inn – Downtown, Chase Park Plaza, Cheshire Inn, Clayton Inn

GATEWAY ARCH
COURSE

This 5,000-meter course begins at the Rodeway Inn. It can be frustratingly busy with downtown activity unless you run before rush hour or late at night. Head north two blocks on Jefferson, and then turn right onto Olive for about 1½ miles to the Gateway Arch. Turn south along Memorial Drive for two blocks to Market Street, and follow Market for the 1½ miles back to the Inn. The YMCA is located along the course, on Locust Boulevard, seven blocks west of the Arch. Terrain is basically flat, and there are not many shade trees.

FOREST PARK

The premier running locale in St. Louis, this vast facility contains excellent bike paths and many of the city's tourist attractions. Chase Park Plaza and the Cheshire Inn are adjacent to the park, at either end. An asphalt bike path skirts the perimeter of the park for a 6.2-mile loop, and a new interior bike path can provide an additional 3 miles.

Runners meet and begin their workout at the fieldhouse next to the handball courts. From here, they usually head in a clockwise direction. Some of the sights along the way include many small ponds, which are used for fish hatcheries, playing fields, heavily wooded areas, and a golf course. Some areas that a runner might want to stop at or come back to include McDonnell Planetarium, the St. Louis Zoo, Steinberg Skating Rink, the Jewel Box Floral Conservatory, Jefferson Memorial, and the St. Louis Art Museum.

Terrain can vary greatly along the route, and some of the hills are challenging. Water fountains can be found periodically, and rest rooms are located at the fieldhouse on the north end, at the Planetarium, ½ mile beyond it, and at the zoo. The park is not considered safe at night.

SHAW PARK

Seven miles west of downtown, this park is located close to the Clayton Inn. From the Inn, run one block south to Bonhomme Avenue, and then three blocks west to the park. A loop just short of 2 miles circles close to the perimeter on a sidewalk and grass pathway. Total distance from the hotel and back measures close to 3 miles. The park is quite shady, and water fountains are available. Runners can train safely here. The area around the park is populated by a number of large corporations.

LONE ELK COUNTY PARK

This is a beautiful 405-acre preserve for a variety of animals including wild elk, bison, deer and mountain sheep. It is located about 20 miles southwest of town, and can be reached by taking I-44 west to State Route 141, then west to North Outer Road, and again west to the park. From the parking area, you can begin a hilly 4.5-mile route along the park road where pedestrians are allowed. Some hills provide 400- to 800-foot rises, and the road travels through some beautiful hardwood forests.

INDOOR TRACKS

The St. Louis YMCA has a banked, 26-laps-per-mile track.

CLUBS AND RACES

The St. Louis Track Club puts on races at least weekly throughout the year. From June through October they also have predicted time runs on Wednesdays at 5:30 P.M. in Forest Park.

TRADITIONAL RACES

Olympiad Memorial Marathon: Last Sunday in February
University City Memorial Day Run, 7 and 3 miles
Green Tree Run, 5 and 2 miles: Mid-October

CONTACTS

Jerry Kokesh, St. Louis Track Club, Marathon Sports Store, 13453 Chesterfield Plaza, Chesterfield, MO 63017. (314) 434-9577.
St. Louis YMCA, 1528 Locust Boulevard, St. Louis, MO 63104. (314) 436-4100.

BOZEMAN

Population: 22,903	Humidity: Low
Elevation: 4,793 ft.	Av. Temperature: Bozeman is reputed to have two seasons—winter and the Fourth of July. (Jan.) 17°F.; (July) 56°F.
Air Quality: Good	Inches of Rainfall: (Jan.) 2.0; (July) 2.9 Raindays: Not available

OVERVIEW

Bozeman sits in a small valley completely surrounded by mountains averaging 9,000 feet at their peaks. This is a wilderness area offering its own particular dangers. At a local race last year, one of the participants was treed by a moose. Also, true to rural communities, dogs can be a serious nuisance, and along the road to the airport is a dog that obviously hasn't been fed in years. Another danger to look out for here is being hit by a wad of chewing tobacco juice from cowboys/cowgirls driving pickup trucks. The final warning is to avoid wooded areas during hunting season.

HOTELS

This is a small enough city to be able to stay at any downtown hotel and be close to a running course.

HYALITE LAKE TRAIL

This run is not to be missed. It's an 11-mile route that goes by five waterfalls on a pine-needle trail around a mountain lake in Hyalite Canyon. Many hawks and an eagle live along the way. Helene Knowlton recommends an early morning run here because of the interesting way the sun shines through the lodgepole pines. The trail can be reached by heading south on 19th Street for 6 miles to the left turn for Hyalite.

TOWN DUMP ROAD

Located 2 miles north of town, this dirt road is surrounded by open pastures with cattle and horses, streams, wildflowers and berry patches. Run north from town on Rouse Road, bearing right onto Bridger Drive, and then make a left at the Town Dump Road. You can run several miles through the hilly netherlands between the town and the mountains.

MSU PHYS. ED. COMPLEX

There are other runs that local runners are familiar with. There is a general meeting place midday, between 11:00 and 1:00, at the Montana State University Physical Education Complex. MSU is slightly south of the center of town, and the Phys. Ed. Complex is on top of the hill, just east of 11th and Grant.

TRACKS

The MSU Fieldhouse has a dirt track, 10 laps per mile. The University also has an outdoor track.

CLUBS AND FUN-RUNS

With one of the fanciest names in the west, the Big Sky Wind Drinkers carry on an active schedule of fun-runs and races. Every Wednesday night when it's not snowing, a group runs at the MSU track.

TRADITIONAL RACES
Froze Noze Run, 5.3 miles: February
Colter Run ("7 miles of pure hell"): September
Bank Run, 7 miles: October
Up to Bridger Run, 3, 7, 10, 19 miles: November

CONTACT
Helene Knowlton, P.O. Box 1686, Bozeman, MT 59715. (406) 586-3732.

LINCOLN

Population: 171,000	Humidity: Not available
Elevation: 1,167 ft.	Av. Temperature: (Jan.) 24°F.; (July) 77°F.
Air Quality: Fair	Inches of Rainfall: (Jan.) .6; (July) 3.9 Raindays: 96

OVERVIEW
Runners here are really appreciated. A mixture of college town and the state capital, Lincoln has an active, aware population. Enthusiasm runs deep at races, when large audiences turn out to cheer on the competitors.

With a varied terrain and the Great Plains wind, local running can be challenging. There are good courses available year 'round with shady summer runs, well-plowed winter roads, and a 7-lap-per-mile indoor track.

HOTELS
Clayton House, Lincoln Hilton

OAK LAKE ROUTE
For a flat 3½- to 4-mile run from downtown, start at your hotel and run north on 10th Street over the Viaduct. On the other side, turn left at Charleston (at traffic light) and follow Charleston until you see Oak Lake on your right. Run around the two connecting lakes, and return on Charleston to 10th and back to downtown. For additional mileage, you can run extra loops of the lakes at 1½ miles per loop. Much of the footing around the lakes is on grass. A water fountain and rest room are available at the lake. Beware of traffic on 10th Street.

WILDERNESS PARK
For a longer run, go south on 7th or 8th for about 1½ miles to South Street. Go right, and when the road forks, go left. This brings you to Van Dorn Street. Cross the little bridge and go left on 1st Street (a gravel road). In about ¼ of a mile you will come to the northern edge of Wilderness Park. At this point you will have already run about 2½ to 3 miles.

The park is flat and its proportions are about 1 mile by 11 miles. There are many dirt trails for high mileage, but there is a possibility of losing your way. Trail markers showing north and south will help you maintain your direction.

PIONEERS PARK
If you use the same route to Wilderness Park, but continue on Van Dorn for an additional 2 miles, you will reach Pioneers Park. There is a 4-mile loop here over a very hilly road.

TRACKS
The hotels are convenient to the University of Nebraska Campus, where you will find a good outdoor track. A lot of runners socialize here. Under the football stadium is an old indoor track, 7 laps per mile. Enter at the door by the northeast corner of the fieldhouse.

RACES AND FUN-RUNS	The Lincoln Track Club has frequent races, mostly on Sundays. A group of runners leaves the Downtown YMCA in the early morning and at noon for daily runs.
TRADITIONAL RACES	Statehood Day, 10 miles: February Lincoln Marathon: May Buffalo Run, 5 miles: September
CONTACTS	Downtown YMCA, 139 North 11th Street, Lincoln, NE 68508. (402) 475-9622. Tim Lewis, Lincoln Track Club, 2900 John Avenue, Lincoln, NE 68502. (402) 489-4130.

OMAHA

Population: (met.) 580,000	Humidity: 68%
Elevation: 960 – 1,272 ft.	Av. Temperature: (Jan.) 23°F.; (July) 77°F.
Air Quality: Fair	Inches of Rainfall: (Jan.) .8; (July) 3.7 Raindays: 98

OVERVIEW

Although Omaha is a plains city with clean, wide open spaces, the climate makes it difficult for running; the winds here are quite strong. Local runners will tell you that there is nothing to stop the winds blowing in from Canada over the 550 miles from the border except barbed wire and fence posts. This gives winter an extra chill. Summers can be extremely hot and humid, with coolness only in the early morning. Some areas are flat, but much of the city has long, rolling hills.

Omaha Airport, only 3½ miles from downtown, offers the prettiest running courses. Carter Lake, right across the road, and the nearby Missouri River attract many local runners. With its close proximity to town, the airport is perhaps the best place to stay.

HOTELS

Ramada Inn – Airport, Airport Inn, Hilton Hotel, Holiday Inn – I-80, Ramada Inn – I-80, Howard Johnson's, Granada Royale Hometel

CARTER LAKE

The Hilton, downtown at 16th Street and Dodge Street next to the Convention Center, is close to the river and the road to the airport. Go out the back door of the Hilton and head east down Capitol Avenue for ⅓ mile to Abbott Drive. Run over the bridge, and then stay on the shoulder of Abbott for 2.4 miles to Locust Avenue. Ramada Inn will be on your right and Kiwanis Park will be on your left. Carter Lake is here, and the shoreline parallels Abbott Drive. A dirt road follows along the shore to the airport entrance. It is 3.5 miles to this point from downtown. The Airport Inn is located here.

To extend your mileage, a loop around the lake is just over 3 miles. The entire course is flat with some areas close to the lake in shade. Part of the loop around the lake lies in Iowa. Water and rest rooms can be found at the north end of the lake.

AIRPORT TO MISSOURI RIVER

At the airport entrance, if you head away from town, you will find an enjoyable route to the Missouri River. The first mile of the course, on Pershing Drive, will eventually contain a city-kept jogging trail. After this, you can run on the road, shoulder, or in roadside parks or meadows. When you reach the "OPPD" sign you will have gone 3.3 miles. Up to this point, the course is flat with little shade, but the terrain and shade change for the better as you continue on.

At about 3.9 miles you will be alongside the Missouri River dividing Nebraska and Iowa. At 4.4 miles you will see a "Florence Plant" sign, and at 5.4 miles is the "Oakridge Road" sign. The only water and rest rooms can be found at the first ½ mile from the airport.

72ND STREET AND
GROVER

Many travelers stay in an area west of town just north of I-80 at 72nd Street and Grover. This area is distinguished solely by a close grouping of motels. It has nothing else to offer. The Holiday Inn, Ramada Inn and Howard Johnson's form the complex, with the Granada Royale Hometel ½ mile north on 72nd Street.

A good 4½-mile hilly loop can be run from these accommodations. Starting on Grover at 72nd Street, head east down Grover for .9 miles, taking a left to go north on 60th Street. After crossing Center Street you will be on a long, steep hill for ⅓ mile before reaching the Elmwood Park entrance at 60th and Leavenworth Avenue. To this point it's 2 miles. Turn left going through the park (keeping to your left) and at the exit, take a right onto Pacific Street at 2.8 miles. After .4 miles, take a left onto 72nd Street, going south for the final 1.4 miles.

ELMWOOD PARK

The most popular running spot in town is at Elmwood Park. From downtown, it's about 5 miles out Dodge Street to 60th Street. A roadway cuts through the middle of the park, with a golf course on either side. You will see a chain-link fence lining the road on both sides. This was built as a tribute to runners by the city to express its concern over the runner's use of the city's links. Briefly, it was golfers, yes, runners, no. Since the runners' taxes were paying for the golfers' exclusivity, a court battle ensued and runners are now tolerated on the course.

The Omaha RRC meets at the big tree on the northside golf course, next to the parking lot. If you are driving, the parking lot will be filled to capacity weekdays and Friday evenings. The preferred route is around the 1-mile perimeter of the northside course. Hills and shade are plentiful. Rest rooms can be found along the course, but the only water fountain is at the parking lot.

MEMORIAL PARK

Across Dodge Street from Elmwood Park is Memorial Park. The grass has very bad footing so it is suggested that you stay on the perimeter walkway. There is not much shade, and no water for the 1.8-mile loop.

TRACKS

Adjacent to Elmwood Park at Dodge Street is the University of Nebraska at Omaha Fieldhouse. An outdoor ¼-mile, all-weather track is open to all runners from sunup to sundown. You can park in the lot at the Fieldhouse, and bring a towel as showers are available.

During winter months you can use the indoor 10-laps-per-mile track during available hours. Call ahead to check on the schedule.

The Downtown YMCA has a poor-quality, 30-laps-per-mile indoor track.

CLUBS, FUN-RUNS
AND RACES

The Plains Track Club holds a fun-run every other Sunday in Elmwood Park at 3:00 P.M. A wide variety of races are put on throughout the year. The Omaha Pacers meet Saturdays at 9:00 A.M. for a group run starting at Hayworth Park. They run to the Fontenelle Forest area along Belleview Boulevard.

TRADITIONAL RACES

Nike United 10-Kilometer: Third Saturday in May
Omaha River Run, 15 kilometers: Third Sunday in June
Omaha Marathon: First Sunday in August

Dick McMahon, Director, Plains Track Club, Box 14003, West Omaha Station, Omaha, NE 68124. (402) 289-3182.

Sport Tred, 13212 West Center Street, Omaha, NE 68144. (402) 322-8645.

UNO Athletic Department, (402) 554-2305.

LAS VEGAS

Population: (met.) 346,000	Humidity: 27%
Elevation: 2,016 ft.	Av. Temperature: (Jan.) 40.9°F.; (July) 91.7°F.
Air Quality: Fair	Inches of Rainfall: (Jan.) .7; (July) .5 Raindays: 23

OVERVIEW

If you think Las Vegas has some secret, terrific, great place to run, you should correct that thought. The one thing runners here have going for them is vast open space to get away from congested areas. The flat, busy streets turn quickly to desert as you aim out of town. Numerous golf courses offer possibilities, although local runners favor a route to the west of town near Sunset Park. Many runners also use the track and ball fields at the University of Nevada, Las Vegas.

Summer heat is intense, and mileage should be limited during the hot months.

HOTELS

Most of the hotels are on Las Vegas Boulevard South ("The Strip")

SUNSET ROAD

This flat road stretches 5 miles from The Strip to Sunset Park. Check the mileage markers on your right at each mile. The first mile or two, depending on which hotel you start from, runs along The Strip, and after that you'll see mostly desert with little traffic and no dogs. You will find water only at the park. Johnny Clark, from the local running store, did a survey and found that three out of every four camels like this course.

DUNES HOTEL GOLF COURSE

The Dunes Hotel tolerates runners using the golf course very early in the morning. A 2-mile loop can be run here. Water is available.

24-MILE DESERT RUN

Not a very scenic course, this 24-mile out-and-back bicycle path remains obstacle-free. You can have your choice of ¼- or ⅕-mile markers. Located several miles outside of town, you can get there by taking the Las Vegas Freeway to the West Charleston exit. Drive west on Charleston until you come to Rainbow Boulevard. There is a 7-Eleven store where you can park your car.

SUNSET PARK

Located at the far end of the Sunset Road course, this park has a 1.1-mile loop along its roadway. A 2-mile loop involves jumping over several fences. Shade is found under occasional large trees, and water and rest rooms prevail.

UNIVERSITY TRACK

About 1½ miles from The Strip, via Flamingo Road, you will come upon the University of Nevada, Las Vegas, track. This ¼-mile Tartan surface sits below a grassy bank that can be used for some hill training. A fence surrounds grassy fields and running alongside the fence will provide you with a .45-mile course.

Showers are available at the university gym after your run over these shadeless routes.

RACES

The Las Vegas Track Club holds races every Saturday, and from April to October, Tuesday night races.

TRADITIONAL RACES

Las Vegas Marathon: First Sunday in February
Las Vegas Mini-Marathon, 13.1 miles: November

CONTACTS

Johnny J. Clark, The Running Store, 602 South Maryland Parkway, Las Vegas, NV 89101. (702) 382-3496.
Las Vegas Track Club, Tony Gerardi, 5020 Lancaster Drive, Las Vegas, NV 89120. (702) 451-4060.

CONCORD

Population: 30,000	Humidity: 71%
Elevation: 342 ft.	Av. Temperature: (Jan.) 20.6°F.; (July) 69.7°F.
Air Quality: Fair	Inches of Rainfall: (Jan.) 2.67; (July) 3.14 Raindays: 120

OVERVIEW

This busy running town is loaded with challenging hills. The state capital, located in the southern part of the state, is typical of New England, with a plethora of races that can be found every weekend within short traveling time.

Many runners can be found in White's Park, only 1 mile west of town. Just beyond the park, Memorial Field is the starting point for a number of street routes. Running on streets and sidewalks is common here, and there are no problems with dogs on suggested courses.

The Turtletown Athletic Club has taken its name from a section of town that was given the nickname in the nineteenth century. Club members figure it will give them an edge against unsuspecting competitors.

HOTEL

Ramada Inn

WHITE'S PARK

From the Ramada, go west on Route 4 (Bridge-Center Street). Head uphill until you crest the hill, then you will see a park to your right on the downhill side. The park is 1 mile from the motel via sidewalk. It contains a 2.1-mile grass and gravel trail over flat and hilly terrain. There is good shade, and water is available.

MEMORIAL FIELD ROUTE

To reach the field, continue on the road from the motel, past White's Park, to a five-way intersection. Turn left to the end of the road, then turn right. The high school will be on your right when you make a left onto Fruit Street; continue straight to the field. This ½-mile route from the park to the field is very hilly.

For a 5-mile loop, run south across the field to a right turn on Clinton Street. Run all the way uphill on the pale-blue bike path shoulder to the blinking lights at the top. This will be 2 miles from the start. From here, the course is all flat or downhill. Turn right on Silk Farm Road for close to a mile before it ends. Turn right onto Dunbarton Road, and follow it through the grounds of St. Paul's School. Drinking water is in the parking lot at the gym. Take Dunbarton until it ends, and turn right on the Pleasant Street Extension until you reach the gas station at the high school. Turn right on Fruit Street, which will bring you back to the field.

OUTDOOR TRACKS

Memorial Field has a ¼-mile, all-weather track. St. Paul's School has a cinder, 3-laps-per-mile track.

INDOOR TRACKS	The downtown YMCA does not have a track, but a lot of runners use the gym floor which measures 30 laps per mile.
CLUBS, FUN-RUNS AND RACES	The Turtletown AC holds fun-runs during the summer at Memorial Field at 5:30 P.M. on Tuesdays and Thursdays. During cooler months, fun-runs are held on Sunday mornings. The club also schedules races.
TRADITIONAL RACES	Mid-July 5-Mile Race Turtletown AC 20-Kilometer and 5-Kilometer Run: Mid-August Domes Shadow 10-Kilometer (Women only): September
CONTACTS	The Long Run, 138 North Main, Concord, NH 03301. (603) 225-5605. Concord YMCA, 15 North State Street, Concord, NH 03301. (603) 224-5351.

Atlantic City

Population: 50,000 plus	Humidity: 71%
Elevation: 0– 15 ft.	Av. Temperature: (Jan.) 32.7°F.; (July) 75.1°F.
Air Quality: Fair	Inches of Rainfall: (Jan.) 3.56; (July) 4.36 Raindays: 112

OVERVIEW

Atlantic City lies on the northern end of Absecon Island along the southern Jersey shore. Now that gambling is in here, the explosive growth of the resident as well as the tourist population will pour large numbers of runners onto the famous Atlantic City Boardwalk. This influx should not crowd anyone, as the boardwalk is 60 feet wide. An active group of "Boardwalk Runners" provide seasonal running events.

Although northeastern winters can be uncomfortable, the seaside climate is generally more moderate than inland. In summer, this moderation again prevails to offer cooler temperatures.

HOTELS

Any hotel near the ocean.

BOARDWALK

Close to an ideal course, the only items lacking here are good shade and hills. The boardwalk extends for 5¾ miles from the northern tip of the island to below the city of Ventnor. Mileage markers have been stenciled onto the boardwalk at ½-mile intervals. The major start-off point in Atlantic City is Albany Avenue. A 10-mile out-and-back course can be run from the northern inlet south to Cornwall Avenue in Ventnor. Night lighting makes evening runs very pleasurable. Water and rest rooms are available along the route.

BEACHFRONT

Of course there is always beach running. Round trip on the island is approximately 17 miles.

CLUBS AND FUN-RUNS

The Boardwalk Runners hold fun-runs in the evenings during the summer: Thursdays at 7:00 P.M. at Albany Avenue in Atlantic City, and Mondays at 7:00 P.M. and Sundays at 10:00 P.M. at Cornwall Avenue in Ventnor.

TRADITIONAL RACES

Atlantic City Marathon: September
Absecon Island Beach & Boardwalk, 16.6 miles: Late September
St. Patrick's 20-Kilometer: March

CONTACT

Paul Purcell, Boardwalk Runners, 103 South Pembroke Avenue, Margate, NJ 08402. (609) 822-2223.

NEWARK

Population: 350,000	Humidity: 66%
Elevation: 0–258 ft.	Av. Temperature: (Jan.) 31°F.; (July) 76°F.
Air Quality: Fair to poor	Inches of Rainfall: (Jan.) 2.9; (July) 4 Raindays: 122

OVERVIEW

Newark would not seem a likely place to find a lot of runners—its urban environment does not provide the greatest incentive for challenging the rolling terrain. Fortunately, Mayor Kenneth Gibson is a marathon runner who has done much to promote the sport in his city. Each year, the Newark Distance Run draws a large and competitive field.

Located only 30 minutes from New York City, Newark has a couple of popular parks located near its downtown area. There are no hotels close to these parks, and a 1¾-to-2-mile run on city streets is necessary to reach them. Many runners use the streets, including the mayor, but once you get to the parks, excellent training facilities are available.

Running is active in the suburban areas and many races are held, especially if you include the New York City area as well. No clubs have been organized within the city, but close to town, the elite New Jersey Athletic Attic runs out of Willowbrook Mall in Wayne. Tom Fleming, the world-class marathoner, trains at Cedar Grove Reservoir, only 10 to 12 miles northwest of Newark.

HOTELS

Robert Treat Hotel, Gateway Downtown Motor Inn

BRANCH BROOK PARK

Located 1¾ miles northwest of downtown, this park must be reached via city streets. One way to get there, although indirect, would be to run the Newark Distance Run 12-mile course. The course begins at the southwest corner of Military Park. Head south, on Broad Street, to Lincoln Park, then left around the park and back to the starting point at the 2¼-mile mark.

Go north on Broad Street to Bloomfield Avenue and turn left (west) uphill to Branch Brook Park at the 4-mile mark. Make a right in front of the park, going north on Lake Street for one block, and then enter the park. Make a right on the park road and run to Mill Street at the 6-mile mark. Turn right, go under two overpasses, and make a left onto a dead-end road. Go up the road ¼ mile, and turn around and make a right at Mill Street.

When you get back to the Park Road, make a half-left in order to be on the right side of the ball fields. When you come to a triple-fork (at the 9-mile mark), stay right, going under the Bloomfield Avenue Bridge, and at the next triple-fork, take the center road onto Park Avenue, and then after 100 yards, turn north onto Lake Street (10-mile mark) and run to Bloomfield Avenue. From here, it is the same route back to Military Park for the last 1¾ miles.

If you do not wish to run the entire course, and would prefer to put more mileage on in the park, you can utilize the different loops available. The park is basically flat and shaded, and a 2.2-mile dirt and gravel path can be found close to the park road. This makes an extended loop around the ball fields. For a 4.5-mile loop, run on the park road going further west around the lake. An adequate number of water fountains and rest rooms are available.

WEEQUAHIC PARK — This park is located about 2 miles south of downtown, and about 1½ miles south of the Gateway Inn. Its challenging hills and excellent shade make it a favorite among local runners. A 2¼-mile dirt road circles around a pretty lake; and a 2½-mile paved road stays close to the perimeter of the park. An old racetrack provides a ½-mile grass loop, bordered by a blacktop track. Water fountains and rest rooms can be found at the playgrounds and in the stadium.

CEDAR GROVE RESERVOIR — Ten to 12 miles northwest of town, this reservoir has a 2.35-mile paved circumferential road. It is mostly flat, and mostly shaded. No water or rest rooms are available.

INDOOR TRACKS — Seton Hall University, about 15 minutes north on South Orange Avenue, has an old, wooden, 11-laps-per-mile banked track which is not officially open to the public. Local runners do wander in, though.

CLUBS AND RACES — The Central Jersey Road Runners Club holds weekly races at Cedar Grove Reservoir Sunday mornings at 10:00 A.M., and, when daylight prevails, at 6:45 on Wednesday evenings. North of Newark, the North Jersey Masters Track and Field Club is mostly a competitive team, and they hold one or two races a year. Closer to New York, in Jersey City, the Warren Street Social and Athletic Club meets at Shannon's Bar. They are a rip-roaring competitive club that enjoys a good time. Its two leaders, Hugh Sweeney and Paul Fetscher, have turned many a quiet race into quite a happening!

TRADITIONAL RACES — Newark Distance Run, 12 and 4 miles: February
Ridgewood 10- and 5-Kilometer: Memorial Day

CONTACTS — Richard Welch, 819 South 19th Street, Newark, NJ 07108. (201) 371-4926.
John Fitzgerald, Department of Recreation and Parks, 2 Cedar Street, Newark, NJ 07102.
James Nicholas, Central Jersey RRC, 86 East Shore Road, Denville, NJ 07834.
Manfred D'Elia, North Jersey Masters Track and Field Club, 144 Spencer Place, Ridgewood, NJ 07450.
Hugh Sweeney, Warren Street Social and Athletic Club, 212 Warren Street, Jersey City, NJ. (201) 332-8480, 344-6355 (work).

TRENTON

Population: 105,000	Humidity: Not available
Elevation: 55 ft.	Av. Temperature: (Jan.) 32°F.; (July) 76°F.
Air Quality: Fair to poor	Inches of Rainfall: (Jan.) 2.8; (July) 4.7 Raindays: 121

OVERVIEW

The Delaware River runs along the southern edge of Trenton, separating it from neighboring Pennsylvania. Although it is the state capital, the city is quite small, and not very much running is done in the downtown area. Many people run in their suburban neighborhoods, and Philadelphia, only 20 miles to the south, attracts Trentonians to its numerous running events.

A new running path has been installed in downtown Trenton, between the river and the highway, to take advantage of the best unobstructed route. Up the river to the northwest, a park surrounds the place where Washington crossed the Delaware to attack the British-held town. Now runners cross the Delaware on pedestrian bridges to attack the miles of roads in the park on each side of the river.

HOTEL

Inn of Trenton

"JOHN FITCHWAY"—ROUTE 29

The Inn is located on the corner of Calhoun and East State streets, adjacent to Route 29. Across Route 29, along the river, a new "Fitness Trail" has been built, measuring 5 miles, one way. It is mostly blacktop with some grass alongside, and the predominantly flat terrain receives cover from adequate shade.

Popularly known as the "John Fitchway," this course gets most attention during the day, as night running is not considered safe. Mileage markers and water fountains add to the route's attractiveness.

CADWALDER PARK

About 8 miles to the south, this popular park has many runners traveling over its roadway. There are also many paths to wander around. Terrain is varied and shade is plentiful. The park is surrounded by a rough neighborhood, so it would not be a good place to run at night.

WASHINGTON CROSSING STATE PARK

Take Route 29 northwest to Lambertville and follow signs to the park, which is open until 6:00 P.M. weekdays, and 9:00 P.M. weekends. There are no particular routes here, and paths go back and forth along both sides of the river. The park's 783 acres allow for plenty of mileage. Terrain is varied, and there are numerous water fountains and rest rooms.

INDOOR TRACK

The YMCA has a 29-laps-per-mile track.

CLUBS   No clubs exist at the present time.

TRADITIONAL RACES   Princeton Half-Marathon: September
Run for Freedom Race, 12 and 3.5 miles: Early October
Lawrence Lions Club Run for Fun, 5 and 1 miles: Mid-October

CONTACT   Trenton YMCA, 2 South Clinton Avenue, Trenton, NJ 08609. (609) 392-5168.

Albuquerque

Population: (met.) 400,000	Humidity: 42%
Elevation: 5,314 ft.	Av. Temperature: (Jan.) 35.2°F.; (July) 78.7°F.
Air Quality: Fair	Inches of Rainfall: (Jan.) .3; (July) 1.4 Raindays: 58

OVERVIEW

The Rio Grande flows through this high altitude city, providing many miles of flat riverside trails. Dry air can keep you comfortable in all seasons, though dehydration is a threat with little or no water available on any of the popular routes. In spring, small dust storms might present a temporary deterrent, if not just a distraction.

The Sandia Mountains, northeast of town, rise up over 10,000 feet, creating some interesting foothill runs, and a challenging course up the La Luz Trail to the summit of Sandia Mountain. Without having to run up the mountain, you can enjoy running along the crest by taking the Tramway to Sandia Peak. The extreme altitude and moderate hills will provide excellent training. Your only company might be some quiet hang-gliders as you look out 80 to 90 miles across the desert.

Back in town, the University of New Mexico has two golf courses; the north campus course has a popular route around its perimeter. The track at University Arena has been under controversy for some time. During the summer of 1978, Lionel Ortega, winner of the Nike Marathon, was found working out on the track, and summarily handcuffed and toted off to jail. Even though the trespassing charges were dropped, an amicable agreement with local runners for use of the track has yet to be worked out.

HOTELS

Best Western Four Seasons Motor Inn, Howard Johnson's—Midtown, Airport Marina Hotel

NORTH CAMPUS GOLF COURSE

From Howard Johnson's, run ¾ of a mile east. The medical buildings next to the course will be in sight. From the Four Seasons, run south on Carlisle for two blocks to a right turn onto Constitution, which will take you to the course after about 1¼ miles.

A 2-mile loop circles the perimeter of the course on a dirt trail. Orange poles have been set up to guide you over the mostly flat route. A shorter, unmarked variation runs on the inside of the law school campus, and meets up with some hilly terrain. Many runners work out here at night, as the course is partially lit by outside streets.

RIO GRANDE RIVER

The Rio Grande flows north-south about 1½ miles west of downtown. Take

Central Avenue all the way to the bridge. Along the riverbank, you will find a levee with dirt footing that goes 9 miles north to Corales Bridge. Further back from the river, a paved bicycle trail begins in Kit Carson Park, and parallels the river for 7 miles north through landscaped terrain with cottonwood trees.

SANDIA FOOTHILLS

About 6 to 7 miles northeast of town, the Sandia East and West Developments have miles of hilly, traffic-free roads to wander over. Tramway Boulevard runs parallel to Sandia Mountain, providing rolling terrain, while dirt roads lead off into hilly neighborhoods. Take Montgomery Boulevard from town to Tramway Boulevard, where you can park along the road. If you run 5 miles north on the Boulevard, you will come to a sign directing you to Juan Tabo Picnic Grounds, 2 miles to the east.

LA LUZ TRAIL

Beginning at Juan Tabo Picnic Grounds, this dirt trail rises 3,500 feet on a 7-mile route to the top of Sandia Mountain. Footing is safe, and the trail is well marked. You can either run down or take the Tramway. A restaurant at the summit can provide sustenance after you run.

SANDIA CREST RUN

From the Tram Station at the top of the mountain, run north along the crest to Delaqua Overlook, 3 miles away, and then doubleback on the trail just below the crest (the top part of the La Luz Trail) for a 7-mile run. The trail will lead you through many stands of pine trees on a spongy, humus-type of footing. There are two moderate hills along the crest, one 1 mile and the other ¾ of a mile in length. Altitude will remain just over 10,000 feet. Looking north, you will be able to see the southernmost part of the Colorado Mountains.

AIRPORT, DESERT RUN

From the Airport Marina Hotel, the desert spreads out to the west. Many dirt roads and open country are available for free running. Footing can be treacherous on the rocky ground. It is unadvisable to run here at night, as it is possible to become lost or to turn an ankle and be stranded.

CLUBS, FUN-RUNS AND RACES

The New Mexico Track Club puts on a number of races during the year, and the Parks and Recreation Department holds a series of weekly races in the summer.

Dr. Otto Appenzeller has a weekly clinic and fun-run every Sunday at 8:00 A.M., at the North Campus Golf Course. At 9:00 A.M., the New Mexico Track Club meets there for group runs.

TRADITIONAL RACES

La Luz Trail Race, 7.5 miles: Early August
New Mexico Track Club, 10 miles: End of August
New Mexico Heart Institute, 4 miles: Early October
Tour of Albuquerque Marathon: October

CONTACTS

Gilbert Duran, New Mexico Track Club, Box 4071, Albuquerque, NM 87106. (505) 268-7682.
Ron Garcia, Parks and Recreation Department, 1801 Fourth, N.W., Albuquerque, NM 87102. (505) 766-7427.

SANTA FE

Population: 55,000	Humidity: 52%
Elevation: 6,990 ft.	Av. Temperature: (Jan.) 30°F.; (July) 70°F.
Air Quality: Fair	Inches of Rainfall: (Jan.) .7; (July) 2.4 Raindays: 38

OVERVIEW

This colorful area of the old southwest retains its historic flavor, providing scenic and interesting runs. The downtown area, with its famous Plaza, has excellent and convenient hotels for runs to the north and east into sparsely populated canyons. Routes south and west have too much traffic for the frequent use of public roads by local runners. Leash laws are not strictly enforced, and the more populated the area, the more dogs you have to fight off.

Altitude in Santa Fe of nearly 7,000 feet will challenge the heartiest runners, and good hills will make running a cinch when you get down to lower elevations. Dry air provides comfortable running whatever the temperature, but be careful about dehydration in warm weather. The most popular running course heads out the Old Santa Fe Trail, still a dirt road after it fell into disuse over 100 years ago.

HOTELS

La Fonda Hotel, Santa Fe Hilton, Garrett's Desert Inn, La Posada, Best Western Inn at Loretto

ROUTE EAST FROM DOWNTOWN

Starting from the above downtown hotels, run east along either Palace Avenue or Alameda Street next to the Santa Fe River. Few cars use these roads and you will cross only a few intersections. Palace Avenue curves south and crosses Alameda Street just before it reaches Canyon Road. Thus, you will end up on Canyon Road after about 2 miles along either of these streets. They both have some shade, although Palace Avenue is the shadier. A slight incline accompanies the 2 miles.

From the 2-mile point, continue east along Canyon Road. For the next 1½ miles, the route tours through a scenic and quaint part of town. This is a tourist area of little shops and restaurants. During evenings, especially in summer, there will be some traffic on this part of the route.

As the road curves south, you will come to Upper Canyon Road, where you can take a detour, going left up into the canyon along a slight incline for 1½ miles until you hit a dirt road. It is best to turn back here, as there are some bothersome dogs for the short distance that the road continues ahead.

Returning to Canyon Road and continuing south, the road turns into Camino Cabra for the most difficult part of the run. It is a 440-foot rise over a 1-mile distance, and there is no shade. Once you get to the top, you can go downhill for a while.

Once over the hill, the road curves west and becomes Camino Cruz Blanca. In about ½ mile you will reach the track at St. John's College. Of course you could have turned back anywhere along the way, but if you have come this far, you will have gone about 5 miles from the start.

You can head back along an easier, more direct route: 300 yards west of the track, turn north onto Camino Monte del Sol, and run downhill for about 1½ miles. Turn left onto a beautiful, very shady street called Acequia Madre. This is a favorite street for many local runners. Follow it for almost a mile to Paseo de Peralta. Turn right on the paseo and head north across the Santa Fe River to

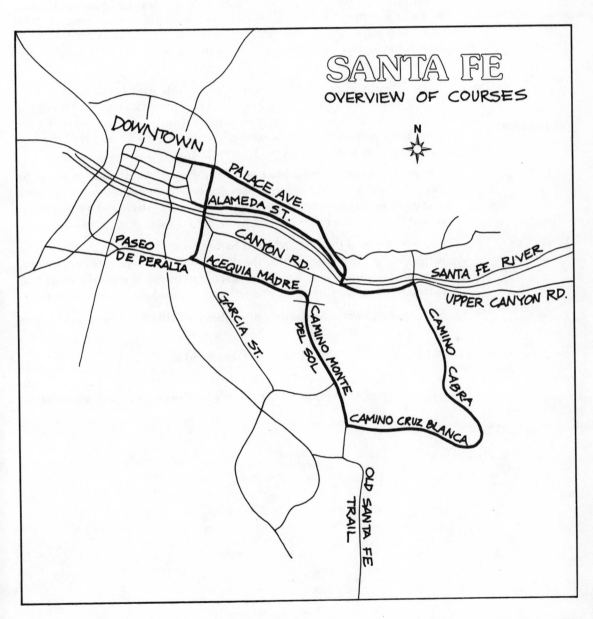

SANTA FE
OVERVIEW OF COURSES

N

DOWNTOWN
PALACE AVE.
ALAMEDA ST.
CANYON RD.
PASEO DE PERALTA
ACEQUIA MADRE
SANTA FE RIVER
UPPER CANYON RD.
GARCIA ST.
CAMINO MONTE DEL SOL
CAMINO CABRA
CAMINO CRUZ BLANCA
OLD SANTA FE TRAIL

Alameda Street or Palace Avenue. You will be 1 mile east of the start along either of these streets.

Water fountains are not easy to come by in Santa Fe. Local runners are known to carry water, or to deposit a cache somewhere along the road.

OLD SANTA FE TRAIL

To run this course, most people meet at the track at St. John's College. From here it is less than ½ mile to the trail. Head west on Camino Cruz Blanca for 300 yards to a left turn on Camino Monte del Sol. Then after ¼ mile you will arrive at the trail.

The first ¼ mile (heading south) is paved, but from there on the footing is dirt. Many juniper trees line the course, but they are too small to provide a lot of shade. Hills persist along the route, but their difficulty varies. If you run to the power plant and back to the track, the distance is a measured 5 miles. The trail goes on for many miles. At the 4-mile point, you will cross a bridge, beyond which you will face a 1½-mile hill. For longer runs, there are many interesting detours to take through villages and along riverbeds. Local runners will be glad to show you the way.

BISHOP LODGE ROAD

Running north from the Plaza in downtown, this road heads right into the foothills to provide a tough, hilly workout. Many mountain trails and residential roads branch out to create a variety of courses. After ¾ of a mile, you will come upon Artist Road, which heads east up into the mountains. A 6-mile trip, one way, from here will take you to Hyde Park. It is a hard climb.

OUTDOOR TRACKS

The most popular meeting place in town, this 420-yard cinder track at St. John's College is 5 miles or less from downtown, according to the previous directions. Regardless of its poor condition and lack of shade and water, runners appreciate its proximity to the Old Santa Fe Trail and other good courses.

FUN-RUNS

Fun-runs are held the first and third Saturdays at 9:00 A.M. at the track at St. John's College. In cooler weather the time is 10:00 A.M., and in winter the runs are not held. A cross-country route is used, and distances normally range from ¼ mile to 10 miles. Runners also meet each weekend for group workouts.

CLUBS

No formal clubs exist at the time of publication, although a new club is in the process of formation.

TRADITIONAL RACES

Old Santa Fe Trail Run, 10 and 5 kilometers: Labor Day

CONTACTS

Norm Mugleston, 141 East Lupita Road, Santa Fe, NM 87501. (505) 983-2110. Dr. Barry Barr, 709 Juniper Drive, Santa Fe, NM 87501. (505) 988-2502.

ALBANY

Population: 106,500	Humidity: 70%
Elevation: 18–300 ft.	Av. Temperature: (Jan.) 24°F.; (July) 73°F.
Air Quality: Fair	Inches of Rainfall: (Jan.) 2.4; (July) 3.5 Raindays: 133

OVERVIEW

Albany, located along the Hudson and Mohawk rivers in upper New York State, is a busy port city and the capital of the state. Most of the running centers around the State University of New York at Albany (SUNY-Albany) and the adjacent New York State Office Campus, both located about 5 miles west of downtown. Bike paths are being built along the rivers and eventually will provide runners with long, scenic runs.

The city receives typical upstate weather with cold, windy winters and lots of snow.

HOTELS

Ramada Inn, Tom Sawyer Motor Inn, Albany Travelodge

SUNY–ALBANY AND NYS OFFICE CAMPUSES

The SUNY campus sits very close to the above motels. Most runners start off at the Phys. Ed. Building which can be found on the perimeter road to your left after you enter the campus. This mostly flat, 3-mile loop has a few grades, one moderately long (¼ to ½ mile, depending upon direction headed). The footing is mostly macadam road, and a side loop of not quite a mile can take you around the campus pond, where there are shaded, firm gravel paths. Water fountains and rest rooms can be found in the Phys. Ed. Building, and in the summer a water fountain is available along the track at the back of the building.

A ¼-mile bike path and/or parking lot connects SUNY with the NYS Office Campus. The perimeter road around this campus is 2 miles.

The annual Marathon consists of four laps around the two perimeter roads.

WASHINGTON PARK

In downtown Albany, this is a moderate-size park with grassy areas and roads of minimal traffic. The YMCA on Washington Avenue is adjacent to this 1½-mile perimeter course.

EMPIRE STATE PLAZA

There is a ½-mile loop around the reflecting pools in the Plaza, located in the downtown area.

MOHAWK RIVER AND SCHENECTADY BIKE TRAILS

Although the bike path is in the initial stages of construction, a couple of areas are now open. There is a 10-mile stretch from Colonie Town Park, off Route 9, to Knoll's Atomic Laboratory in Niskayuna. This trail cannot be easily reached on foot. Terrain is flat, and the trail runs along the Mohawk River through very scenic countryside.

Another stretch of the bike path begins at the Schenectady Community College in downtown Schenectady, about 15 miles from Albany. The trail heads west for about 7 miles, also along the Mohawk. A third segment will soon be built along the Hudson north from Albany.

CLUBS AND RACES   The Hudson-Mohawk Road Runners Club has bi-monthly races beginning at the SUNY-Albany Phys. Ed. Building. Race day is usually Sunday.

TRADITIONAL RACES   HMRRC Hangover Half-Marathon: January 1
Bankathon U.S. 30-Kilometer Championship: March
HMRRC Marathon: March
Troy Turkey Trot, 5 and 2.5 miles: Thanksgiving

CONTACTS   John Aronson, Hudson-Mohawk RRC, 3 Leda Lane, Guilderland, NY 12084. (518) 456-7414.

T. Bick, Math Department, Union College, Schenectady, NY 12308. (518) 370-6246 or 372-0248.

BUFFALO

Population: 400,000	Humidity: 73%
Elevation: 571–699 ft.	Av. Temperature: (Jan.) 24°F.; (July) 70°F.
Air Quality: Fair to poor	Inches of Rainfall: (Jan.) 2.9; (July) 2.9 Raindays: 165

OVERVIEW

One of the larger cities in the country, Buffalo sits at the mouth of Lake Erie along the Niagara River. The downtown section provides no unobstructed running for the 3 miles from Niagara Square, the heart of downtown, to Delaware Park, the popular running area. Unfortunately, there are no major hotels within a couple of miles of the park.

The airport appears to be the most convenient area to stay for out-the-door running. Short drives to Niagara Falls and the Canadian side of the river will bring you to some scenic runs.

Buffalo receives unusually abundant snowfalls, yet the city handles it well, and running continues all winter over well-plowed roads.

HOTELS

Hotel Statler, Holiday Inn–Midtown, Holiday Inn–International Airport, Executive Motor Inn, Howard Johnson's–Genesee Street

DELAWARE PARK

It's city street running from downtown to Delaware Park. Both the Holiday Inn and the Statler are located along Delaware Avenue, the main artery on the route to the park. Running north along Delaware from the Statler, you will reach the Holiday Inn after 1 mile. Continue north for another 1¼ miles to Gates Circle. Then head northwest for about ½ mile on Chapin Parkway to Soldiers Place (another circle), and then north on Lincoln Parkway for the final ¼ mile to the park.

The first area of the park that you will reach is the lake with a 1.2-mile loop over a mixture of grass, mud, macadam, and cinder paths. The terrain has some steep but short upgrades. On the far side of the lake, you'll reach the Meadow Road around the park golf course. One loop around the golf course will take you 1.8 miles over a choice of grass or pavement on fairly flat terrain. Meadow Road has been well plowed in winter ever since a Park Department employee took up running. Both areas of the park have rest rooms with water.

AIRPORT ROUTE

This route starts at the corner of Genesee Street and Sugg Road in front of the Holiday Inn. The Executive Motor Inn and Howard Johnson's are nearby. Head north on Sugg, bearing left onto Aero Drive under the airport runway tunnel. Then turn right on Youngs Road to Erie Community College Campus

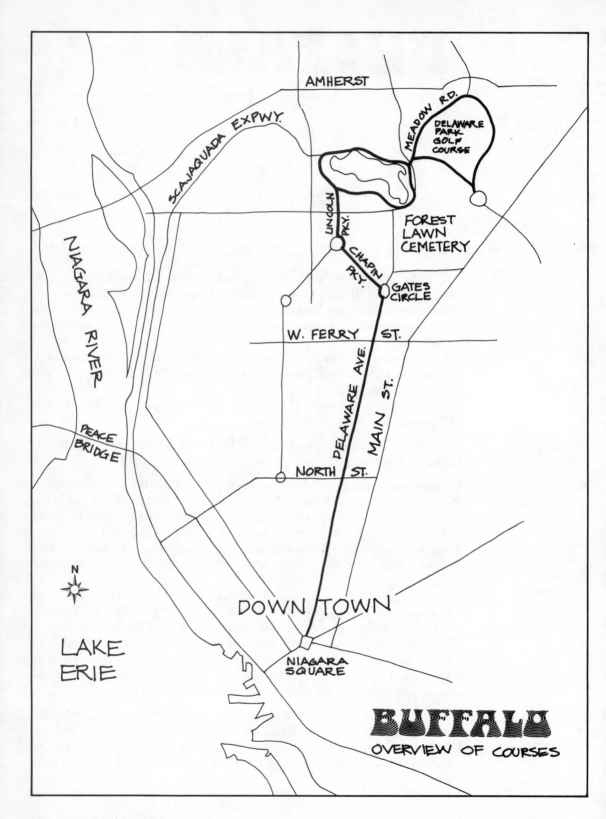

at 1¾ miles. Each loop around the campus is another 1¾ miles. The route to the campus will take you through some quiet residential neighborhoods.

NIAGARA RIVER PARKWAY

Fort Erie sits on the Canadian side of the river, looking out at the Buffalo cityscape. A run north from the fort on Niagara Parkway is part of the famous Skylon Marathon course. If you're up for it, the falls are 19.2 miles away. Back at the fort, you can take a dip in the river and replace some carbohydrates at the refreshment stand.

CLUBS AND RACES

Many local runners compete for the Belle Watling Athletic Club, which also sponsors some races, but most running events are handled by the Niagara Association AAU, with a busy schedule of races going on throughout the year. Local runners enjoy a good relationship with some of the city's taverns that sponsor a number of races, notably, Checkers Tavern, Grover's Ale House, and the Locker Room Tavern.

TRADITIONAL RACES

Blossom Festival 20-Kilometer: Mid-May
Fredonia Farm Festival 10-Kilometer: August
Skylon Marathon: Late October

CONTACT

Richard Kendall, President, Belle Watling Athletic Club, and Long Distance Chairman, Niagara Association AAU, 3925 Harlem Road, Buffalo, NY 14226. (716) 839-1996.

NEW YORK

Population: 7,420,000	Humidity: 65%
Elevation: 0–41 ft.	Av. Temperature: (Jan.) 33°F.; (July) 75°F.
Air Quality: Poor	Inches of Rainfall: (Jan.) 2.9; (July) 3.9 Raindays: 121

OVERVIEW

Many people wonder how New Yorkers do it. Out-of-towners always suggest that it must be a very difficult city to run in, what with crime, pollution, traffic, and of course the mile after mile of urban buildings and pavement. True, a lot of that does exist, but New York has some of the best and most convenient running sites that you can find in America. Central Park is the gem of the city, and from the dark hours of early morning until the late hours of night, it is flooded with runners over the myriad routes that its 840 acres provide.

In the five boroughs of New York, each one has a very popular park and plenty of other excellent runs. The sport has always had a home in this city, and many founders of the Road Runners Club of America who reside here still participate in organizing year 'round events. In the early days they were focused in the Bronx, at McCoombs Dam Park, next to Yankee Stadium. Then, in 1970, after Central Park was closed to automobiles on weekends, many races shifted to this natural facility.

Runners all around the country who competed for their college cross-country teams will remember national events held in Van Cortlandt Park in the Bronx. It remains a great cross-country training and racing site, and many Road Runners Club competitions are held there.

Manhattan is the predominant borough for courses, as well as having a huge running population. A 1.58-mile dirt loop around the reservoir in Central Park has become the most popular course, and the Engineers Gate, at 90th Street and 5th Avenue, is where most people either begin their workouts, or at least stop to chat for a while before beginning another loop around the reservoir or Park Drive.

The borough is surrounded by water, and parks or sidewalks can be found along most of its perimeter. Riverside Park, on the west side of Manhattan, begins at 72nd Street and goes north. Although the park stops occasionally, you can run north on Riverside Drive as far as the George Washington Bridge, a distance of close to 6 miles. From there runners often go over the bridge to New Jersey, or continue north on the sidewalk next to the parkway.

A good friend, Don Handal, lives in the suburbs and works in midtown. He enjoys coming into the city early in the morning for runs around the bottom of the island. Heading over to the East River, he then goes south through parks, under the Manhattan and Brooklyn bridges, through the lively Fulton Fish Market, past the South Street Seaport Museum, and down into Battery Park at the southern tip. Then he heads north beside the World Trade Center and past old piers along the Hudson River. It is an exciting way to experience New York as it wakes up to a new day.

Many competitive clubs in New York have a long history, such as the Millrose AA, with its elite ultra-marathoners. Other clubs are fairly new, including the Greater New York AA with its world-class women's team. All city clubs come under the umbrella of the New York Road Runners Club, the largest and most active running club in the world. More than twenty years old, the club has originated many of the race ideas and concepts in use today. Women only mini-marathons and the Corporate Challenge are two ideas that have recently blossomed. Of course, nothing compares to the New York City Marathon, one of the most elaborate and ambitious events in the world. Its director, Fred Lebow, has long been the creative and energetic force behind it.

HOTELS

There are probably thirty to forty good hotels within ½ mile of Central Park. The following are directly across the street from the park:
Mayflower Hotel, Barbizon-Plaza Hotel, Plaza Hotel, Marriott's Essex House, Park Lane Hotel, St. Moritz Hotel, Sherry-Netherland Hotel, Hotel Navarro, Hotel Stanhope
The U.N. Plaza Hotel, on the east side of Manhattan, supplies jogging maps to its guests.

CENTRAL PARK

In the middle of Manhattan Island, Central Park is an oasis amidst the hubbub of city life. Numerous hotels at the southern end, and miles of apartment buildings surrounding the park, are prime living spaces in great demand by runners. Extending from 59th Street along its southern border to 110th Street 2½ miles north, the park reaches from the plushest sanctum of the city into the southern quarters of Harlem.

A roadway circles through the park, measuring 6 miles, 33 yards. It is a very popular course, especially when vehicles are excluded on weekends, and during warm months on weekday evenings. In summer, cars are restricted on weekdays between 10:00 A.M. and 4:00 P.M. Terrain is constantly rolling, with major hills on the east side between 74th and 80th streets, and at the northern end. Grass and dirt footing beside the road can be helpful along the sections where it exists. Shade covers much of the course, and water fountains can be found periodically. Rest rooms are located only at the 97th Street Fieldhouse, when it is open, along the West Drive at around 79th Street, and at the 74th Street Boathouse.

A lower loop of the park, between the south end and the 72nd Street cutoff, measures 1.71 miles. An inside bike path will protect you from cars when the park is open to them. The only other crossroad is at 102nd Street; using it will eliminate a mile at the top of the park. In the same fashion, the 72nd Street cutoff eliminates a mile of the lower section.

In the middle of the park, the reservoir has a flat, 1.58-mile dirt path along the fence next to the water. Just below it is a bridle path which provides a slightly rolling loop of 1⅔ miles. Footing on the bridle path is uneven and often extremely soft. The path next to the water has little shade, whereas the bridle path is well protected from the sun.

Just south of the reservoir bridle path is the Great Oval. This paved walkway circles around several ball fields for a distance of slightly over ½ mile. Every ⅛ mile is marked, and many people use the flat loop for interval workouts. There are water fountains nearby, but shade is sparse. A narrow dirt trail skirts the inside of the walkway.

During winter, the Great Oval is normally runable when other parts of the park are snowed in.

Central Park is not as dangerous as most visitors think. Men can run alone at all hours, especially along the Park Drive, but women should run in groups, except perhaps during the busiest hours. Late at night, when cars are using the Park Drive, it might be safest to run the sidewalk loop around the outside of the park, next to the stone wall. The distance here is 6.2 miles. Terrain is flat, and during the daytime shade is abundant.

RIVERSIDE PARK

Wednesday evenings, groups leave from the West Side YMCA on 63rd Street for long runs. They start with two laps around the lower loop of Central Park, and then head up to 72nd Street where they run west on city streets for about ¾ of a mile to Riverside Park. Here they run north on the sidewalk just inside the park up to 79th Street. After crossing busy 79th Street, they can either go into the park, continuing north, or stay outside the park on the wide sidewalk. If they go into the park, the walkway soon opens up into a long, flat mall with a choice of pavement or dirt path. The sidewalk outside the park has rolling terrain.

At 95th Street, there is another road to cross, and again a choice of a flat mall in the park, or a rolling sidewalk along the outside. The sidewalk here is built with hexagonal pavement stones which are slightly convex in elevation, thus creating uneven footing. This segment of the park goes up to 120th Street, about 2½ miles north of 72nd Street. If you reach 120th Street in the park, you must climb two long flights of stairs to continue north on Riverside Drive.

From 120th Street, it is about 3 miles north to the George Washington Bridge. This part of the course is strictly sidewalk, next to Riverside Drive. Terrain varies between short, steep hills and long, gradual inclines and declines.

Much of the run lies in shade, except for intervals between park sections where there are excellent views of the Hudson River. Water fountains are frequent, but there are no rest rooms.

EAST RIVER DRIVE

On the east side of Manhattan, runners use the walkway along the East River which runs from a garage at 120th Street, south to the Heliport at 60th Street, a distance of close to 3 miles. This route has no shade, and being next to East River Drive, has a high level of exhaust fumes. However, there are good views of the river and Roosevelt Island.

At 23rd Street, the course picks up again, traveling under the highway to 19th Street, and then on a sidewalk along the river to 13th Street, at the entrance to East River Park. One loop to the bottom of the park along the river, and then back north beside the highway, measures 2½ miles. Terrain is flat, and footing is all asphalt. The pathway beside the river has clean air, due to the park separating runners from the highway. Shade is adequate, and rest rooms can be found near the tennis courts. An overpass crosses the highway at 6th Street.

Below East River Park, the route goes under a few bridges and passes the sites mentioned in the overview. From the northern entrance of East River Park to the bottom of Manhattan in Battery Park is about 4 miles.

BROOKLYN BRIDGE An exciting detour would be a run over the Brooklyn Bridge. If you are coming down the East River route, run west under the bridge to its furthest end in Manhattan. This will be right across the street from City Hall. Here you will see a sidewalk running up the middle of the bridge. Run up the sidewalk for about ¼ mile to a stairway which will put you on a wooden walkway a level above traffic. Bridge cables line the path for the mile or so distance to the Brooklyn side. Not only is the bridge a dramatic structure, but the vistas of Manhattan and the river are thrilling.

FLUSHING MEADOW PARK Flushing Meadow Park, in Queens, has twice been used as a World's Fair site. In 1939, and again in 1964, it was transformed into an elaborate city of pavilions. Now it is an attractive park with a well-groomed lake and the remaining Unisphere structure. The park can be reached from Manhattan via the Long Island Expressway. Take the Van Wyck Expressway exit south, and immediately exit from that into the parking lot at the park's boathouse.

One section of the park, south of the Long Island Expressway, contains the lake, and a section north of the Expressway contains the Unisphere. A paved bike path, walkway, and a road circle around the lake. The distance on the road measures 2¼ miles and 11 feet over fairly flat terrain. This course has been used for a 100-mile race. Almost none of the water fountains you will see here actually work. Shade is hard to find, but you can expect a cool breeze close to the lake. Rest rooms are at the boathouse at the south end of the lake.

You can extend the run into a 5-mile loop by heading over the bridge to the north section. A pathway follows the perimeter. In this part of the park, there are many working fountains.

PROSPECT PARK Located in Brooklyn, this elaborate park was designed by the same two men who designed Central Park, Frederick Olmsted and Calvert Vaux. Its well-landscaped, 526-acre site draws many local runners for daily workouts. If you follow Park Drive, which forms a loop close to the perimeter, you can run 3½ miles. The Drive is closed to vehicles on weekends, and at other times, the inside lane is reserved for runners. Two other roads cut through the park for shorter loops. Many walkways and bridle paths can be used as well.

The park has some rolling hills, but running here is not considered difficult. Water fountains can be found throughout the park, and rest rooms are located at the south corner and along the East Drive. Shade trees cover much of the route. Lockers and showers can be found near Parkside and Coney Island avenues, close to the tennis courts. The Brooklyn Botanic Gardens, across Flatbush Avenue from the park, has 50 acres of unusual flora.

Occasional races are scheduled here, and the Prospect Park Track Club uses this territory for training and club events. Often, they run on the sidewalk surrounding the exterior wall of the park, just short of 3¾ miles.

To reach Prospect Park by subway from Manhattan, take the F train to Fort Hamilton Parkway. Sit in the last car, and from the station, walk two blocks to the park.

BROOKLYN SHORELINE Brooklyn is the largest and most populated borough of New York. Its shoreline extends from Far Rockaway, on the ocean, 15 miles east to the Verrazano

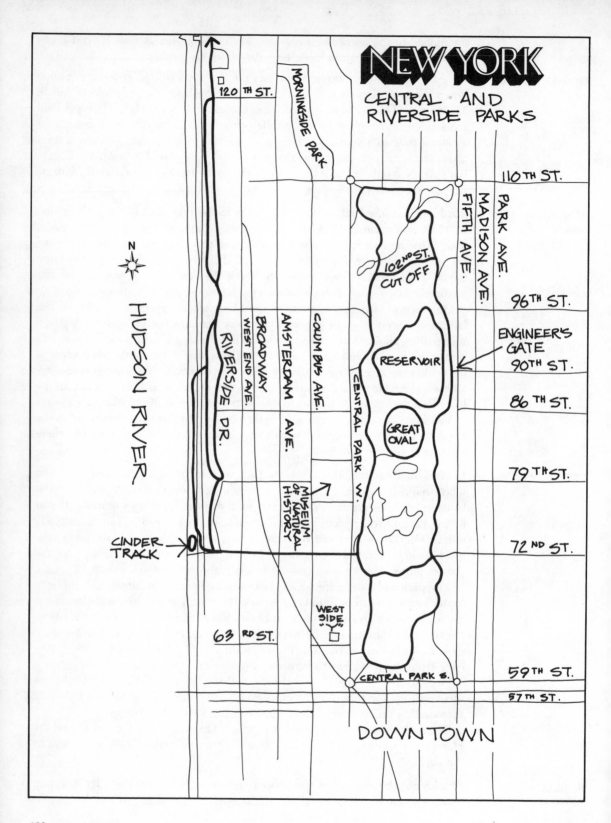

Bridge, and then north along the East River, opposite downtown Manhattan. Boardwalks and bike paths have been built along much of the shore. One exciting run follows a bike path under the Verrazano Bridge (the famous bridge at the starting point of the New York City Marathon). The route reminds me of the Promenade in San Francisco, under the Golden Gate Bridge. Both runs have great channel and city vistas.

CLOVE LAKE PARK On Staten Island, Clove Lake Park can be reached by bus #6 from the Staten Island Ferry, or by taking the Clove Road exit after crossing the Verrazano Bridge. The park is located in the northern section of the island. Its interior lake has a figure-eight bike path circling around and across it, measuring about 1.5 miles. Terrain is flat under ample shade. Water fountains and rest rooms are available.

The park also contains a wooded section with dirt trails winding over some good-sized hills. The Staten Island YMCA, on Broadway, is located just across the zoo from the park.

VAN CORTLANDT PARK Located in the Bronx, this park is an excellent cross-country facility. It can be reached from Manhattan via the Broadway subway to the end of the line, or by driving up Broadway, or by taking the West Side Highway to the Broadway South exit. You can park in the street next to the park.

A large, flat, ball field area contains part of the route around its perimeter. On the east side of the field, take the dirt path between the hill and the golf course. It soon comes out of the woods to a bridge over the highway. If you make a sharp left turn into the hill you just skirted, you will be tackling famous Cemetery Hill, which has claimed many a runner in grueling races.

Continuing over the bridge into the hilly woods in the northern section, you can loop left, returning to the bridge, and then make a sharp right, downhill to the ball field. Not counting Cemetery Hill, the course is close to 3 miles. Water fountains and rest rooms can be found to the south, at the swimming pool or the track.

OUTDOOR TRACKS In Manhattan, a ¼-mile, good-quality cinder track is located in East River Park, at about 10th Street. Riverside Park, next to the river at about 74th Street, contains a cinder 220-yard track. Traction is poor.

In the Bronx, Van Cortlandt Park has a ¼-mile cinder track, and McCoombs Dam Park, next to Yankee Stadium, also has a ¼-mile cinder track. Randall's Island, in the East River, has a ¼-mile, all-weather track in Downing Stadium. There is also a lot of good grass running around the island.

In Jamaica, Queens, St. John's University has a new 400-meter, all-weather track.

INDOOR TRACKS In Manhattan, there are many indoor, banked tracks. The West Side YMCA has a 23.6-laps-per-mile track, and the McBurney YMCA has a 32-laps-per-mile track. The 92nd Street YMHA has a 32-laps-per-mile track. The Parks and Recreation Department has three indoor facilities. At 348 East 54th Street, there is a 28-laps-per-mile wood track, and at Seventh Avenue and Varick Street, there is a 38-laps-per-mile cork track. At 135th Street, between Lenox and Fifth avenues, there ia a 36-laps-per-mile cork track. These city facilities are free, along with lockers and showers, but you must bring your own lock and towel.

In Brooklyn, the Prospect Park and the Twelve Towns YMCA's both have 32-laps-per-mile, banked tracks.

CLUBS AND RACES The New York Road Runners Club, founded in 1958, is the largest city club in the country, with over 8,000 members. It organizes many races during the year, most of them taking place in Central Park. These events are usually held on Sundays. A weekly clinic and group run is held every Saturday at 10:00 A.M. at 90th Street and Fifth Avenue, in Central Park. There is also a race-walking clinic held on Sundays at 11:00 A.M. at the same location. The club also has enrolled classes for beginners and intermediates on Tuesday and Wednesday nights. Special clinics are held in the evenings at different times during the year.

A Winter Series and Summer Speed Program account for many of the events during those seasons. The Manufacturers Hanover Corporate Challenge has become a successful Wednesday evening program, with three races during the summer.

The L'eggs Mini-Marathon, for women, and the New York City Marathon are the club's biggest productions. A newsletter, up to 64 pages, is published each quarter. Members do not compete for the club in races. Many runners in New York belong to smaller competitive clubs and run for them in New York Road Runners Club events.

Among the major clubs that compete in New York races, the Millrose AA and the Central Park Track Club have many longtime, experienced runners. The Greater New York AA, consisting of both men and women runners, has an elite women's team. The Vanderbilt, West Side, and McBurney YMCA's all have active teams. The Warren Street Social and Athletic Club has some out-

Central Park, New York City

standing runners, as well as some outstanding socializers. The East Side Track Club specializes in race-walking.

Each borough has good club representation. Staten Island has two clubs, the Staten Island Athletic Club and the North Shore Track Club. Brooklyn has the Prospect Park Track Club; Queens has the Flushing Meadow Track Club and the Cahit Pacers; and the Bronx has the Van Cortlandt Park Track Club.

TRADITIONAL RACES
Snowflake 4-Mile: Late January
Mike Hannon Memorial 20-Mile: Early February
Bob Preston Memorial 5-Mile: Early March
Manufacturers Hanover 10-Mile: Mid-March
Seven-Mile Reversible Run: Early April
Bronx Historical 5-Mile: Mid-May
Yonkers Marathon: Late May
L'eggs Mini-Marathon, 10 kilometers: Early June
Manufacturers Hanover Westchester Half-Marathon: Mid-June
Prefontaine Memorial 5-Kilometer: Mid-July
Hispanic Half-Marathon: Late August
Women's Half-Marathon: Early September
Atlantic Antic, 2.5 miles: September
NYC Marathon 20-Kilometer Tune-up: Early October
Henry Isola Memorial 4-Mile Cross-Country: Early October
NYC Marathon: Late October
Women's Perrier 4-Mile Run: Early November
Met AAU 50-Mile: Early November
RRCA Age Group Cross-Country Championships: Early November

CONTACTS
Fred Lebow, New York RRC, Box 881, F.D.R. Station, New York, NY 10022. (212) 595-3389, 595-4141.
Metropolitan Association AAU, Room 321, 15 Park Row, New York, NY 10038. (212) 267-7334.
West Side YMCA, 5 West 63rd Street, New York, NY 10023. (212) 787-4400.
McBurney YMCA, 215 West 23rd Street, New York, NY 10011. (212) 741-9216.
92nd Street YMHA, 1395 Lexington Avenue, New York, NY 10028. (212) 427-6000.
Prospect Park YMCA, 357 9th Street, Brooklyn, NY 11215. (212) 768-7100.
Twelve Towers YMCA, 570 Jamaica, Brooklyn, NY 11208. (212) 277-1600.

$\mathcal{N}$IAGARA $\mathcal{F}$AL$_L$S

Population: 80,000	Humidity: 73%
Elevation: 590 ft.	Av. Temperature: (Jan.) 24°F.; (July) 70°F.
Air Quality: Fair to poor	Inches of Rainfall: (Jan.) 2.9; (July) 2.9 Raindays: 165

OVERVIEW

About 15 miles north of Buffalo, Niagara Falls is located about midway along the Niagara River between Lake Erie and Lake Ontario. Although many tourists come here to see the falls, runners are not often aware of the potential for magnificently scenic long runs. The New York State Department of Parks and Recreation has done an excellent job of maintaining this unusual environment.

Goat Island, in the river between the falls, provides a spectacular loop around its perimeter. Passing the American falls, you can see a rainbow almost every day. The falls are not only great to look at, they also provide a refreshing spray on each lap. In winter, the perimeter pathway gets plowed, and is only closed on rare days when a cold wind hitting the spray creates a dangerous icy condition.

Parks are maintained along the river north of the falls, and a long run can include views of the whirlpool rapids, a few miles away. The downtown area abuts the falls, and motels are located at the bridge to Goat Island.

HOTELS

Holiday Inn, Ramada Inn, Red Coach Inn

GOAT ISLAND

From the above motels, run across the bridge from Buffalo Avenue onto the island. Along the perimeter, you will find a paved pathway measuring 1.6 miles. The course is generally flat, and there is not much shade. Two water fountains and two rest rooms can be found along the route.

Taking either of the two bridges off the island, turn left along the river and head up to the Observation Tower, ¼ to ½ mile away. Here you will find more water and rest rooms.

From the tower, the route goes north, under the Rainbow Bridge after ⅓ mile, and up to the Schoelkopf Museum after another ½ mile, circling around the building and heading back to the Goat Island bridges.

WHIRLPOOL STATE PARK

To continue north from the Schoelkopf Museum, run north on the shoulder of the Robert Moses Parkway for about 200 yards, and then go left toward the river where you will find a small dirt path in the park. The path stays on the bluff, and after about 2 miles you will be able to look out over the famous Whirlpool Rapids. Continuing north, the path eventually reaches a small caretaker's building where the course doubles back. Total distance from the museum and back is about 10 miles.

CLUBS   The city is closely connected with Buffalo, and runners from here belong to the Belle Watling Athletic Club.

CONTACTS   John Chew, or Larry Hailey, Carborundum Corporation, (716) 278-2000.
John Richardson, New York State Telephone Company, (716) 282-9923.

Rochester

Population: 280,000	Humidity: 71%
Elevation: 244 – 743 ft.	Av. Temperature: (Jan.) 24°F.; (July) 72°F.
Air Quality: Fair to poor	Inches of Rainfall: (Jan.) 2.2; (July) 2.9 Raindays: 153

OVERVIEW

It seems that cities located in adverse climates produce an inordinate number of elite runners. Rochester takes its place with Minneapolis and Eugene, Oregon, in turning out these top athletes. Dick Beurkle, Paul Stemmer, Charlie McMullen and Jim Ferris are all Rochester-bred. The heavy snows that bury this city each winter have hardened many a local runner.

Excellent parks around the city provide challenging runs over scenic, hilly trails. Durand Eastman Park sits about 30 minutes north of town along the shore of Lake Ontario. The Genesee River flows through town, and has some scenic routes along its banks as it passes the University of Rochester and the adjacent Genesee Valley Park. These are located about 3 miles from downtown. An interesting attraction, only 30 minutes south of town, is the newly improved Barge Canal path.

Downtown hotels are not close to the parks, but an interesting run on 2 miles of city streets will take you to Cobbs Hill Park. Rochester is a hotbed of racing activity, and many quality events are held throughout the year.

HOTELS

Holiday Inn – Downtown, Americana Hotel, Downtowner Motor Inn, Rochester Downtown Travelodge, One Eleven East Avenue Hotel, Depot Motor Inn

COBBS HILL PARK

From downtown hotels, run east on Main Street ½ mile to Liberty Pole, a gigantic flagpole, and make a half-right onto East Avenue. Continue on East Avenue for 1½ miles to a right turn on Culver Road and into the park. The run is mostly flat with little shade. Along the way you will pass the George Eastman House, the Rochester Museum, and the Historical Society.

Cobbs Hill Park has a reservoir with a ¾-mile dirt-and-paved pathway encircling it. You must run up a hill to this loop. Great views of downtown Rochester can be experienced from here. At the back side of the reservoir, there are many wooded trails over rolling hills. Water fountains and rest rooms are located at the ball fields. It is not recommended to run in any city park at night.

UNIVERSITY OF ROCHESTER CAMPUS AND GENESEE VALLEY PARK

Three miles east of downtown, the University of Rochester Campus and Genesee Valley Park provide fine facilities for free footing. The park is being broken up by a new highway, and routes will need to be changed, but you can still get some good cross-country workouts on the two golf courses. This is one of the flatter parks in the city.

DURAND EASTMAN PARK	Here you can enjoy hilly terrain on many different running surfaces. Horse trails meander through the park around many little ponds. Of course there are roads, and you can also do some grass running on the golf course. The park can be reached 7 miles north on Kings Highway.
ELLISON PARK	Located in a valley about 10 minutes east of town, this park has the toughest hills you can find in Rochester. Horse trails follow winding creeks through a very scenic environment.
MENDON PONDS PARK	Many ponds dot this pretty park where horse trails and roads wind over moderate hills. As with all Rochester parks, there are plenty of large, beautiful shade trees, and water fountains and rest rooms are easy to find. This park can be reached within 20 minutes south from downtown.
BARGE CANAL	If you stay at the Depot Inn in Pittsford, you will be right next to the Barge Canal. There is a flat, gravel path along its edge that extends for many miles in both directions. However, shade is variable, and no water is available.
OUTDOOR TRACKS	Many excellent tracks can be utilized in Rochester. The one favored by elite runners is at Jefferson High School, located in the inner city. Monroe Community College and Rochester Institute of Technology both have all-weather tracks. RIT also has an open, grassy campus that many runners use. The University of Rochester has a cinder track. You can use these tracks almost all the time, except at night, since they are not lit.
CLUBS, FUN-RUNS AND RACES	Fun-runs are held every other Sunday at Monroe Community College. The Greater Rochester Track Club schedules meets year 'round. During the summer, track meets are held every Tuesday Evening at Rochester Institute of Technology.
TRADITIONAL RACES	Irondequot July Fourth 5-Mile Race Corn Hill 10-Kilometer: July Phelps 20-Kilometer: Early August Fredonia 10-Kilometer: Mid-August Rochester Marathon: Labor Day Fulton 10-Mile: Early September
CONTACT	Paul Gesell, Greater Rochester Track Club, 4472 Main Street, Hemlock, NY 14466. (716) 367-2875.

Syracuse

Population: 180,000	Humidity: 71%
Elevation: 363 – 840 ft.	Av. Temperature: (Jan.) 24°F.; (July) 72°F.
Air Quality: Fair	Inches of Rainfall (Jan.) 2.7; (July) 3.1 Raindays: 167

OVERVIEW

Syracuse has had a long history in the sport, yet it is curious they even have an active running population. Many of the amenities runners are used to barely exist in this city. Winters are especially tough, with snowfall constantly accumulating over very hilly terrain. In other cities, this would force runners out onto the streets, but in Syracuse that is where they run normally. No large parks have been built, and most popular downtown routes wander informally through city and residential streets to small, distant parks and back. This makes early morning the most popular, and safe, running time.

Two routes are available to the east and southeast that offer less obstructive workouts. A towpath road alongside the Erie Canal is flat and has little traffic, and a hilly loop around a golf course has no intersections and again, few cars. Many running club events are held over these courses.

HOTELS

Holiday Inn – Downtown, Treadway Inn, Hotel Syracuse

BURNET PARK

At Columbus Circle, close to Hotel Syracuse, large groups leave from the Downtown YMCA to several different parks within a couple of miles from the start. Each park is found up a sharp rise on a hill, so these morning groups call themselves the Mountain Goats. The runs basically head out on sidewalks, taking different streets as the mood prevails, and upon reaching the parks, make a quick circle around and head back.

Burnet Park, west of downtown, can be reached by heading west out Fayette Street for about 1¼ miles to a left turn on Geddes Street. At the high school on the right, cut through the parking lot and school grounds to Wilbur Street in back of the school, and go right up the hill into the park. A small loop circles around the zoo. Total distance, out and back, is about 4 miles.

WOODLAND PARK

Southwest of downtown, this park can be reached by heading in that direction on Onondaga Street, passing a fountain at Tallman Street, and after about 1¾ miles, making a left onto Geddes Avenue, reaching the park after about ⅓ mile. A loop circles around the reservoir before the route turns back. The park is on a high hill, providing excellent views of the city skyline.

THONDEN PARK

The closest of the parks to downtown, and near Holiday Inn and Treadway Inn, this park can be reached by heading east on East Genesee Street to a right onto Comstock Avenue, and then taking the second left onto Madison Street. You will see a lot of students here, as the park is very close to the Syracuse University Campus.

Southeast of downtown, this popular route can be reached by heading toward Thonden Park but continuing beyond the park south on Comstock Avenue for another 1½ miles to Colvin Street. This is where the Manley Fieldhouse is located. Turn left on Colvin and continue for another 1⅓ miles to the course.

An exact 3-mile route follows the roads around the perimeter of the golf course. Head south on Waring Road to a left onto Nottingham Road, which takes you slightly downhill. Turn left onto Peck Hill Road for a tough climb of about 2 kilometers. As they come over this hill, many runners enjoy the sight, especially at sunset, of a Russian church in the distance. Christine Hubbard runs this course to get a feeling of being in Russia. At Randall Road, turn left and head back on the shoulder of this busier road to Waring, where you turn left, back to the start.

If you had taken a right on Randall Road, you would have reached a track at Christian Brothers Academy, after .35 miles. Some summer races start from there, and then head out onto the loop around the golf course.

ERIE CANAL
TOWPATH

Head east on East Genesee Street for about 5 miles to Lyndon Drive. Turn left, and after about 1 mile, you will reach Cedar Bay Park, and the Erie Canal Museum. From here, you can run many flat miles on a road along the old canal. The road gets plowed in winter, when you must alter your runs depending on wind direction. Because the road only heads east/west, be sure to begin into the wind, so you will have it at your back for the last half of your run.

Drinking water is hard to come by on this and the other popular courses in town.

OUTDOOR TRACKS

The Christian Brothers Academy, on Randall Road, has a ¼-mile cinder track. Nottingham High School has a ¼-mile cinder track along Euclid Avenue.

INDOOR TRACKS

Manley Fieldhouse, at Syracuse University, has an 8-laps-per-mile synthetic surface track. University identification is checked during busy hours.

The downtown YMCA has a 27-laps-per-mile, banked track.

CLUBS AND RACES

The Syracuse Track Club, affiliated with the YMCA, puts on a few large races each year as well as a summer program of fourteen weekly races at Nottingham High School, on Wednesdays at 6:30 P.M. Distances are 5 to 10 kilometers. The club also publishes an annual race calendar.

The Syracuse Chargers are affiliated with Syracuse University. They hold six to ten races a year, and during spring and fall, put on a weekly series of races on Tuesday nights at Christian Brothers Academy.

The Baldwinsville Harriers are a small but active club. Among other events, they put on a summer series of races at Durgee Junior High School on Thursday nights.

TRADITIONAL RACES

Liverpool Marathon and 10-Kilometer: Third Sunday in May
Blue Cross 10- and 5-Kilometer: Second Sunday in June
Casanovia Round-the-Lake, 10 miles: Fourth of July
Marcellus Gorge 10- and 5-Kilometer Run: Late July
Neil Pratt Memorial Run, 10 and 5 kilometers: Second Saturday in August

GROOT Race, 10 kilometers: Early September
Fulton 10-Mile Race: Second Sunday in September
YMCA Fitness Day, 10 and 5 kilometers: Mid-October
Erie Canal Towpath Run, 20 and 5 kilometers: Late October
Turkey Day Run, 10, 5, 3 and 1 miles: Thanksgiving Day

CONTACTS   Syracuse Track Club, Downtown YMCA, 340 Montgomery Street, Syracuse, NY 13202. (315) 474-6851.

Nick Wetter, Syracuse Chargers, Athletic Department, Manley Fieldhouse, Syracuse University, Syracuse, NY 13210.

Chuck Wiltse, 7909 Glenbrook Drive, Baldwinsville, NY 13027. (315) 638-4162.

Charlotte

Population: (met.) 460,000	Humidity: 68%
Elevation: 765 ft.	Av. Temperature: (Jan.) 42°F.; (July) 78°F.
Air Quality: Fair to poor	Inches of Rainfall: (Jan.) 3.5; (July) 4.4 Raindays: 110

OVERVIEW

One of the larger cities in the South, Charlotte retains much of its traditional Southern flavor, while expanding rapidly into a modern metropolis. A couple of small parks south of town constitute the major running courses. Although downtown hotels necessitate street running to reach these parks, the routes are not difficult and many runners can be seen here.

This city cannot be called a hotbed of running activity. Two Phidippides stores have taken responsibility for the organization of running here, and are directing the Charlotte Track Club. Visiting runners are fortunate that one of the stores is located in the Radisson Plaza Hotel.

In winter, do not be fooled by the city's southern location, as it can get very cold. The downtown area is often 10 degrees colder than its environs.

HOTELS

Radisson Plaza Hotel, Sheraton – Center Inn

LATTA PARK

From the two downtown hotels, you can reach Latta Park by running south on either McDowell, Brevard or College streets. After $^8/_{10}$ of a mile on city streets, turn left on Morehead, and follow it for ½ mile to a fork. Take the right onto Dilworth at the fork, and continue ½ mile to a right at the first light. After 100 yards you can enter the park.

The perimeter road around the park measures just 1 mile. The entire course is basically flat, and shade covers a majority of the road. Sidewalks are available throughout.

FREEDOM PARK

This popular area is located in the residential Queens Road section, about 2¾ miles from downtown. It can be reached by running south for $^8/_{10}$ of a mile to Morehead, turning left and staying on Morehead for 1 mile to Kings Drive at the five-point intersection. Turn right and follow Kings Drive for $^7/_{10}$ of a mile to the first light at East Boulevard. Take a right for $^2/_{10}$ of a mile to the entrance at Freedom Park. Up until now, the route has been mostly flat with a slight upgrade, and about 80 percent shaded.

Take the entrance road for $^8/_{10}$ of a mile past open fields and ball parks to the lake. One loop around the lake measures $^8/_{10}$ of a mile. This part of the course is also in shade, and the road is flat. You will find adequate drinking fountains in the park.

INDOOR TRACKS	The Central Branch YMCA on Morehead Street near Latta Park has a non-banked, 22-laps-per-mile track. Visiting runners must belong to another Y to use these facilities.
CLUBS, FUN-RUNS AND RACES	The Charlotte Track Club holds fun-runs every second Saturday at 9:00 A.M., beginning at Phidippides at the Radisson Plaza Hotel. Clinics and races are generally held once a month.
TRADITIONAL RACES	Dilworth, 10 kilometers: Early August James K. Polk, 15 kilometers: Mid-November *Charlotte Observer* Marathon and 10-Kilometer: Mid-December
CONTACTS	Don Plyler, Randy Layman or Gary Church, Phidippides, Two NCNB Plaza, Charlotte, NC 28280. (704) 375-1152; or 4400 Sharon Road, Charlotte, NC 28211, (704) 366-1213. Central Branch YMCA, 400 East Morehead Street, Charlotte, NC 28202. (704) 333-7771.

Greensboro, Winston-Salem

Population: Greensboro— 170,000 Winston-Salem— 150,000	Humidity: 70%
Elevation: 838— 884 ft.	Av. Temperature: (Jan.) 39°F.; (July) 77°F.
Air Quality: Fair	Inches of Rainfall: (Jan.) 3.2; (July) 4.4 Raindays: 117

OVERVIEW

This twin city area lies in the west-central part of North Carolina, close to the foothills of the Piedmont and Smoky Mountains. Thirty miles distant, the cities together comprise an important industrial complex of tobacco, furniture and apparel.

Landscape throughout the region is heavily wooded and residential with rolling hills. Rainfall is above average. Most of the running in Greensboro takes place a few miles northwest of town on bike paths and residential streets. Winston-Salem's focus is at Hanes Park, 1½ miles west of town, where runners head out on flat, residential streets. Many runners end up a few miles northwest of the park, at Reynolda Estate, the former estate of R. J. Reynolds, and the adjacent Wake Forest University.

A few miles south of Winston-Salem is the restored Old Salem, originally founded by Moravians, an Old-World, craft-skilled, religious sect. An historically scenic run can be had through its streets.

The Twin City Track Club is mostly run out of Winston-Salem, but many members are from Greensboro, and identify with the club as a regional organization.

HOTELS

Greensboro: Journey's End Motel, Maplewood Motel, Guest Quarters Motel
Winston-Salem: Holiday Inn—Coliseum, Hilton Inn, Sheraton Motor Inn, Hyatt House, Downtowner Inn

GREENSBORO GRIMSLEY HIGH SCHOOL

A bike path begins at the Grimsley High School, about 3 miles northwest of downtown. From the corner of Friendly and Elam streets, it heads out 4½ miles, one way. Gradual hills roll through residential neighborhoods, and the course is covered with moderate shade. Every ½ mile and kilometer are marked.

JAYCEES PARK

Five miles northwest of downtown Greensboro, this very hilly park has a 1.6-mile loop around a pond. Water and rest rooms can be found here. The park is located along Battleground Avenue, down the road from the Journey's End and Maplewood Motels.

One-half mile west of the park, along Battleground Avenue, is the start of another route which begins at Westridge Street. Follow Westridge southwest for 3.2 miles to Friendly Street. The run goes through a pretty residential area on a quiet, wide street. Terrain is mostly flat under heavy shade.

WINSTON-SALEM **HANES PARK**	From the Hyatt and Downtowner, in the center of town, run west on 4th Street for 1½ miles to the park. The city is on a hill, so you will have about ¾ of a mile downhill. This route is safe, as it passes through a neighborhood of gracious, old homes. Hanes Park contains the Family Y, and has a 1½-mile loop around its perimeter. It is a very popular running site. A dirt path describes a 1-mile loop beginning at the baseball diamond. It winds through the park, crossing streams, and is easy to follow. Several water fountains are available. From the park, a number of different courses can be run through residential neighborhoods. If you head west on Runnymeade, you will reach Stratford Road after 1 mile. Continuing west, Runnymeade becomes Reynolds, which runs into Country Club Circle. Out and back from the park to the circle is 5 miles. If you turn north on Stratford, you will reach Reynolda Road and the Reynolda Estate after 3 miles from the park. The Estate has beautiful gardens which are open to the public. Many miles of well-maintained trails meander through wooded areas. Terrain is flat at the park, along the residential streets, and at the estate. Shade is abundant, and the streets have little traffic. For a long run, you can begin just north of Hanes Park, on Reynolda Road, and follow it northwest for 8 to 10 miles one way. A ½-mile hill is located about ¾ of a mile from the park. The road is wide and there is some traffic, but runners use this route frequently.
WAKE FOREST **UNIVERSITY**	The Wake Forest Campus is located adjacent to Reynolda and Graylyn Estates. Parking is available on Faculty Drive near the Chapel and Theater. You can run into either estate, or follow courses posted on the bulletin board in the weight room at the gym. One course goes from the gym, left on Wingate for ⅛ mile, to a right onto Faculty Drive for ¼ mile, where you will see a paved bike path on the left. Follow the path through a forested area for ⅝ of a mile to the dam at Lake Catherine. Return along the same route. Holiday Inn is located near the university, which can be reached by running 1 mile west from the hotel, and then north on Cherry for two blocks to a left on University for ½ mile to the entrance.
OUTDOOR TRACKS	Grimsley High School has a rubberized asphalt ¼-mile track. Wake Forest University has a 400-meter Tartan track, and officials prefer visitors to use the outside lanes when the track is being used by the school. Hanes Park has a 400-meter cinder track.
INDOOR TRACKS	The Family Y at Hanes Park has a 10-laps-per-mile, banked track.
CLUBS, FUN-RUNS **AND RACES**	The Twin City Track Club puts on a number of events throughout the year. Fun-runs are held on the first and third Sundays of each month at 4:00 P.M. during warm months, and 3:00 P.M. beginning in November. These are at Hanes Park.
TRADITIONAL RACES	Natural Light Classic Half-Marathon and 10-Kilometer: March Schlitz Street Scene, 10 kilometers: September Holiday Classic, 10 kilometers: December
CONTACTS	Jon C. Lewis, Twin City Track Club, 826 Austin Lane, Winston-Salem, NC 27106. (919) 727-0502.

Phil Falkenberg, Twin City Track Club, 321 Avaln Road, Winston-Salem, NC 27104. (919) 725-0169.

Winston-Salem Family Y, 775 West End Boulevard, Winston-Salem, NC 27104. (919) 722-1163.

Frank Parker, Phidippides Running Store, Quaker Village Shopping Center, Greensboro, NC 27410. (919) 852-3555.

Raleigh, Durham & Chapel Hill

Population: Raleigh — 150,000 Durham — 110,000 Chapel Hill — 38,000	Humidity: 70%
Elevation: 363 – 501 ft.	Av. Temperature: (Jan.) 41°F.; (July) 78°F.
Air Quality: Fair	Inches of Rainfall: (Jan.) 3.2; (July) 5.1 Raindays: 112

OVERVIEW

The area encompassed by these three cities is known as the Research Triangle, due to the concentration here of three major universities — North Carolina State at Raleigh, Duke at Durham, and the University of North Carolina at Chapel Hill.

Cross-country running and track are celebrated sports at these universities, and popular running courses utilize the competitive facilities. Gymnasiums at each school post maps showing suggested training routes. In each town, head to the campus to pick up the best courses. In Chapel Hill and Raleigh, runs begin at the university track, and in Durham, at the entrance to the school's golf course. Chapel Hill, the most rural of the towns, has many dirt roads that runners can enjoy, while the other two more paved towns rely heavily on cross-country courses.

Durham and Chapel Hill have a close association with each other. The Carolina Godiva Track Club draws runners from both towns. Most runners in Raleigh belong to the North Carolina Track Club. Of course, Raleigh also has the Raleigh Rats, a celebrated competitive women's team anchored by the world-class Shea sisters, Julie and Mary, and Ellison Goodall.

HOTELS

Raleigh: Mission Valley Inn, John Yancy Motel, Hilton Inn, Velvet Cloak Inn
Durham: Hilton Inn
Chapel Hill: Carolina Inn

RALEIGH
CROSS-COUNTRY
COURSE

Starting at the university track, the sawdust and dirt trail winds through a mile of woods and a couple of miles of grass fields. There are several hills with 80 feet the biggest rise in elevation. Outside the gym next to the track, you will find a map posted with directions. A fountain at the track provides the only water.

Several other courses have maps posted describing the routes. You can run to Lake Raleigh and Lake Johnson from the track. These routes make use of shouldered roads, dirt and gravel roads, and grass fields. You will also travel through woods, and past tobacco fields and plenty of cows. Be cautious about slippery footing in wet weather.

DURHAM
CROSS-COUNTRY
COURSE

At Duke University, the rolling cross-country course consists of four different loops of approximately 1 mile each. It starts at the entrance to the golf course, about .8 mile from the gym. Check the map at the start or at the gym for directions. Most of the route follows the periphery of the golf course and utilizes some of the wooded areas for shade.

DUKE FOREST

Contiguous to the Duke Campus lies 4,000 acres of forest providing miles of graded dirt roads for tranquil, pleasurable runs. Although drinking water is not available, the cool forest air and streams to refresh in allow for safe, comfortable runs on hot days.

CHAPEL HILL
CROSS-COUNTRY
COURSE

This course is more complicated than the others, involving some residential streets and the University Botanical Gardens. Starting point is at Fetzer Field, where you can find a map of the route.

OUTDOOR TRACKS

The tracks at these universities are among the best in the nation. At Duke, the track is available twenty-four hours a day because the coach, Al Buehler, a former Olympic manager, allows visiting runners to work out with his team. At Fetzer Field at UNC and the track at NC State, you might be asked not to use the track during team practice. All three tracks are 400 meters, and are lit at night.

INDOOR TRACKS

Duke University has an indoor running concourse in its gym, not a true track.

CLUBS, FUN-RUNS
AND RACES

The Carolina Godiva Track Club holds fun-runs or races on most Saturdays. Training runs are held on weekday evenings once a week. An informal social run takes place every Sunday, beginning at the Friends School in Durham at 8:00 A.M. Directions to the school are complicated, so call ahead to Peter Klopfer for directions. These short to long runs utilize the Duke Forest.

The North Carolina Track Club holds races twice a month.

TRADITIONAL RACES

Southeastern Masters Track Championship: Early May
Great Raleigh Road Race, 10 kilometers: June
Chapel Hill Bob Holiday Cross-Country, 10 miles: June
WDBS Godiva 10.7 Road Race, 10.7 miles: Labor Day
Durham First Marathon and 10 Kilometers: October First

CONTACTS

Peter Klopfer, Carolina Godiva Track Club, Route 1, #184, Durham, NC 27705. (919) 383-3237.
Walter High, Carolina Godiva Track Club, Box 16, Carolina Union, UNC-CH, Chapel Hill, NC 27514.
Don Jayroe, North Carolina Track Club, 602 Wimbleton Drive, Raleigh, NC 27602. (919) 787-7858.

BISMARCK

Population: 40,000	Humidity: 70%
Elevation: 1,670 ft.	Av. Temperature: (Jan.): 8°F.; (July) 71°F.
Air Quality: Good	Inches of Rainfall: (Jan.) .5; (July) 2.2 Raindays: 97

OVERVIEW

This modern city, in the south central part of North Dakota, displays an unexpected skyscraper character. The Missouri River flows through town, and provides scenic river runs. Most courses use city streets, as traffic here is never a problem, and dogs are well contained by city ordinance. Terrain varies, and some good hills can be found on the north side of town. South side and river runs are flat.

Climate is only a problem in winter, when the city remains frigid for months. Running persists, although in the winter race last year, you could not find one runner in shorts. Vaseline is heavily used on faces and hands to protect against the cold.

The city boasts about its clean air, due to lack of industry and little traffic.

HOTELS

North side: Holiday Inn, Town House Motor Inn
South side: Best Western Kirkwood Motor Inn

DOWNTOWN COURSE

From the YMCA, you can run a loop of 2.6 miles. To reach this course from the Town House Motor Inn, run west on Divide Avenue for about 1 mile. From the Holiday Inn, run east on Memorial Highway for ½ mile to Rosser Avenue, continuing east for another ½ mile to Washington Street, and then north for another ½ mile to Divide Avenue. The YMCA is on the corner of Washington and Divide.

To run the loop, head west ½ mile on Divide, turning south on Ward Road for about ¾ of a mile to Avenue C. Follow C for a short distance to Griffin Street, turning north for not quite ½ mile to Boulevard Avenue. Turn east on Boulevard for the last bit of mileage back to the YMCA. You will find three good-sized hills along the course. There is no shade.

ROUTE TO MISSOURI RIVER

From the YMCA, head west on Divide Avenue. After ½ mile, Divide turns into Ward Road. Continuing west for another ½ mile, you will run over the interstate, and then ½ mile later there will be a steep ½-mile downhill which will take you to the river.

RIVER ROAD AND SERTOMA RIVERSIDE PARK

If you head south on River Road from Ward Road, you will reach the park after 2½ miles. The road through the park measures 1 mile. A water fountain is located at the zoo in the park, and rest rooms can be found in a number of different places off the park road. Shade is adequate along this route.

BIKE TRAIL FROM RIVERWOOD GOLF COURSE

A paved trail measuring 2½ to 3 miles has been built through the woods along the river. The trail starts on the road at the golf course, and can be reached by driving toward the river on Route 83 to 7th Street, south to Bismarck Avenue, and then west to Riverwood Golf Course.

SOUTH SIDE ROUTE TO THE RIVER

The Kirkwood Motor Inn sits next to the Elks Club, where many runners head out for their noontime workout. The route heads south on Washington Avenue for 3 miles to the riverbank. It is a flat, easy run. You can add additional mileage along the river.

CLUBS, GROUP RUNS AND RACES

The Missouri Valley Running Club organizes events in Bismarck, and the YMCA also has an active group of runners. Only two races were held in 1978. The club travels to almost all other races in the state to lend its support.

A group meets on the north side of town every Sunday at 10:00 A.M. for a workout; the address is 104 Seminole.

INDOOR TRACK

The YMCA has a 20-laps-per-mile, banked track.

OUTDOOR TRACK

Hughes Field, at the high school on Washington Avenue, ½ mile south of the YMCA, has a ¼-mile, all-weather track.

TRADITIONAL RACES

Frigid Frolic 10- and 5-Kilometer: January
Mandan Fourth of July Race, 10 kilometers
Road Runner Road Race, 15 kilometers: Last Saturday in July

CONTACTS

Tom Zimmerman, YMCA, Washington and Divide, Bismarck, ND 58501. (701) 255-1525.
Dr. Joe Cleary, 104 Seminole Avenue, Bismarck, ND 58501. (701) 223-1333.

FARGO

Population: 57,000	Humidity: 71%
Elevation: 900 ft.	Av. Temperature: (Jan.) 6°F.; (July) 71°F.
Air Quality: Good	Inches of Rainfall: (Jan.) .5; (July) 3.2 Raindays: 102

OVERVIEW

Many North Dakotans cannot do hill work. There just aren't any hills in this part of the state to practice on! From Fargo you have to drive clear out of the state to reach some hills, and they are not very steep. Fortunately, Fargo lies along the Red River on the Eastern border of the state adjacent to Minnesota.

Even without hills, local runners are very tough. Winter running is as difficult as you can find. There is always a stiff breeze of about 20 m.p.h. or more, and the temperature gets to around 20 below. Top this off with a constant ground cover of snow, and you get tough.

HOTELS

Town House Motel, Oak Manor Motel

RED RIVER BIKE PATH TO LINDENWOOD PARK

The Town House is located on 3rd Avenue North. If you head down 3rd Avenue to the Red River, you will reach a bike path that follows the river south for about 2½ miles from downtown at 2nd Avenue to Lindenwood Park. The park has a perimeter road measuring 1.9 miles. From the Oak Manor Motel, at U.S. 10 and I-95, you can reach the park by running north on 10 to 18th Avenue and then east to the park.

Many runners use this scenic course along the river. A few water fountains are available en route. Warning: During heavy rains, the riverbank can flood onto the bike path creating very sloppy footing.

FUN-RUNS

The YMCA has fun-runs every Saturday at Lindenwood Park.

INDOOR TRACK

There is an indoor track at the YMCA, 20 laps per mile.

TRADITIONAL RACE

Red River Run, 15 kilometers: Early August

CONTACT

YMCA, 400 1st Avenue South, Fargo, ND 58102. (701) 293-9622.

AKRON

Population: 245,000	Humidity: 74%
Elevation: 1,080 ft.	Av. Temperature: (Jan.) 26°F.; (July) 72°F.
Air Quality: Fair	Inches of Rainfall: (Jan.) 2.7; (July) 3.8 Raindays: 141

OVERVIEW

Located south of Cleveland in the Lake Erie region, "The Rubber Capital of the World" provides simple, convenient routes for visiting runners. Redeveloped around the modern Cascade Plaza, the downtown area contains a square running route of four streets. The University of Akron, with its active running population, takes up much of the area within this route. The Goodyear Tire and Rubber Company, just east of downtown, has an indoor track, and a little further east, Goodyear Heights Metropolitan Park offers a wooded environment for countrified running.

HOTELS

Holiday Inn – Downtown, Holiday Inn – Cascade Plaza

DOWNTOWN ROUTE

Four straight streets constitute this route. Exchange Street runs along the south, and is the longest leg of the course. Brown Street, along the eastern side, borders the university for its full length. Mill Street, the shortest leg, runs along the north, and Main Street constitutes the western border. Although the route is very popular, it has not been exactly measured; most runners estimate the distance at about 2½ miles.

Holiday Inn – Downtown, along Exchange Street near the southeastern corner of the course, sits across the street from the university. Holiday Inn – Cascade Plaza sits on the northwest corner, at the intersection of Main and Mill. From either of these motels, you can run the course in either direction. Only a few streets along each leg actually intersect the course, so runs are fairly unobstructed. Terrain is mostly flat, with a couple of small hills, and the sidewalk provides hard footing under very few shade trees. You can stop for water at gas stations or at the university. During rush hours, auto exhaust can be a problem.

GOODYEAR PARK

This is an excellent training facility with miles of dirt paths through heavily shaded woods. It can be reached from Holiday Inn – Cascade Plaza by running east down Mill Street, and taking a half-left onto Forge Street at the same intersection that you meet Brown Street. Take Forge a few hundred yards to a right turn onto Market Street. Head east on Market for just over 1 mile to a left turn on Case Street. Stay on Case for about a ¼ mile to a right turn on Newton Street, and follow Newton for about 1¾ miles to the park. Total distance is about 3¾ miles.

From Holiday Inn—Downtown, head east along Exchange Street for just over a mile to Market Street. Make a right on Market, and then a quick left onto Case Street and follow the last part of the route as above. Total distance is about 3 miles.

Once in the park, a sign will direct you to the start of the different trails. Five to six trails are available. At the beginning of each trail, a sign will show the distance and code markers to guide you along the way. Terrain in the park is generally rolling. Rest rooms can be found at the park entrance, and signs along the trails will direct you to other rest rooms.

OUTDOOR TRACKS

The University of Akron has a ¼-mile, all-weather track across the street from Holiday Inn—Downtown. Lee Jackson Field, surrounding the track, has a ¾-mile grass perimeter.

INDOOR TRACKS

The University of Akron is in the process of building a 220-yard indoor track which will be available to the public upon request during most hours. The gym at the Goodyear Plant on East Market Street has a balcony track measuring 180 yards. This is also available upon request. Six to 7 miles north of town, at Cuyahoga Falls, the Natatorium has a 13-laps-per-mile track.

CLUBS, FUN-RUNS AND RACES

The major organization for running here is the Summit Athletic Club. They have a fun-run every Saturday morning at Hampton Hills Park on Akron Peninsula Road at 9:00 A.M. The fun-run is followed by a training run, and then a group breakfast. The club also holds races during the year.

TRADITIONAL RACES

Lake Erie AAU 15-Kilometer Championships: March
Greater Akron 10 and 20 Kilometers: Early June
Lake Erie AAU 10 and 25 Kilometers: Late September

CONTACTS

Summit Athletic Club, P.O. Box 9148, Akron, OH 44305.
Cletus Griffin, Summit AC, (216) 794-0507.
University of Akron Athletic Department, (216) 375-7080.
Goodyear Tire and Rubber Company, (216) 794-2121.

CINCINNATI

Population: 1,450,000	Humidity: 68%
Elevation: 433 – 960 ft.	Av. Temperature: (Jan.) 35°F.; (July) 78°F.
Air Quality: Fair to poor	Inches of Rainfall: (Jan.) 3.4; (July) 4 Raindays: 134

OVERVIEW

The downtown area of Cincinnati is a flat basin with the Ohio River on one side and steep hills to the north and east. Your choice is to run along the flat river-bank, not especially pretty, or in the beautiful, hilly parks. This charming city has many small communities of well-kept homes. Some areas of the city that you can reach by foot afford beautiful vistas of these communities and the river. I went for a night run with the Clifton Track Club through a residential area of old, architecturally exquisite homes. Occasionally, we could look out from hundreds of feet above downtown Cincinnati and see the skyline, city lights, and the bridges over the Ohio River.

HOTELS

Terrace Hilton, Stouffer's Cincinnati Towers

EDEN PARK

This attractive and exciting park can be easily reached on foot from the above downtown hotels. If you start at 8th Street and Vine, head east and you will swing left onto Gilbert Avenue. After ¼ mile, going uphill, turn right onto Victory Parkway at the Eden Park entrance. If you run the bottom and top loops one time each, and head back along the same route to the starting point, you will have covered 5½ miles.

At both the bottom and the top loops, you will have beautiful vistas of the Ohio River. Many runners use this course throughout the day. The park provides good shade, and plenty of water fountains and rest rooms. The footing in the park is mostly on road, with some grass at times along the road. Terrain is very hilly.

MEHRING WAY

From downtown, you may also run a flat course by heading down Broadway toward the river to Mehring Way, which runs east and west along the river. As you run into Mehring, it's a T, and if you turn right and run to the end, staying left, and then turn back and run east on Mehring, passing Broadway, until you reach the boat basin, and then back to Broadway, you will have covered 4.5 miles, all on Mehring Way. This is an industrial area and should be avoided during the early morning hours. During the afternoon, the street is practically empty.

RIVERFRONT STADIUM AND THE COLISEUM

These two facilities sit between downtown and the river. They are easily reached from downtown by pedestrian bridges. In heavy snow, this area is

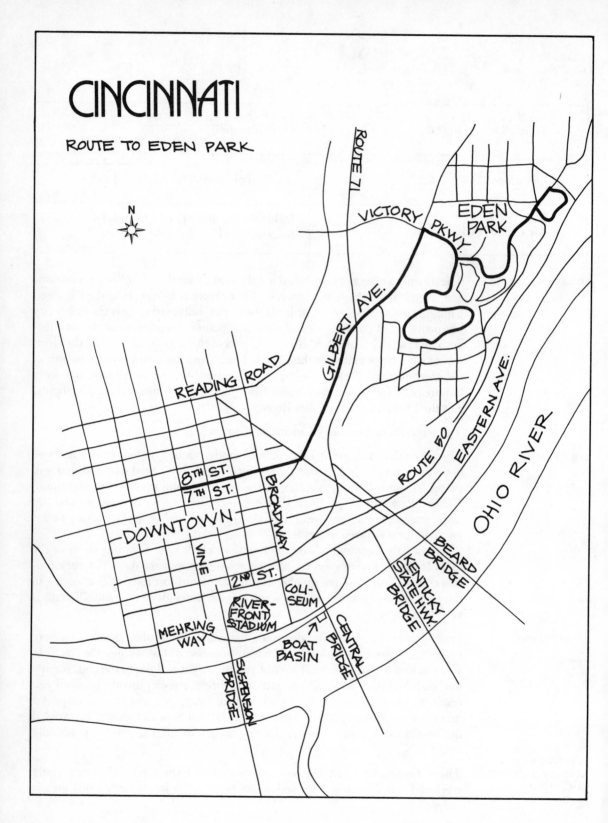

CINCINNATI

ROUTE TO EDEN PARK

ROUTE 71

VICTORY PKWY.

EDEN PARK

GILBERT AVE.

READING ROAD

ROUTE 50

EASTERN AVE.

OHIO RIVER

8TH ST.

7TH ST.

BROADWAY

DOWNTOWN

VINE

2ND ST.

COLISEUM

RIVER-FRONT STADIUM

MEHRING WAY

BOAT BASIN

CENTRAL BRIDGE

SUSPENSION BRIDGE

KENTUCKY STATE HWY. BRIDGE

BEARD BRIDGE

shoveled clear, and many runners put in mileage by running figure eights around the two buildings. The route falls just short of 1 mile.

LUNKEN AIRPORT BIKE PATH Located about 8 miles east of downtown via Columbia Parkway, this new asphalt bike path circumvents Lunken Airport for a loop of 5.8 miles. One mile of the course runs on top of the Little Miami River Levee. There is no shade available and water can be found only at the playground at the north corner and the airport building at the west corner.

MILL CREEK VALLEY You can run a flat course from downtown north on Central Parkway. This goes through Mill Creek Valley along a broad avenue. After about 1 mile of moderately busy intersections, there are long stretches of pleasant, tree-lined sidewalks. You can actually run 7½ miles out this way to Mt. Airy Forest. At 4½ miles the road "T's" at Ludlow Viaduct. Go left for about ⅓ mile to the six-way intersection where you take a left onto Hoffner, followed after ¼ mile by a right onto Colerain. Take Colerain uphill to the park entrance.

MT. AIRY FOREST This enormous 1,459-acre park can be found 7½ miles north of town. Many hiking trails exist here over the typical Cincinnati hills. Directions are easy to follow as the trails are well marked and the starting gates have posted mileage. The central roadway lies mostly flat, with many legs extending off into picnic areas. If you run each leg, you will do about 3.5 miles. There is plenty of shade throughout the park, and a sufficient number of water fountains and rest rooms, mostly at picnic areas. The park gets very crowded during the middle of the day and on weekends.

BURNET WOODS The University of Cincinnati sits about 4 miles north of downtown. Burnet

Eden Park, Cincinnati

Woods, an attractive park, is located adjacent to the university campus. The grass perimeter around the park measures 1¼ miles, and you may also run the open grassy areas and paved walkways in the park. Although not steep, terrain is all up or down. Plenty of shade and water are available.

INDOOR TRACKS

Two downtown indoor tracks are available, but unfortunately, they are only open to men. The Central YMCA has a 26-laps-per-mile track and the Fenwick Club has a 31-laps-per-mile track.

OUTDOOR TRACK

The University of Cincinnati has a ¼-mile, all-weather track available to visiting runners.

CLUBS, FUN-RUNS AND RACES

The Clifton Track Club is the major running organization in Cincinnati. An evening meeting is held on the second Monday of each month, after which there is a 3- to 5-mile fun-run. After the run, the club socializes at Fries Cafe at 3247 Jefferson, in Clifton, adjacent to the University of Cincinnati. The club holds many varied running events.

Fun-runs are held the first and third Saturday at 9:00 A.M. every month at Sharon Woods, about 15 miles northeast of town, and on the second and fourth Wednesdays at 6:00 P.M. at Winton Woods, about 15 miles north of town.

TRADITIONAL RACES

Mini-Marathon, 15 kilometers: Late March
Memorial Day 5-Kilometers
Labor Day 5-Miles
Thanksgiving Day Race (since 1910), 5 miles.

CONTACTS

Mike Boylan, Clifton Track Club, 3401 Brookline, #12, Cincinnati, OH 45220. (513) 961-6755.
Don Connolly, 1445 Sigma Circle, Cincinnati, OH 45230. (513) 474-1399.
The Athlete's Foot, 2629 Vine, Clifton, OH 45220. (513) 861-6200.
Craig Harms publishes the *Miami Marathon Newsletter* out of Oxford, Ohio, which contains many Ohio entry blanks and results: 6458 Contreras Road, Oxford, OH 45056.

Cleveland

Population: (met.) 2,255,000	Humidity: 72%
Elevation: 570– 1,050 ft.	Av. Temperature: (Jan.) 29°F.; (July) 74°F.
Air Quality: Fair to poor	Inches of Rainfall: (Jan.) 2.6; (July) 3.5 Raindays: 153

OVERVIEW

Cleveland abounds with running clubs, events, and many running facilities to fulfill the needs of this robust city along the shore of Lake Erie. Although there are interesting courses downtown, much of the activity spreads out to the surrounding communities. Just east of downtown, the terrain rises sharply up to the Appalachian Plateau upon which are the towns of Cleveland Heights, Shaker Heights, and University (Case Western Reserve University) Heights. To the west lie the towns of Lakewood and Parma, and to the south lie Bedford and Maple Heights.

All of these towns, and the city of Cleveland, lie within the "Emerald Necklace," an encircling string of city parks called the Metroparks System totaling 18,500 acres. The average distance from downtown to these parks is 15 miles. Many of the outlying industrial and commercial areas, where traveling runners might be staying in hotels, are within a short driving distance of the Metroparks System.

Cool lake breezes blow in from Lake Erie during the summer to make it a comfortable running season.

HOTELS

Holiday Inn– Lakeside, Bond Court Hotel, Hollenden House, Cleveland Plaza, Sheraton Inn– Rocky River

MARGINAL AREA

This run along the lakefront is the most convenient and popular in the downtown area. Head over to 9th Street and then north to the lakefront at the Naval Reserve Building. Turn right onto North Marginal Drive and you will have an almost straight, very flat run, for 3 miles out to East 55th Street. Also known as the Marginal Area, this route travels along the lakefront and part of the Municipal Airport. You will have an excellent view from here of the Cleveland skyline. The downtown hotels are within a couple of blocks of East 9th Street and about ⅓ mile from the lakefront. There is no shade or water at the Marginal Area. Lighting is sufficient for night running.

THE FLATS

A secondary area that provides interesting downtown running is the Flats, an old warehouse and steel mill area just east of downtown and next to the Cuyahoga River. This tiny river is used by giant ore boats. Although the river is very busy, the adjacent roads are fairly quiet with quaint restaurants amidst mostly unused industrial buildings. There seem to be half a dozen little draw-bridges to run over, and the streets are winding and confusing, but you can always work your way back along the river to where you started. The Flats are really flat, except for the substantial hill from the downtown area to get there. Superior Avenue or St. Clair Avenue are your two access roads. You will have to run for time here, as there is no prescribed route to follow. No trees grow in the Flats; water might be obtainable in some of the commercial establishments.

UNIVERSITY
HEIGHTS

Case Western Reserve University is located about 4 miles east of downtown, at University Circle. The campus and surrounding area create an interesting running environment, including some small parks and museums. It is a haven for runners due to the wide open sidewalks and the scenic location. Again, there are no prescribed routes to follow.

Just below University Circle is an attractive, though littered park through which runs Liberty Boulevard. A low-income neighborhood borders the park, and it is not considered safe to run here alone. There is a mostly flat, shaded run along the boulevard of about 3 miles, one way.

FOREST HILLS PARK

Further east, you will find Cleveland Heights, where you should head directly to the Cleveland Heights Recreation Pavilion at 1 Monticello Road. Dressing rooms and showers are available before heading directly behind the pavilion to Forest Hills Park. At the edge of the parking lot you will see the start of a measured 2¼-mile paved bike path. The course winds through wooded and grassy areas, is mostly flat, and has good shade and water. The park is also conducive to free running over its grassy lawns and occasional rolling hills.

There is also another bike path across Monticello Road, and this one measures 2.3 miles in length.

ROCKY RIVER
RESERVATION

Located west of Cleveland, this 5,680-acre park is the largest and most popular among runners in the Metroparks System. A 5-mile bicycle path travels south through an exciting gorge with challenging hills to either side. Many picturesque miles can be logged here if you take advantage of the numerous roads and trails. The Cleveland West RRC focuses most of their activities in this park.

BEDFORD
RESERVATION

Within the Metroparks System to the southeast lies Bedford Reservation. Though only one-fourth the size of Rocky River Park, this is a beautiful hilly facility with excellent trails and roads. The Southeast Running Club utilizes this park.

CHAGRIN RIVER
RESERVATION

Located further to the east, this very hilly park offers some of the most challenging runs in Cleveland.

OUTDOOR TRACKS

At Case Western Reserve University, Finnegan Field has a new all-weather, 400-meter track. Call the University Athletic Department for permission to use.

INDOOR TRACKS

The Central YMCA on Prospect Avenue has a 23-laps-per-mile track. In Cleveland Heights, the Jewish Community Center on Mayfield has a 20-laps-per-mile track. The Cleveland Heights Recreation Pavilion houses a large gymnasium containing a running loop, not a track, of 10 laps per mile. Call ahead for its schedule of availability.

The Cleveland State University has a beautiful 10-laps-per-mile indoor track. Unfortunately, only students, faculty, and staff may use it. Many local runners

The Flats, Cleveland

overcome this limitation by enrolling in an inexpensive course and thus gain full track privileges during the winter semester.

CLUBS, FUN-RUNS AND RACES

The Cleveland West Road Runners Club is the largest running club in the city. Every Saturday morning at 7:30, members meet for a group workout at the Detroit Road entrance to Rocky River Reservation. On Sunday mornings, they hold a fun-run at the same location, at 9:00 A.M. Races are held frequently.

The Southeast Running Club meets for workouts on Sunday mornings at 9:00 A.M. at the Bedford Reservation. The club holds races about once a month.

The University Circle Striders hold a fun-run every Sunday at 9:00 A.M. at Forest Hills Park.

The Cleveland Women Running Club is designed to meet the needs of women runners. They hold fun-runs on Saturday mornings at 9:00 A.M. at Forest Hills Park. Clinics and races are also scheduled throughout the year.

The Cleveland Heights Parks and Recreation Department and the Shaker Heights Recreation Board hold many weekday running programs organized by John O'Neill.

TRADITIONAL RACES

Revco Marathon and 10-Kilometer: May
Southeast RRC Annual 7.5-Mile Run: August
Heart-A-Thon Half-Marathon: Early September
Octoberfest 10-Kilometer: October
Rocky River 30-Kilometer Championship: Early December

CONTACTS

Cleveland West Road Runners Club, P. O. Box 16243, Rocky River, OH 44116.
Southeast Running Club, Roger McKain, 6549 Forest Glen Avenue, Cleveland, OH 44139.

John O'Neill, University Circle Striders, 3690 Randolph Avenue, Cleveland, OH 44121.

Cleveland Women Running, Linda Creighton, 3286 Ardmore, Shaker Heights, OH 44120.

Cleveland Heights Recreation Pavilion, 1 Monticello Road, Cleveland Heights, OH 44118. (216) 321-0100, ext. 283.

Central YMCA, 2200 Prospect Avenue, Cleveland, OH 44115.

Ted Creighton, The Complete Runner, 2218 Lee Road, Cleveland Heights, OH 44118. (216) 321-1679.

COLUMBUS

Population: 550,000	Humidity: 72%
Elevation: 685–893 ft.	Av. Temperature: (Jan.) 28°F.; (July) 74°F.
Air Quality: Fair to poor	Inches of Rainfall: (Jan.) 2.9; (July) 3.2 Raindays: 134

OVERVIEW

This central Ohio city has excellent opportunities for convenient and interesting runs. The Scioto River passes through the downtown area, providing a fast escape from the urban environment on a scenic riverside bike path. Several suburban parks have excellent running facilities so that many runners need only to stay in their communities for satisfying daily mileage.

Ohio State, one of the largest universities in the country, plays a major role in city life, and contributes to a great share of the running population. Campus routes focus mainly around the ball fields next to the stadium.

The Columbus Police Department has an overzealous jaywalking enforcement program. They have even gone so far as to arrest the front runner in a race for running in the street, and only five blocks from the finish. One of the best restaurants in Columbus, The Place Upstairs, is owned by Earl Bradley, a 2:32 master marathoner.

HOTELS

Downtown: Sheraton–Columbus, The Neil House, Holiday Inn–Downtown
University: Stouffer's University Inn, Holiday Inn–Ohio State
North: Sheraton Motor Inn–North, Holiday Inn–North, Ramada Inn–North
East: Ramada Inn–East, Holiday Inn–East, Red Roof Inn, Budgetel, Knights Inn

SCIOTO RIVER BIKE PATH

From the downtown hotels, go a few blocks west to Front Street, and then a few blocks south to Bicentennial Park. Across the street from the south side of the park, the bike path begins. Follow it 1½ miles south to the Whittier Street Bridge. Go over the bridge to South Front Street and turn right for three blocks to Greenlawn Bridge. Go over the bridge and follow the bike path signs. Take the bike path south another 2 miles to the bottom of Southview Park, and follow the same route back to the start. Total distance measures 8 miles out and back. The course is basically flat with nice wooded scenery. Water and rest rooms are available at the service station near Greenlawn Bridge.

BLACK LICK WOODS PARK

East side motels are located no more than 1½ miles from this busy park. A variety of loops within the park range from 1.8 to 4.5 miles over paved and gravel roads and trails. Terrain is flat to rolling, through both shaded and open areas. The park office has maps of the different trails. Weekly fun-runs are held at this park—the meeting place is at the nearby Reynoldsburg High School track.

WHETSTONE PARK

Five and a half miles north of downtown along the Olentangy River, this park has a 2½-mile, out and back, bike path. The park is only 3 miles north of Ohio State, and can easily be reached from university motels. Run or drive north on the Olentangy River Road to East North Broadway. Turn right and proceed ¾ of a mile to North High Street, turning left for another ¾ of a mile to the park. The bike path begins at the parking lots close to the river. It extends 1½ miles to the north, and 1 mile south over flat, scenic terrain.

SHARON WOODS PARK

A 3.8-mile circular loop bike path here goes through beautifully wooded areas and over several steep hills. One of the two rest shelters along the way contains a water fountain. The park is located in the northeast part of Franklin County, about 12 miles north of downtown, at the intersection of Cleveland Avenue and Schrock Road.

INDOOR TRACKS

The Sheraton Motor Inn—North has a newly built indoor track available to guests. The track measures 20 laps per mile. The Central YMCA has a track measuring 15 laps per mile, and the new North Side Branch YMCA has a 13-laps-per-mile track.

If you are visiting someone associated with Ohio State, they can obtain a guest pass for you to use the indoor track at French Fieldhouse. This beautiful 8-laps-per-mile facility is available when not in use by the university.

OUTDOOR TRACKS

The ¼-mile track at Ohio State Stadium can be used by visitors when the stadium is not in use by the football or track teams.

CLUBS, FUN-RUNS AND RACES

The Columbus Roadrunners hold fun-runs on the first and third Sundays of every month at 10:00 A.M. at the Worthington High School track, and the second and fourth Saturdays of every month at the Reynoldsburg High School track. Runs are on both the track and the road. A group run is held during the summer at 5:45 P.M. at Black Lick Woods Park. The club also puts on a number of races throughout the year.

TRADITIONAL RACES

Citizen's Journal Race, 10 kilometers: Mid-June
Granville 5 Miles: July 4th, A.M.
Bexley 5 Miles: July 4th, P.M.
Olentangy Run, 10 and 3 miles: Mid-September
Columbus Day Run, 14.92 kilometers: Early October

CONTACTS

Columbus Roadrunners, P.O. Box 15584, Columbus, OH 43215.
Don Fox, 321 Highland Avenue, Worthington OH 43085. (614) 888-6754.
Central Branch YMCA, 40 West Long Street, Columbus, OH 43215. (614) 224-1131.
North Side Branch YMCA, 1640 Sandalwood Place, Columbus, OH 43229. (614) 885-4252.
Ohio State University Track Office, (614) 422-2931.

DAYTON

Population: 195,000	Humidity: 71%
Elevation: 715–983 ft.	Av. Temperature: (Jan.) 28°F.; (July) 75°F.
Air Quality: Fair	Inches of Rainfall: (Jan.) 2.8; (July) 3.5 Raindays: 128

OVERVIEW Dayton is one of Ohio's more attractive cities. At the confluence of several rivers which are crossed in town by twenty-eight bridges, the most popular running course here is known as the River Corridor. The Kettering Striders, a famous Midwest club, is located in Kettering, Ohio, a suburb of Dayton. Steve Price, the coach, is constantly developing national class runners, and his women's team is always highly ranked nationally.

HOTELS Holiday Inn–Downtown, Stouffer's Dayton Plaza, Ramada Inn Stratford House

RIVER CORRIDOR ROUTE In the downtown Dayton area, a river corridor bikeway was built in 1976. The Holiday Inn is situated alongside the bikeway. The Ramada Inn is less than ¼ mile away, and Stouffer's is less than ½ mile away.

The course is a loop with a blacktop surface for its 8.2-mile length. Most of the bikeway is down at river level with the north and south ends rising up to street level for about 1½ miles. There are also rises at the three crossed bridges. Mileage markers can be found every ½ mile. Water is seldom found along the route, though since the bikeway goes through the downtown area it is possible to find water nearby. The YMCA is located along the bikeway and is a good watering spot as well as a place to start and end a run as there are good shower and locker room facilities within. The route passes a city park with a number of ball fields and softer footing.

SUGARCREEK RESERVE This route, south of Dayton, has miles of cut grass trails along a river and through woods and fields. Steve Price considers it one of the most beautiful running areas in the state.

INDOOR TRACK The Central YMCA has a Tartan smooth-surface, 28-laps-per-mile track open 7:00 A.M. to 9:30 P.M.

CLUBS, FUN-RUNS AND RACES The Ohio River Roadrunners Club has events scheduled at least twice a month, usually on Saturdays. The YMCA also sponsors running events.

TRADITIONAL RACES YMCA 8.6-Mile Run: late Spring
Dayton River Corridor Classic, 13.1 miles: Mid-October

The Central Branch YMCA is a general meeting place for runners and has information about all running events in town. The Kettering YMCA also attracts many runners.

Steve Price, Kettering Striders, 1117 Pursell, Dayton, OH 45420. (513) 253-4395.

Felix LeBlanc, Ohio River Roadrunners Club, (513) 426-5340.

Harry L. Bradbury, Central Branch YMCA, 117 West Monument Avenue, Dayton, OH 45402. (513) 223-5201.

TOLEDO

Population: 363,000	Humidity: 72%
Elevation: 571 – 627 ft.	Av. Temperature: (Jan.) 25°F.; (July) 72°F.
Air Quality: Fair to poor	Inches of Rainfall: (Jan.) 2.0; (July) 3.2 Raindays: 132

OVERVIEW

This busy port city on the Ohio-Michigan border along Lake Erie, producing much of the nation's glass products, has aptly named its local Glass City Marathon. The University of Toledo's Engineering Department must have some enthusiastic runners as they have accurately measured every quarter mile along the city's most popular running course. Toledo also has a large Metropolitan Park System with an abundant variety of running trails. The active Toledo Road Runners Club uses a number of these parks for its weekly races.

HOTEL

Sheraton – Westgate Inn

BROOKSIDE AVENUE COURSE

A 10-mile, residential out-and-back course starts from the University of Toledo Health Building. Head west along the river on Towerview Road, crossing Secor Road (the Sheraton is along Secor) and taking Brookside Avenue. The first mile presents the only traffic problem over this flat route. The residential streets provide good summer shade, and they are well plowed in winter. Runners can use this route day and night.

WILDWOOD PARK

After running on the Brookside course for 5 miles out, you can cross Central Avenue into Wildwood Park to extend your run along beautiful wooded trails. The green, blue and red trails are each 2 to 3 miles long and well marked.

METRO PARKS SYSTEM

The Metro Parks System provides Toledo with a number of excellent running trails at the different parks throughout the suburbs. No hotels are particularly close to any of these parks. Terrain is generally flat over the 3- and 4-mile routes that you will find.

Secor Park has a 2¾-mile wooded trail. Swan Creek Park's 3-mile loop is marked with mileage posts. Oak Openings Park is larger with longer trails.

INDOOR TRACKS

The University of Toledo has two indoor tracks, available if you are accompanied by a student or other university sponsor. The downtown YMCA has a 22-laps-per-mile track available if you are a member of another Y.

CLUBS

The Toledo Road Runners Club sponsors an event in the area every weekend. The *Toledo Blade* lists the weekly event in its Friday Sports/Road Running section.

FUN-RUNS AND RACES

The Toledo RRC weekly events are mixed 50/50 between fun-runs and races.

TRADITIONAL RACES   Heartwatchers Marathon: March
Glass City Marathon: June (Father's Day)
Run Against Cancer, 10 kilometers: August

CONTACTS   Tom Kovacs, Toledo RRC, 3262 North Reach Drive, Oregon, OH 43616.
(419) 698-3487.
Sy Mah, University of Toledo, Toledo, OH 43606. (419) 537-2741.
Downtown YMCA, 1110 Jefferson Avenue, Toledo, OH 43624. (419) 241-7131.
University of Toledo Athletic Department, (419) 537-4184.

Oklahoma City

Population: 370,000	Humidity: 66%
Elevation: 1,050–1,334 ft.	Av. Temperature: (Jan.) 37°F.; (July) 82°F.
Air Quality: Fair	Inches of Rainfall: (Jan.) 1.1; (July) 2.7 Raindays: 90

OVERVIEW

Many cities have ideal running facilities within easy reach of downtown hotels. Oklahoma City does not. 1½ to 2 miles of city streets are necessary to traverse before reaching the few small parks that offer unobstructed pathways. Most local downtown runners have adjusted to the busy streets. After 6:00 P.M. traffic diminishes. The city is laid out in a grid pattern, so it is hard to get lost. About seventeen blocks total 1 mile.

The environment downtown can be quite pleasant, with trees and wide sidewalks on mostly flat terrain. Local runners use their residential neighborhoods, or head to Lakes Hefner and Overholser, west of town. Most running events take place around these lakes.

HOTELS

Skirvin Plaza Hotel, Sheraton Century Center Hotel, Holiday Inn–Central

DOWNTOWN RUNS

Many runners prefer to head north to 36th or 38th streets and then west for several blocks where a couple of parks provide loops around their grass perimeters. Guy James Park is at 400 N.W. 36th Street. One lap around measures about ¾ of a mile. A smaller park at 500 N.W. 38th Street has a ½-mile loop. The parks are well shaded, but water is not available.

Woodson Park can be found at May and S.W. 25th Street. Reach it by running west for twenty blocks and south for twenty-five blocks from downtown. It is about a 2- to 2½-mile run to get there. A perimeter loop of the park measures a little over 1 mile. All of these parks have flat terrain.

STATE FAIRGROUNDS

At May Avenue and N.W. 10th Street, this facility is only about 1 mile from downtown. Its main draw are unobstructed roads. The area is flat and has few trees. Water fountains are available, and you can do about a 3-mile loop around the area.

LAKE HEFNER

About 7 miles northwest on Oklahoma 3, this pretty lake provides a 10-mile loop on a paved road. Terrain is flat and shaded and you will find some traffic on the road. Water and rest rooms are available on the south side of the lake at Stars and Stripes Park, and the golf course. Mileage markers have been painted on the left side of the road on the pavement.

LAKE OVERHOLSER

Eight miles west of downtown on U.S. 66, this lake offers a 7- or 8-mile run around its shore on a paved road. Terrain is flat and shaded; only one water fountain and rest room can be found here, but I do not know where they are.

OUTDOOR TRACK	A popular track is located at Northeast High School, N.E. 30th Street and Kelly Avenue.
INDOOR TRACKS	The Central Branch YMCA has recently built an air-conditioned, banked, 18-laps-per-mile track. The Y is only about four blocks north of downtown hotels. A banked rooftop track of 23 laps per mile is also available there.
CLUBS AND RACES	The Oklahoma City Running Club holds monthly races, usually on the third Saturday morning.
TRADITIONAL RACES	Oklahoma City Marathon: Early November
CONTACTS	Dr. Dan Metcalf, 2240 N.W. 114th Street, Oklahoma City, OK 73120. (405) 232-8861.
	Central Branch YMCA, 125 N.W. 5th Street, Box 778, Oklahoma City, OK 73101. (405) 232-6101.

TULSA

Population: (met.) 505,000	Humidity: 66%
Elevation: 620–810 ft.	Av. Temperature: (Jan.) 39°F.; (July) 83°F.
Air Quality: Fair	Inches of Rainfall: (Jan.) 1.4; (July) 3.5 Raindays: 90

OVERVIEW

This cosmopolitan city has developed from the proceeds of the oil industry. Its interest in cultural and recreational activities has launched a new park area along the Arkansas River. Not far from the downtown area, the first stages of the park have been completed. As this is the model for the park being developed all along the river, it has been named the "Model Park." This is the most popular running area including a 5-mile bike path that runs through the park and extends south along the river.

Tulsa can often be a windy city, and the Tulsa Running Club cautions runners to beware of thunderstorms in the spring and summer.

HOTELS

Holiday Inn–Civic Center, Fairmont Mayo Hotel, Williams Center Hotel, Camelot Inn, Sheraton Skyline East

MODEL PARK

Head south from the downtown hotels: Holiday Inn, Fairmont Mayo or Williams Center, for 1 to 2 miles along such streets as Denver or Houston to the Model Park bike paths. These streets are well traversed by runners, particularly from the YMCA on Denver Avenue. The bike path distance through the Model Park is 1.3 miles, beyond which the paved path becomes crushed limestone, which is really good to run on unless there is a lot of rain.

The route crosses an old railroad bridge which belongs to the park and has been converted to a pedestrian bridge. Camelot Inn is near the crushed limestone portion of the path. A more elaborate area of the park is being developed across the river, and a new bridge is being built at 11th Street.

When Tulsa RC members head out in groups from the park for a long workout, they will occasionally cross the river farther south and run up a wooded hill called Turkey Mountain to view the city skyline. This is not a good place to run without a local guide because it's so difficult to find access.

Rest rooms (often locked) and drinking fountains can be found in the park near Denver Avenue and Riverside Drive. Shade trees are not plentiful along the path, but street lights are, and runners do use the park safely at night.

MOHAWK PARK

Located immediately northeast of the airport, Mohawk Park is the site of most Tulsa RC races throughout the year. The course is very flat, so it's possible to have a fast race when it isn't too windy. Some runners train in this park, but it's rather remote from residential areas. Unfortunately, it is on the far side of the airport from the terminal building and not very accessible for air travelers. Running is possible through the residential areas south of the airport.

TRACKS

The Sheraton Skyline East, about 9 miles southeast of downtown, has an all-weather metric track across the back fence.

CLUBS AND RACES

The Tulsa Running Club has at least one race day a month, always on Saturday mornings. There are also members who meet in small groups on Sunday mornings between 7:00 and 8:00 A.M. at 56th Street and Riverside Drive for training runs.

Also, groups run from the Downtown YMCA at 515 South Denver.

TRADITIONAL RACES

Oil Capital Marathon: Late March
5-Mile Riverside Run: June
8- and 2-Mile Zoo Run: July
10- and 2-Mile Riverside Run: Early October

CONTACT

Art Browning, Tulsa Running Club, 1211 East 27th Place, Tulsa, OK 74114. (918) 743-9089, 836-5511, ext. 2360 (work).

EUGENE

Population: 100,000	Humidity: 77.5%
Elevation: 426 ft.	Av. Temperature: (Jan.) 39°F.; (July) 67°F.
Air Quality: Good	Inches of Rainfall: (Jan.) 5.4; (July) 0.3 Raindays: 143

OVERVIEW

Eugene is Steve Prefontaine's town. At the University of Oregon's Hayward Field, Steve broke numerous American records in front of tumultuous crowds screaming "go Pre, go Pre." It was also in this town that Steve met his tragic death in an automobile accident after celebrating his last victory. He will not be forgotten here, for his dedication to running is being rewarded by a dedicated population of runners.

The Willamette River flows through Eugene on its way to Portland, 110 miles to the north. Here the river is smaller and not used for shipping. The valley between Eugene and Portland produces the nation's grass seed, and people with hay fever or sinus problems are sometimes affected by this. In the summer, after the seed is harvested, the grass is burned and the air in Eugene is, at times, polluted by smoke.

The terrain in Eugene is generally flat, particularly in the North, with out-croppings of small, steep hills or buttes in the southern part of town. With this varied terrain and mild year 'round weather, it's no wonder that many of the nation's top runners come here to train. The University of Oregon is always a powerhouse in running competition and draws many of our future greats. Nike's Athletics West, a running club, operates from here with its coach, Harry Johnson.

HOTELS

Valley River Inn, Holiday Inn, Thunderbird Motel, New Oregon Hotel

PRE'S TRAIL

The foremost tribute to Steve Prefontaine, and the pride of Eugene, is Pre's Trail. This 4½-mile wood chip trail in Alton Baker Park runs through a beautiful area alongside canals and into rustic wooded glades. Its running surface is very well built with a gravel foundation and many inches of wood chip and sawdust above it. Due to excellent drainage, the wet seasons cannot hinder the fine footing. Another feature of the trail is its day and night availability; the entire trail being lit early morning and evening.

The Valley River Inn, along the Willamette River, is located about 1 mile west of Alton Baker Park. The river has a bicycle path along both sides for easy access to the park, and loops can be run from bridge to bridge. The Thunderbird and Holiday Inn (with a Holidome) are located on Coburg Road, about ½ mile north of Alton Baker Park. Run a direct route down Coburg to the Ferry

Bridge where you will find the park to your left on the near side of the river. When you run through the pond area, go along under the power lines to your left and you will reach Pre's Trail at the end of the gravel walk. This is at one end of the Green Loop, so you can take the trail to the left or the right and after about ½ mile, arrive at the sign with a map of the trail. You can continue on from here over the Red Trail, the Yellow Trail or the Blue Trail.

The New Oregon Hotel is located on Franklin Avenue at the University of Oregon. This is just over the river from Pre's Trail, which can be reached by a convenient footbridge.

HAYWARD FIELD

If you have a car, you can park at Hayward Field at the University where you will have a choice of routes to head for. Adjacent to the field is a ¼-mile track used only for training. It is not the track used for meets. A number of ball fields are also available for good grass running. You can head north for a few hundred yards to Franklin Avenue and then cross over the footbridge to Pre's Trail.

HENDRICKS PARK

To the southeast looms the beautiful and hilly Hendricks Park, only 1 mile from Hayward Field. Run down any of the streets heading south from the University to 19th Street. Turn left and follow 19th straight to Fairmount. Here you will see signs directing you to the park. (It's right on Fairmount and then left onto Summit which will bring you into the park.)

A steep grade leads you up to this small, but beautifully wooded park containing towering fir trees which give excellent shade. The north side of the park contains a rhododendron garden. Roads here are short and hilly, so it is best to take swings out along some of the residential streets from the park.

MCKENZIE RIVER TRAIL

Jon Anderson, a former Boston Marathon winner living in Eugene, recommends the McKenzie River Trail as being "fantastic." Drive one hour east on Highway 126 near the McKenzie Bridge. The best starting point is at Paradise

Pre's Trail, Eugene

Campground, where the trail crosses the entry road about 50 meters in from the highway. Heading east upstream, you can follow a smooth, soft forest trail along the river for 15 picturesque miles, one way. It parallels Highway 126 until it ends. During the wet winter months the trail might be muddy. Some runners also enjoy rafting down this river.

CLUBS, FUN-RUNS AND RACES
The Oregon Track Club holds monthly fun-runs every third Sunday at Alton Baker Park. They also hold monthly races at various locations in Eugene.

INDOOR TRACKS
The Eugene Family YMCA has a modern indoor track, 13 laps per mile.

TRADITIONAL RACES
Butte to Butte, 10 kilometers: Fourth of July
Pre's Trail Run, 5 miles: Labor Day
Nike Marathon: Early September

CONTACTS
Bob Gray, The Running Company, 24th and Willamette, Eugene, OR 97405. (503) 345-4786.
Sugar Pine Ridge, 877 East 13th Street, Eugene, OR 97403. (503) 345-5584.
The Athletic Department, (503) 342-5155.
Eugene Family YMCA, 2055 Patterson Street, Eugene, OR 97405. (503) 344-6251.

PORTLAND

Population: (met.) 1,109,000	Humidity: 75.5%
Elevation: 0 – 1,073 ft.	Av. Temperature: (Jan.) 40°F.; (July) 69°F.
Air Quality: Good	Inches of Rainfall: (Jan.) 5.4; (July) .42 Raindays: 153

OVERVIEW

Portland has a reputation for its high-density running population. One might wonder why a city with an excess of rainfall would turn out a large number of splashers. Some people have explained that flooded ball fields are no fun and you get tired of staying indoors. Road running is the answer.

It is a pretty city with much greenery and a sense of intimacy about the environment. A feeling of meeting nature up close rather than in wide open spaces.

There are some great running courses, especially on the west side of the Willamette River, which divides the city in two. Hills are abundant and offer interesting views. Although participation in the sport is high, very few running events are held to bring the population together.

HOTELS

Red Lion Motor Inn, Portland Motor Inn, Portland Hilton, Riverside West Motel, Benson Hotel, Holiday Inn – Coliseum, Travelodge at the Coliseum, Sheraton Hotel

DUNIWAY PARK

This is the major starting point for running in Portland. Convenient to downtown, it provides three ideal situations: a beautiful ¼-mile, all-weather outdoor track tucked into a verdant hillside, an adjacent modern YMCA with a fancy 14-laps-per-mile indoor track, and the opportunity to take off into the hills on a scenic route you can follow for up to 13 miles, round trip.

Duniway Park can be reached from the west side downtown hotels by running south for no more than a mile along S.W. 4th Avenue. The Red Lion Motor Inn is the closest.

The Holiday Inn, Travelodge and Sheraton are over a mile further away on the east side of the river. Obtain individual instructions from your hotels for the ½-mile or more route to the Steel Bridge. Cross the bridge and take the stairway at the west end of the bridge down to the river walkway going south for about 1 mile along one of the cleanest city rivers in the world. There are plans to extend this walkway further along the river. Take a right up to S.W. 4th Avenue and head south a short distance to Duniway Park.

TERWILLIGER
BOULEVARD

The most popular route in town is the hilly road leading up the hill from the track at Duniway Park. Many runners take a few laps around the track to warm up and then head off on Terwilliger Boulevard. Mostly uphill for the first couple of miles, the elevation provides a terrific vista of the downtown area. A sidewalk offers even footing along the way. Be skeptical about mileage markers, as many people have painted in their own personal markers.

Terwilliger Boulevard, Portland

At 2.6 miles you will reach the first intersection at Capitol Highway. Picking up the path across the road, it is another .9 mile to Barbur Boulevard. Then backtrack this route for a 7-mile total. Water fountains and rest rooms can be found at the track and at 1¼ miles. Sunrises are a specialty of the course.

WILDWOOD TRAIL

Within the city limits, to the northwest is a wilderness area called Forest Park, which contains about 7,000 acres of seldom used trails. This park actually dwarfs the downtown area and very few people make use of it. Just to the south of Forest Park are the Pittock Mansion Acres, the Hoyt Arboretum, and Washington Park.

Wildwood Trail follows the west hills through these parks for a total of 16¾ miles. The trail begins at the Western Forestry Center on Knights Boulevard behind the main building. A large sign there will show distances and directions. You will see many side trails, roads and fire trails for over 50 miles of potential running.

MT. TABOR PARK

Located about 3½ miles west of the river, Mt. Tabor Park covers 200 acres on the site of an extinct volcano. Some runners can be found using its hilly roads.

CLUBS, FUN-RUNS AND RACES

The Oregon Road Runners Club holds weekly fun-runs on Sundays at 8:00 A.M. at the Forestry Center at Washington Park. Races, when held, are on Saturdays at 9:00 A.M.

TRADITIONAL RACES   Seaside Trail's End Marathon: February
Oak Hills T-Shirt Run, 7 miles: April
Cascade Run-Off, 15 kilometers: Mid-June
ORRC Picnic Run, 5 miles: July
Portland Marathon: Thanksgiving Saturday

CONTACTS   Stephen W. Gould, Oregon Road Runners Club, 2139 S.W. Edgewood Road, Portland, OR 97201.

Portland YMCA, 2831 S.W. Barbur Boulevard, Portland, OR 97201. (503) 223-9622.

HARRISBURG

Population: 60,000	Humidity: 66%
Elevation: 327 ft.	Av. Temperature: (Jan.) 30°F.; (July) 76°F.
Air Quality: Fair to poor	Inches of Rainfall: (Jan.) 2.6; (July) 3.7 Raindays: 124

OVERVIEW

The capital of Pennsylvania, Harrisburg is a moderate-sized city lying amidst rolling hills. Its eastern edge borders the wide Susquehanna River, along which many runners ply their way back and forth in Riverfront Park. A number of bridges cross the river from downtown providing scenic mileage from bank to bank, and an accessible island mid-river provides alternative routing. Away from the urban area, hilly country roads can be enjoyed, and a bike path along a creek west of the city receives a lot of attention.

HOTELS

Holiday Inn–Town, Best Western Nationwide Inn, Host Inn, Penn Harris Motor Inn

RIVERFRONT PARK

The YMCA located at Front and North streets is a good place to start a run. The Holiday Inn and Nationwide are only a couple of blocks away. If you run across Front Street to Riverfront Park and head north, after a few hundred yards you will be at Front and Foster streets where a white post will mark the start of the YMCA 1-mile distance to just short of Front and McClay streets. The route is paved and you can run out on the upper part of the bank and return closer to the river. Usually there is a noticeable head wind going north. Some large trees offer occasional shade.

BRIDGE LOOP

An interesting loop has been set up utilizing two bridges situated only about 300 yards apart crossing to the west bank of the river. The course has been precisely measured to 2.86 miles to be used for a 100-kilometer race.

Run ¼ mile south of the YMCA through Riverfront Park to the Walnut Street Bridge. Cross to the west bank and turn left for 300 yards to the Market Street Bridge. Cross back to Harrisburg and take a left (north) to Front and Foster streets and then turn back to your starting point in Riverfront Park.

To increase your mileage, you can run from either bridge onto an island in the river and run on the roads around the island. There is no measured route.

CONODOQUINET CREEK

On the west side of the river, in Camp Hill, a 6-mile loop has been measured along Conodoquinet Creek. Take the Harvey Taylor Bridge to the west bank and run 1 mile uphill on Bypass 15 to a right turn on 21st Street. Follow 21st for ½ mile until you are opposite Holy Spirit Hospital. Pick up Center Boulevard and turn right just before the bridge and head down to the creek. It is about 3 miles to this point.

A paved bike path follows a loop along the creek over a very hilly 6 miles. It is an interesting run along the water and there are a number of beautiful mansions. Keep a close eye out for bike path signs and you will not get lost. Follow the same route back to the east bank of the river.

The Penn Harris Motor Inn is located in Camp Hill on Bypass 15. If you follow Bypass 15 to 21st Street, you will reach the above route to the creek bike path. You can drive to the start of the creek loop.

COUNTRY ROAD
BEHIND HOST INN

Carol Fridley, a local world-class runner, once stayed at this inn, and found a good country run behind it. Head to the far side of the golf course and take the road left over undulating hills, past farmhouses and cows at pasture. The road travels on for many peaceful miles.

CLUBS, FUN-RUNS
AND RACES

The Harrisburg Area Road Runners Club holds a running event every Sunday. These are usually at 1:30 P.M. in cool weather, and at 6:30 P.M. during hot weather. The format is mostly informal, with no entry fee and no prizes. The club schedules more formal races occasionally throughout the year.

TRADITIONAL RACES

Capital 5,000-Meter Run: Early June
YMCA Quarter-Marathon: June
Kipona 10,000-Meter Run: Labor Day
Harrisburg National Marathon: Early November
Marine Corps 5 Miles: November
Mechanicsburg Glenn Timmons Memorial Half-Marathon: Saturday before Thanksgiving

CONTACTS

Walt Greene, Harrisburg ARRC, 431 Springhouse Road, Camp Hill, PA 17011. (717) 761-5178.
Paul Hurley, Harrisburg ARRC, 28 South 29th Street, Camp Hill, PA 17011. (717) 737-3286.
Jim Kuntz, Central YMCA, Front and North Streets, Harrisburg, PA 17101. (717) 234-6221.

Philadelphia

Population: (met.) 5,320,000	Humidity: 67%
Elevation: 0–441 ft.	Av. Temperature: (Jan.) 35°F.; (July) 78°F.
Air Quality: Fair to poor	Inches of Rainfall: (Jan.) 3.9; (July) 4.1 Raindays: 115

OVERVIEW

Philadelphia has been through a major reconstruction in recent years to clear slums and industrial areas and clean up the downtown area, which is now attractive and safe. While visiting the city, I had never seen so many police cars cruising along the major running routes.

If New Yorkers think that Central Park is the most convenient, large park to be found in America's cities, they have not seen Fairmount Park in Philadelphia: nine and a half times the size of Central Park, and only ¾ of a mile from Center City. Most runners who have seen the park are familiar with the flat loop along the Schuylkill River. This beautiful run draws the greatest number of local runners. East Park, and the more popular West Park sections of Fairmount Park, provide more varied terrain. The northwest section of the park contains Wissahickon Creek, along which Forbidden Drive offers a run through a secluded wilderness environment.

The Philadelphia Art Museum sits in the southern corner of the park, closest to Center City. The steps leading up to the museum were used for the dramatic setting in the film *Rocky*. Part of the Philadelphia Marathon cuts across the upper level of the museum, and past this famous spot. Coming from Center City, a wide boulevard leads directly to the museum and the park.

Suburban parts of the city are popular running areas, and many small clubs hold fun-runs and races. The city of Camden, New Jersey, directly across the Delaware River from Philadelphia, attracts many runners from across the river to its loop along Cooper River. Some visitors to Philly prefer to stay at an inn next to this course.

HOTELS

Franklin Motor Inn, Sheraton Hotel, Penn Center Inn
Camden, New Jersey: Country Squire Inn
Valley Forge: Holiday Inn–Valley Forge, Stouffer's–Valley Forge

ROUTE TO
FAIRMOUNT PARK

Benjamin Franklin Parkway runs diagonally northwest from the heart of downtown (Center City) to the Art Museum. Logan Circle, along the Parkway, can be reached only a few blocks east of the Sheraton. From Logan Circle to the statue of George Washington astride his horse, in front of the museum steps, is .7 miles. Follow the Parkway on sidewalk through a shaded, grassy mall beside the road. Franklin Motor Inn is on the Parkway, close to the museum.

RIVER DRIVE RUN

From George Washington's statue, you can go either left or right to run the 8.379-mile loop along the Schuylkill River. Most runners head counterclockwise, so go right, following the East River Drive sign, staying along the sidewalk. At about .45 miles you will reach a building on your left called Plaisted Hall, next to the "Bike Rental" sign. This is the major starting point for races and training runs. You can obtain water and use the rest rooms here. Several buildings along the road here constitute Boat House Row. Schuylkill River is famous for its crew races.

Continue along the river on the sidewalk, where mileage markers are painted on the walkway every ½ mile. Many trees line the course, and often there are grass and dirt trails beside the pavement. A number of bridges cross the river, but are unreachable by foot, until you come to Falls Bridge. Cross the river on this bridge, and head back down West River Drive. This will bring you back to the Art Museum. No water fountains or rest rooms can be found along West River Drive. On East River Drive, a fountain is located at the 1.5-mile mark. The course is completely flat and quite safe, even at night, when it is lit and frequently used.

FORBIDDEN DRIVE

Drive, or run, up East River Drive past Falls Bridge, on Wissahickon Drive, continuing along the river. After about 2 miles, there will be a road to your left with some room to park. About 40 yards up the road, you will see a sign saying "Forbidden Drive—No Motor Vehicles Permitted."

The course begins here on a dirt and gravel road over fairly flat, scenically wooded terrain for 5½ miles, one way. Following alongside Wissahickon Creek, you will reach Valley Green Inn after 2½ miles. Water and rest rooms can be found here. Continuing on Forbidden Drive for 3 more miles will take you to the edge of the park, and the northwest boundary of the city. This is a favorite route for many local runners.

BELMONT PLATEAU

In West Park, Belmont Plateau has open, grassy fields over challenging hills. Dirt cross-country trails cross over the fields and through wooded areas. At the crest of the hill, near the flagpole, there is a good view of the city skyline. Water and rest rooms are available at the snack bar. Many schools and colleges hold their cross-country meets here over 3-, 5-mile, and 10-kilometer courses. They are not clearly marked.

The plateau can be reached from Center City by heading to Fairmount Park and traveling up West River Drive for about 2 miles to a left at the second traffic light. Then proceed uphill for about ½ mile, where you will see the plateau's open fields to your right.

WEST PARK

Heading uphill on the roads from West River Drive, will take you into West Park. Many miles of roads and sidewalks are here, and few people, as this part of the park is not heavily used. For this reason, it is often used by runners who enjoy quiet, isolated workouts. Along the top of the park roads are flat, but there are good hills running east-west. Few trees provide adequate shade; occasionally you will see a water fountain or rest room. Mileages have not been measured, and most people run here for time. This part of Fairmount Park is also considered safe.

EAST PARK

Heading uphill on the roads from East River Drive will take you into East Park. This section of Fairmount Park is perhaps a little more dangerous than others,

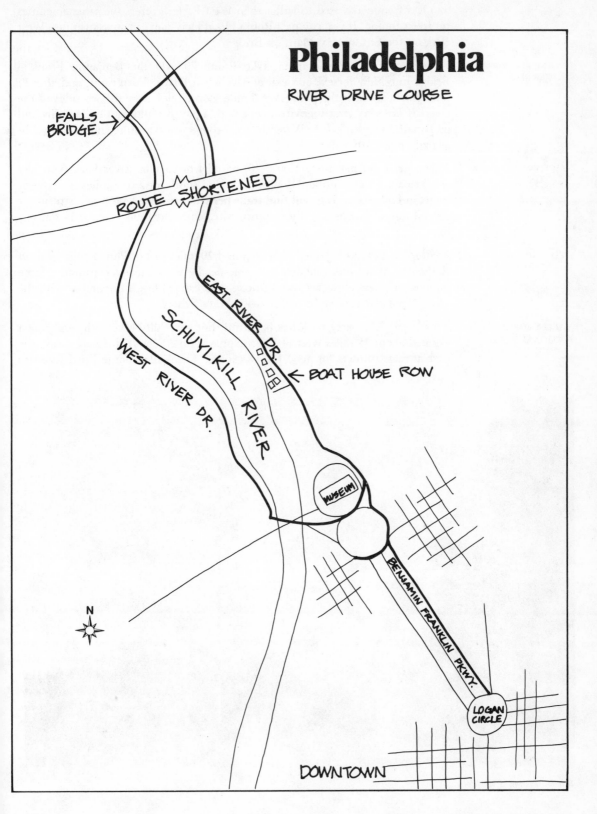

Philadelphia
RIVER DRIVE COURSE

FALLS BRIDGE

ROUTE SHORTENED

EAST RIVER DR.

SCHUYLKILL RIVER

WEST RIVER DR.

← BOAT HOUSE ROW

MUSEUM

BENJAMIN FRANKLIN PKWY.

LOGAN CIRCLE

N

DOWNTOWN

and less frequently used. Shadier than West Park, it offers the same amenities for free running. If you run past Robin Hood Dell, you can cross over into West Park on the Strawberry Mansion Bridge.

COOPER RIVER PARK   From downtown Philadelphia, take Route 70 over the Benjamin Franklin Bridge into New Jersey, and exit at McClellan Drive. Turn right, and after ¼ mile you will reach the park. A 3.6-mile loop circles around both sides of the river. It is a very pretty environment with a paved walkway beside a dirt and grass path. Terrain is flat. Water and rest rooms are available, and the area is lit at night and fairly safe.

NEWTON LAKE PARK   If you drive further along Route 70, parallel to Cooper River Park, you will come to an exit at Cuthbert Boulevard. Head south for 2 to 3 miles to arrive at Newton Lake Park. You will find trails here that run the length of a stream for several miles. This is a really beautiful site, with dirt trails over fairly flat terrain.

MEDFORD LAKES   Medford Lakes, New Jersey, can be found 20 miles east of Philadephia, just off Route 70. Many miles of dirt and pine-needle trails meander around a large number of lakes. However, be warned—you can get lost if unfamiliar with the area. A popular trail starts at Shawnee High School.

VALLEY FORGE
NATIONAL PARK   This large, 2,255-acre park has beautiful, but very hilly bike paths and trails. Located about 25 miles west of Philadelphia via the Schuylkill Expressway, the park attracts runners for good hill workouts. The Valley Forge Road Runners

Belmont Plateau, Philadelphia

meet for their workouts in the park at the Covered Bridge on Route 252. You will find runners heading out from this spot at all hours of the day.

Paved bike trails and dirt horse trails wind through all sections of the park. Routes have been measured, but not marked, so it is best to run with local runners who know the way. If you stay to the far outside of the park, you can run a perimeter loop of 12 miles. Asphalt paths are about 25 percent shaded, and dirt trails are fully shaded. Automobiles are no problem on these courses, and water and rest rooms are scattered throughout.

OUTDOOR TRACKS

Franklin Field, at the University of Pennsylvania, has a 400-meter, all-weather track, which is available usually until 7:00 P.M. During July and August, the track is closed earlier and on weekends.

CLUBS, FUN-RUNS AND RACES

Many groups hold weekly fun-runs and races. The Middle Atlantic Road Runners Club has races which are usually on Sunday. During the summer, they hold occasional Wednesday evening races. Browning Ross, one of the founders of the Road Runners Club of America, puts on low-key races every Sunday at 10:00 A.M. in nearby Woodbury, New Jersey, starting at the YMCA. In the summer, he holds Wednesday evening races at 7:00 P.M.

The Delco Joggers, in Collingdale, Pennsylvania, a southwest suburb, hold fun-runs at least twice a week at three different locations, totaling at least nine runs per week. These are in Collingdale, Swarthmore and Springfield. Contact Byron Mundy for time and place (see address and phone numbers below).

Other competitive clubs around the city include the Plaisted Harriers, Philadelphia Masters, Penn AC, and Haverford AC.

TRADITIONAL RACES

Penn Relays Marathon: End of April
Phoenixville 4½-Mile Race: May
River Run, 10 kilometers: June
Provident Marathon: Mid-October
Valley Forge Turkey Trot, 10 kilometers: Second Weekend of November
Philadelphia Marathon: End of November

CONTACTS

Chris Tatreau, Middle Atlantic RRC, Memorial Hall, Philadelphia, PA 19131. (215) MU6-1776.
Seth Bergmann, Middle Atlantic RRC, 2222 Green Street, Philadelphia, PA 19130. (215) 568-4387.
Browning Ross, Sports East, 240 South Broad Street, Woodbury, NJ 08096. (609) 845-1894.
Byron Mundy, Delco Joggers, 713 Beechwood Avenue, Collingdale, PA 19023. (215) LE4-2833, (215) LU3-1200 (work).
Bob Parks, Valley Forge Road Runners, 388 Radar Drive, King of Prussia, PA 19406. (215) 265-3927, (215) 265-3900 (work).
Raymond K. Reighn, Valley Forge Road Runners, Pawling Road, Phoenixville, PA 19460. (215) 933-6517.
Franklin Field, (215) 386-0961.

PITTSBURGH

Population: (met.) 2,200,000	Humidity: 69%
Elevation: 710–1,370 ft.	Av. Temperature: (Jan.) 33°F.; (July) 75°F.
Air Quality: Fair to poor	Inches of Rainfall: (Jan.) 2.8; (July) 3.6 Raindays: 145

OVERVIEW

Although Pittsburgh has been heavily into steel and coal production, it has tempered its industrial development with a redevelopment of its downtown environment. The "Golden Triangle" consists of clean, modern buildings and spacious parks. The triangle is formed by the confluence of the Allegheny and Monongahela rivers coming together to create the Ohio River. Point Park, at the tip of the triangle, has been built to enhance the occasion. An exciting and scenic running course takes advantage of the park, the riverbanks, and the several bridges crossing the rivers.

Residents are disgusted with the dilapidated city transportation, and recommend visitors to utilize downtown facilities, when possible. If you do wish to wander away from the "Golden Triangle," you will immediately notice the change from a flat to a very hilly terrain. Blanketed over these hills can be found some large, naturally preserved parks with many miles of roads and trails. They are all very safe at daylight hours.

HOTELS

Hilton Hotel, Sheraton Inn, William Penn Hotel

GOLDEN TRIANGLE
COURSE

This 5-mile course begins along the wharf at the Monongahela River, underneath the Smithfield Street Bridge. Run along the wharf to Point Park, a distance of about ¾ of a mile. Go around the "point" at the park's beautiful giant fountain and continue up the wharf, now along the Allegheny River, to the first bridge you reach. This is the 6th Street Bridge. Head up the steps and cross the bridge on the sidewalk, turning left at the end of the bridge onto the walkway heading into Roberto Clemente Park. Staying along the bank of the Allegheny, follow the walkway to Three Rivers Stadium. Circle the stadium and head back along the same route.

The river can be crossed at any of the four bridges along the Allegheny to alter the mileage of the course. Naturally, you can even run loops over the bridges.

Many runners use this course during the week, particularly at noon. The YMCA has daily group runs here. Traffic is no problem, and the course is very safe during the day, although safety is debatable at night. Water fountains are readily available.

SECOND AVENUE ROUTE	If you care to explore Pittsburgh's industrial environment, you can head out 2nd Avenue which runs along the Monongahela River for about 5 miles to Hazelwood. The route is safe, but you do have to deal with commercial traffic and occasionally noxious air.
SCHENLEY PARK	This park is located close to downtown and adjacent to Carnegie-Mellon University on Forbes Avenue, in Oakland, which is also the home of the University of Pittsburgh. Many students utilize the 456-acre park and its 10-kilometer cinder and dirt trail. The trail zigzags its way over a hilly, wooded terrain. Perimeter sidewalks of the park are lit at night. Water can be found at the bottom of Flagstaff Hill, in the parking lot near Carnegie-Mellon.
VIRGINIA MANOR LOOP	You will have to drive to this course which cuts through one of the richest neighborhoods in the Pittsburgh area. There are few cars, the course is flat, and the scenery is excellent. To get there, follow Route 19 south for 3 to 4 miles to the intersection of Beverly and Cochran roads. Turn right on Cochran to Osage Road and park about 100 yards up on your left.
	Run along Osage Road for 1 mile until you reach Valleyview Road on your left. Turn left on Valleyview and follow it 1 mile back to the start.
SOUTH PARK	South Park is located 12 miles south of town on PA 88. For the easiest route, follow the main road (Corrigan Drive) out and back. It measures about 2 to 2½ miles one way. The road is flat and not heavily traveled. Away from Corrigan Drive the park is very hilly and there are many paved paths that branch off and meander over the hills. Water can be found at some of the picnic groves.
NORTH PARK	North Park can be found 14 miles north on Route 19. It contains a lake circumvented by a 5-mile bike trail. The course is almost flat and about three-fourths shaded. Start from the Boathouse Parking Lot where there is water and rest rooms.
FRICK PARK	This 499-acre park, east of Schenley Park on Beechwood Boulevard and English Lane, provides runners with many nature trails that wind through ravines, along creeks, and over hills. A gravel path follows a creek through a grassy valley.
OUTDOOR TRACKS	The nearest track to the Golden Triangle is located about 3 miles to the east on Route 51. Baldwin High School's all-weather track can be seen from the highway on a hill to your left at that point.
INDOOR TRACKS	An old indoor track is available to the public, and can be found in South Park at Schoonemaker Hall. The hall is a barn-type building, not well heated in winter, and with no showers. The 12-laps-per-mile dirt track is a somewhat primitive facility. The Golden Triangle YMCA has a new 30-laps-per-mile, banked track.
CLUBS, FUN-RUNS AND RACES	Three active clubs maintain a busy schedule of events throughout the year. Fun-runs are held by the Allegheny Mountain RRC on the second and fourth Saturdays at 9:30 A.M. at the Mt. Lebanon High School upper parking lot. The club also holds races once a month.
	The Greater Pittsburgh Road Runners Club holds monthly road races. These are on Sundays, and during cold weather, begin at 1:00 P.M. A 2-mile run is always included with a longer distance.
	The West Penn Track Club holds track and cross-country events, which are most frequent during their particular seasons.

Boston Qualifier Marathon: Early March
Meet of Miles, 1 mile: June
GPRRC 10-Mile Regional Race: September
The Great Race, 10 kilometers: Late September

Skip Brown, Greater Pittsburgh RRC, Kimberly Estates, Route 3, Box 497J, Mt. Pleasant, PA 15666. (412) 547-5679.

Shirley McDaniels, Allegheny Mountain RRC, 721 Vallevista Avenue, Pittsburgh, PA 15234. (412) 343-1327.

John Harwick, West Penn Track Club, 467 Beverly Road, Pittsburgh, PA 15216. (412) 561-0338.

Golden Triangle YMCA, 304 Wood Street, Pittsburgh, PA 15222. (421) 261-5820.

Providence

Population: 160,000	Humidity: 70.5%
Elevation: 0–253 ft.	Av. Temperature: (Jan.) 28°F.; (July) 72°F.
Air Quality: Fair to poor	Inches of Rainfall: (Jan.) 3.5; (July) 2.9 Raindays: 123

OVERVIEW

This busy running town has a number of universities which add a young population of runners to the city's streets. Streets are the byword here, as the city has no central parks or waterside runs that can be utilized. One downtown course, along Blackstone Boulevard, appears to be the most popular route, but unfortunately is not close to any motels. To run from a motel, you must resort to the locally normal use of city streets. Motorists are usually very considerate about sharing the road with runners.

Many competitive clubs offer excellent training runs. Unfortunately, no club is interested in putting on races, which are left to commercial sponsors. Many events in nearby Connecticut and Massachusetts provide a complete year 'round schedule.

HOTELS

Marriott Inn, Howard Johnson's – Pawtucket

BLACKSTONE BOULEVARD

Blackstone Boulevard runs through a very nice residential community and here you will find a safe environment for running at all hours. Although there are few lights, runners do use the course at night.

The course is flat and shady, with few intersections to cross. You can run 1.7 miles, one way, on grass along the inside median, or on the road. Swan Point Cemetery, along the boulevard, can be used for additional mileage. The cemetery personnel do not hassle runners here. There are no rest rooms along the route, but water spigots can be found in the cemetery.

Both motels listed are about 2 miles away. Directions to the boulevard are complicated, and it would be best to obtain a map, or inquire at your motel.

LINCOLN WOODS STATE PARK

This is a good place to do hill work, about 3 miles northwest of downtown. A 2½-mile broken asphalt road loops around the park lake. Most hills are rolling, except for one steep 300-yard-long rise. Also, take in the .6-mile-long hill at the entrance to the park from Great Road. This park is not considered safe for night running. Water and rest rooms can be found at the main beach.

ROGER WILLIAMS PARK

This 450-acre park, 3 miles south of town, is *not* recommended by local runners.

TRACKS

Brown University has an outdoor ¼-mile track and an indoor 12¾-laps-per-mile

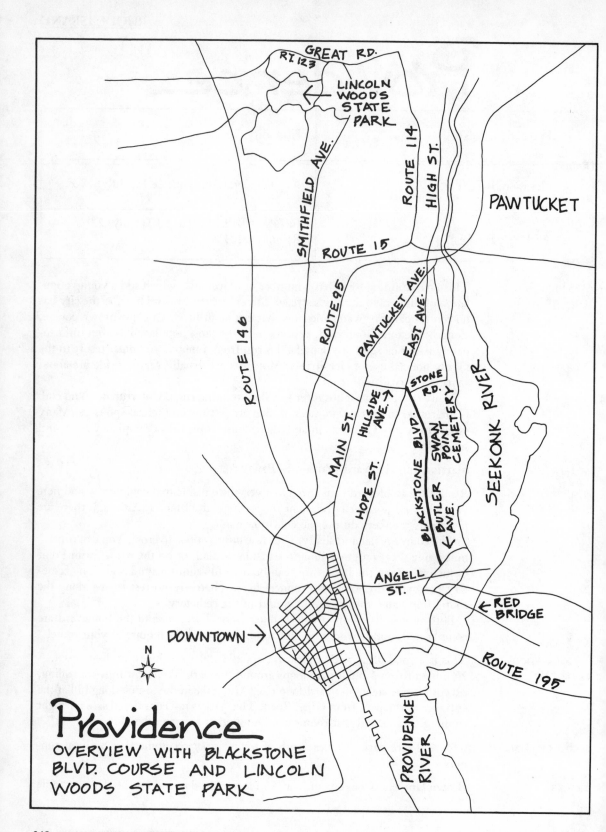

Providence

OVERVIEW WITH BLACKSTONE
BLVD. COURSE AND LINCOLN
WOODS STATE PARK

track. Both of these are available to members of the Brown Spike Shoe Club, and membership is open to the public. Both tracks are closed to non-students between the hours of 2:00 and 6:00 P.M., but are open to the public mornings and evenings.

CLUBS

The following clubs compete in local events: Johnson and Wales Athletic Club, Ocean State Track Club (young women), University of Rhode Island Track Club, Providence College AA, Brown Spike Shoe Club, and the Pawtucket Valley Striders.

TRADITIONAL RACES

West Warwick St. Patrick's Race, 5 miles: March
Lincoln Road Race, 10 miles: June
Point Judith Galilee Road Race, 10 miles: July
Block Island Race, 10 miles: August
Old Stone Bank Race, 10 kilometers: October
Ocean State Marathon: Late October
Seekonk Road Race, 5 miles: November

CONTACTS

Bobby Doyle, Doyle's Sport Center, 133 Broad Street, Pawtucket, RI 02860. (401) 723-6655.
Brown University Track Office, (401) 863-2211.

Charleston

Population: 58,000	Humidity: 76%
Elevation: 0–12 ft.	Av. Temperature: (Jan.) 49°F.; (July) 80°F.
Air Quality: Fair	Inches of Rainfall: (Jan.) 2.9; (July) 8.2 Raindays: 115

OVERVIEW
This charming, aristocratic city affords visiting runners a magnificent scenic route along its historic harbor. Conveniently located to downtown hotels, the course draws many local runners over the busy, yet unobstructed roadway.

Summer months are characterized by high heat and humidity, and early or late runs are recommended.

HOTELS
Battery Carriage House, Vendue Inn, Mills Hyatt House, Holiday Inn, Golden Eagle Motel, Heart of Charleston Motel, Best Western King Charles Inn, Indigo Inn

HARBOR RUN
From your hotel, head east a few blocks to East Bay Street, and turn south. From the traffic light at East Bay and Broad streets, it is exactly 1½ miles to the Coast Guard Station. This run follows the famous Charleston Battery, with the harbor on one side, and lovely mansions on the other. Sailboats to the left, and eighteenth- and nineteenth-century mansions to the right. When you come to the bend in the course, you are at the point where the Civil War began. To your left, you can see Fort Sumter.

A rest room is located at the Exxon station near the beginning of the course, and you will run through a park where there is a water fountain.

For a slightly longer route, turn west on Ashley Avenue, two blocks north of the Coast Guard station. Go five blocks to a small lake, which will provide you with a ½-mile loop. Many runners can be found here.

CHARLES TOWNE LANDING
Take I-26 north 5 miles to Cosgrove Avenue, and follow the signs. At this historic state park you will find a beautiful 2½-mile cross-country loop on a dirt and pine-needle trail.

KIAWAH ISLAND INN
This luxury resort is located about 23 miles from downtown. Here you will find a 10-mile flat beach, and a system of bike trails, golf cart roads, and a parcourse. Many runners come here to do their long mileage.

CLUBS, FUN-RUNS AND RACES
The Charleston Running Club and the Complete Runner store put on races and fun-runs about twice a month.

TRADITIONAL RACES
Kiawah Island 10 Miles: February

Cooper River Bridge Run, 10 kilometers: Early April
Women's Distance Classic, 3 miles: October

CONTACTS Bob Schlau, Charleston Running Club, 7½ Bennett Street, Charleston, SC 29401. (803) 577-6669.
The Complete Runner, 401 Coleman Boulevard, Mt. Pleasant, SC 29464. (803) 884-1298.

COLUMBIA

Population: 115,000	Humidity: 71.5%
Elevation: 332 ft.	Av. Temperature: (Jan.) 45.4°F.; (July) 81.2°F.
Air Quality: Fair	Inches of Rainfall: (Jan.) 3.44; (July) 5.65 Raindays: 110

OVERVIEW

Located near the geographical center of South Carolina, Columbia is a broad-boulevarded capital with streets laid out in a grid pattern. After the city burned down during the Civil War, the downtown area was redesigned with streets four to eight lanes wide. The State House lies directly across the street from the large University of South Carolina Campus, where many of the city's runners head out on well-measured and marked courses. Actually, the most famous course, the 15-miler used for the Governor's Cup Race, begins in front of the State House.

These courses turn back and forth through stately residential communities with many large, old trees lining the lightly trafficked roads. Most of the runners prefer to stay on the roads, rather than using sidewalks, and apparently dogs have long given up the effort to bother them.

Group running is very popular, and on Saturday mornings you can see many small units of runners working their way around town. A couple of different clubs are active in the area.

HOTELS

Holiday Inn—City Center, Carolina Inn, Sheraton Motor Inn

GOVERNOR'S CUP COURSE

This course, beginning at the State House, heads out from the intersection of Gervais and Main streets, the two major thoroughfares in town. Run east on Gervais for one block and turn south on Sumter Street. Then turn east again onto Senate Street and follow it for about 1 mile, where you make a couple of quick rights to head back toward the university. Remember that this course is well marked to indicate every turn, so these incomplete directions are basically to give you an idea of the course, rather than a turn by turn description.

After a few more turns you arrive back at Main Street and then make a left on Wheat Street to pass the university's Physical Education Center where rest rooms are available. This is about 2½ miles from the start, and the course until now has been relatively flat along streets with modest traffic. From here, you travel into Heathwood, a very wealthy neighborhood, and Shandon, a community of old, attractive homes. About ½ mile from the university you come to Saluda Hill, ½ mile up on a 20 percent grade. Then it is rolling hills followed by a slight downhill to 8 miles, when you reach the back side of Lake Catherine. Here the course makes a 4-mile loop around the lake. It then heads back to downtown on a gentle 2-mile uphill before meeting some monster hills, including Tomaca Hill at 10¾ miles. This hill is about 300 yards long on a 100-foot rise. Once you are through the hills, the course remains flat to rolling back to the finish. Water fountains can be found at occasional small parks.

10-KILOMETER COURSE FROM DOWNTOWN

Start from the ramp in front of the Physical Education Center and head east on Wheat Street for about 2 miles to Bonham Street. Turn right, and after two blocks, right again onto Duncan Street. Follow Duncan for about 1 mile to a left on Maple Street, followed by an immediate left onto Monroe Street, and take Monroe for about 1 mile back out to Bonham. Make a right on Bonham and an immediate right onto Hayward Street for 1½ to 2 miles west until you reach Saluda Street. Take Saluda downhill to Wheat Street, where you make a left back to the Physical Education Center.

The course is mostly flat and travels almost entirely through quiet Shandon with its heavy shade trees.

IRMO-CHAPIN RECREATION CENTER COURSES

Several miles north of town, numerous marked courses begin at the recreation center and travel through residential communities. To reach the center, take the St. Andrews Road exit on I—26 to Leisure Lane across from Allied Chemical. Mileage and directional markers for each course have been painted on the road. During early morning hours, you will find groups of runners heading out over the rolling hills to take advantage of the cool morning air.

OUTDOOR TRACKS

A ¼-mile asphalt track is located on the University of South Carolina Campus, close to Rosewood Street. At the Irmo High School, an all-weather track measures ¼ mile.

INDOOR TRACKS

The Columbia YMCA has a new Tartan indoor, banked track of 20 laps per mile.

CLUBS, GROUP RUNS AND RACES

The Columbia Track Club has the most active racing schedule with both track and road races. The Columbia Runners and Joggers put on one event each year, the Governor's Cup Race, and otherwise function in an informal and social manner.

A group meets for a training run every Saturday at 9:00 A.M. in front of Steve Sparrows house on Edisto Street in Shandon, near Saluda Street, south of Hayward Street.

The Irmo Sunrisers meet every morning at the Irmo-Chapin Recreation Center. The Irmo Track Club meets Mondays, Wednesdays and Fridays at 5:00 P.M. at the Irmo High School track.

TRADITIONAL RACES

Carolina Marathon: First Saturday in February
Palmetto Cup Road Race, 15 and 5 miles: Second Saturday in March
Governor's Cup Road Race, 15 miles: First Saturday in October
State Fair Race, 10 kilometers: Mid-October
Turkey Trot, 10 kilometers: Saturday of Thanksgiving Weekend

CONTACTS

Dr. Tom Trotter, President, Columbia Track Club, 811 Rolling Wood Trail, Glendale, SC 29210. (803) 772-5917.
Richard Harris, Columbia Runners and Joggers, 2436 Robin Crest Drive, West Columbia, SC 29169. (803) 794-0345.
Columbia YMCA, 1420 Sumter Street, Columbia, SC 29201. (803) 799-9187.

GREENVILLE

Population: 55,400	Humidity: 68%
Elevation: 1,040 ft.	Av. Temperature: (Jan.) 43°F.; (July) 79°F.
Air Quality: Fair	Inches of Rainfall: (Jan.) 4.2; (July) 4.6 Raindays: 115

OVERVIEW
This quiet, friendly South Carolina town sits in the western part of the state. With some rolling hills and tree-lined streets, Greenville offers a bucolic running environment. Furman University contributes its track, campus, and golf course for runs just north of town, and downtown runners can enjoy Cleveland Park alongside the Reedy River.

HOTELS
Sheraton Motor Inn, Howard Johnson's—Downtown, Downtowner Motor Inn

REEDY RIVER TRAIL
Within a mile of the above hotels and only about 700 yards south of the Sheraton can be found the entrance to Reedy River Trail. Go south on Church Street to Bell Tower Shopping Center. Behind the center, the entrance sits below the parking lot. The run stays entirely within Cleveland Park over a distance of approximately 3½ to 4 miles. The trail is actually a bicycle path alongside the river over a mostly flat terrain. There is one hilly ½-mile section that goes over a ridge. Water fountains and rest rooms are available and the course is lit and safe at night. Shade trees are abundant.

FURMAN UNIVERSITY ROUTES
Follow highway 25 and 276 north for 5 miles to Furman University. The campus has a relatively flat 2½-mile road around a 30-acre lake. The 18-hole golf course has rolling hills and is available for grass running, and the ¼-mile track is open to visiting runners.

PARIS MOUNTAIN STATE PARK
This 1,275-acre park contains three lakes surrounded by 8 to 10 miles of trails. The area offers good hills with one particularly steep mountain trail. Fountains and rest rooms can be found in different areas.

CLUBS
The Greenville Track Club holds races or fun-runs about three times a month. They also have a monthly meeting on the first Tuesday at Pizza Inn, LeGrand Boulevard, at 6:30 P.M.

FUN-RUNS
From May to August, there are Thursday night track meets at Furman University; fun-runs are held there the first three Saturdays each month.

TRADITIONAL RACES
Reedy River Run, 10 kilometers: Late April
Paris Mountain 20-Kilometer: First Saturday in December

CONTACTS
Bill Keesling, 5 Rollingwood Drive, Taylors, SC 29687. (803) 268-8967.
Adrian Craven, Woodhaven Drive, Greenville, SC 29609. (803) 233-0333, (803) 242-6600 (work).

RaPiD CiTY

Population: 500,600	Humidity: 60%
Elevation: 3,140 ft.	Av. Temperature: (Jan.) 22°F.; (July) 73°F.
Air Quality: Fair	Inches of Rainfall: (Jan.) .5; (July) 3.0 Raindays: 95

OVERVIEW

A busy tourist town, Rapid City lies on the eastern edge of the Black Hills, only 25 miles from Mt. Rushmore. The heavy influx of tourist traffic in the summer months can make local street running somewhat hazardous. Hometown runners favor two courses, offering you a good chance to find running companionship.

HOTELS

Best Western Gill's Sun Inn, Alex Johnson Hotel

SIOUX PARK BICYCLE PATH

Gill's Sun Inn is only four blocks northeast of this grass, or concrete, 4-mile loop. The park is on the west side of town. Follow Canyon Lake Drive to the "Rapid City Recreation Department" sign. Turn left, and the course begins at the parking lot. Most of the way, the path follows Rapid Creek and passes Canyon Lake and a golf course. Do not drink water from the creek or the lake. The course is very winding with some short hills and is occasionally interrupted by parking lots. Drinking fountains can be found at picnic areas.

SKYLINE DRIVE

This is a hilly, challenging course with a very scenic aspect. It runs along a razorback hill with excellent vistas of the city below to your left and to your right. Begin at the corner of Quincy and Mt. Rushmore Road, at J. B. Big Boy. Run west on Quincy, and when the road curves left it becomes Skyline Drive. Stay on the main road for as long as you wish, then doubleback. Dinosaur Park is located 1 mile from the start, and the Wax Museum is 5.6 miles. The environment is mostly open country and there is some shade.

TRACKS

There is a ¼-mile outdoor Tartan track at the School of Mines and Technology on the east edge of town. The YMCA will have an indoor track completed in 1980.

FUN-RUNS AND RACES

There is no official local club, although weekly fun-runs are held throughout the year. Most of the year, these are held at noon on Sundays at the Sioux Park Bicycle Path. During the summer, they are held on a weekday evening. For more details, contact the runners listed on the following page.

TRADITIONAL RACES

Mystic Mountain Run, 6⅜ miles (in the back woods of the Black Hills): Mid-July

Spearfish Canyon, 9 miles (downhill): Mid-November

Terry Peak Railroad Race, 6.5 miles: Early August
Angostura Road Race, 6 miles: June

CONTACTS   Larry Robertson, 1302 Racine Street, Rapid City, SD 57701. (605) 341-3916.
Bill Marquardt, 216 San Marco, Rapid City, SD 57701. (605) 343-0132.

SIOUX FALLS

Population: 90,000	Humidity: 67%
Elevation: 1,422 ft.	Av. Temperature: (Jan.) 14°F.; (July) 73°F.
Air Quality: Fair	Inches of Rainfall: (Jan.) .6; (July) 2.9 Raindays: 93

OVERVIEW

A small and quiet city, Sioux Falls sits at the eastern edge of the state, close to Minnesota and Iowa. Surrounded by barren, flat plains, it is an oasis of hills and trees. The Sioux River winds its way through and around town, and many parks have been developed along its banks. From downtown, a new bike trail has been built along the river for a total of 11.7 miles.

Lincoln High School has long been a powerhouse in track and cross-country, and much of their success comes from training in hilly Tuthill Park, near the river. Race activity has been infrequent here, with much of the focus directed 65 miles north in the smaller town of Brookings, the running capital of the state.

Winter and summer produce difficult conditions due to extreme temperatures and plenty of humidity.

HOTELS

Holiday Inn—Downtown

SIOUX RIVER BIKE TRAIL

The trail begins at the Statue of David, on 9th Avenue, about four blocks east of Holiday Inn, and runs alongside the eastern bank of the river as it curves its way to the south. At about 3½ miles, the trail crosses over to the western bank on a dam and continues on that side of the river, which curves west after another mile. The trail eventually ends at Western Avenue.

Many runners prefer a small dirt road which runs along both sides of the river. Known as The Dike, it can be found where the bike trail has not yet replaced it. The uneven footing keeps bicyclists away.

Shade covers many parts of these trails, and the bike trail runs through parks that have drinking fountains and rest rooms. You can also find water at the Statue of David.

TUTHILL PARK

About 4½ miles south of downtown, running on the bike trail, you will come to a footbridge that crosses the river into the park. Here you will find large grassy areas on lower and upper sections, and a long, steep hill.

INDOOR TRACKS

The YMCA has a 17-laps-per-mile track (see address below, under Contacts).

CLUBS, FUN-RUNS AND RACES

A new club, the Sioux Empire Striders, has recently been formed in order to provide more running events. During the summer a 3-mile road race is held every Monday night at Lincoln High School at 6:00 P.M. The high school can be

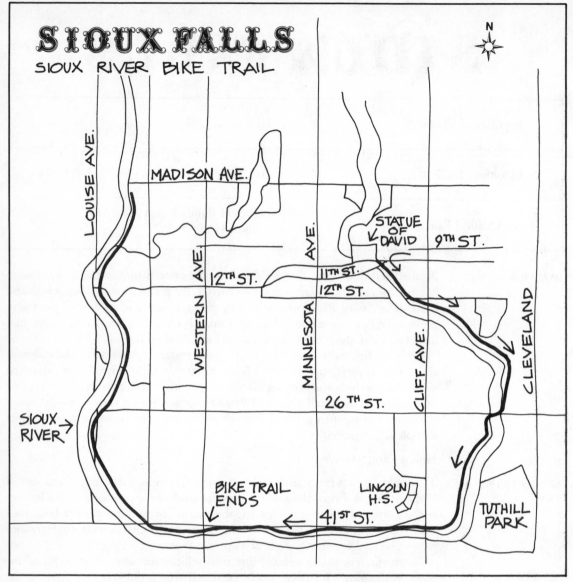

SIOUX FALLS
SIOUX RIVER BIKE TRAIL

reached by running down the bike trail to Cliff Avenue, and then north ¼ of a mile.

The Prairie Striders, in Brookings, have a fun-run or race almost every week.

TRADITIONAL RACES   Brookings Jackrabbit, 15 miles: June
Sioux Falls Marathon: Mid-September
Sioux Falls to Harrisburg Road Race, 6 miles: Early December

CONTACTS   Sioux Falls YMCA, Sioux Empire Striders, 230 South Minnesota Avenue, Sioux Falls, SD 57102. (605) 336-3190.
Bob Bartling, Prairie Striders, Bartling Furniture Store, Brookings, SD 57006. (605) 692-2414.

Chattanooga

Population: 165,000	Humidity: 70.5%
Elevation: 672 ft.	Av. Temperature: (Jan.) 40°F.; (July) 79°F.
Air Quality: Fair	Inches of Rainfall: (Jan.) 5.38; (July) 5.14 Raindays: 131

OVERVIEW

Spirited by the famous song "Chattanooga Choo-Choo," runners here have worked up plenty of steam in developing an active running environment, and the local Athletic Attic store has now taken the place of the "Chattanooga Shoe-Shine Boy."

The city is located in the East Tennessee Valley, along the southern border of the state, and is surrounded on three sides by mountains. Lookout Mountain dominates the landscape, and the name Chattanooga comes from its Cherokee Indian description.

The Tennessee River curves its way through town, and a popular downtown course travels along its banks. Many runners key on the Central YMCA to begin this convenient route. Not far from the city, the famous Chickamauga Battlefield draws many runners to its rolling terrain.

HOTELS

Holiday Inn—I-124

YMCA—CENTRAL COURSE

The Holiday Inn is located just a few blocks from the YMCA. This is a rolling 3- or 5-mile course starting from the entrance to the YMCA on 6th Street. Proceed up a moderate hill for ¼ mile to 9th Street, and then straight across onto Gateway Avenue, down an easy graded hill to Riverfront Parkway at the entrance of the Combustion Engineering Company at a point 1 mile from the start. Turn right here and follow Riverfront Parkway for 1½ miles to the base of the Market Street Bridge. This 1½-mile stretch borders John Ross Landing Park. John Ross was the Cherokee Indian Chief who founded the city. For the 3-mile course, turn right two blocks short of the bridge onto Chestnut Street for the ½ mile back to the YMCA. For the 5-mile course, turn back at the bridge and repeat the 2½-mile route back to the YMCA.

CHICKAMAUGA NATIONAL MILITARY PARK

This is the 5,000-acre site of the Chickamauga Battlefield where one of the fiercest battles of the Civil War took place. Located 9 miles south of Chattanooga on U.S. 27, a 10-mile course starts at the Headquarters Building. You can run other distances, and directions for these can be found at the Headquarters.

For the 10-mile course, follow U.S. 27 .3 miles south to the first left, following that for 1.3 miles to Brotherton Road, swinging left for 1 mile to Jays Mill Road. Then turn right for 1 mile and back onto another paved road for .3 miles, and then make a right onto the next paved road for 2 miles.

At 6 miles, turn right again for approximately ¼ mile, then turn right on Cravens Tower Road. Follow this road for 1 mile to Cravens Tower and then another ½ mile back to Brotherton Road. The course continues over Snodgrass Hill for the 2 miles back to the Headquarters.

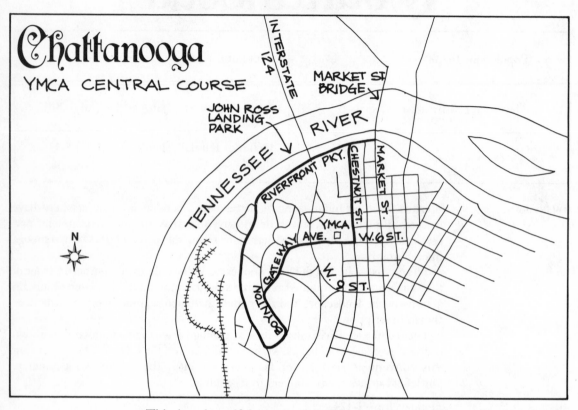

This is a beautiful course, heavily wooded, and the running is between monuments and cannons. The annual Chickamauga Chase takes place over this course.

INDOOR TRACKS   The Central YMCA, on West Sixth Street, has an indoor track.

CLUBS   The Chattanooga Track Club is a well-organized club, featuring about one race each month. There is a Summer Track and Field Program and these events are listed in the *Chattanooga News—Free Press*. Many runners meet and run from the Central YMCA.

TRADITIONAL RACES   Chickamauga Chase, 10 miles: Early Spring
Chattanooga Chase, 5 miles: Late April
First Tennessee Marathon: Mid-Fall

CONTACTS   Earl Mahler, Editor of *Jogging Around*, the CTC Newsletter, First Tennessee Bank, 701 Market Street, Chattanooga, TN 37401. (615) 757-4499.
Central YMCA, 301 West Sixth Street, Chattanooga, TN 37402. (615) 266-3766.
Dick Ramsey, Chattanooga Track Club, 3124 Rose Terrace, Chattanooga, TN. 37401. (615) 622-7596.

KNOXVILLE

Population: 190,000	Humidity: 70%
Elevation: 936 ft.	Av. Temperature: (Jan.) 41°F.; (July) 78°F.
Air Quality: Fair to poor	Inches of Rainfall: (Jan.) 4.67; (July) 4.70 Raindays: 132

OVERVIEW

In the eastern section of the state, Knoxville is part of the lush Tennessee Valley, just 35 miles north of the Great Smoky Mountains. Headquarters for the Tennessee Valley Authority, the city has more of a commercial than agricultural environment. Even without a plantation atmosphere, it expresses a lot of southern charm with its gracious residential areas and streets lined with beautiful dogwood trees.

The Tennessee River flows through town, providing a popular, scenic course close to its banks and through one of its finest neighborhoods. Close to downtown, the University of Tennessee has an active running group who often meet and run from the university track. The mostly flat campus functions as an active training ground. Knoxville is a busy running city, with races about every other week.

HOTELS

Holiday Inn–Central, Sheraton–Campus Inn

CHEROKEE
BOULEVARD COURSE

This is a beautiful, residential, grass 5-mile course located about 1½ miles west of the above hotels which are at the University of Tennessee. From the hotels you can either run through busy streets or take public transportation to the start of the course. To get there, follow Cumberland Avenue, which becomes Kingston Pike. You will reach Cherokee Boulevard on your left, easily recognizable by its grass median strip and large stone archway.

Over rolling hills, part of the course follows the Tennessee River. Stay on the Boulevard until it reaches Kingston Pike. You will have run 2½ miles and you will be 1 mile along the Pike from the start. It is recommended to repeat the 2½-mile course back rather than take the 1-mile congested route along the Pike.

There is little traffic along the Boulevard and dogs have become bored with the runners. The street is well lit and popular for night running. Residents are very tolerant of polite runners using their outdoor water faucets. There is an historical Cherokee Indian burial mound directly on the course, and the Civil War-famous Cherokee Bluffs are across the river.

CADES COVE

In the Smoky Mountain National Park, 40 minutes south of Knoxville, there is a 10-mile loop course at Cades Cove. This is considered an outstandingly beautiful site with excellent hill running at about 2,800 feet in altitude. On summer mornings, the air is cool and fresh. There is a lot of wildlife in the area, and campsites are available. The course is paved and easy to follow, with water and rest rooms along the route. Within an hour's drive from the Cove, you can get to 7,000 feet for real altitude training.

CLUBS AND RACES

The Knoxville Track Club has an annual twenty-six race program. In the summer there are evening fun-runs at the University of Tennessee track.

TRADITIONAL RACES

Smoky Mountain Marathon: February
Expo 10-Kilometer Road Race: Late May
"Run Fer The Hills," 10-kilometers, Gatlinburg: June
Cobbly Nob International Cross-Country Meet: November

CONTACT

Harold Canfield, Knoxville Track Club, 502 Alexander Road, Knoxville, TN 37920. (615) 577-1537.

MEMPHIS

Population: 685,000	Humidity: 70%
Elevation: 331 ft.	Av. Temperature: (Jan) 41°F.; (July) 82°F.
Air Quality: Fair	Inches of Rainfall: (Jan.) 4.9; (July) 3.5 Raindays: 112

OVERVIEW

This large southern city along the Mississippi River has a beautiful, clean and safe downtown area. Unfortunately, it does not help runners because no decent, unobstructed courses can be found here. River industry developed long before any thought was given to riverside parks or pathways.

A promising situation is in the works to solve the downtown problem. Sitting directly below the skyline, City Island retains its natural wooded state, offering miles of rustic running. In the near future, a bridge will connect the Civic Center to City Island, now commonly known as Mud Island, and soon to be named Volunteer Island. In the meantime, it is a 3-mile run to get onto the island.

Good running parks can be found east of downtown, with excellent accommodations nearby. Two universities near these parks produce a lot of runner traffic.

The Memphis Runners Track Club has created much excitement with frequent and interesting runs. You can usually find a running event on both weekend days.

HOTELS

Holiday Inn – Central, Hyatt Regency Ridgeway

OVERTON PARK

Located 3 miles east of downtown, this is the most popular running area in the city. To reach the park from downtown hotels, you can run straight out Poplar to the park entrance. It is a broad, open avenue with wide sidewalks. Traffic can be heavy during the day. The most convenient hotel is Holiday Inn, just ½ mile along McLean to Poplar, and a quick right into the park.

The park offers a diversity of routes and footing. One loop on the roadway closest to the perimeter will be 3 miles. The shaded roads are closed to automobile traffic on weekends. At other times you might want to avoid the roads, as some are highly crowned and you would want to run down the middle. A large section of the park is wooded, and many trails provide good cross-country workouts. The golf course has a grassy path around its perimeter. Terrain is mostly flat with some gradual hills. Water fountains and rest rooms are available.

SOUTHWESTERN UNIVERSITY CAMPUS

Adjacent to the north side of Overton Park, many runners do a loop around the

Overton Park, Memphis

university campus. A dirt path has been worn into the surrounding lawns. Once around is 1.6 miles; parts of the flat course are on sidewalk.

CITY (MUD, VOLUNTEER) ISLAND

Once the bridge to this island is completed, the downtown area will be one of those rare places in America where you can reach semi-wilderness within a few blocks of the central business area. Until then, you must run north on 2nd Street for 3 miles until you can make a left onto the island. Follow the dirt road on the island along the riverbank for 3 miles south, and then head back along the same bank, enjoying the skyline, or follow the pathway north on the other side of the island for the 3 miles back. The island is virtually flat, with plenty of shade trees. When muddy conditions prevail, use the paved road further in from the riverbank.

AUDUBON PARK

Seven miles east of town, Audubon Park receives a lot of attention from runners in the neighboring residential areas. Memphis State University is only about 1 mile north of the park. One loop around the park road is 3 miles. From here you can run north on Goodlett Street to Memphis State, and close to the university, you can run the perimeter of the Galloway Golf Course.

HYATT REGENCY

This hotel is located between two parallel roads that make up a pretty, residential route. An annual race is held over the course. Head north on Sweet Brier or East Shady Grove for 1½ miles to Shady Grove Road, then cross over and take the other street back. The road is lined with shade trees and some small hills break up the flat terrain.

If you head left (west) on Shady Grove Road you can have a long run over to Audubon Park and back. Stay on Shady Grove Road for 2½ to 3 miles to a left on Perkins, and then a quick right onto Central Avenue. After 1 mile, make.a left on Goodlett for another mile to the park. If you head back without going into the park, you will have a 12- to 13-mile run, out and back.

OUTDOOR TRACKS

Memphis State University has an all-weather, ¼-mile track. The track is off Goodlett, about 1 mile north of Audubon Park.

INDOOR TRACKS

The only indoor track is at the Urban Division YMCA. It measures 27 laps per mile.

CLUBS, FUN-RUNS AND RACES

The Memphis Runners Track Club holds a race and a fun-run every weekend. The race day alternates with the fun-run day to allow local runners a chance to race if they have to work one day a weekend.

The Memphis-Shelby Track Foundation is one of the more ambitious age-group programs in the country. Many fine college runners have developed through their meets.

TRADITIONAL RACES

26.2 Memphis: Late February, early March
Memphis in May 10-Kilometer: Early May
Overton Park 5-Miles: Late August
Overton Park 5-Miles: Late September

CONTACT

Bud Joyner, Memphis Runners Track Club, Joyner Sporting Goods, 683 New York Street, Memphis, TN 38104. (901) 274-1358, 276-3690.

NASHVILLE

Population: (met.) 560,000	Humidity: 70%
Elevation: 550 ft.	Av. Temperature: (Jan.) 39.9°F.; (July) 80.2°F.
Air Quality: Fair	Inches of Rainfall: (Jan.) 4.8; (July) 3.8 Raindays: 120

OVERVIEW

Known as the "Athens of the South" and the Country Music Capital of the World, Nashville is also developing a reputation for being a friendly and active city of runners. With variable weather as well as variable terrain, you can find some challenging and enjoyable runs here. Sitting between northern and southern climates, the city may be hot one day and cold the next. Nashville is a pretty city, small and clean, with comfortable access to Centennial Park, a popular running spot containing a replica of the famous Greek Parthenon.

HOTELS

Holiday Inn – Nashville, Hyatt Regency, Spence Manor, Sheraton – Nashville, Best Western Hall of Fame Inn

CENTENNIAL PARK

Many downtown runners use this park during the week. Located next to Vanderbilt University, it also receives a lot of attention from the school population. For an easy route to follow from downtown, go straight out Church Street for the 1½ miles to the park. Many runners meet at the YMCA, downtown on Church Street, and run out in groups starting at about 6:15 each morning. The Holiday Inn sits directly across the street from the park.

The terrain here is mostly flat, and a 1-mile loop circles the Parthenon building and a small duck pond. You can run on the road or alongside on the adjacent grassy lawns. A hilly area in the western section circles up and around for another ½ mile. Traffic is allowed on the park roads, but since the roads are not thoroughfares, a slow speed limit is usually observed. A public building in the park contains rest rooms and water fountains.

SHELBY PARK

Lying along the Cumberland River, about 2 miles east of downtown, this attractive park contains a good 5-mile loop. Most of the run along the river is flat, with a choice of using the hilly riverbank.

Park police assure safety here while the park is open until 11:00 P.M., and night lighting provides extra hours of training.

The park is not well used by runners, as it is located in a low-income part of town.

PERCY WARNER PARK

You've heard of Nashville's Grand Ole Opry—well this is its "grand ole park." Local runners are proud of this park and make good use of its hilly terrain. Many running events are scheduled here over its marked courses of 1.6, 5.8 and

11.2 miles. Located about 8 miles southwest of downtown, the park can be reached by following West End Avenue until it becomes Harding Road, and then turning left onto Belle Meade Boulevard to the park entrance. You can park inside the entrance where the courses begin.

The hills here are very tough, and can intimidate all but the best runners. Ed Leddy, a local world-class runner, before a race remarked to some anxious competitors that he was going to sprint the hills as hard as he could and at the top he was going to turn it on. It worked for him, as he finished way ahead of the field.

When I ran the course and was duly fatigued after a short distance, my companions chuckled and said we would be reaching the hills soon. Finally, at the higher elevations in the park, you can experience beautiful vistas of the Nashville countryside and skyline.

Autos are allowed into the park, but traffic is usually negligible. Bring your own refreshment, or if you meet up with Tom Raynor, a top Nashville runner, he keeps a well-stocked supply of beer in his van. The park is heavily wooded and provides excellent shade. All intersections are well marked, making it easy to follow each course.

INDOOR TRACKS

The Nashville YMCA has a 22-laps-per-mile indoor track and a 17-laps-per-mile rooftop track.

CLUBS, FUN-RUNS AND RACES

The Nashville Striders is an active, innovative organization providing a full schedule of yearly events. Fun-runs are held every Saturday morning at Percy Warner Park at 8:00 A.M., and on Wednesday evenings at Centennial Park at 5:15. A new and popular fun-run takes place once a month, usually on Tuesdays, during the full moon. Runners meet at 10:00 P.M. at the first picnic area in Edwin Warner Park (the southern part of Percy Warner Park) for a night run.

Centennial Park, Nashville

Races are held almost once a month, and clinics are usually coordinated with them. The club also holds monthly meetings and has a picnic twice a year.

TRADITIONAL RACES
Music City Run, 1.6, 5.8 and 11.2 miles: March
Old Hickory Run, 1.6, 5.8 and 11.2 miles: October

CONTACTS
David Wood, Nashville Striders, 5972 Asberry Court, Nashville, TN 37221. (615) 646-4685.
Kent Rea, Nashville YMCA, 1000 Church Street, Nashville, TN 37203. (615) 254-0631.
The Athlete's House, 1700 Portland Avenue, Nashville, TN 37202. (615) 292-8110.

Population: 320,000	Humidity: 66%
Elevation: 650 ft.	Av. Temperature: (Jan.) 50°F.; (July) 84.5°F.
Air Quality: Fair	Inches of Rainfall: (Jan.) 2.35; (July) 2.18 or less Raindays: 82

OVERVIEW

The Colorado River flows through downtown Austin. Hydroelectric dams cross the river, creating a continuous series of lakes. Thus, where you once had a river, you now have Town Lake and Lake Austin. Most of the running here is done along Town Lake. Shoal Creek runs into Town Lake, creating another opportunity for an interesting run.

Austin is proud of its running courses, and the Parks and Recreation Department has printed a brochure about utilizing them. The large student population (University of Texas) adds its feet to these popular routes, keeping the running traffic active both day and night. Like all Texas towns, summer heat can be wicked, and running is advisable either in the early morning or in the evening. You will have plenty of company at these hours.

HOTELS

Stephen Austin Hotel, Sheraton Crest Inn, Driskill Hotel, Holiday Inn–South, Villa Capri Motor Hotel, Ramada Inn–Downtown

TOWN LAKE ROUTES

The lake lies within close proximity, south of downtown hotels and the State Capitol. When you reach the lake, you can follow courses both east and west. Congress Avenue, running down from the Capitol, divides the courses to either side.

The course to the east of Congress Avenue is not a loop, as it only includes part of the southern bank. Following the pathway out and back, including the few spurs and connectors, the distance measures 4.9 miles.

The course west of Congress Avenue loops around both sides of the lake, and includes two spurs, one of them reaching into Eilers Park at the western end of the run. This distance measures 4.7 miles. Both courses hug the shore most of the way. Terrain is mostly flat over paved or gravel footing, and landscaping is maintained to provide ample shade. Drinking fountains are frequently available.

SHOAL CREEK TRAIL

Shoal Creek Trail is a popular route that heads north from Town Lake, through the downtown area. The completed distance now measures 3.7 miles, one way, with a proposed addition of 1.3 miles when the trail will eventually reach 45th Street. It now ends at 38th Street.

The city is very responsible about maintaining the scenic beauty of its running courses, and this route will not disappoint you. Plenty of drinking water can be found along its flat, paved or gravel, shady miles.

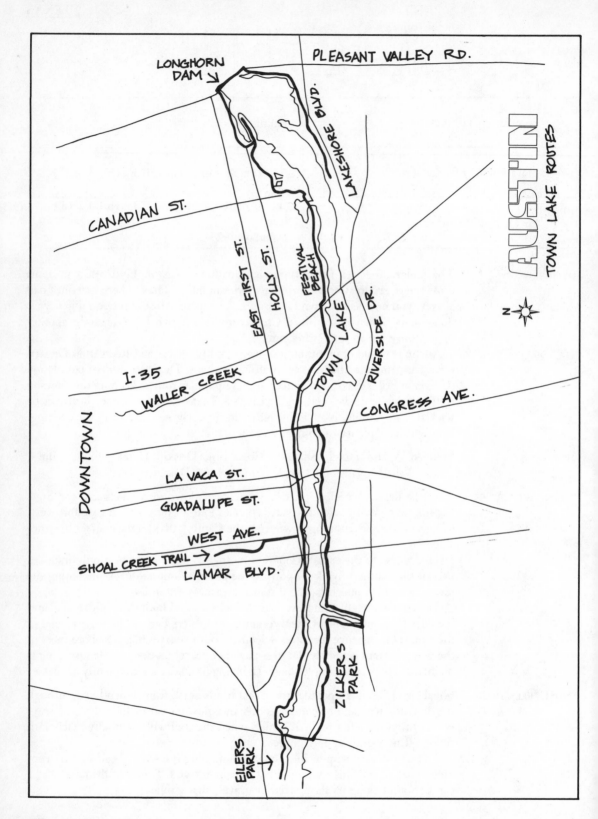

AUSTIN
TOWN LAKE ROUTES

N

PLEASANT VALLEY RD.

LONGHORN DAM

LAKESHORE BLVD.

CANADIAN ST.

EAST FIRST ST.

HOLLY ST.

FESTIVAL BEACH

TOWN LAKE

RIVERSIDE DR.

I-35

WALLER CREEK

CONGRESS AVE.

DOWNTOWN

LA VACA ST.

GUADALUPE ST.

WEST AVE.

SHOAL CREEK TRAIL

LAMAR BLVD.

ZILKER'S PARK

EILERS PARK

Both Town Lake and Shoal Creek are considered very safe for both day and night running.

OUTDOOR TRACK   The University of Texas Memorial Football Stadium contains a ¼-mile Tartan track. It is available during the day and at night with good lighting. The Villa Capri Motor Hotel is located six blocks from the track.

INDOOR TRACK   The Austin YMCA, located across the street from Town Lake, has an indoor track of 16 laps per mile.

CLUBS, FUN-RUNS
AND RACES   The Austin Runners Club has an active schedule of fun-runs and races.

TRADITIONAL RACES   Capitol 10,000 Race: March
Texas Relays Marathon: April

CONTACTS   Larry Mack, Austin Runners Club, 5824 Trailridge Drive, Austin, TX 78731. Austin YMCA, 1100 West 1st Street, Austin, TX 78703. (512) 476-6705.

DALLAS

Population: (met.) 2,500,000	Humidity: 63.5%
Elevation: 390−686 ft.	Av. Temperature: (Jan.) 44°F.; (July) 86°F.
Air Quality: Fair to poor	Inches of Rainfall: (Jan.) 2; (July) 1.8 Raindays: 79

OVERVIEW

Dallas is a great city for meeting and working out with other runners. Two lakes, located near downtown, have become the focus of attention among local runners. Bachman Lake, adjacent to Love Field Airport, has a 3.1-mile loop attractive to many beginners and intermediates. White Rock Lake, northeast of town, with its 10.81-mile perimeter, draws many veterans. For many Dallas runners, these are the only two courses that exist in the city. To facilitate more convenient workouts and to create a variety of courses, some other routes have been mapped out by adventurous runners. Closer to midtown, these runs have deterrent factors, such as city street traffic, or difficult footing in adverse weather. One of these courses, beginning downtown at the YMCA, quickly moves onto residential streets, and with complicated directions, passes by some beautiful roadside parks and attractive communities, making it all worth the effort.

The Cross-Country Club of Dallas, its growth molded by the concentration of runners on few courses, has a very social and hospitable nature. It is an easy town to feel right at home within the running environment.

HOTELS

Royal Coach Inn, Hilton Inn, Sheraton-Dallas Hotel, Dallas-Hilton Hotel, Holiday Inn−Downtown, Baker Hotel, Aldolphous Hotel, Hyatt Regency Hotel

BACHMAN LAKE

A fairly new paved path around the lake has made this course a great new attraction to local runners. Royal Coach Inn, perhaps the most convenient hotel to any running course in town, is located across the road from the lake. The winding pathway lies flat under intermittent shade. Markers have been set every ¼ mile over the 3.1-mile course. A rest room and water fountain are located on either side of the lake.

Bachman Lake can be found about 6 miles northwest of town between Love Field Airport and Northwest Highway.

WHITE ROCK LAKE

This is the pièce de resistance of running in Dallas. Most runners meet at the Big Thicket Cabin on East Lawther Drive along the northeast side of the lake. From the way the name sounds, you might envision a heavily wooded area, with a primitive trail snaking its way through the underbrush around the lake.

Quite the contrary is true. A good paved road circles the lake, with many open spaces. Some areas do have good shade.

The road lies fairly flat with a few short hills. Mileage markers begin at the Big Thicket Cabin and can be found every ¼ mile for 6½ miles of the 10.81-mile loop. They go 3 miles north and west, and 3½ miles south. There are five roadside rest rooms, plus three buildings along the road with rest rooms. Water fountains are every 3 to 3½ miles.

NOR-BUC PARK

Located just north of White Rock Lake, at Northwest Highway and Buckner Boulevard, this grassy, hilly park can provide good cross-country running. Three laps around its perimeter will give you close to a 6-mile run.

TRINITY RIVERBED AND LEVEE

This route seems to be the answer for runners staying at hotels downtown close to Union Station (*i.e.*, Holiday Inn and Hyatt Regency), and at hotels along Stemmons Freeway between Oak Lawn Avenue and Mockingbird Lane, 1½ to 5½ miles from midtown.

A levee follows alongside the riverbed, most of which is normally dry. You can either run up on the levee on its dirt path, or on the riverbed itself, where you can work your way around trees and through underbrush. The levee, 27 miles long, contains no amenities, and its dirt footing can be difficult in wet weather. Footing on the riverbed is impossible when wet, and the driest month, July, is too hot for running here, with little to no shade and no water.

This course can be reached from downtown along the Commerce Street Viaduct, crossing under Stemmons Freeway behind the County Courthouse. From the hotels along the freeway, viaducts run south to the river about 1 mile apart. Head south to Irving Boulevard and follow Irving east or west until you reach one of these viaducts, and then continue south until they cross the levee.

TURTLE CREEK

Many runners from downtown head out along the Turtle Creek route. This begins at the YMCA at North Ervay and Patterson. Follow Ervay north into Akard and bear right on Cedar Springs, passing Maple at the 1-mile mark. At Cedar Springs and Carlisle (Grandma's Salad Company sign on right), make a right onto Carlisle, following it to the top of the hill. At the top, go left downhill on Lemmon Avenue West to the first street on your right, after going under the railroad overpass. Take a right on this unmarked street through the Dallas Theater Center parking lot to a right on Blackburn Street. Proceed up a small hill to Turtle Creek Drive, turning left, and proceeding to its intersection with Stonebridge Drive at the bottom of the hill. Turn right on Stonebridge and head up one of the more difficult hills on the course, continuing to a left on Fitzhugh. After half a block, turn right on Abbott Avenue. After three blocks you will reach the 3-mile mark. Continuing on Abbott, the 4-mile mark is at Beverly Drive.

Since these directions are complicated, you might wish to follow the same route back from here, for an 8-mile run. If you want to continue on for the duration of the 9.6-mile route, stay north on Abbott to Drexel Drive (this is one block south of the SMU campus and track). Turn left on Drexel and follow it as it curves in a southwesterly direction, passing Beverly Drive at the 5-mile mark. One block later, take a right onto Miramar and run to Lakeside Drive. At Lakeside, turn left and run alongside scenic Turtle Creek to Armstrong. Turn left and go one block to a right on St. Johns Drive, and then follow St. Johns to a left onto Fitzhugh, at the 6-mile mark. Run up the hill, and turn right onto

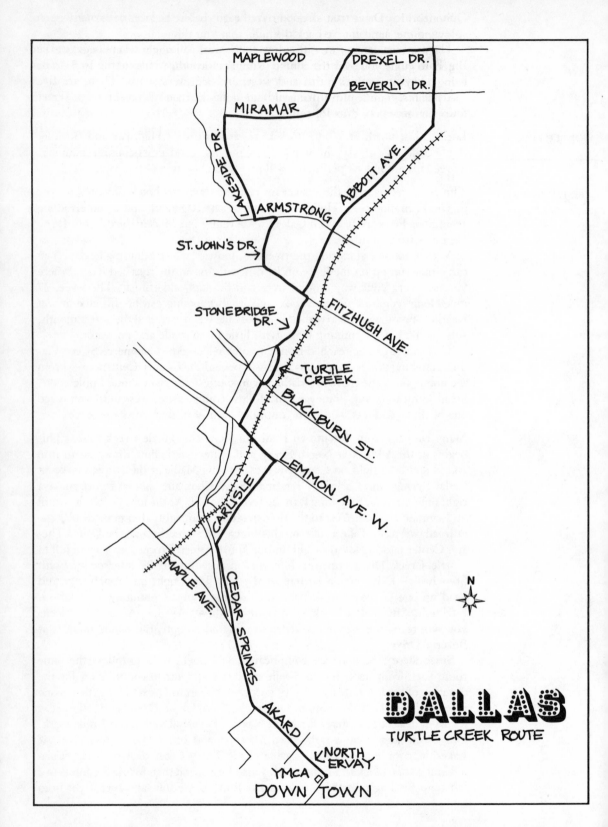

MAPLEWOOD

DREXEL DR.

BEVERLY DR.

MIRAMAR

LAKESIDE DR.

ABBOTT AVE.

ARMSTRONG

ST. JOHN'S DR.

STONEBRIDGE DR.

FITZHUGH AVE.

TURTLE CREEK

BLACKBURN ST.

LEMMON AVE. W.

CARLISLE

MAPLE AVE.

CEDAR SPRINGS

N

AKARD

NORTH ERVAY

YMCA

DOWN TOWN

DALLAS

TURTLE CREEK ROUTE

Stonebridge Drive (last street on your right before the railroad overpass), following the same course back to the Y that you came out on.

These instructions are difficult to follow and you might want some local runners to guide you over the course. Runners leave the Y frequently in the morning and at noon during the week to run this course.

Running surfaces are primarily sidewalks and asphalt streets, although the opportunity does exist for some running on grass. Terrain is generally flat with some hills. Service stations along the route near downtown and in Highland Park on Knox Street, about one block from the Abbott and Knox intersection (3½ miles), have rest rooms and drinking water. Be sure to obey traffic signals in the downtown area, as they are enforced.

White Rock Lake, Dallas

The route travels through neighborhoods with exquisite homes and beautiful landscaping.

UNIVERSITY PARK, HIGHLAND PARK AREA

Hilton Inn, at North Central Expressway and Mockingbird Lane, sits adjacent to these two attractive communities. No defined routes go through these neighborhoods, but they might make for interesting runs. The Southern Methodist University Campus is located only a couple of blocks west of the hotel along Mockingbird Lane. Its open, grassy areas can provide excellent casual workouts.

MOUNTAIN CREEK LAKE

This large, pretty lake sits about 14 miles southwest of town. Many runners enjoy coming here to run on the eastern shore along Florina Road. A park between the lake and the shore also provides some good running paths. Terrain is flat, and you can do about 5 miles in one direction.

CLUBS, FUN-RUNS AND RACES

The Cross-Country Club of Dallas provides a broad scope of running activities. Fun-runs are held every Sunday at 9:00 A.M. at the Big Thicket Cabin at White Rock Lake. Races are held at the same place on the first Saturday of every month.

OUTDOOR TRACKS

The ¼-mile outdoor track at Southern Methodist University is available and popular. Another track, of 400 meters, is located in University Park at University Boulevard, adjacent to the Dallas North Tollway. This one is also quite popular.

TRADITIONAL RACES

Bunny Hop, 6 miles: Mid-April
Texins Half-Marathon: Early November
Turkey Trot, 8 miles: Thanksgiving Day
White Rock Marathon: First Saturday in December

CONTACTS

Dale Hager, President, Cross-Country Club of Dallas, (214) 327-2992.
Don Lucas, 3203 Beverly Drive, Dallas TX 75205. (214) 521-8983.
Downtown YMCA, 605 North Ervay Street, Dallas, TX 75201. (214) 742-3251.

EL PASO

Population: 400,000	Humidity: 39%
Elevation: 3,762 – 6,700 ft.	Av. Temperature: (Jan.) 44°F.; (July) 81°F.
Air Quality: Fair	Inches of Rainfall: (Jan.) .4; (July) 1.8 Raindays: 44

OVERVIEW

This desert city, in the far west corner of Texas, has many obstacles that have hindered the growth of running. Hot summers, no shade, and scarce water create unappealing, if not unhealthy, conditions. In addition, the only soft footing you can find here is loose desert sand. Runners here are sometimes greatly harassed by drivers and prefer to train in populated areas where vulnerability is lessened. Winter climate here can be very pleasant.

El Paso sits across the Rio Grande from the Mexican city of Juarez. The occasional races held here often have a fair percentage of good Mexican runners, as well as members of the celebrated University of Texas at El Paso (UTEP) track team, including their world-class African runners.

HOTELS

Best Western Tom Penny Inn, Granada Royale Hometel, Holiday Inn – Airport, Howard Johnson's, La Quinta Motel, Rodeway Inn, Sheraton Motor Inn, Hilton Inn

I-10 FRONTAGE ROAD

This most popular course utilizes the service road along I-10, a couple of miles east of downtown. It combines the security of a moderately busy street with the availability of drinking water at frequent gas stations. The above hotels, except for the Hilton, are located along the course. The Frontage Road can be found along the east side of the highway, so if your hotel is on the west side of the highway, you must use an underpass to get to the other side.

Footing is concrete on this flat route, and you can run at least 10 miles one way. One excellent aspect of this course are the mileage markers along the highway.

MONTANA AVENUE

This road runs along the eastern edge of the airport, providing a 4- or 5-mile route, one way, from the Hilton Inn. It is a frontage road, and, unfortunately, has sections that do not exist, forcing one to detour a few blocks until it begins again.

TRANS MOUNTAIN ROAD

Drive about 10 miles north to the intersection of I-10 and the North-South Gateway. Get off the highway here, and follow the signs to Trans Mountain Road. Park in the lot at Wilderness Park Museum. The road travels up and over a mountain for 12 miles, one way. The top of the pass, after a 1,200 foot rise in elevation, can be reached at 6 miles. There is no water along this concrete road. The museum has water only when it is open—from 10:00 A.M. to 5:00 P.M.

This road is safe due to its limited access, but occasionally runners have been bothered in isolated or hilly areas outside of the city.

OUTDOOR TRACKS

The track at the UTEP Campus is available most of the time. It is advisable to call ahead to find out the hours—it might be closed during team practice.

CLUBS, FUN-RUNS
AND RACES

The Half Fast Track Club holds a fun-run every Sunday at 8:00 A.M., starting in Zaragosa Park at the Ysleta exit from I-10, about 12 miles east of downtown. Races are held on an occasional basis.

TRADITIONAL RACES

The only traditional race, a marathon, was cancelled last year due to lack of interest.

CONTACTS

Half Fast Track Club, 2727 Montana, El Paso, TX 79900.
Track Office, UTEP, (915) 747-5812.

FORT WORTH

Population: 350,000	Humidity: 66%
Elevation: 513–766 ft.	Av. Temperature: (Jan.) 45.7°F.; (July) 84.4°F.
Air Quality: Fair to poor	Inches of Rainfall: (Jan.) 2.0; (July) 1.75 Raindays: 78

OVERVIEW

Although Fort Worth shares much of its attention with neighboring Dallas, it maintains a distinctly informal western character and a strong self-identity. The Trinity River flows through downtown, and heading west, several parks have been developed alongside it. A bicycle path has been built next to the river, and constitutes the major running route in town. The Fort Worth Runners Club has been very responsible about measuring and marking it. Typical Texas summer heat can be a problem, and until the club's campaign to put in water fountains along the trail is successful, you must be careful about dehydration.

Downtown hotels are concentrated in an area more than eight blocks south of the river, creating a possible, if not pleasable, convenience.

HOTELS

Holiday Inn—Midtown

FORT WORTH BIKE TRAIL

The Fort Worth Bike Trail presently runs along the Clear Fork of the Trinity River, from the bridge at Main Street, in downtown, to the Southwest Loop 820 Highway. Total distance one way is 7.94 miles.

Holiday Inn is located about five minutes from downtown on I-20, and about 40 yards east of the bike trail. From the Inn to town, on the trail, is 2.8 miles, passing through Trinity Park for most of the distance. The Trinity Park section has the only shade along the trail, late afternoon being its most effective time. Asphalt covers the full length of the trail, with mileage markers painted white at every ½ mile. The only water fountain presently on the trail can be found at the Main Street end. No rest rooms are available.

OVERTON PARK BIKE TRAIL

This bike trail, located southwest of downtown, will soon have a connection to the Fort Worth Bike Trail. Overton Park is a narrow strip of land running south. The bike trail begins in the north at Pebblebrook Drive and travels through Overton Park, coming out the bottom of the park, and traveling along a residential road for about ⅓ mile. It then enters Foster Park for the last ¾ mile to Trail Lake Drive. Total distance is 2.65 miles. Two water fountains have been installed at the northern part of Overton Park, but there are no rest rooms. Shade covers most of the trail.

INDOOR TRACKS

The Downtown YMCA has the only indoor track, and it measures 30 laps per mile. At noon, runners leave the Y in a group for a run along the river.

CLUBS, FUN-RUNS AND RACES

The Fort Worth Runners Club has an informal "social and training run" every Saturday morning at 8:00 A.M. They meet at the Fort Worth Bike Trail where Rogers Road crosses the Trinity River at Colonial Cafeteria, west of 1849 Village on University Drive. Races are scheduled throughout the year.

The Mid-Cities Running Club meets for runs on the second Saturday of every month.

TRADITIONAL RACES

Fort Worth Trinity Trot, 4 miles: Early June
Fort Worth Fall Classic, 20 kilometers and 7 kilometers: October

CONTACTS

Dwain D. Camp, President, Fort Worth Runners Club, 4821 Langley, Fort Worth, TX 76114. (817) 626-1103.

T. Price Stone, President, Mid-Cities Running Club, P.O. Box 53, Bedford, TX 76021. (817) 589-0111.

Downtown YMCA, 512 Lamar, Fort Worth, TX 76102. (817) 332-3281.

HOUSTON

Population: (met.) 2,350,000	Humidity: 74%
Elevation: 0 – 41 ft.	Av. Temperature: (Jan.) 51°F.; (July) 82°F.
Air Quality: Poor	Inches of Rainfall: (Jan.) 3.6; (July) 4.1 Raindays: 103

OVERVIEW

Situated close to the Gulf, Houston has as hot and steamy a climate as you will find in America. For most runners, summer here can be unbearable, yet people train here for marathons, and even ultra-marathons, during these difficult months. Eight runners from Houston competed in the London to Brighton 52-Mile Run in 1978. When asked how they were able to train, the answer was "very slowly." Out-of-towners might look at Houston race results and figure they can clean up. When they try, they usually find these times are a product of high heat and humidity.

Many runners begin workouts as early as 4:00 A.M., and most people like to be done before the sun comes up. Of course, the early morning humidity is a trade-off for the higher temperatures later in the day.

Courses here are mostly limited to three popular areas. Beginning from downtown, Buffalo Bayou, the river responsible for the city's development, runs west, bordered on both sides by a greenbelt. The bayou flows into Memorial Park, 5 miles west of town, where many trails can be run. At the southwest corner of the park, the Arboretum, with its "Do Not Run" sign, attracts many you-know-whats, who ignore the sign.

Houston is a town of many running clubs and plenty of competition. Over 200 races per year are scheduled within 75 miles of the city. Few races are held during the summer. Although only several clubs carry most of the responsibility for events, there are fifteen to seventeen registered competitive clubs, some of which squeeze their own events into the yearly race calendar.

HOTELS

Hyatt Regency, Marriott – West Loop, Warwick Hotel, Holiday Inn – Medical Center, Houston Oaks Hotel, Holiday Inn – Downtown

BUFFALO BAYOU

Beginning in the western part of downtown, the bayou flows west for 2½ miles through a greenbelt. Asphalt paths can be found on either side of the 200-yard-wide park. The paths work their way up and down along the embankment, creating some hill work. Most runners head out one side of the bayou and come back along the other to make a 5-mile loop (minus 100 yards). Mileage markers have been placed by different groups who start at different places. Try to key on the same type of marker to avoid confusion. Water can be found at the far end of the Shepherd Bridge, close to the turnaround point. The Hyatt

Regency and Holiday Inn are close to this course, and other downtown hotels are not far.

MEMORIAL PARK JOGGING TRAIL

Continuing west along the bayou, you will reach this park after another 2½ miles. The greenbelt stops and houses line the bayou most of the way, so you will have to run on residential streets through the well-to-do River Oaks community. The Marriott and Houston Oaks Hotels are located a short distance from the park.

A jogging trail has been built along the exterior of the golf course at the park. The course runs in the shape of a triangle for 3 miles on wood-chip footing. Water and rest rooms can be found at the Tennis Center, where you can also use showers and lockers.

MEMORIAL PARK HILL TRAIL

Buffalo Bayou runs through the park and a pathway can be found traveling up and down its banks for a 3-mile, out-and-back course. The area is well shaded to provide some coolness on hot days. Water and rest rooms are located at the baseball diamond. Many other routes can be run through the park as well. Trails crisscross a lot, but you will not have to repeat your steps for 10 to 12 miles.

McASHAN ARBORETUM

At the southwest corner of Memorial Park, the entrance to the Arboretum has a sign telling runners not to use this beautiful 265-acre site. Since the sign is not enforceable, the locale is heavily used by local runners. A 2-mile loop through a pine-tree forest provides cool runs over a dirt trail. Water can be found at the office.

HERMANN PARK JOGGING TRAIL

Several miles south of downtown, across the road from Rice University, this park contains a 2-mile jogging trail around its golf course. The course travels through considerable shade on pine-bark footing. Terrain, as characteristic of Houston, is flat. Water and rest rooms can be found at the clubhouse. The Warwick, Holiday Inn, and Tides II hotels are near the park.

OUTDOOR TRACKS

There are many tracks in Houston, but few are open to the public. Rice University has a ¼-mile cinder track that many people use by just walking through the holes in the fence.

INDOOR TRACKS

The Downtown YMCA has a banked, Tartan, 28-laps-per-mile, air-conditioned track.

CLUBS AND RACES

The Houston Road Runners Club puts on races about once a month. These are generally 6 miles and under, although they also have one 10-mile race.

The Gulf Association AAU holds races about once a month of generally 6 miles and up, including some ultra-marathons. They also publish the annual calendar of events.

The Houston Harriers also sandwich a number of races into the schedule each year. The Houston Masters Sports Association holds meetings the first Sunday of each month, followed by a group run, and then a social gathering. The Bay Area Running Club, south of Houston at the NASA Space Center, is active with races and fun-runs.

TRADITIONAL RACES

Houston Marathon: January
Bayou City Fun-Run, 6 miles: March

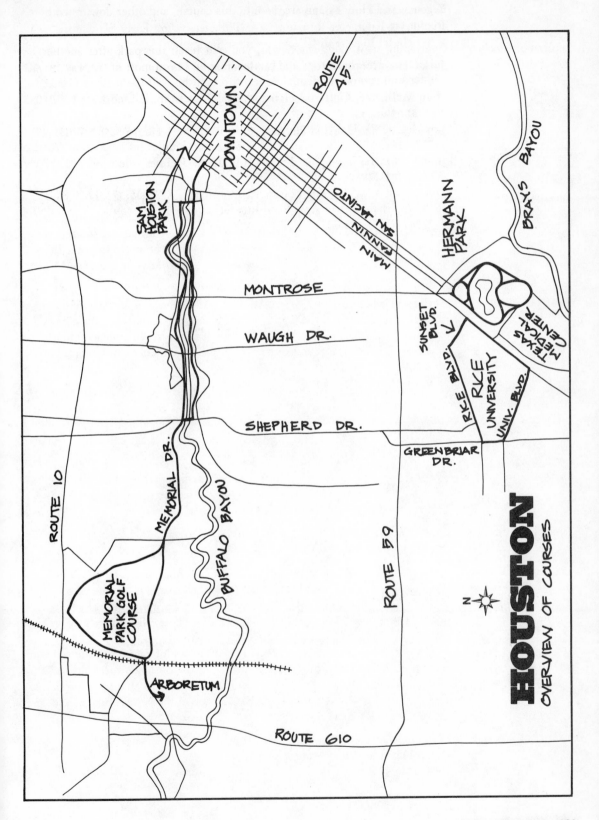

HOUSTON
OVERVIEW OF COURSES

Watermelon Run, 3 miles: Early July
Biathlon 4-Kilometer Run and 300-Millimeter Swim: Early September
KILT/Pearl Light Fall Classic, 5 miles: September

CONTACTS

Jock Geller, Houston RRC, 4132 Meyerwood, Houston, TX 77025. (713) 667-9746.

Tom McBrayer, Gulf Association AAU, 7733 Moline, Houston, TX 77087. (713) 649-6832.

Jim McLatchie, Houston Harriers, 8618 Birdwood, Houston, TX 77035. (713) 777-8339.

Jimmy Gilbert, Terlingua Track Club, 12168 Beamer, Houston, TX 77089. (713) 481-1298.

Downtown YMCA, 1600 Louisiana, Houston, TX 77006. (713) 659-8501.

Richard Arbaugh, Bay Area Road Runners, Route 2, Box 469W, Pearland, TX 77581. (713) 482-0032.

San Antonio

Population: (met.) 950,000	Humidity: 66.5%
Elevation: 805 – 1,000 ft.	Av. Temperature: (Jan.) 51°F.; (July) 84°F.
Air Quality: Fair	Inches of Rainfall: (Jan.) 1.74; (July) 2.09 Raindays: 79

OVERVIEW

San Antonio is the city of the Alamo and the modern Hemisfair. A city that boasts good running weather all year 'round, it has active running clubs with full racing and fun-run schedules, and attractive parks that truly cater to runners. Plans are underway to maintain shower facilities for runners in the city's major parks.

Winters are generally moderate, and summer running can be pleasurable in the morning when the skies are often cloudy and a Gulf breeze cools the air.

The flat downtown area, with the San Antonio River meandering through it, becomes a congested tourist area during the day. Morning runners use the Hemisfair Plaza's 92.6-acre grounds for an interesting workout. The San Pedro Creek, which also runs through the city, has a newly built running path providing the best opportunity for unobstructed runs from the downtown area.

Hilly neighborhoods surround the city and offer scenic parks with challenging courses.

HOTELS

Hilton Palacio de Rio, Holiday Inn – Alamo Area, La Mansion, Menger Hotel, St. Anthony Hotel

HEMISFAIR PLAZA

One block south of the Alamo, and across the street from the Hilton, is the Hemisfair Plaza, a 92.6-acre conglomerate of Civic Center—a 16,000-seat indoor sports arena, the 750-foot Tower of the Americas, tourist amusements and museums. The grounds of the Plaza are empty and available in the early morning, offering numerous walkways and roadways to run on. No main routes exist, so it is impossible to measure mileage. You can run for over half an hour without retracking. Overpasses and dips offer some short hill work. Very little shade can be found, and water fountains and rest rooms are available.

SAN PEDRO CREEK PATHWAY

This popular downtown course starts from the San Fernando Gymnasium at 19 West Travis. The gym is free and open to the public on weekdays, with shower facilities available for both men and women. You can run north or west for several blocks from the downtown hotels, or you can park your car in the lot adjacent to the building.

From the gym, head west one block to the San Pedro Creek and turn north on the flat, grassy, riverside path. You can run for 1 mile to a turnaround marker.

Eventually the park will be extended another ¼ mile to reach San Pedro Park. In the meantime, you can follow North Flores for several blocks to the park. This square park, measuring about ⅓ mile on a side, contains many roads and pathways to wander around. Few people use the park, so you will have a lot of freedom to move around. There are water fountains available in the park.

WOODLAWN LAKE

This lake is located about 2½ miles northwest of downtown. An interesting route to here would be to follow the same course to San Pedro Park, and at the northwest corner of the park, head west along Ashby for about 1 mile to Zarzamora and turn left (south) for one block to Cincinnati. Turn west again for one and a half blocks to the lake.

At the near end of the lake, you will find a gym with free showers available. Around the lake is a dirt and grass path that when followed along the road, will create a flat 1½-mile loop. Water fountains are available at either end of the lake.

ROUTE TO
BRACKENRIDGE PARK
GOLF COURSE

Brackenridge Park Golf Course is located about 1¾ miles from downtown. The Central YMCA on North St. Mary's has many runners heading out to the golf course from downtown during the day. They run up St. Mary's two blocks, then turn right onto 9th Street for one block, and then left onto Avenue B, following it to the golf course. It is 1½ miles to this point. A flat 2½-mile paved path circles around the perimeter of the course.

BRACKENRIDGE PARK

North of the golf course is Brackenridge Park proper. There are many running trails here, although none are presently marked. You can run several miles without much repetition on the paved trails. The park has abundant water foun-

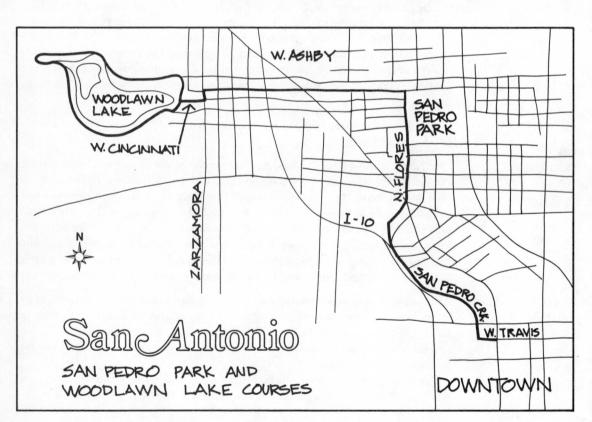

tains and rest rooms. The best route to the park entrance is to follow Broadway for the 2½ miles from downtown.

MISSION COUNTY PARK

The real gem of running in San Antonio begins 4 miles south of downtown in Mission County Park. A 20-kilometer course, out and back, follows a beautiful section of the San Antonio River. This course is known as the hike and bike path and meanders past some beautiful, old missions. The paved path contains some dips and short hills, and several wooden bridges are interspersed along the course. These bridges can be fine if you cross them alone, but another runner or two will set the bridge in motion and footing will only be guesswork. Kilometer markers are very vivid, but mileage markers are not always noticeable. Water can be obtained in the park at the beginning or end of the course.

McALLISTER PARK

About 10 miles north of town, the park is also only about 3½ miles north of the airport. On the entrance road, after ¼ mile you will see a pavilion behind which a 2-mile marked loop begins. The course stays on the park road, as the area is heavily wooded and not well groomed. Some unmarked courses are used by local runners, but they would have to guide you through them.

The interior of the park is mostly flat, but the perimeter is quite hilly and many runners utilize the 13-mile loop around the outside. Water fountains and rest rooms can be found in many areas of the park. Avoid coming here in the afternoons when the park is crowded.

INDOOR TRACK

The Central YMCA has an indoor track of 26 laps per mile.

OUTDOOR TRACK

Trinity University has an all-weather, ¼-mile track adjacent to the west side of Brackenridge Park. It is always available.

San Antonio River, near Mission County Park

CLUBS, FUN-RUNS AND RACES

The most active running club in town is the San Antonio Road Runners. Each weekend throughout the year they have a race or a fun-run.

At 9:00 A.M. on the second Sunday of each month, there is a uniquely named race that takes place simultaneously in Mission County Park and McAllister Park. If the Dick Tracy Stick-to-Your-Guns Run does not excite you, perhaps the Dagwood-Bum-A-Long will pique your interest. Each month the run is devoted to a different comic strip character.

On the third Saturday of each month, there is a fun-run in McAllister Park with varying distances. These runs are named after famous runners and coaches, such as Ron Hill, Miruts Yifter and Arthur Lydiard.

TRADITIONAL RACES   Fiesta Mission Run, 10 kilometers: Late April
San Antonio Fireworks Run, 3 miles: Early July
Independence Midnight Run, 4 miles: Late July
Mission Trails Half-Marathon: Early December
Las Colonias Marathon: Late May

CONTACTS   David DeBell, San Antonio Road Runners, Box 12474, San Antonio, TX 78212. (512) 494-6377.
Diego Vacca, Central YMCA, 903 North St. Mary's Street, San Antonio, TX 78215. (512) 227-5221.
Leonard Stern, Majestic Men's Shop, 160 East Houston Street, San Antonio, TX 78205. (512) 226-8812.

Salt Lake City

Population: 164,500	Humidity: 52%
Elevation: 4,209 – 8,005 ft.	Av. Temperature: (Jan.) 27°F.; (July) 77°F.
Air Quality: Poor	Inches of Rainfall: (Jan.) 1.5; (July) .6 Raindays: 88

OVERVIEW

Salt Lake City is on a panorama desert with great vistas of the Wasatch Mountains looming up from the very edge of the downtown area. At 4,200 feet and up, there is high altitude running here whether you are in the valley reaching out to the Great Salt Lake, or climbing the many canyons and mountains to the east and north of town.

The city streets are laid out in a grid and numbered in an easy-to-follow order starting at the Mormon Temple on the north edge of town. There are approximately seven blocks to a mile, so distances along city streets are easy to figure out.

Most of the downtown activity is adjacent to the Temple Square. This includes the State Capitol and the Salt Palace. There is a bench area that rises up 200 to 300 feet and forms a plateau at the foot of the mountains north and east along the edge of the city. The State Capitol sits on the bench at the north edge just above Temple Square.

HOTELS

Hotel Utah, International Dunes, Howard Johnson's

MEMORY GROVE PARK AND CITY CREEK CANYON

There is an excellent canyon run starting only two blocks northeast of Temple Square. The above hotels are within three to four blocks from the start of the course. Head north to 2nd North and turn east until you are a half block past State Street (Mormon Temple) where you will take a left onto Canyon Road. About ⅓ mile north you will reach the entrance to Memory Grove Park. Here, with City Canyon Creek on your right, is a gradual uphill route for 1.1 miles. Most of the running is on the road and occasionally you can run on grass alongside under the trees. At the north end of the park you will cross a road and begin a canyon run on one of the most beautiful city courses in America. The road becomes rollingly steeper, and you can follow it through real wilderness for about 3.5 miles. This canyon has magnificent foothills on either side and towering snow-capped mountains looming ahead. You will likely see interesting animals along the way, such as beaver, deer and geese, and happily, no dogs, since no dogs are allowed in the canyon. Also, the canyon road is closed to cars on Mondays and Wednesdays. Signs will occasionally point to roadside water fountains, and there are rest rooms at picnic areas.

The canyon creek is pure water for drinking, as it is en route to the city's drinking fountains. You will even pass a couple of small purification plants along the road. If you decide to run on any of the paths you see up the canyon walls, always utilize the cooler south side, as it is less likely to attract rattlesnakes with a penchant for sunbathing. The road reaches a gate that is normally closed to persons not having a reservation with the Water Department to proceed beyond it. You can either call the Department in advance or ignore the gate and probably not upset anyone.

Local runners claim that winter snows are not deep enough nor last long enough to interfere with year 'round use of canyon roads.

LIBERTY PARK

There are two other parks downtown that are available for running. Liberty Park is the more central, although it is over 1 mile from the nearest hotel. To run there from your hotel, head south to 9th South, turn left and you will reach the park at 5th East. The park has many old and beautiful trees to shade runners on the 1.4-mile loop around the perimeter on the inside of the roadway. If you run along the outside of the roadway, the distance is 1.5 miles. Both sides of the road have excellent grass surfaces. The terrain here is virtually flat. One water fountain is located at the southeast corner of the park, and a couple of rest rooms are located along the route. More water and rest rooms can be found in the interior of the park.

HOTELS

There is a major grouping of hotels around 6th South and 3rd West near the freeway entrance. This area is not very convenient to running courses. Liberty Park is the best bet following the above directions for the 2¾ miles to the park. You might also run up to Memory Grove Park, about 2⅞ miles away. The route to Liberty Park would be less congested during working hours. With fairly long blocks and little commercial and industrial crowding in the downtown area, city street running can be tolerable.

SUGARHOUSE PARK

Sugarhouse Park is a new facility built on the grounds that originally housed the State Penitentiary. It is located at 21st South and 13th East. This is on the bench area overlooking the city. You will find a rolling 1.4-mile loop alongside the roadway, or a 2-mile loop around the perimeter. There are few trees here to block the view of the towering, craggy mountain range jutting up from the east end of the park. A pretty stream and pond are located in the center. Every Saturday morning at 8:30, the Parks and Recreation Department holds a fun-run here, excluding the winter months.

RED BUTTE CANYON

If you are at the University of Utah, situated on the mountain bench about 3½ miles north of Sugarhouse Park, you are near a beautiful hill run on the Red Butte Canyon Road. It starts on the east side of the Fort Douglas Compound and extends for about 1½ miles into the canyon before a gate will turn you back. There are terrific vistas of the valley below and distant mountain ranges.

From the university, you can follow Wasatch Drive south to a left on Sunnyside Avenue which will take you up to the "This is the Place" Monument where Brigham Young entered the valley and said something I can't remember. This is a hilly, 10-mile loop.

BEEHIVE TRACK CLUB

Salt Lake City has a busy-bee population of runners and a number of challenging traditional races. The founder and chief energizer of the Beehive Track Club is Jan Cheney, who was solely responsible for years of race organization. Now, with the support of President Darel Neilson, the club is continuing to meet the

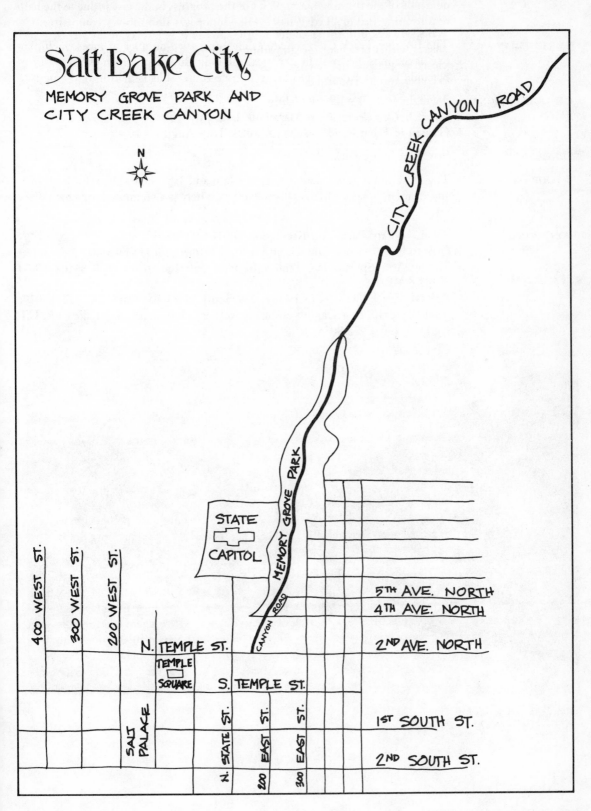

Salt Lake City

MEMORY GROVE PARK AND CITY CREEK CANYON

CITY CREEK CANYON ROAD

MEMORY GROVE PARK

CANYON ROAD

STATE CAPITOL

400 WEST ST.

300 WEST ST.

200 WEST ST.

N. TEMPLE ST.

TEMPLE SQUARE

S. TEMPLE ST.

SALT PALACE

N. STATE ST.

200 EAST ST.

300 EAST ST.

5TH AVE. NORTH

4TH AVE. NORTH

2ND AVE. NORTH

1ST SOUTH ST.

2ND SOUTH ST.

demands of the running boom. A lot of the progress in the city is due to the help of a running mayor, Ted Wilson. His Honor is a fine sub-vet competitor.

BAIR GUTSMAN RACE The Beehive Track Club schedules an impressive number of races, including one of the most grueling in America, the Bair Gutsman, which climbs 940 feet per mile for the first 5 miles of its 10-mile route. Ths is held in mid-August.

OTHER TRADITIONAL RACES Twilight Run, 4 miles: Mid-July
Salt Lake City Deseret News Marathon: Late July
Garden of Eden Road Race, 11.6 miles: Late August

FUN-RUNS See Sugarhouse Park, above.

INDOOR TRACKS The Deseret Gym is a new facility at Main and 1st North. Open for both men and women, it has a 15-laps-per-mile track. There is a nominal charge for a daily rate.

CONTACTS Salt Lake City Parks and Recreation, (801) 535-7856.
Governor's Advisory Council on Physical Fitness, (801) 533-6120.
Mountaineer Sports, 155 Trolley Square, Salt Lake City, UT 84102. (801) 363-6003.
Beehive Track Club, Jan Cheney, 289 South 200 East, Kaysville, UT 84037, (801) 376-5072; or Darel Neilson, 1956 West 3300 South, Salt Lake City, UT 84119. (801) 972-8076.

City Creek Canyon, Salt Lake City

BURLINGTON

Population: 38,000	Humidity: 72.5%
Elevation: 332 ft.	Av. Temperature: (Jan.) 16.8°F.; (July) 69.8°F.
Air Quality: Fair	Inches of Rainfall: (Jan.) 1.74; (July) 3.54 Raindays: 148

OVERVIEW

Burlington, in northern Vermont, has some outstanding trails with excellent hills and beautiful scenery. Lake Champlain lies just west of town, and the Green Mountains rise up to the east, with the Winooski River flowing along the north edge of town. Flat runs here can be found only on the track.

There are as many courses here as roads, since the environment is quite rural, and traffic presents no problem. A few dogs might show their snoots, but local runners can think of no past difficulties short of mild intimidation.

The University of Vermont, perched on a hilltop, supplies the town with a good-size running population. A favorite route for them is the perimeter of a neighboring golf course.

Members of the Green Mountain AA meet frequently on weekends for long runs. The club also puts on races and stages competitions with the university teams.

HOTELS

Holiday Inn, Howard Johnson's Motor Lodge, Econo Lodge, Ramada Inn

BURLINGTON COUNTRY CLUB GOLF COURSE

The above motels are all about ½ mile downhill from this popular golf course route. A 3-mile dirt course is marked around the perimeter of the Burlington Country Club. The rolling terrain has adequate shade, and water fountains can be found on the golf course. A map of the course can be found on a giant sign at the south end of the track at UVM.

RED ROCKS PARK

A couple of miles south of town, next to Lake Champlain, this small, attractive forest park has some well-maintained dirt trails. You can run 1- to 3-mile loops here without any interference.

Beautiful views of the lake can be experienced from the cliffside trails.

GRAND ISLE

About 20 miles north of town, bridges will take you onto this large island in the middle of Lake Champlain. A marathon is held here each year because the 25-mile perimeter is a natural for the distance. To begin a workout, park at Folsom School. From the start, you can head north on Route 2 for 3 miles to Town Line Road, or west for 1½ miles on paved South Street to a right turn on West Shore Road, which has a dirt surface. If you run all the way on West Shore Road to Moccasin Avenue and back, the distance will be 20 miles. Plan ahead, as you will find no water to drink along the way. The course has rolling terrain, and scenery, of course, is spectacular.

Winter running in Vermont

OUTDOOR TRACKS	The University of Vermont has a ¼-mile, rubberized, asphalt track, as does the Essex Educational Center in Essex Junction, about 8 miles northeast of Burlington.
CLUBS, FUN-RUNS AND RACES	The Green Mountain AA holds about twelve to fifteen events during the year. They also have summer fun-runs, May to October, on Wednesdays at 6:00 P.M. on the track at Essex Educational Center.
TRADITIONAL RACES	Burlington Winter Carnival, 5 kilometers: February Spring Opener, 5 kilometers: April Cambridge Pleasant Valley 5-Kilometer: May Montpelier 10-Mile Road Race: Late June Green Mountain Island Marathon: August Archie Post 5-Mile Cross-Country: September Vagabond 10-Kilometer: October Arthur Tudhope Memorial 10-Kilometer: Late October
CONTACT	Leighton Walker, Green Mountain AA, 2 Redwood Terrace, Essex Junction, VT 05452. (802) 878-2322.

ПORFOLK

Population: Norfolk—280,000 (met.) 764,000 Virginia Beach—281,000	Humidity: 71%
Elevation: 13 ft.	Av. Temperature: (Jan.) 42°F.; (July) 77.6°F.
Air Quality: Fair to poor	Inches of Rainfall: (Jan.) 3.4; (July) 5.6 Raindays: 115

OVERVIEW

Norfolk has a large metropolitan area comprising Newport News, Hampton, Virginia Beach, Portsmouth and Chesapeake. The area, located at the mouth of the Chesapeake Bay, is one of the most important shipping and trade centers in the country. It also provides excellent recreational and resort facilities.

The Norfolk Botanical Gardens are adjacent to the airport and provide the best running environment in that city.

Virginia Beach is near the Seashore State Park, a preserved nature area which offers mossy trails, sand dune hills and jungle-like paths.

HOTELS

Quality Inn—Airport, Holiday Inn Scope—Downtown, Omni International—Downtown
Virginia Beach: Many beachfront motels

NORFOLK BOTANICAL GARDENS

There is an entrance fee of fifty cents, but runners can normally get through from near the airport for free. A paved path follows the perimeter of the gardens for approximately 2⅔ miles. The terrain is flat, and water and rest rooms are available.

THE HAGUE RUN

The only running downtown is around a body of water known as The Hague. For 2 kilometers, the perimeter follows Brambelton Avenue, Mowbray Arch and Dundaff Avenue over a flat course. The Holiday Inn Scope is ½ mile from The Hague near Brambelton Avenue. From the Omni International it's 1½ miles via a left on Waterfront Drive to Boush then to Brambelton and left to The Hague. The course is paved and flat.

VIRGINIA BEACH BOARDWALK

Along the beachfront there is a concrete boardwalk for about 2 miles. The fresh morning ocean air and the rising sun will create an appreciation for early runs. Later in the day, summer crowds can be a nuisance.

SEASHORE STATE PARK

This park contains 2,770 acres of one of the finest natural preservation areas on the Atlantic coastline. If you are a nature runner, this is an area not to pass up. An entrance is located at 64th Street and Atlantic Avenue, 2½ miles from the boardwalk at 25th Street. The main entrance is 3½ miles down the main trail from the 64th Street entrance. Trails in the park vary in length from 1 to 5 miles.

VIRGINIA BEACH CLUBS, RACES AND TRAINING RUNS	These are held at least monthly and there is a six-week track and field program in the summer. The Tidewater Striders welcome all runners to train with them at Seashore State Park.
TRADITIONAL RACES	Shamrock Marathon: March International Azalea Festival 8-Mile Run: April Ghent Art Festival 6-Kilometer Run: May
CLUB	The Tidewater Striders
CONTACTS	Charlie George, Tidewater Striders, 801 Yearling Court, Virginia Beach, VA 23462. (804) 467-1509. Norfolk YMCA, 312 West Bute Street, Norfolk, VA 23452. (804) 622-6328.

RICHMOND

Population: 225,000	Humidity: 71.5%
Elevation: 0–312 ft.	Av. Temperature: (Jan.) 38°F.; (July) 78°F.
Air Quality: Not available	Inches of Rainfall: (Jan.) 2.9; (July) 5.6 Raindays: 113

OVERVIEW

Richmond is rich in the history of the South. In runs through town, you can experience southern ambience along tree-lined boulevards, passing statues of Civil War generals. Monument Avenue, with a beautifully scenic and historic flavor, runs to the west from downtown. Most running activity can be found in this direction, as the University of Richmond track, even further west, draws the greatest number of local participants. A little nearer to the business district, Byrd Park provides a comfortable environment for daily workouts.

Although the city does not have a running club, that fact does not seem to be a detriment to marathon fever. The Richmond Marathon, in 1978, had a field of 2,500 runners, of which 90 percent were hometown residents.

HOTELS

Holiday Inn–Downtown, John Marshall Hotel, Richmond Hyatt House

MONUMENT AVENUE

The downtown hotels are located on West Franklin Street, which runs east-west through town. To reach Monument Avenue, head west on Franklin, passing Monroe Park after ¼ mile, and then the Virginia Commonwealth University Campus before reaching the statue of Jeb Stuart. The course along Franklin is basically flat, on a wide sidewalk. Monument Avenue is the continuation of Franklin Street and stays westerly from its start between the statue of Stuart and the one of Robert E. Lee.

The course from here follows a wide grass median bordered by cobblestone streets through a section of old, well-kept, residential brownstones. The first 4 miles have a small, gradual incline covered with many shade trees. From 4 miles to the end of the course at 6 miles, it becomes increasingly hillier and the cool protection of trees disappears.

There are no water fountains or rest rooms along this route, and it has almost no light at night. Many people resort to the sidewalk where streetlights are helpful.

BOULEVARD

At about 1½ miles along Monument Avenue, you will come to Boulevard. The intersection contains a statue of Stonewall Jackson. Turn south (left) here, and follow Boulevard for close to a mile along its shaded sidewalk to Byrd Park. Quite a number of intersections along this road can be a nuisance. Terrain remains flat.

BYRD PARK

This is a very pretty park for daytime running. It would not be safe to run here at night. A 2-mile loop on the perimeter road circles around three lakes. Terrain in the park is flat and shaded. Water can be found at a spring at the south end, and there are rest rooms in the park.

MAYMONT NATURE CENTER

The entrance to the center can be found at the southern end of Byrd Park. Here you will have some interesting, hilly runs along fenced-in meadows and fields containing bison, deer and bear. There are no set routes or distances over the many paved, intersecting pathways.

COURSE FROM RICHMOND HYATT HOUSE TO MONUMENT AVENUE

This is one of the most popular hotels in town, although it is not ideal for runners. You can reach Monument Avenue by heading east on West Broad Street along its busy sidewalk and road for about 1 mile to a right turn on Bremo Road, at the Golden Skillet Restaurant, and follow Bremo's suburban, semi-shaded, two-lane street for another mile to Monument Avenue.

UNIVERSITY OF RICHMOND CAMPUS

Many runners meet at the track next to the Robins Athletic Center. A 10-mile road course is well traveled from here, but it is unmarked, and directions are complicated. It is best to find local runners who can show you the way.

Six-mile and 3-mile cross-country courses run on dirt paths over the semi-hilly, English Gothic campus. Shade is moderate, and there is a water fountain at the track and rest rooms at the Athletic Center. Both courses are well marked for direction.

MONROE PARK

Located ¼ mile from downtown along West Franklin Street, this park has a 1-mile perimeter route on a wide sidewalk. Terrain is almost flat, and you will find a water fountain and rest room here.

OUTDOOR TRACKS

The University of Richmond has a ¼-mile Chevron, eight-lane track, which is semi-lit at night. The university is located in West Richmond at University Drive. Five miles from downtown, it can be reached by heading out Grove Avenue to a right turn on Three Chapt Road, followed by a left onto Towana Road, and continuing on Towana to the university.

INDOOR TRACKS

The Central YMCA has a 32-laps-per-mile, slightly banked track on the roof of the building. A covering protects runners from adverse weather.

Robins Athletic Center at the University of Richmond has a route inside the building that circles around the basketball courts and the viewing sections. There are 9 or 10 laps per mile. The track is not always available, so call ahead.

CLUBS, FUN-RUNS AND RACES

The Richmond Track and Field Club puts on a number of events at the University of Richmond Track. They are most active in the summer, with all-comers meets every other week. Fun-runs are held every Tuesday night. Many runners are talking about starting a road runners club, which could be in existence by the middle of 1979.

TRADITIONAL RACES

Richmond 10-Mile Road Race: Third weekend in August
Run for the Arts, 6, 3 and 1 miles: Late September
Richmond Newspapers Marathon: Early October

CONTACTS

Jim Holdren, Richmond Track and Field Club, 6005 Pollard Drive, Richmond, VA 23226. (804) 282-3289.
Bill Buckman, 6505 Wessex Lane, Richmond, VA 23226. (804) 285-3135 or 353-6611 (work).
Central YMCA, 2 West Franklin Street, Richmond, VA 23220. (804) 644-4611.
Robins Athletic Center, (804) 285-6375.

SEATTLE

Population: (met.) 1,855,000	Humidity: 75%
Elevation: 0 – 520 ft.	Av. Temperature: (Jan.) 41°F.; (July) 66°F.
Air Quality: Good	Inches of Rainfall: (Jan.) 5.5; (July) .7 Raindays: 162

OVERVIEW

Few cities in the country can give you the feeling that they were really designed for runners. Seattle is loaded with trails, waterfronts and vistas to offer numerous opportunities for your running enjoyment. The city lies on a strip of land between Puget Sound and Lake Washington. Many of the long routes can be found along the eastern edge of the city on the shores of Lake Washington. Along Puget Sound, on the western edge, there is a downtown waterfront run, as well as a peninsula run in the south along Alki Beach.

And all this does not include the most popular route of all, around Green Lake, a few miles north of downtown. With so much water around, and bluffs, beaches and parks, it is no wonder why this is a runners haven, and why local runners appreciate their city so much. Of course, it takes a local runner to be used to the great amount of rainfall most of the year. Be sure to pack your raingear and an extra pair of shoes when traveling to Seattle.

HOTELS

Washington Plaza, Hilton, Olympic Hotel, University Towers, Sherwood Hotel

WATERFRONT ROUTE

The downtown area itself is not the most convenient place to stay if you want to run from your hotel to one of the popular courses. The best you can do here is run down to the waterfront, only about three or four blocks away, and head north or south between the Seattle Marine Aquarium to the south and Pier 89 to the north. The total distance between the two is about 2¼ miles. The lower half of the course passes piers and shops and the upper 1½ miles runs through a new park with many small, young trees. The entire course is flat.

BURKE-GILMAN TRAIL

This old railroad right-of-way has been recycled into a long, flat, traffic-free route. It begins along Lake Union, part of the waterway that cuts between Lake Washington and Puget Sound, and heads east, passing through the University of Washington Campus. The University Towers and Sherwood Hotel are located close to the trail here.

The trail then winds toward the northeast, eventually hugging the lakeshore until it completes its 12.1-mile distance at the northern tip of the lake. An extension of 12 miles is on the planning boards. Shade trees line the route along both sides for a majority of the course. Water fountains can be found in the occasional

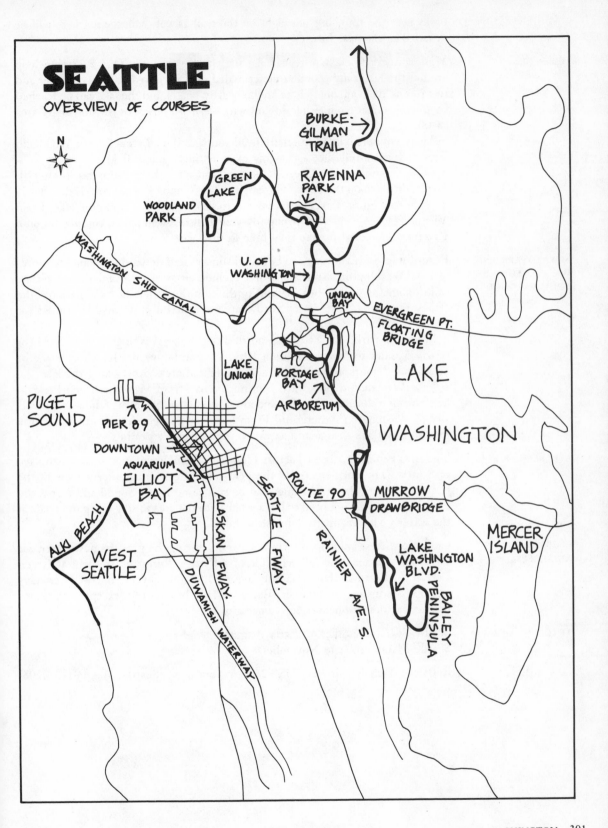

SEATTLE

OVERVIEW OF COURSES

N

BURKE-GILMAN TRAIL

RAVENNA PARK

GREEN LAKE

WOODLAND PARK

WASHINGTON SHIP CANAL

U. OF WASHINGTON

UNION BAY

EVERGREEN PT. FLOATING BRIDGE

LAKE UNION

PORTAGE BAY

ARBORETUM

LAKE

WASHINGTON

PUGET SOUND

PIER 89

DOWNTOWN

AQUARIUM

ELLIOT BAY

ALASKAN FWAY.

SEATTLE FWAY.

ROUTE 90

MURROW DRAWBRIDGE

MERCER ISLAND

ALKI BEACH

WEST SEATTLE

DUWAMISH WATERWAY

RAINIER AVE. S.

LAKE WASHINGTON BLVD.

BAILEY PENINSULA

parks near the trail, but not right on the trail as yet. Mileage markers will be installed in the near future.

GREEN LAKE

Most runners flock to Green Lake for their workouts. This 2.78-mile loop around the lake can become quite crowded over its paved pathway. Water and rest rooms are available. There are no nearby hotels, but the lake can be reached by public transit from either downtown (#5 or #6 buses) or the university area (#48).

Many runners will additionally head south to the adjacent Lower Woodland Trails for extra mileage, zigzagging over its hilly, grassy fields.

From the university, Green Lake can be reached by running north on 17th Street, or north on the Burke-Gilman Trail to Vienna Place. From 17th, after ½ mile, head west on Ravenna Boulevard for the next 1¼ miles to the lake. From Vienna Place you can run through Ravenna and Cowan parks, coming out onto Ravenna Boulevard for the final mile to the lake.

SEWARD PARK AND WASHINGTON BOULEVARD ROUTES

Beautiful lakeside running can be found southeast of downtown along the shores of Lake Washington. Runs along here include vistas of Mt. Ranier and the Cascade Range, as well as boating and birdlife on the water. Seward Park, on the Bailey Peninsula, has a beach road that skirts the hilly, woodsy land mass for almost 3 miles.

From the park, you can head north along Lake Washington Boulevard for nearly 5 miles to Madrona Beach Park. Choose between a lakeshore route or occasional detours up into parks and residential areas overlooking the lake.

Lake Washington Boulevard continues north from Madrona Beach Park inland through some small parks, and after 1¼ miles reaches the fabulous University of Washington Arboretum. From here you can continue north for ¾ of a mile to Montlake Bridge and across to the university campus.

ALKI BEACH RUN

The Alki Peninsula, located across Elliot Bay from downtown, is the birthplace of Seattle. The northern tip of the peninsula offers a magnificent view of the Seattle skyline. Elaborate routes can be run along Puget Sound and across the Peninsula. You do not need to be familiar with the area to stay along the roads at the water's edge for many interesting miles.

CLUBS, FUN-RUNS AND RACES

Club Northwest holds many running events during the year. Its newsletter, *the nor'wester*, contains the full schedule of activities. Fun-runs are held at Green Lake at the East Fieldhouse on Sundays at 11:00 A.M. all year, and on Thursdays at 6:00 P.M. during the summer. Races are held bi-monthly, except in the summer when they are held at least once a week.

TRADITIONAL RACES

Seattle Seafair Summerun: Early August
Seattle Marathon: Late November

CONTACT

Bill Roe, Club Northwest, 2557 25th Avenue East, Seattle, WA 98112. (206) 325-3167.

SPOKANE

Population: 180,000	Humidity: 64.5%
Elevation: 1,898 ft.	Av. Temperature: (Jan.) 25°F.; (July) 70°F.
Air Quality: Good	Inches of Rainfall: (Jan.) 2.5; (July) .4 Raindays: 118

OVERVIEW

Spokane makes life very easy for traveling runners. Weather conditions are usually excellent, with very little of the rain that the northwest coastal area receives. The city developed in the early days as an access through the Rockies. It lies as a basin surrounded by mountains which creates the dry, temperate climate so enjoyed by local runners. The Spokane River runs through the downtown area offering pleasant river runs.

The downtown area was redeveloped for Expo '74 and the pride of Spokane, Riverfront Park, was created on the site of an old railroad yard. This convenient park is the most popular running area in town.

HOTELS

Sheraton Hotel, Holiday Inn – Downtown, Ridpath Hotel, Travelodge River Inn

RIVERFRONT PARK

The Sheraton is located right at Riverfront Park. An interesting 1-mile loop begins at the Sheraton heading west on the path between the Convention Center and the river. Turn north onto the bridge over the river and continue past the YMCA, crossing a second bridge. Then take the path east (right) all the way down under the car bridge and back up a slight hill, turning south onto a wooden footbridge. Stay on the path across the park to the Convention Center.

This run is flat, and very pretty, with the falls, the U.S. Pavilion from Expo '74, an antique carrousel, a quiet section of the river with ducks, and lots of green grass. There are many other paths, so you can change course for variety and distance. The park is very safe and there is no traffic and no dogs. Drinking fountains are in four different locations.

The YMCA, located along the course, is a popular meeting place and can provide a shower after your run. The other downtown hotels are within a short warm-up of the park.

HIGH DRIVE

For more hills, head west on any east-west street from downtown to Monroe, then take Monroe south. It goes up and up for several miles. Once up to about 29th Avenue, go west to High Drive and take it south. This gives a very pretty view of a valley from a cliff. Stay on High Drive for as long as you wish, then just turn around and head back. The distance can be anywhere from 6 to 15 miles.

SPOKANE RIVER RUN   This beautiful, slightly hilly, 15-mile run follows along both sides of the Spokane River. Head east on Fort Wright Drive from Spokane Falls Community College across the bridge and then west along the river past Downriver Golf Course where the road curves right. Soon after the curve, take Aubrey White Parkway to the left past the sewage treatment plant (the only bad part of the run) and past Riverside State Park, staying along the river past the Gun Club where the road curves left and continues to the 7-Mile Bridge.

Cross the bridge and take the road to the left, back toward the start. The road eventually comes out on a highway on which you go left for about a mile to Fort Wright Drive, turning left to the college.

CLUBS, FUN-RUNS AND RACES   The Bloomsday Road Runners Club organizes most of the running events in Spokane. In the summer, they sponsor the Spokane Marathon Clinic on Sundays at 7:00 A.M. at Spokane Falls Community College. The YMCA and the Heart Association sponsor "Heart Runs" on the third Saturday of every month.

TRADITIONAL RACES   Bloomsday Run, 8.2 miles: Early May
Newman Lake 25-Kilometer: Early June
Spokane Biathlon: Labor Day Weekend
Spokane Marathon and 10-Mile: Early September
Cheney Marathon and 20-Kilometer: November

CONTACTS   Sandra Micklewright, Bloomsday Road Runners Club, Box 645, Spokane, WA 99210. (509) 838-3577.
Spokane YMCA, North 507 Howard, Spokane, WA 99201.
Don Kardong, Human Race, Spokane, WA 99201. (509) 838-6264.

TACOMA

Population: 150,000	Humidity: 77%
Elevation: 21 – 250 ft.	Av. Temperature: (Jan.) 40°F.; (July) 64°F.
Air Quality: Good	Inches of Rainfall: (Jan.) 5.8; (July) .6 Raindays: 160

OVERVIEW

Tacoma has running trails that offer the full experience of the Pacific Northwest's scenic beauty. Only a few miles north of town, you can find a peaceful rain forest with dramatic views of Puget Sound and the Olympic Mountain Range.

A visitor to Tacoma will need a map to make any sense out of the curved and confusing streets over this hilly, scattered city. Fortunately, there is still a north and a south, and they can get you to the appropriate courses. Typical northwest precipitation can be expected here, but remember it is all a state of mind. Some local runners refer to it as "That nice gentle rain."

HOTELS

Doric Tacoma Motor Hotel, Olympus Hotel

POINT DEFIANCE PARK

This could be one of the best city routes in the west. Located only about 3½ miles north of downtown, the park can be reached by city buses that will drop you off in the park at the Japanese Pagoda, along the 5-mile drive. This drive follows a 5-mile loop around the park, and constitutes the major running route. Roadway footing can be alternated with adjacent trails over the hilly terrain. Tree cover is so dense, it will protect you from light to moderate rain. This same tree cover keeps temperatures cool in the park when the rest of the city is hot. Water is available at the top of the final hill at Fort Nisqualli.

The new YMCA on South Pearl Street would be a good starting point to run to the park entrance at North Pearl Street. It is a distance of 1½ miles downhill.

SHUSTER PARKWAY TRAIL

From the above hotels, go north on Pacific Avenue about ½ mile to Old City Hall. The trail starts a half block up the hill at a large wooden marker. Follow the trail for 1½ miles through a rustic-wooded, vine-hanging hillside over a comfortable sawdust path. The elevation provides excellent vistas of Commencement Bay. At the end of the trail, stay on Shuster going north for another ¾ of a mile, and then continue along the waterfront on Rustin Way for another ½ mile to the smelter. A bike path adjoins the road along Rustin Way. You can return along the same route.

FORT STEILACOOM PARK

This popular running area can be found 10 miles south of town in the Lakewood suburb. Most runs start at Lake Waughop, a small duckpond in the park.

Routes are very complicated, so it is best to run with the local runners. The area is quite open, with a few big trees. Most of the terrain lies flat, although there are some distinct hills.

GIG HARBOR

Across the Narrows Bridge, you will find this small New England-type town. It is hilly and picturesque. Many runners utilize the residential streets for pleasant, scenic mileage. Traffic is sparse, and shade is plentiful. No routes are prescribed, so just meander around enjoying the views of Puget Sound, and run for time.

ISLAND RUNS

From Point Defiance Park, a ferry can be taken to Vashon Island where you can wander over many miles of roads. Fort Steilacoom also has a ferry that will take you to Anderson Island for a 10-mile loop starting at the ferry dock.

INDOOR TRACKS

The YMCA on South Pearl Street is a new facility with a beautiful 11-laps-per-mile indoor track.

CLUBS, FUN-RUNS AND RACES

The Fort Steilacoom Running Club holds fun-runs on the second and fourth Sunday of each month at Fort Steilacoom Park. Races are usually held on the third Saturday.

TRADITIONAL RACES

Lakewood Super Summer Halfathon, 13.1 miles: Mid-May
Sound to Narrows, 7.6 miles: Early June

CONTACTS

Steve Cole, Steilacoom Running Club, 9406 South 50th Court, Tacoma, WA 98467. (206) 564-7168.
Tacoma YMCA, 1002 South Pearl Street, Tacoma, WA 98406. (206) 564-9622.

Charleston

Population: 68,000	Humidity: 70%
Elevation: 900 ft.	Av. Temperature: (Jan.) 38°F.; (July) 76°F.
Air Quality: Fair	Inches of Rainfall: (Jan.) 3.8; (July) 5.4 Raindays: 152

OVERVIEW

Lying in the small Kanawha Valley, Charleston provides flat, easy runs along the scenic Kanawha River. Adjacent to the river, the downtown area is bordered by steep hills rising up quickly on each side. Hotels are conveniently located along the river course.

Running away from the river can be complicated, as roads twist and turn through the hillside neighborhoods. No one here lives on flat terrain, so many runners come down to the river for their easier workouts.

The city is well known for its Charleston Distance Run, which draws a large field every Labor Day weekend.

HOTELS

Four Holiday Inns are located along the river in the downtown area.
Daniel Boone Hotel

KANAWHA RIVER RUN

A sidewalk extends 7 miles, east and west, next to Kanawha Boulevard at the riverbank. The route is well shaded by crab apple and maple trees, and there are nice views of the hills across the river. Occasional gas stations on the course will provide water and rest rooms.

KANAWHA STATE FOREST

Only 7 miles southeast, off U.S. 119, this 6,597-acre park offers an excellent environment for hill training. A dirt road and a paved road travel parallel to each other through the park, at about ¼ mile apart. A 12-mile loop is normally run by heading out on the dirt road, which leads onto the paved road at 6 miles, and running back on the paved road. The dirt road provides no amenities other than softer footing and plenty of shade. Coming back on the paved road, you will reach a water fountain at the 8-mile mark, and then you will pass fountains frequently. Three rest rooms are also spaced along the paved road, and it does have mileage markers, but these are from two different starting points and can be confusing.

OUTDOOR TRACKS

Laidley Field, ten blocks east of downtown, has a newly built ¼-mile, all-weather track. An indoor track is in the planning stages for the field.

CLUBS, FUN-RUNS AND RACES

The Kanawha Valley Road Runners are an active organization with some interesting ideas. They give an annual award to members for running the most consecutive days during the year. They hold fun-runs once a month, on Sundays at 2:00 P.M. They also put on races about twice a month.

TRADITIONAL RACES   Union Carbide, 10 kilometers: April
St. Albans Lions Club, 10 kilometers: Late June
Putnam County Great Teays,10 kilometers: Late July
Putnam County Hurricane, 5.8 miles: Late July
Charleston Distance Run, 15 miles: Saturday of Labor Day Weekend
Dunbar Wine Cellar Classic, 10 kilometers: Early October

CONTACTS   Jim Jones, Kanawha Valley RRC, Box 2022, Charleston, WV 25327. (304) 949-2711.
Al Anson, President, Kanawha Valley Road Runners, (304) 722-5314, 348-5883 (work).
Fred Waybright, President, St. Albans Track Club, (304) 722-2485, 727-2381 (work).

MORGANTOWN

Population: 30,900	Humidity: Not available
Elevation: 892 ft.	Av. Temperature: (Jan.) 32°F.; (July) 73°F.
Air Quality: Fair	Inches of Rainfall: (Jan.) 1.1; (July) 3.9 Raindays: Not available

OVERVIEW
: Morgantown is an educational center situated in the northern part of West Virginia along the Monongahela River. It's a hilly city with most of the running focused around West Virginia University.

HOTEL
: Holiday Inn, Beechurst Avenue

WEST VIRGINIA UNIVERSITY COURSE
: The Holiday Inn is located ½ mile from the West Virginia University Coliseum. For a 6- or more mile run, proceed to the Coliseum, turn left onto Patterson Drive, and go ½ mile to the stoplight. Go through the light and around the bend for another ¾ of a mile. Turn right at the four-way stop onto Chestnut Ridge Road and follow that for ½ mile to WVU Golf Course. Here you can do a 2-mile loop around the perimeter of the course. For a great view of Morgantown, you can climb Law School Hill for a ½-mile loop. Backtrack the course to the Holiday Inn. Traffic is moderate to heavy on Beechurst, and moderate on Patterson and Chestnut Ridge Road.

WVU ARBORETUM
: Arboretums are always a special treat to runners as they are usually traffic-free, and contain interesting varieties of flora and fauna. This arboretum is extremely hilly and extends out to the Monongahela River. You will find the entrance on Beechurst right above the Coliseum.

COOPERS ROCK STATE FOREST
: The largest state forest in West Virginia, this area is about 12 miles north of town. There are numerous roads and trails, and in this "Mountain State" you can be sure the scenery is spectacular.

TRACKS
: WVU has a good outdoor track about ¼ mile along Beechurst Street from the Holiday Inn. A new 200-meter Tartan indoor track will be available in 1979.

RACES
: The West Virginia Track Club has races about once a month at the WVU track.

TRADITIONAL RACES
: Mountaineer Relays: April
West Virginia Club Relay: September

CONTACT
: Chris Gaidrich, Athletic Attic, 5000 Greenbag Road, Mountaineer Mall, Morgantown, WV 26505. (304) 296-7755.

WHEELING

Population: 45,000	Humidity: Not available
Elevation: 678 ft.	Av. Temperature: (Jan.) 30°F.; (July) 74°F.
Air Quality: Fair	Inches of Rainfall: (Jan.) 2.8; (July) 3.7 Raindays: Not available

OVERVIEW

Wheeling is located along the Ohio River in the thin northern strip of West Virginia that is squeezed between Pennsylvania and Ohio. Its highway system makes it much more accessible to these other two states than to its own. Pittsburgh can be reached within a 50-mile drive.

Running in Wheeling predominantly centers around a 6-mile stretch of highway heading west out of the downtown area. This is the last 6 miles of the annual Wheeling Distance Race course. Apparently, the friendliness and camaraderie of local runners supercedes the inherent difficulties of running amidst traffic and exhaust fumes. Wheeling drivers do have a reputation for being very polite, and of course, there are times when few cars are on the road.

A couple of nice parks are not far from town, so if highway running makes you nervous, you can run in a peaceful environment.

HOTELS

Downtowner Motor Inn, Howard Johnson's, Wilson Lodge

NATIONAL ROAD

Local runners are so enthused about their Wheeling Distance Race that they run the course all the time for practice. The race officially starts and finishes at the Civic Center, so that is as good a place as any to start a workout. If you head away from the river to 14th Street and turn left onto Chapline, you can keep going straight out of town and you will be on National Road. When you reach the top of the Big Wheeling Hill, you will have run 1½ miles. Elby's Family Restaurant is at the 3-mile mark. At 4 miles, you will be on "Chicken Neck" Hill, where the road curves south. Stay on National Road for 1/10 of a mile past the Triadelphia Junior High School, where you will make a left at about 5 miles.

The road enters Wheeling Park where you can do a 1-mile loop past the swimming pool, continuing on the road to the exit. Head back National Road to the finish line. Total distance for this course is 11 miles, although you can turn back anywhere along the way. The road through the park is shady and you can find water and rest rooms there. Both the road and park are well lit at night, but the park would not be safe at night for a woman running alone.

If you wish to run the entire 20-kilometer race course, do not turn into Wheeling Park. Instead, continue south on National Road past Elm Grove and over a small river to a left turn onto Bethlehem Boulevard after 1½ miles from the park road. Heading west on Bethlehem, you will go up a long hill, crossing Route 88, and then downhill on Valley Boulevard. The road then runs into 29th Street where you will give up the luxury of a sidewalk on a heavily trafficked street. Follow 29th Street right, and then make a left onto 27th Street and a right onto Main Street. Follow Main Street into town all the way to 10th Street, make two quick rights, heading back on Market Street to 14th Street, and turn right to the finish line.

Unfortunately, if you follow these directions, you will have run the course in reverse. If you are willing to turn these directions around, then you deserve to deal with the hardships of the southern part of the course. The National Road part of the course is much safer, and most runners prefer to stay on it.

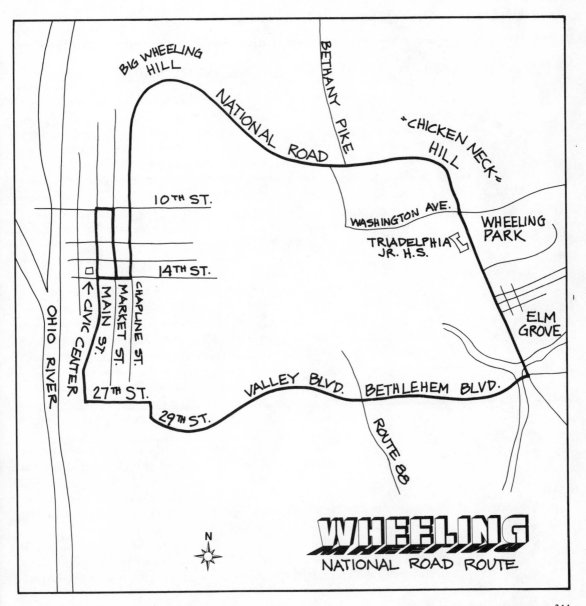

OGLEBAY PARK

Three miles from town, on National Road, take a left onto Bethany Pike and proceed 3 or 4 miles to Oglebay Park. This giant 1,460-acre park provides a rustic setting for a hilly workout. Wilson Lodge is located in the park. An easy-to-follow road will give you a 5-mile loop. Shade is variable, and occasionally you can run on grass alongside the road. Only parts of the road are lit at night. The park is very safe, and water and rest rooms are available.

INDOOR TRACKS

The YMCA, located downtown on 20th Street, ¼ mile south of the Civic Center, has a 32-laps-per-mile track. Many runners meet here to run the National Road course.

CLUBS, FUN-RUNS AND RACES

The Country Roaders Road Runners Club holds monthly races. Fun-runs are held once or twice a month at John Marshall High School in Glen Dale, about 10 miles south of town, and at Martin's Ferry.

TRADITIONAL RACES

Wheeling Distance Race, 20 kilometers: Late May

CONTACTS

John Nally, Country Roaders RRC, 334 West Cardinal Avenue, Wheeling, WV 26003.

Wheeling YMCA, 32 20th Street, Wheeling WV 26003. (304) 233-3560.

EAU CLAIRE

Population: 48,000	Humidity: Not available
Elevation: 880 ft.	Av. Temperature: (Jan.) 13°F.; (July) 70°F.
Air Quality: Fair	Inches of Rainfall: (Jan.) 0.9; (July) 3.6 Raindays: Not available

OVERVIEW On the shores of the Eau Claire and Chippewa rivers, Eau Claire sits in the northwest sector of Wisconsin in the Chippewa Valley. This lumber town is sometimes known as "Sawdust City." Most of the running here is done in Carson Park, not far from the downtown area. Although winters are very cold, Eau Claire runners are proud of their year 'round activity.

HOTELS Holiday Inn, Howard Johnson's, Exel Inn

CARSON PARK From the above hotels, head west on Highway 12 for about 1 mile to Menomonie Street. Turn right on Menomonie and run about ⅛ of a mile to the entrance of Carson Park. A Dairy Queen is on the corner. Turn left and run into the park and up the hill to the large train engine. Then turn left and run past the tennis courts and the Historical Museum, and on to the playground area where you run to the right down a small hill and follow this road around to where you were. Then turn right and down the hill to the Dairy Queen and retrace your steps back to the motels. The total run will be about 4.3 miles. Each loop of the park is 1.8 miles.

Traffic exists on Highway 12, but there is ample room on the side of the road. Water fountains are available in the park at the tennis courts, and on the playground.

INDOOR TRACKS The YMCA has an indoor track, 17 laps per mile.

CLUBS The Indianhead Track Club puts on four races each year. It also has meetings on the second Tuesday of every other month.

The YMCA has no formal club, but many people run at and from the Y. A group heads out weekdays at noon.

TRADITIONAL RACES Carson Park 10-Mile: Early May
Sawdust City Days, 6 miles: Late June
Four-Miler: Late August
Frigid Eight: Early December

CONTACTS Jerry Foote, Indianhead Track Club, 606 4th Avenue, Eau Claire, WI 54701. (715) 834-5923.
Eau Claire YMCA, 700 Grand Avenue, Eau Claire, WI 54701. (715) 832-3433.

MADISON

Population: 168,000	Humidity: 71%
Elevation: 849 ft.	Av. Temperature: (Jan.) 17°F.; (July) 72°F.
Air Quality: Fair	Inches of Rainfall: (Jan.) 1.5; (July) 3.8 Raindays: 115

OVERVIEW

Sandwiched on an isthmus between Lake Mendota and Lake Monona, Madison sits in the southcentral part of Wisconsin. The rolling hills and verdant streets make this a comfortable running town. Lakefront runs dominate the scene, and a large university population makes for busy running courses. The downtown hotels offer convenient accommodations for a direct route to the Lake Mendota run, and a slightly longer route to Lake Wingra, the most popular running area.

HOTELS

The Concourse, Inn on the Park, Howard Johnson's—Downtown, Best Western National Motor Inn

LAKE WINGRA

From the downtown hotels, run approximately 1 to 1½ miles southwest to Vilas Park on Lake Wingra. Beginning in Vilas Park, you can take either direction for the 6.2 miles around the lake. The footing is paved road or sidewalk, with many shade trees overhead. Rolling hills take you past the Arboretum Wildlife Refuge where you can pick up about 20 miles of trails. Water fountains can only be found along the beach on the 6.2-mile route. In winter, the route is plowed. No lights exist for night running.

LAKE MENDOTA

This course begins at Capitol Square in the heart of downtown. Follow State Street west until it ends after ¾ of a mile of busy city life. Turn right on Lake Street for 200 yards and you will be at the lake. Take a left and then stay right along the lake for the 2⅛ miles to Picnic Point. Return to downtown along the same route. The course is flat with good shade, but no water fountains. There are no lights at night along the lakefront, and in the winter the area is not plowed, yet it is usually runable. The course, adjacent to the University of Wisconsin, gets heavy student use.

CLUBS

The Hash House Harriers and the Vilas Running Club are the two active clubs in town. The same people head up both clubs. The Harriers are the more socially oriented group, carrying on parties after their weekly fun-runs.

FUN-RUNS AND RACES

During warm months, the Hash House Harriers hold cross-country fun-runs Wednesday nights at different locations within the city. During the same months, the Vilas Running Club holds fun road runs Thursday nights in small towns around Madison.

During cold months, fun-runs are held on Saturday afternoons. Races are scheduled monthly year 'round.

TRADITIONAL RACES
Vilas Half-Marathon: Mid-March
Syttende Mai 20-Mile Race: Mid-May
Madison Marathon: End of June
Monona 20-Kilometer: Mid-July

CONTACTS
Peter Senzig, 3613 Hovde Road, Madison, WI 53704.
Bill Hauda, 1210 Ellen Avenue, Madison, WI 53716.
Movin' Shoes, 1115 South Park Street, Madison, WI 53715. (608) 251-0125.

MILWAUKEE

Population: (met.) 1,382,000	Humidity: 72%
Elevation: 579–799 ft.	Av. Temperature: (Jan.) 22°F.; (July) 71°F.
Air Pollution: Fair to poor	Inches of Rainfall: (Jan.) 1.6; (July) 2.5 Raindays: 121

OVERVIEW

For many runners, Milwaukee would be heaven. This is the number one city for that popular carbohydrate replacement, beer. Unfortunately, after a long run you can't drink it right out of the rivers or lakes, but you will not find it far away.

This clean, attractive city sits on a bluff overlooking Lake Michigan. Its spacious, open atmosphere allows for comfortable downtown running. A short warm-up will bring you to the lakefront.

One caution about running on downtown streets: runners have been ticketed here for jaywalking. In one incident, a policeman nearly caused a five-car pileup with his car while chasing down two runners who had stepped off the curb a moment too soon. Larry Brown, coach of the Denver Nuggets, was another runner ticketed for this.

HOTELS

Downtown: Pfister Hotel, Marc Plaza, Milwaukee Inn, Ramada Inn
Wauwatosa: Holiday Inn–West, Best Western Midway Motor Lodge, Sheraton Mayfair, Howard Johnson's

THE LAKESHORE COURSE

Head down Wisconsin Avenue from your hotel to the lakefront, and take the entrance road to the War Memorial Center. On the left, a road heads downhill going north onto Lincoln Memorial Drive. Here you will be on a bicycle path alongside a peaceful lagoon with a large duck population. After 1 mile, the pathway runs along the lake next to some narrow beaches. There is grass along the pathway at times. At other times, you can cross the road for grass running and good shade. Just past the bathhouse is the 2-mile mark. At 2¾ miles you will reach the first hill which will give you a good workout to the 3-mile turn-around into the park along the top of the bluff.

The route returns through a winding pathway in the park. Here the terrain is flat and scenic with plenty of shade. At Lafayette Street head left downhill back onto Memorial Drive, where you will be slightly over 1 mile from the starting point.

The bluffs along the lakefront create the best conditions when temperatures are extreme. In summer, the lakefront is generally much cooler than inland, and even the run on top of the bluffs is much warmer than down below. In winter, the opposite is true, and a run along the lake will be 10 to 15 degrees warmer than elsewhere. Occasionally, northeasterly winds over the water can make a run here difficult.

<table>
<tr><td>UNDERWOOD PARK AND EXTENDED ROUTES</td><td>Wauwatosa, located about 7 miles west of town, has some closely connected parks which provide excellent running. Many local races are staged here. Runners meet in the parking lot along the drive in Underwood Park. Courses are out and back from the parking lot.</td></tr>
</table>

UNDERWOOD PARK AND EXTENDED ROUTES

Wauwatosa, located about 7 miles west of town, has some closely connected parks which provide excellent running. Many local races are staged here. Runners meet in the parking lot along the drive in Underwood Park. Courses are out and back from the parking lot.

For a 6-mile run, go left to the end of the park drive. Turn left along Swan Boulevard for a few hundred feet, making a right into Hoyt Park. Follow the pathway here until it ends at Church Street. Repeat the course back to the parking lot and continue to the end of the park drive and then return again to the parking lot. There are some small rolling hills here, and occasional shade. Water fountains are numerous in season, and rest rooms are adjacent to the parking lot. A lot of woods and grassy areas here give you a choice to run on soft terrain.

For a longer run, instead of turning right into Hoyt Park, go about 100 feet further and make a left onto Menomonee River Parkway. Here you can run north along the river, either on a sidewalk or on grass, for about 3½ miles, and even continue further north from there for another few miles along a small bicycle path.

A number of hotels are situated within a mile from these courses. From the Sheraton Mayfair and Howard Johnson's, head east on North Avenue to Menomonee River Parkway. If you turn right onto the Parkway, you will arrive at Swan Boulevard, where another right will put you between Hoyt and Underwood parks. If you turn left onto the Parkway, you will have the long river run mentioned above.

If you are at the Holiday Inn—West (with health club facilities) or Midway Motor Lodge, head north on Mayfair Road, making a right onto Watertown Plank Road. About 100 yards up, turn into Underwood Park.

LONG RUNS FROM DOWNTOWN

For a 20-mile run, continue from the 3-mile mark on the lakefront route, following Lake Drive (Route 32) to the north. At 9½ miles, turn right onto Dean Street and it is another ½ mile to Doctor's Park. Lake Drive is residential and there are not many crossroads.

A second choice is to pick up a bicycle path on the west side of Memorial Drive just south of the lagoon. Go left uphill for about 1 mile and continue for another 2½ miles on the pathway. This used to be a railroad track. You will then arrive in Estabrook Park. Then continue on the path for almost 2 miles until you reach Lincoln Park. After heading west in the park for about ½ mile, take the path to the right and you can run north for a little more than 2 more miles. Overall, it is about 8 miles out.

SHERIDAN PARK NEAR THE AIRPORT

Runners are often harassed around the airport neighborhood. If you drive east for about 4 miles on Layton Avenue you will arrive at Sheridan Park on the lakefront. A paved footpath extends 3 miles in each direction north and south from the parking lot. Only the northernmost 1½ miles are along the beach. The rest of the course is through parks on the bluff above the lake. You will find occasional shade, water and rest rooms.

CLUBS AND RACES

The one large club in Milwaukee, the Badgerland Striders, holds races about once a month. Evening meetings are usually held on Wednesdays in the middle of the month. On weekend mornings, members meet at the parking lot in Un-

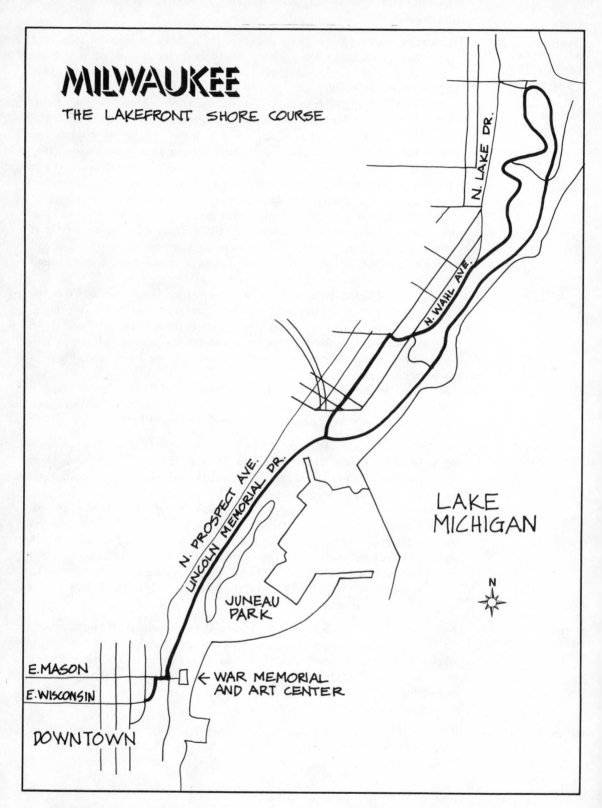

MILWAUKEE

THE LAKEFRONT SHORE COURSE

N. LAKE DR.

N. WAHL AVE.

N. PROSPECT AVE.

LINCOLN MEMORIAL DR.

LAKE MICHIGAN

N

JUNEAU PARK

E. MASON

E. WISCONSIN

← WAR MEMORIAL AND ART CENTER

DOWNTOWN

derwood Park. The University of Wisconsin at Milwaukee puts on a number of developmental indoor and outdoor track meets.

INDOOR TRACKS
: The Marquette YMCA on Wisconsin Avenue and 10th Street has a new indoor track equipped with pacing lights. The distance is 18.7 laps per mile.

TRADITIONAL RACES
: Wisconsin Mayfair Marathon: Late May
Badgerland Striders Half-Marathon and 5-Mile Run: October
Badgerland Striders Turkey Day 10- and 2-Mile Run: Sunday before Thanksgiving

CONTACTS
: Mary Belling, Badgerland Striders, 20655 Van Winkle Court, Waukesha, WI 53186. (414) 782-7333.
Neal Robinson, University of Wisconsin at Milwaukee Athletics, Box 413, Milwaukee, WI 53201. (414) 963-5151.

Lincoln Memorial Drive, Milwaukee

Cheyenne

Population: 45,000	Humidity: 56%
Elevation: 6,062 ft.	Av. Temperature: (Jan.) 25°F.; (July) 66°F.
Air Quality: Good	Inches of Rainfall: (Jan.) .46; (July) 1.82 Raindays: 98

OVERVIEW

This authentic cowboy town boasts the Frontier Days Rodeo, the world's largest event of this kind. No longer do horses dominate the scene, because now the Frontier Days Marathon makes running an important part of the festivities.

Cheyenne is located in the southeast corner of the state on a 6,000-foot plateau, making it one of the highest cities in the country. The most stringent altitude considerations should be given to your workouts here.

Broad sidewalks downtown provide trouble-free running to two city parks from centralized hotels. Motorists are somewhat considerate, especially after a celebrated incident when an elderly woman driver became so distracted while berating runners that she demolished her car.

The close proximity of the YMCA to Holiday Park makes the park a small but popular site for local runners. North of town, and quite a bit further from hotels, Lions Park has much more territory for distance training.

HOTELS

Downtown Motor Inn, Plains Hotel

HOLIDAY PARK

Hotels are located downtown close to the U.P. Depot, near the railroad tracks. Sixteenth Street, considered the "main drag," parallels the tracks and a run of about ¾ of a mile east on 16th will take you to Holiday Park. One lap circling the perimeter of the park measures 1 mile. You can also run through the park, alongside Lake Minnehaha. The YMCA is located on Dunn Avenue, just one block from the southeast corner of the perimeter route. You can find many other runners here, and also use the Y's rest rooms and water fountains.

LIONS PARK

Two miles north of downtown hotels, via Carey Avenue, you can run into this busy and attractive park, where a lot of recreational use is made of Sloan's Lake. Many bike paths circle in and around the lake, and for a measured course, you can run the perimeter to enjoy a 3-mile loop. Most park roads are blocked off to traffic. Three gas stations at the southwest corner of the park can provide water and rest room facilities.

MEDICINE BOW NATIONAL FOREST

This popular recreation area, about 30 minutes from downtown, has over one million acres of beautiful mountain territory for long, thrilling runs. A measured 15-kilometer course, on dirt roads, begins at the Lincoln Monument, close to I−80. Elevation for this run is 8,640 feet.

INDOOR TRACKS	Visitors can use the 160-meter Pro-turf track at Cheyenne Central High School. Call ahead to check out available times.
CLUBS, FUN-RUNS AND RACES	Although small, the Cheyenne Track Club tries to keep its members busy with a number of running events during the year. Fun-runs are held daily at the Cheyenne Family YMCA at 12:00 noon.
TRADITIONAL RACES	Summit Run Relay, 43 miles: June Frontier Days Marathon: Late July 15-Kilometer Mountain Championships: Early June Cheyenne Track Classic: Early June Annual Hour Run: First Saturday in October
CONTACTS	Brent Weigner, Cheyenne Track Club, 421 East 28th, Cheyenne, WY 82001. (307) 632-2602. Don McMahill, Cheyenne Family YMCA, 1401 Dunn Avenue, Cheyenne, WY 82001. (307) 632-9374. Cheyenne Central High School, (307) 632-9264.

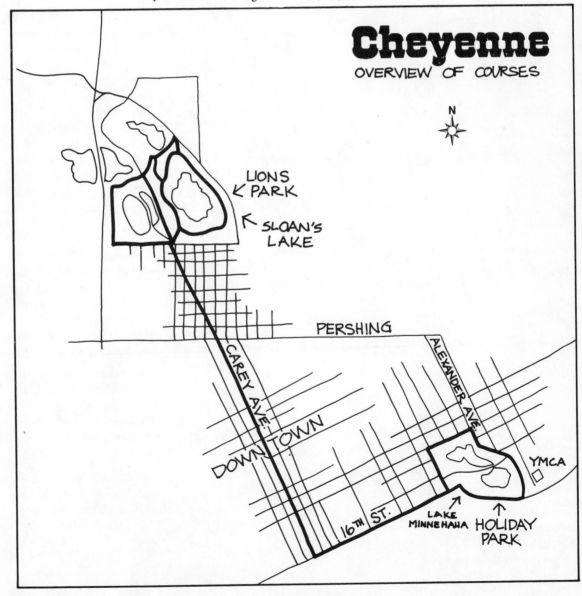

Cheyenne
OVERVIEW OF COURSES

RUNNING STORES

If, during your travels, you find you are short of running supplies or need advice or information, the following stores will be most helpful—The Athlete's Foot, Athletic Attic and Phidippides. These can be found at the locations listed below for the cities included in this book:

THE ATHLETE'S FOOT

Alabama

727 B. Brookwood Village Mall
Shades Creek Parkway
Birmingham, AL 35209
(205) 870-0480

Arizona

Chris-Town Mall
1729-B West Bethany Home Road
Phoenix, AZ 85015
(602) 249-2211

9611 Metro Parkway West
Phoenix, AZ 85021
(602) 944-3301

Arkansas

3929 McCain Boulevard
North Little Rock, AR 72116
(501) 758-7600

9700 Rodney Parbem Road
Little Rock, AR 72207
(501) 225-7624

California

335 Eastridge Mall
San Jose, CA 95121
(408) 274-5262

Colorado

The Citadel
750 Citadel River Drive East
Colorado Springs, CO 80909
(303) 596-2368

Connecticut

Chapel Square Mall
New Haven, CT 06510
(203) 789-0000

Delaware

Branmar Plaza II
1808 Marsh Road
Wilmington, DE 19810
(302) 475-1636

Florida

Sunrise Mall
2488 East Sunrise Boulevard
Ft. Lauderdale, FL 33304
(305) 561-1330

3433 North State Road 7
Ft. Lauderdale, FL 33319
(305) 484-0470

Omni International Mall
1601 Biscayne Boulevard
Miami, FL 33132
(305) 358-5994

20505 South Dixie Highway
Miami, FL 33170
(305) 253-3900

7563 Dadeland Mall
Miami, FL 33156
(305) 661-1500

10 Colonial Plaza Mall
Orlando, FL 32803
(305) 894-8411

Pinellas Park
St. Petersburg, FL 33730

2106 University Square Mall
Tampa, FL 33612
(813) 977-7159

Tampa Bay Center
3302 West Buffalo Avenue
Tampa, FL 33607
(813) 877-8555

1675 Forum Place
West Palm Beach, FL 33401
(305) 689-1990

Georgia

1372 Cumberland Mall
I-285 and U.S. 41 N.W.
Atlanta, GA 30339
(404) 432-1222

Lenox Square Mall
3393 Peachtree Road, N.E.
Atlanta, GA 30326
(404) 261-5246

Idaho

Cole Village
3447 North Cole Road
Boise, ID 83704
(208) 377-2370

Illinois

Century Shopping Center
2828 North Clark Street
Chicago, IL 60657
(312) 327-7333

330 South Michigan Avenue
Chicago, IL 60604
(312) 663-1464

124 South Franklin Street
Chicago, IL 60606
(312) 782-2521

Sheridan Village Shopping Center
Sheridan and Lake Streets
Peoria, IL 61614
(309) 685-3668

Indiana

57 Monument Circle
Indianapolis, IN 46204
(317) 635-4050

Washington Square Mall
East Washington Street and Mitthoefer Road
Indianapolis, IN 46229
(317) 894-7080

Iowa

1245 Merle Hay Mall
Des Moines, IA 50310
(515) 278-1651

332 Southridge Mall
Des Moines, IA 50320
(515) 287-2823

Kansas

1438 Towne East Square
7700 East Kellogg
Wichita, KS 67207
(316) 681-3741

Kentucky

Bashford Manor Mall
Bardstown Road
Louisville, KY 40218
(502) 456-1140

Oxmoor Center
Louisville, KY 40222
(502) 426-3242

Louisiana

8110 Hampson Street
New Orleans, LA 70118
(504) 866-7478

730 Canal Street
New Orleans, LA 70130
(504) 566-0050

142 Mall Saint Vincent
Shreveport, LA 71104
(318) 227-2881

Maryland

Eastpoint Mall
7817 Eastern Avenue
Baltimore, MD 21224
(301) 284-7500

Mississippi

Deville Plaza
5050-D, I-55 North
Jackson, MS 39211
(601) 956-9229

1345 Metrocenter
Jackson, MS 39209
(601) 354-8997

Missouri

Country Club Plaza
Seville Square
500 Nichols Road
Kansas City, MO 64112
(816) 931-6007

Crown Center, Suite 104
2450 Grand Avenue
Kansas City, MO 64108
(816) 474-8187

22 Crestwood Plaza
St. Louis, MO 63126
(314) 962-4010

Nebraska

1213 Q Street
Lincoln, NE 68508
(402) 474-4557

208 Alpine Mall
102nd Street and Dodge
Westroads Shopping Center
Omaha, NE 68114
(402) 391-4411

Nevada

The Boulevard Mall
3486 Maryland Parkway
Las Vegas, NV 89109
(702) 731-6400

New Mexico

2116 Central Avenue, S.E.
Albuquerque, NM 87106
(505) 842-5992

New York

1201 Amsterdam Avenue
New York, NY 10027
(212) 222-6444

34 East 8th Street
New York, NY 10003
(212) 260-0750

500 Fifth Avenue
New York, NY 10036
(212) 575-1680

739 Third Avenue
New York, NY 10017
(212) 697-7870

16 West 57th Street
New York, NY 10019
(212) 586-1936

170 West 72nd Street
New York, NY 10023
(212) 874-1003

5322 Kings Plaza Mall
Brooklyn, NY 11234
(212) 253-7555

North Carolina

North Park Mall
135 Eastway Drive
Charlotte, NC 28213
(704) 596-1152

241 Four Seasons Mall
Greensboro, NC 27407
(919) 292-2402

774 Hanes Mall
Winston-Salem, NC 27103
(919) 768-4054

North Dakota

510 East Main Street
Bismarck, ND 58501
(701) 255-4394

Ohio

Rolling Acres Mall
Romig and Harlem Roads
Akron, OH 44322
(216) 745-6355

Northgate Mall
9715 Colerain Avenue
Cincinnati, OH 45239
(513) 385-8696

1792 Northland Mall
Columbus, OH 43229
(614) 268-1343

603 Southwyck Shopping Center
Toledo, OH 43614
(419) 866-0687

Oklahoma

1829 Penn Square
Oklahoma City, OK 73118
(405) 848-5505

Fontana Shopping Center
7903 East 50th Street
South Tulsa, OK 74145
(918) 664-5656

237 Williams Center Forum
Tulsa, OK 74103
(918) 599-7161

Woodland Hills Mall
6941 South Memorial
Tulsa, OK 74133
(918) 252-5656

Oregon

9510 Southwest Washington Square Road
Portland, OR 97223
(503) 639-8328

Pennsylvania

Gallery at Market East
9th and Market Streets
Philadelphia, PA 19107
(215) 627-1285

Roosevelt Mall
2383 Cottman Avenue
Philadelphia, PA 19149
(215) 338-9761

139 South 13th Street
Philadelphia, PA 19107
(215) 928-1217

3935 Forbes Avenue
Pittsburgh, PA 15213
(412) 681-6510

520 Wood Street
Pittsburgh, PA 15222
(412) 471-1880

South Carolina

Charles Towne Square
North Charleston, SC 29405
(803) 747-0631

Marion Square
King and Calhoun Streets
Charleston, SC 29401
(803) 722-2381

Woodhill Mall
6000 Garners Ferry Road
Columbia, SC 29202
(803) 776-0141

South Dakota

Empire Plaza
4001 West 41st Street
Sioux Falls, SD 57106
(605) 332-4800

Tennessee

Northgate Mall
Chattanooga, TN 37415
(615) 870-1168

1725 Cumberland Avenue, S.W.
Knoxville, TN 37916
(615) 525-1119

Bavarian Village
4004 Hillsboro Road
Nashville, TN 37215
(615) 383-1181

Hickory Hollow Mall
Nashville, TN 37013
(615) 331-6666

White Station Plaza
599 Erin Road
Memphis, TN 38117
(901) 683-2449

Texas

2526 West Anderson
Austin, TX 78757
(512) 458-3454

1104 Valley View Center
Dallas, TX 75140
(214) 387-2112

North Oaks Mall
4617 FM 1960 West
Houston, TX 77069
(713) 440-4887

558 Westwood Mall
U.S. 59 and Bissonnet
Houston, TX 77036
(713) 771-4150

242 North Star Mall
San Antonio, TX 78216
(512) 349-2718

Windsor Park Mall
7900 IH35N
San Antonio, TX 78218
(512) 349-2718

214 Wonderland Mall
Loop 410 at IH10
San Antonio, TX 78201
(512) 734-6819

Virginia

367 Independence Boulevard
Virginia Beach, VA 23462
(804) 499-2640

Washington

517 Northgate Mall
Seattle, WA 98125
(206) 365-2006

4343 University Way
Seattle, WA 98105
(206) 632-3032

West 510 Riverside
Spokane, WA 99201
(509) 455-7525

West Virginia

1005 Quarrier Street
Charleston, WV 25301
(304) 345-2810

Wisconsin

45 West Towne Mall
Madison, WI 53719
(608) 836-9511

Bay Shore Mall
5906 North Port Washington Road
Milwaukee, WI 53217
(414) 962-4405

ATHLETIC ATTIC

Alabama

250 Century Plaza
Birmingham, AL 35210
(205) 592-7379

Bel Air Shopping Center
Airport Boulevard and I – 65
Mobile, AL 36616
(205) 479-1963

California

200 El Paseo de Saratoga
San Jose, CA 95130
(408) 374-3540

Connecticut

Charter Oak Mall, #A-13
940 Silver Lane
East Hartford, CT 06101
(203) 569-3589

Delaware

Georgetown
3432 "M" Street, N.W.
Washington, D.C. 20007
(202) 338-3188

Mazza Gallerie Mall
Concourse Level
Western and Wisconsin Avenue, N.W.
Washington, D.C. 20015
(202) 362-1180

Florida
826 – 828 North Federal Highway
Ft. Lauderdale, FL 33304
(305) 761-1131

Gainesville Mall
2510 Northwest 13th Street
Gainesville, FL 32601
(904) 378-2426

Oaks Mall
6357 Newberry Road
Gainesville, FL 32605
(904) 377-8846

Westside Mall
3411 West University Avenue
Gainesville, FL 32607
(904) 376-7423

Regency Square
9501 Arlington Expressway
Jacksonville, FL 32211
(904) 724-7272

Orlando Fashion Square
3201 East Colonial
Orlando, FL 32803
(305) 898-6511

Tyrone Square, #760
6901 22nd Avenue
St. Petersburg, FL 33710
(813) 344-1542

Floriland Mall, #9351
Tampa, FL 33612
(813) 933-5600

Westshore Plaza
Tampa, FL 33609
(813) 876-9347

Oakbrook Square
11594 U.S. Highway 1
North Palm Beach, FL 33408
(305) 622-1215

Georgia
Lenox Square Mall
3393 Peachtree Road, N.E.
Atlanta, GA 30326
(404) 233-3972

1006 Perimeter Mall
4400 Ashford – Dunwoody Roads
Atlanta, GA 30346
(404) 394-2404

Chatham Plaza
7805 Abercorn Street
Savannah, GA 31406
(912) 355-4567

Kansas
The Mall
3975 East Harry
Wichita, KS 67218
(316) 686-0077

Kentucky
Jefferson Mall
4801 – 236 Out Loop
Louisville, KY 40219
(502) 969-2334

The Mall, #315
5000 Shelbyville Road
Louisville, KY 40207
(502) 895-4406

Mississippi
1064 Metrocenter
Jackson, MS 39209
(601) 969-1114

New York
464 Sixth Avenue
New York, NY 10011
(212) 255-5890

1170 Third Avenue
New York, NY 10021
(212) 249-2133

Hylan Shopping Center
2600 Hylan Boulevard
Staten Island, New York City, NY 10306
(212) 987-8750

North Carolina
173 East Franklin Street
Chapel Hill, NC 27514
(919) 967-4527

The New Dilworth Coop
1609 East Boulevard
Charlotte, NC 28203
(704) 377-9898

2520 Hillsborough Street
Raleigh, NC 27602
(919) 821-5085

Oklahoma
Crossroads Mall
7000 Crossroads Boulevard
Oklahoma City, OK 63149
(405) 632-0504

Pennsylvania

4007 Locust Street
Philadelphia, PA 19104
(215) 387-8314

Northway Mall, #2150
Pittsburgh, PA 15237
(412) 367-4151

South Carolina

50 Northwoods Mall
Charleston Heights, SC 29405
(803) 797-7512

Columbia Mall
7201 Two Notch Road
Columbia, SC 29204
(803) 788-2915

Greenville Mall
I—85 Woodruff Road
Greenville, SC 29607
(803) 288-1957

Tennessee

Eastgate Center
Chattanooga, TN 37411
(615) 894-5206

Texas

Grand Central Station Center
8760-A Research Boulevard
Austin, TX 78758
(512) 454-7609

Cielo Vista Mall
8401 Gateway Boulevard West
El Paso, TX 79925
(915) 772-0016

224 Memorial City Shopping Center
Houston, TX 77024
(713) 461-7535

522 Sharpstown Center
Houston, TX 77036
(713) 777-3314

Virginia

Pembroke Mall
Virginia Beach, VA 23462
(804) 499-2101

Regency Square J-22
Quioccasin and Parham Roads
Richmond, VA 23229
(804) 740-1740

West Virginia

Mountaineer Mall
5000 Greenbag Road
Morgantown, WV 26505
(304) 296-7755

PHIDIPPIDES

California

3740 Sports Arena Boulevard, Suite 8
San Diego, CA 92110
(714) 222-7161

Colorado

3101 East Belleview Road
Denver, CO 80237
(303) 770-6305

Florida

775 University Boulevard North
Jacksonville, FL 32211
(904) 743-6063

Georgia

2967-B Cobb Parkway (Akers Mill Square)
Atlanta, GA 30309
(404) 955-5963

3212 Northlake Parkway (Northlake II)
Atlanta, GA 30345
(404) 491-0253

1544 Piedmont Road, N.E. (Ansley Mall)
Atlanta, GA 30324
(404) 875-4268

Kentucky

321 South Ashland
Lexington, KY 40508
(606) 269-8313

Louisiana

5242 Magazine Street
New Orleans, LA 70115
(504) 895-4705

Mississippi

261 Highland Village Mall, I—55N
Jackson, MS 39211
(601) 981-3583

Nebraska

The Atrium Building, 12th and N
Lincoln, NE 68508
(402) 489-0647

North Carolina

Franklin Street, University Square
Chapel Hill, NC 27514
(919) 942-1078

4400 Sharon Road
Charlotte, NC 28211
(704) 366-1213

Quaker Village Shopping Center
Greensboro, NC 27410
(919) 852-3555

Ohio

Madison and Edwards Roads
Cincinnati, OH 45209
(513) 871-7170

5557 Old Troy Pike
Dayton, OH 45424
(513) 233-3866

South Carolina

736 Harden Street
Columbia, SC 29250
(803) 254-3599

Tennessee

4296 Summer Avenue
Memphis, TN 38117
(901) 767-6552

Virginia

Parham Plaza Shopping.Center
Richmond, VA 23229
(804) 270-9494

ACKNOWLEDGMENTS

This book was written with the help of many informed and generous individuals. While I was traveling, the following people devoted a great deal of time to show me their cities, often making excellent running companions, and certainly providing immense hospitality.

Glenn Angelino—*Des Moines*
Mary Belling—*Milwaukee*
Seth Bergmann—*Philadelphia*
Garry Bjorklund—*Minneapolis*
Alex Boies—*Minneapolis*
Mike Boylan—*Cincinnatti*
Marty Cooksey—*Los Angeles*
Mitch Feingold—*San Diego*
Roy Greene—*New Orleans*
Leroy Harvey—*San Antonio*
Steve Hoag—*Minneapolis*
Bill Houston—*Cincinnatti*
Damien Howell—*Fort Lauderdale*
Hans Huseby—*Miami*
Pam Magee—*Portland*
Mike Martorano—*Chicago*
Dick McMahon—*Omaha*

Milan Mitrovic—*Chicago*
Darel Neilson—*Salt Lake City*
John O'Neil—*Cleveland*
Marianne Pugh—*Dallas*
Tom Raynor—*Nashville*
Leal-Ann Reinhart—*Los Angeles*
Michael Reinhart—*Los Angeles*
Andy Riska—*Ft. Lauderdale*
Alan Spanier—*Oakland*
Walt Stack—*San Francisco*
Randy Tindol—*Tampa*
Richard Truly—*Dallas*
Bill Vicic—*Cleveland*
Gene Weis—*Louisville*
Steve Whitehead—*Des Moines*
David Wood—*Nashville*
Charlie Zipprich—*Louisville*

There are many others who spent long hours working on correspondence with me, sending valuable information about the running environments in their cities. Their faith that I would make their time worthwhile is greatly appreciated.

Alabama   *Birmingham*—Versal Spalding; *Mobile*—Charles M. Matlock, Richard W. Overby
Alaska   *Anchorage*—Roy Reisinger; *Fairbanks*—Mark Woldseth
Arizona   *Tucson*—Ken Young
Arkansas   *Little Rock*—Lloyd Walker
California   *Lake Tahoe Area*—Austin Angell; *Palm Springs*—Jack T. Warren; *Sacramento*—Rick Baugher; *San Diego*—Bill Stock; *San Jose*—Ted Pawlak
Colorado   *Boulder*—Dale Scott; *Colorado Springs*—Jay Longacre
Connecticut   *Hartford*—David G. Arnold, George S. Brown; *New Haven*—Stephen S. Mick; *New London*—Amby Burfoot

Delaware *Wilmington* — Wayne S. Kursh

District of Columbia — Jeff Darman, Caroline Hahn, Ellen Wessel

Florida *Jacksonville* — Tom Skordas; *Miami* — Sandy Thiessen; *West Palm Beach* — Justus W. Reid; *St. Petersburg* — Greg Holzwart, Wade Yeakle

Georgia *Savannah* — Bill McClinton, Bob Phillips

Hawaii *Honolulu* — Mid-Pacific RRC

Idaho *Boise* — Bruce Blaser, Basil Dahlstrom

Illinois *Peoria* — Dan Osterman

Indiana *Indianapolis* — John F. Cope, Dr. John Moe, Gene S. Moll, Gary L. Peterson

Iowa *Des Moines* — Jeff Boone

Kansas *Wichita* — Brent Wooten

Kentucky *Lexington* — Jerry Stone; *Louisville* — Gary Daniel

Louisiana *Shreveport* — Richard Rogers

Maryland *Baltimore* — John Roemer

Massachusetts *Boston* — Don Spittle; *Springfield* — Brian T. Cormier

Michigan *Detroit* — Mike Cunney, Ken Isherwood, Dr. Ed Kozloff; *Kalamazoo* — Tom Coyne; *Lansing* — Raymond D. Warner

Mississippi *Hattiesburg* — John L. Pendergrass; *Jackson* — James L. Crosthwait

Missouri *Kansas City* — Rich Ayers, Carl Owczarzak; *St. Louis* — Jerry Kokesh

Montana *Bozeman* — R. Helene Knowlton

Nebraska *Lincoln* — Jim Lewis; *Omaha* — Bill Symolon

Nevada *Las Vegas* — Johnny J. Clark

New Jersey *Atlantic City* — Paul Purcell; *Trenton* — Barbara Stumbaugh

New Mexico *Santa Fe* — Norm Mugleston

New York *Albany* — John N. Aronson, Ted Bick; *Buffalo* — Richard A. Kendall; *Rochester* — Jim Boyle, Jim Ferris; *Syracuse* — Christine Hubbard

North Carolina *Charlotte* — Belvie Jenkins, Don Plyler; *Greensboro* — Jon C. Lewis, Terry Walts; *Raleigh* — Peter Klopfer, Mike Shea

North Dakota *Fargo* — Nancy Hall

Ohio *Akron* — Cletus Griffin; *Columbus* — Donald K. Fox, Hans R. Poehlmann; *Dayton* — Harry L. Bradbury, Steve Price, John Wilderman; *Toledo* — Tom Kovacs, Sy Mah

Oklahoma *Oklahoma City* — Dr. Dan Metcalf; *Tulsa* — Art Browning

Oregon *Eugene* — Jon Anderson; *Portland* — Barbara Gould

Pennsylvania *Harrisburg* — Bud Smitley; *Philadelphia* — Raymond Reighn, Browning Ross, Chris Tatreau; *Pittsburgh* — Ken Balkey, Gregory Leroy

Rhode Island *Providence* — Bobby Doyle

South Carolina *Charleston* — Bob Schlau; *Columbia* — Tom Trotter; *Greenville* — Bill Keesling

South Dakota *Rapid City* — Larry A. Robertson; *Sioux Falls* — Alan Straatmeyer

Tennessee *Chattanooga* — Earl A. Marler, Jr.; *Knoxville* — Harold W. Canfield; *Memphis* — Bud Joyner; *Nashville* — Larry Duncan

Texas *Austin* — Robert T. Renfro; *Dallas* — Miki Hervey, Don Lucas, Tom Spillman; *El Paso* — Allen P. Killam; *Fort Worth* — Dwain D. Camp; *Houston* — Bob Wagner, George Kleeman

Vermont *Burlington* — Kurt Lauenstein

Virginia *Norfolk* — Charlie George; *Richmond* — Bill Buckman

Washington *Seattle* — Bill Roe; *Spokane* — Sandra L. Micklewright, Ruth Van Kuren; *Tacoma* — Craig Hatton

West Virginia *Charleston* — Bob Fretwell; *Morgantown* — Chris Gaidrich; *Wheeling* — D. J. Jebbia

Wisconsin *Eau Claire* — Jerry Foote; *Madison* — Peter Senzig

Wyoming *Cheyenne* — David J. Bliss, Brent Weigner

And special thanks to Dr. Jeffrey Brent, who contributed information for a number of cities.

SPECIAL ACKNOWLEDGMENTS

While traveling around the country researching this book, I moved fairly quickly from city to city. Fortunately, Holiday Inn felt the project was worthy of their support, and gave me the opportunity to stay in their hotels in every city I visited. They were instrumental in making this book possible, and I greatly thank Rick Schneider at Holiday Inn, who showed his company cares about runners, and Nell DeShazo and Dorothy White, his diligent and concerned assistants.

No project of this size can come about without the help and support of close friends. Fred Lebow of the New York Road Runners Club, Mike Shimkin, the conceiver of this project, and his wife, Barbara, have all shown incredible belief in me and were a constant source of energy. Tom Shimkin, Mike's son, worked for weeks through the summer to help compile statistics on climate, and Esta Greenfield provided long hours of needed assistance during the last weeks of the project. Jim Ferris offered excellent feedback, reading segments as the book progressed, and Dale Jagemann's expertise and encouragement as my editor gave me a sense that the project would actually work out. Don Colflesh's enthusiasm in designing the book brought it character, even in the early stages.

Gary Null's encouragement and generosity, and my brother Alan's excitement about the project, were very important. Fellow members and staff of the West Side YMCA and the New York Road Runners Club provided me with a strong foundation in the sport, and I thank them all. Long-distance support came from Guy Thomas and Dr. Mitch Feingold, whose frequent phone calls were very energizing.

My good friends, Jack and Leslie Manes, provided companionship and their home while the book was being written, and their years of caring and support are deeply appreciated.